BEHAVIORAL RESEARCH METHODS IN ENVIRONMENTAL DESIGN

COMMUNITY DEVELOPMENT SERIES

Series Editor: Richard P. Dober, AIP

Volumes Published and in Preparation

CDS/8

BEHAVIORAL RESEARCH METHODS IN ENVIRONMENTAL DESIGN

Edited by

William Michelson
University of Toronto

STROUDSBURG, PENNSYLVANIA

Distributed by
HALSTED
PRESS

A division of
John Wiley & Sons, Inc.

LIBRARY OF CONGRESS CATALOGING IN PUBLICATION DATA

Michelson, William M   1940-
    Behavioral research methods in environmental design.

    (Community development series, v. 8)
    Bibliography: p.
    1. Social sciences--Methodology--Addresses,
essays, lectures. 2. Human ecology--Addresses, essays,
lectures. 3. Cities and towns--Planning--Addresses,
essays, lectures. 4. Design, Industrial--Addresses,
essays, lectures. I. Title.
H61.M4965   300'.1'8   74-10937
ISBN 0-470-60145-0
ISBN 0-470-60146-9 pbk.

Exclusive Distributor: **Halsted Press**
A division of John Wiley & Sons, Inc.

Series Editor's Preface

For several years it has been assumed that designers and their clients would profit from having research techniques applied in programming and other phases of the development cycle. However articulate the claims and desirable the approach, methods have been hard to find, especially those which could be adapted to everyday practice. In my view, receptivity—the desire to advance designs through better research—has grown; methods have not, at least in proportion. What we have here in the work of William Michelson and his colleagues is a useful, informative, instructive book. Ready as it is to come off the shelf, handy, it removes one more barrier between theory and the built environment.

Richard P. Dober, AIP

Preface

Chemistry books normally need no great introductory statement as to what is chemistry. A few words of preface define an author's specific approach and perhaps his or her sources of motivation and guidance. Nor do music books require a statement telling readers what music is, although assessments of its *details* and *variations* do fill books.

But when a book on "behavioral research methods in environmental design" comes into being, its course is less well charted. Although individuals may know very much about specific aspects of design and specific aspects of behavioral science, the context that holds and justifies a particular set of substantive materials joining the two worlds of professional endeavor is one that few people have mastered. And even these few people have not reached the state of systematization, even conceding its possibility.

Rather than to reduce such serious and necessary concerns to the few words of a preface, let me place them instead, in slightly more expanded form, in an Introduction within the volume proper. Concerns about the very nature of this interdisciplinary field surely deserve explicit, on-the-record treatment.

At this point, however, I want to acknowledge my considerable gratitude to other persons who helped to make this book possible, as it is the result of considerable collaboration. Wolfgang Preiser provided the initial spark for the whole enterprise, knowing little what it would lead to. Robert Bechtel shared the initiative with me at the inception of the project, and he and the other authors went beyond the call of duty in the interests of high quality, readability, and comparability of approach, under considerable time pressures. Charles Hutchinson, from the publisher's side, made work on this volume more pleasant and predictable than it would otherwise have been, and Barbara Zeiders provided inestimable technical assistance during the publication process. Cathy Barth provided typing and clerical help in times of dire need. Finally, the Centre for Urban and Community Studies at the University of Toronto proved once again a fruitful home for such an effort. I am grateful to all.

William Michelson

Contents

Editor's Introduction

William Michelson

In recent years, environmental designers have courted the social sciences. Like most courtships, it assumed a happy result from togetherness. Like most courtships, it started with partners not knowing much about each other. Like most courtships, it took many forms and meant many things to many people. And like many courtships, it has seen flirtation, repudiation, and serious commitment.

This collection of papers is one attempt to provide a steady basis for the continued collaboration of social scientists and environmental designers for the benefit of both, each on their own terms. The aim of this book is twofold: to indicate to the environmental designer the usefulness and characteristics of selected social science techniques for some of his ongoing problems, and to indicate to the social scientist a rich lode of context, ready and waiting to serve as a literal new world of application for techniques at his command.

In this introduction I shall describe briefly the content of this collection and the circumstances under which it was written, as well as provide a more general context to surround the substantive material.

When organizing the Fourth International Environmental Design Research Association (EDRA) Conference, held in 1973, Wolfgang Preiser inadvertently laid the groundwork for this volume. He thought it might be helpful to convene a symposium to outline in elementary, concise terms some of the major methodological approaches used by social scientists in design research. Robert Bechtel and I, to whom he turned, agreed with him, largely because of our own feeling that previous meetings had exemplified research techniques in a generally implicit manner, sometimes well and sometimes only poorly. It was our impression that most designers found themselves faced with the prospect of dabbling around in a dilettantish fashion when faced with the vast potpourri of social science effort, with little or no structure available to guide their efforts of selection and utilization. We therefore thought that it would be helpful to provide a symposium in which persons who represented a variety of the social science and design disciplines each gave a relatively uncomplicated but lucid description of the pros and cons of a major social science approach to research in the context of environmental design, together with an equally brief description of how they themselves had utilized their approach in design research. Owing to the format of the conference, the papers presented were extremely short and largely lacking in detail.[1]

Nonetheless, what was perceived to be a most positive reaction to this initial attempt led the participants to consider the creation of a book. The same inchoate relationship between the fields of design and social science, made conceptually more rational in recent years by the appearance of a variety of new books (e.g., Gutman, 1973; Michelson, 1970; Perin, 1970;

Proshansky et al., 1970; Wohlwill and Carson, 1972), but left undeveloped methodologically, argued for the transformation of our efforts for a wider audience at the earliest possible time.

Faced with the usual dilemma of disseminating a narrow range of information at the earliest time as opposed to encountering significant delays while greatly increasing the comprehensiveness of the materials, we opted for a common solution—compromise. We chose to completely rewrite and expand our original papers, with the aim of making the coverage of the original topics more complete and more helpful to the reader and researcher-to-be. We chose also to add selected chapters that would cover topics considered equally crucial but which had not been selected for the EDRA symposium simply owing to the pragmatic but nonetheless absolute limits that has been imposed.

Hence all the chapters in this collection are original and written specifically for the explicit purposes of the volume. Each author attempts to systematically introduce a specific methodological approach, discuss its relevance to research in environmental design, present careful advice about its use, and present a major personal application of the technique within this research context.

Three chapters are authored by sociologists, two by city planners, one by a psychologist, and one by architects. These backgrounds help ensure that a variety of methodological perspectives is tapped. That each author is restricted to a chapter and that the chapters have different emphases necessarily implies that no chapter can be expected to say the last word on the subject it treats. Many volumes, for example, are written about survey research; Robert Marans could hardly been expected then to present a complete manual in his chapter on that subject. The aim of all authors was rather to communicate a basic awareness of the existence and characteristics of the technique to be covered, with references to take the interested reader onward. Obviously, however, subject areas differ in the degree of prior development, and the chapters by Gerald Davis and Virginia Ayers and by Ira Robinson and his colleagues, for example, are very much on the frontier with respect to content.

It becomes clear to the reader in short order that the book as a whole is characterized, first, by selectivity, and, second, by heterogeneity. At a time when the field of design research is expanding exponentially, no volume published at a single point in time could hope to be complete, and we have not attempted to make it so. We begin to explore what are considered to be major alternative approaches, and success lies in whether or not the approaches selected prove fruitful in soliciting relevant design information in the future or in stimulating readers to develop still other approaches.

That there is no single perspective pursued or focused upon in this book is less a function of the will of the editor and contributors than of the substantive context addressed. Clearly, design research calls on the social scientist to use not just a single set of methodological tools or a single theoretical perspective, but in fact many, all relevant to aspects of the design context and the design process.

Since both environmental designers and social scientists are uncertain as to where their interests might meet, it may be desirable to expand upon this question here.

First, the design process, ideally executed, calls on many different types of social science expertise at different points in the process. For example, many design processes start with an examination of the policy alternatives relevant to a problem that faces an individual or collective client. When faced with the question of providing housing for the greater number of persons in society who cannot afford the real cost of new housing, for example, someone has to decide whether it makes more sense for a collectivity such as the government to build housing expressly for these people, or whether it makes more sense to give people money to occupy residences built by other means. The implications of these various general approaches or "targets" are the subject matter of a variety of persons, including sociologists, economists, political scientists, and ecologists from the social sciences. What they might do is quite naturally very different from that done at other points in the design process.

Once, then, general directions are charted on the basis of good information, popular sentiment, and all other relevant inputs, it is usually necessary to identify the potential clients for the program to be developed. In this case, research akin to market research is required, which generally involves persons with competence in demography, economics, and public opinion, at the least.

The discussion to this point might lead one to suspect that the author views design as a purely technocratic process. If this ever was the case, now it is not. There is general recognition that representatives of the public interest should be in a position to evaluate technical solutions before implementation, with such evaluation ranging from only formal political approval, on the one hand, all the way to responsibility for the initiation and as much as possible of the development of the technical details of the program, on the other. Except in those cases when projects are completely self-initiated by existing collectivities, however, the social scientist may be of some value by possessing expertise in the psychological, social, and/or political dynamics of community groups. Public participation does not always just happen; some ways are better than others in tapping representative and fruitful contributions to the design process in which people have so much at stake. The social scientist can hence assist both designer and client in the setting of mutually relevant goals and in the ratification of technical solutions to these goals.

Yet design is considerably more than the mechanical implementation of the newly recognized public will. It is a process whereby the needs and desires of the client are sensitively and accurately accommodated by the creation of certain arrangements of space in preference to others. Doing this is seldom accomplished purely by guesswork or intuition. The interaction of man and space is not a matter of indifference and is subject to observable regularities, which, if in fact observed, parallel practices in other applied sciences that are based on the results of scientific inquiry and widely disseminated results. Although every building or city plan may reflect a unique situation, the component parts of that situation are by no means unique. Prior experience, if monitored systematically and accurately, is of considerable benefit to any new endeavor. The "research-and-development" cycle is of such relevance to environmental design that the wonder is only at its relatively unsophisticated level of development to date. In any case, although sociologists, anthropologists, psychologists, and geographers sometimes are able to perform immediate short-term pieces of research of relevance to the design of a forthcoming building or community, they are more likely able to draw upon *prior* work for the assessment of possible consequences of alternative design suggestions. At the least they are highly relevant to the design process at the point when drawings are made, through contributions of knowledge regarding the fit of man, his activity, and man-made space.

Frequently, however, there is little time available during the creation of a "design solution" to conduct original research. What it might add could in most cases only be marginal (vis-à-vis the body of work already existing), and the amount of time necessary to do it might seriously undermine the act of accomplishment, particularly from an economic point of view. This, of course, by no means rules out original research. Rather, it merely underscores the cruciality of examining the effects of projects *once completed*. The design solution is a hypothesized mode of accommodating a specified number of goals and desires. The genius of a solution is not in its logic or in how well it photographs, but rather in whether it works or not. And there is no way to know the latter except to examine it explicitly. It is highly ironic that few clients provide funds for the evaluation of the solution to their needs or that designers so seldom insist on an examination of the consequences of their work, for this information would help both of them in the long run, as neither in most cases is involved in a terminal act. It is critical to any notion of research and development that research not be omitted at the time when it is most relevant. Airplane manufacturers, for example, customarily assess whether or not their newest planes fly when constructed, finding research and development in that way more fruitful than when restricted to building planes based only on what they can believe from the performance of other people's airplanes, particularly if these other people do not evaluate their own products. Hence the vital feedback to the design solution stage of all future projects comes from the evaluation stage of every project in turn. In this respect, the works of a wide variety of social scientists, particularly those able to utilize experimental research designs, observational techniques, monitoring of ongoing behavior, and the assessment of public opinion, are highly critical.

Finally, although the typical design process is by now completed, studies utilizing a more macroscopic outlook on social, economic, and political structure may be helpful in providing a realistic context for future design activities. It may be a purely scientific and design question, for example, as to whether high-rise apartments are good or ill for family life, as well as the extent to which they can be modified to be made more beneficial. Answers to these questions may be very illuminating and valuable, but unless people become aware of why this housing form has become so preeminent, in terms of land values, profitability, unit costs, and so on, designers and the more microscopic social scientists will remain tilting their pens at windmills.

The preceding exposition was intended to provide some indication of the variety of ways in which social scientists should be collaborating in the process of environmental design. The contents of this book, however, are not spread over all these areas. They concentrate much more specifically on what I consider the crucial heart of collaboration between social scientists and designers — the content of design. What I mean by this is that portion of the design process whereby the fit between man and environment is reduced to observable, empirical considerations — at the point of making a design solution and at the point of evaluating that solution. While the other types of contributions are nonetheless valuable, they are fruitless unless a design project can be made to accommodate the goals and desires it has set out to accommodate. There are without question methodological approaches and techniques worth extensive presentation on the other points in the design process, but we shall start here. Even at just these two points in the design process, however, it becomes evident that a number of diverse perspectives are required.

Dealing with the social science perspectives necessary for a given design solution is not like buying a loaf of bread. When you buy bread, you may have to choose from a wide variety of ryes, wheats, and oats, but you still walk out with a loaf of bread that satisfies your needs. Dealing with social science and design is more like jumping hurdles. Once you have cleared one hurdle, others still lie in your way, until you have disposed of them one by one in a satisfactory manner.

The hurdles represent different perspectives in human life. Many social scientists specialize in only one or possibly two of them, since the pursuit of these perspectives usually involves different interests and skills. All perspectives, nonetheless, are drawn from the single context of man's use of designed environments; hence a satisfactory accounting of man for the purpose of design requires a consideration of all perspectives, complementary as they are. You don't finish the race, let alone win it, until you have cleared all the hurdles.

One such perspective, a vital, imperative first consideration, is whether people have the physical opportunity to perform that which is intended in the designed environment. There is little feeling these days that environment determines what people do, whether they want to or not. The perspective is very much more one of opportunity, rather than determinism. Is the wide range of possible movements and activities permitted by the environment those which were desired to occur? Or, on the other hand, does the design really make them more difficult or even impossible? Too many buildings and communities, in fact, present a positive answer to the latter question.

The behavior that has the opportunity to occur in a given physical setting can be viewed both with respect to desired and undesired types of behavior. Although environment is designed for the most part to accommodate certain explicit and implicit types of behavior, people have also found it necessary to consider plans that carefully eliminate the possibility of certain kinds of undesired behavior. Oscar Newman (1972) brilliantly expounded this theme in describing his attempt to redesign high-density residential settings so as to lessen the possibility of criminal activity.

On a microscopic scale, behavioral needs to be accommodated in housing are frequently referred to by the term *user needs*. Although research in user needs is not particularly well developed, it is nonetheless applied to larger-scale environments, such as concern the city planner. Large-scale entities are the setting for frequent, regular, and important activities that are more or less difficult to satisfy as a consequence of environmental design. Recreation, commercial, and travel patterns are but the tip of the iceberg in this regard; the whole complex of life style is either fostered or stifled in the macroscopic milieu.

If we ask specifically what it is that occurs in designed environments, the most immediate answer is behavior. Hence a first question to ask of any potential or recently completed environment is how it provides the opportunity for specific sets of human behavior. Obviously, then, concepts to discuss and methods to assess behavior itself are required of social scientists by environmental research. Once the opportunity for behavior has been taken into consideration, however, it does not necessarily follow that the desired behavior will in fact ensue. Other perspectives come into play at this time. Perceptual phenomena, for example, are highly important. Opportunity not only has to be there; it has to be perceived for what it is in order that things work out as anticipated. A whole different line of investigation is then necessary to see what types of symbolic representation people in fact identify with as preconditions for their own behavior. Spaces, for example, can be convivial or solitary depending on the array of symbolic properties placed within them, including color, furniture, and decorative touches such as bookcases or bars, crosses or cartoons. Within most societies, or, when necessary, subcultures, there are conventions as to how phenomena are arrayed and as to how people view them. These conventions must be observed; creative activity on the part of the designer starts with these as a basis, for ignoring them in the pursuit of fancy leads to the functional collapse of the product, however imaginative.

Even when the perceptual and opportunity hurdles are cleared, however, we are not yet home free. Although these may be preconditions for a successful design, the latter still must take careful account of people's norms. Edward Hall in

The Hidden Dimension (1966) refers to the fact that in any culture the roles guiding how people deal with one another (with strong social sanctions guarding against violation of the rules) have a strong spatial dimension. Certain activities, ranging from extreme intimacy to public demagoguery, contain implicit but nonetheless real standards of separation between the participants. Notions of privacy differ from culture to culture, but imply identifiable standards within a given setting.

Within this normative perspective, Sommer (1969) has contributed considerable work in institutional settings, through his handling of the environmental implications of interpersonal, spatial norms in such settings as classrooms, libraries, and mental hospitals.

Whether at a microscopic or macroscopic level, studies relevant to the normative perspective may focus, on the one hand, on what people actually do in particular spatial settings and, on the other, but certainly not mutually exclusive, hand, on what they consider right or correct regarding environmental design for people like themselves.

In short, any design project that truly accounts for relevant social science considerations will have at least explored whatever behavioral, perceptual-symbolic, and normative implications may be lodged in the work.

Thus, this is the context in which social scientists and designers find themselves, even at just the design solution and evaluation stages of the design process, it is no wonder that what we consider leading methodological approaches are diverse in character and representative of different social science perspectives.

In the first chapter, Göran Lindberg and Jan Hellberg are concerned with the very first steps in the design of social science research in environmental design. They observe that many considerations in the design of the research project itself play a large part in determining the eventual usefulness of the study. These considerations apply regardless of the specific technique one chooses to pursue in any study. In the latter half of the paper, they develop approaches to environmental description and computer utilization of environmental material; experience makes them uniquely prepared to introduce the innovations described.

The second chapter, written by Robert Bechtel, is the first of the chapters focused specifically on techniques. With strong emphasis on the semantic differential, Bechtel provides a review of pen-and-pencil techniques that, on the one hand, describe to some extent the users of the potential environment, and, on the other hand, elicit the nature of people's perceptions of the designed environment.

In the third chapter, Ira Robinson and his colleagues discuss trade-off games, which attempt in the most realistic possible fashion to assess people's demands and priorities with respect to urban environments. The methods in neither this chapter nor the preceding one observe or measure actual environmental behavior; instead they turn to the valuable question of perceptions and norms.

In the fourth chapter, Robert Marans deals with the social survey, a technique used widely for environmental and other purposes to probe people's attitudes and actions in so far as they can relate them orally. As Marans points out, this technique is surprisingly underutilized in environmental research. While he points out obvious problems in its use, he also points to some of its favorable prospects.

In the fifth chapter, Paul Reed and I develop in greater detail one particular kind of social survey, the time budget. This technique is considered of particularly strong relevance to design research, as it deals explicitly with the interrelations of behavior, social structure, and place, in quantitative terms. Like the other authors, we discuss this technique both generally and with respect to a design-oriented project.

In the sixth chapter, Gerald Davis and Virginia Ayers cross the threshold between precise tools of measurement and physical observation of behavior in environmental contexts. Their focus is on photographic methods of environmental research; but the camera in this case is but a single useful technique to use for the general purpose underlying this book, the relation between human activity and designed environment. Davis and Ayers go into considerable detail on the newest ways to harness the art of photography for this purpose.

Finally, in the seventh chapter, Dagfinn Ås goes to the other extreme of observing behavior in physical settings without the aid of mechanical devices. He first assesses the question of observation as a contrast to approaches where the people actually involved tell you what they think or what they do. Then he discusses some of the main conceptual considerations required when entering into the act of observing behavior. Finally, he goes into considerable detail with respect to one form of observational work, which deals with the symbolic and locational focus of discrete group activities, the behavior – setting approach. Although this is not itself a major form of observation in the behavioral sciences, it has been used with considerable impact in studies on the physical environment, because it deals so directly with the types of *units* that people most consciously and frequently design.

I join with my collaborators in the hope that what we have written encourages students and practitioners alike to seek answers far beyond what we have written and to make this volume soon outdated.

NOTE

1. They may be found in Preiser (1973).

REFERENCES

2. Gutman, Robert (ed.). 1973. *People and Buildings.* New York: Basic Books.
3. Hall, Edward. 1966. *The Hidden Dimension.* New York: Doubleday.
4. Michelson, William. 1970. *Man and His Urban Environ-*

ment: A Sociological Approach. Reading, Mass.: Addison-Wesley.

5. Newman, Oscar. 1972. *Defensible Space*. New York: Macmillan.

6. Perin, Constance. 1970. *With Man in Mind*. Cambridge, Mass.: MIT Press.

7. Preiser, Wolfgang. 1973. *Environmental Design Research,* vol. 2, Symposia and Workshops. Stroudsburg, Pa.: Dowden, Hutchinson & Ross.

8. Proshansky, Harold, et al. (eds.). 1970. *Environmental Psychology*. New York: Holt, Rinehart and Winston.

9. Sommer, Robert. 1969. *Personal Space*. Englewood Cliffs, N.J.: Prentice-Hall.

10. Wohlwill, J. S., and D. H. Carson (eds.). 1972. *Environment and the Social Sciences: Perspectives and Applications*. Washington, D.C.: American Psychological Association.

Strategic Decisions in Research Design

Göran Lindberg and Jan Hellberg

Göran Lindberg is a sociologist, who serves as Universitetslektor (Associate Professor) at the University of Lund in Sweden. In addition to teaching in the Sociology Department, he is connected with the Department of Building Function Analysis in the Lund Institute of Technology, where he conducts research such as that described in the first chapter. His thesis work was on residential segregation, and since then his main concern, both in research and in teaching, has been urban and environmental sociology. He is both editor of and contributor to a book called Urbana Processer: Studier i Social Ekologi *(Urban Processes: Studies in Social Ecology, Gleerup, Lund, Sweden).*

Jan Hellberg is connected with the Department of Building Function Analysis, where he both studies and teaches. His experience includes several years of work in a private city-planning firm.

Methodologists continually try to teach us that many of the choices and assumptions we make in the early stages of a research project will have a great impact on both the project as a whole and its results. Here an attempt is made to discuss, from a methodological point of view, some research design problems pertinent to environmental research. The research area, more specifically, may be called "behavior in environment." This is a field toward which great hopes and interests around the world are directed at present. Social scientists have, of course, recognized this emerging interest and its potential in facilitating financial support for their work. We thus have what is perhaps the first stages of a boom in this field.

The research described in the section "A Practical Strategy for Dealing with Physical Environment" was financed by The National Swedish Council for Building Research in Stockholm and performed at the Department of Building Function Analysis, University of Lund. Other members of the research team are Rune Dahlgren and Sven Laarm.

Optimistic newcomers to the field do not seem to be aware that methodological problems are involved which they might not have met in their previous training and research. To make the interest in the field something other than simply a gold rush, it is time to begin considering its somewhat unique methodology.

For the sake of making the discussion more concrete, let us point out a research problem inside our own field of interest. Assume that we want to study what relations, if any, exist between a set of children's outdoor activities and the built environment. Assume also that our goal is quite practical, as we want our research to result in some kind of advice to designers and planners. We want to gain knowledge that will enable us to tell designers if specific environments (or blueprints of environments) are likely to further the activities we think good; we also want to isolate the disfunctional environments. It is not very likely that we will reach this goal all at once, especially since many theoretical issues about the problem still are (and always will be, to some extent) unsettled. The question here is how we should proceed in *designing* investigations that are useful for our goal and for similar problems.

This book deals primarily with methods and techniques. There is a danger in this subject for the untrained researcher unless he is aware, first, that the most important parts of the research activity have to do with theory and explanation, and, second, that methods are not neutral toward his theories or goals. In line with the rest of the book, we shall not discuss substantial theories that are relevant to our hypothetical research problem or to any other problem inside the field, however important such a discussion would be. Instead, we shall discuss somewhat *broader* theoretical and methodological problems that must be encountered when we try to design research for the hypothetical problems inside the field. At the end of the section we shall return to the hypothetical problem and indicate how we think we might design research on it.

But, as we shall see, there appear to be some crucial technological barriers against the ideal research design that we proposed. To be bound by already existing social science research techniques in the choice of environmental research problems may, at least in the long run, lead to unfortunate consequences (i.e., some factors in the designing and planning of built environments might get improper weights, while others might be overlooked). Thus we have felt forced to develop new techniques that concern the collection, description, and handling of specifically *environmental* data. Later these methods are described and explained.

EIGHT PAIRS OF OPTIONS

In Table 1, the methodological questions discussed here are arranged in the form of eight pairs of options. They are certainly not all on the same level of generality, nor are they necessarily independent of one another (i.e., the choices made on some options will often make other options rather illusory). But, explicit or not, the choices on these options will have to be made while doing research about behavior in environ-

Table 1
Eight Pairs of Options with Consequences for Research About Behavior in Environment

The option of seeing	1. Behavior as actions or as acts.
	2. Man in terms of aggregates or as an individual.
	3. Man as a whole or as an abstract part of a social system.
	4. Man as the prime client or as an object of investigation.
	5. Environment at an aggregate or at a nonaggregate level.
	6. Environment as an objective or as an experienced structure.
The option between	7. Direct or indirect measurement of environment.
	8. Man or environment as the primary sampling unit.

ment, and the way we choose will have important impact on our research.

Actions Versus Acts

The first pair of options applies to the choice of behavioral units. *Action* is here thought of as having the same meaning as in Alfred Schutz's usage of the concept. He defines it as "conduct which is devised in advance" (i.e., "based upon a preconceived project"). In the definition "conduct" is a term for behavior that embraces "all subjectively meaningful experiences emanating from spontaneous life" (Schutz, 1970, p. 125). Thus this category excludes behavior of the reflexive type and other types that occur without conscious volition by the individual, such as breathing or transpiring.

The other kind of behavioral units, *acts*, is a much more general concept. The term here is used with the same meaning as in natural science. It can be defined as "every change of state of matter/energy or its movement over space from one point to another" (Miller, 1965, p. 193). Obviously, all actions consist of acts. However, an action is something other than just a heap of acts. To qualify as an action, a set of acts has to be consciously organized by a human being; this brings in the notions of volition, the meanings of the act to the actor, and nondeterministic links of causality. In other words, the concept of action brings us directly to the unique problems of the social sciences.

There is certainly a place for both act-unit studies and action-unit studies within the field we are discussing. Difficulties arise when a researcher mixes the units together without a clear understanding of what is what in the mixture. One of the largest faults of the past has been the treatment of action units as if they were plain act units. The reverse is also a fault, of course, but is more seldom found. The research annals are full of instances where researchers have gone out to search for deterministic kinds of relations be-

tween environment and what, without the realization, are actions and not heaps of acts. Behaviors such as crime, leisure activity, migration, divorce, suicide, and child-rearing practices are actions and cannot very successfully be studied as though they were just acts without further qualifications. The results from such research are most often very disappointing for the scientists involved. The researchers are rarely able to demonstrate the deterministic kind of relations that they seek.

As an example of act-level reasoning with negative results, we can point to research about the social effects of slums and public housing. Many studies have been able to establish significant statistical correlations between slum living and a number of problematic behaviors, such as crime, drug abuse, vandalism, and child beating. But to find a correlation is not automatically the same as demonstrating a causal relation. This became a disillusioning insight for many researchers, as well as for planners and politicians, when they realized that just moving slum people to physically better housing conditions did not automatically reduce problematic behavior to any significant extent.

Fortunately, many researchers in the field show an emerging recognition of the distinction between action-unit research and act-unit research. These researchers do not pretend that it will ever be possible to state the full relations between man's behavior and environment as nomic laws or to represent the relations in elegant mathematical formulas. But they persist in the conviction that much insight can be gained by looking at nondeterministic kinds of relations and by introducing explanatory variables such as perceptions, norms, and values, which have for long been at the core of social science research in other fields (e.g., Michelson, 1970).

An action-level research of potential value for planning and research may take various forms. An example is the community study tradition, for which the classic Middletown books by the Lynds

(1929, 1937) can be taken as some sort of model. Such studies are normally made through intense and long participant observation of a milieu and of individuals in the performance of sustenance and other important human activities. Their strength is the deep understanding they can offer about man's relations to the surrounding world. Their weakness from the physical planning point of view is that it is not immediately obvious what part of the results relates specifically to the built environment, on the one hand, and to the social structure on the other. Some would also say that the mainly qualitative data analysis found in the community study tradition is a weakness as well. But by accompanying the qualitative data with descriptive quantitative data, it is often possible to get a sense of the quantitative weights of the insights into causal relations.

A slightly different but related form of action-level research is the use of interviews, which are in greater depth than is customary in surveys. A rather well-known study in which this technique was used (along with standardized, formal interviews to get quantification) with illuminating results is Young and Willmott's investigation, *Family and Kinship in East London* (1957).

An interesting variant of research that belongs to the category we now discuss is *action research*. Action here refers, first, to the behavior of the investigator himself. Contrary to what is usual in nonexperimental research, the investigator is not a passive observer of what is going on in a setting but is actively trying to change what he believes to be important parameters or factors in the situation (e.g., the consciousness level of the people). He is then trying to observe and to evaluate what actions among the individuals studied come from his own actions. If the consequential actions are what he had expected, he takes this as a sort of confirmation of his theory. Interesting as the approach is, it may often raise ethical questions and doubts about the possibility of the researcher being even remotely objective in situations that will naturally engage him emotionally. Perhaps this study design might be improved by having a parallel, but more nonempathetic, research team making the record.

The described approaches have been used so far mainly for analyses of rather infrequent though extremely important actions, such as "choosing a career" or "finding a marriage partner." We think it essential that similar methods be developed also for studying more everyday, routine kinds of actions, such as shopping, playing, and the like.

Certainly, not all research in the field has to be confined to the action perspective. In particular, two related subfields in which research is on the act level, and for which this approach seems to be quite appropriate, can be mentioned. The first is a substantial part of the *medical* environmental research that aims at detecting how abnormal conditions in the environment (e.g., pollution) affect our organisms. Second, to a certain extent *stressor* research might be said to belong to the same category. Perhaps in this context it should also be mentioned that some important portions of research about environmental perception may successfully be performed on the act level.

Thus the point is not that we all should choose the action perspective on research, but rather that we should spend some time exploring the nature of the phenomena we have decided to investigate before we settle our research design. If the nature happens to be in the category of actions, we had better turn to the social sciences for design models. If, after careful consideration, we find that an act level of research seems to be appropriate, we should then look for design models in the natural sciences.

Man in Aggregate or as an Individual

The second pair of options is a somewhat biased way of expressing the choice between individual-level and aggregate-level analysis. The classical recognition of the fallacy of making an interpretation on the individual level from aggregate-level data, made by Robinson, is still valid (Robinson, 1950).

By aggregate-level data, in this context we mean data that refer to a collection of people as the basic unit described, assuming that group characteristics apply equally well to members of the group (for further clarification see Lazarsfeld and Menzel, 1961). If the group is a residential neighborhood, examples of aggregate data could be the proportion of foreign-born people, the number of crimes committed during a certain period, or the number of people dying from liver cancer during a 10-year period. Aggregate-level research is characterized by the researcher's inability to "break down" group data through cross-tabulations utilizing subgroupings of members with attributes whose comparison would aid explanation. Often such breakdowns are made impossible from the way the data have been collected. For example, if official statistics are used, there is most often no other possibility than to stick to aggregate-level research.

If we regard this question from a practical point of view, it will probably most often be found that an aggregate research design is cheaper and more easily handled. Quite often such research can produce very "interesting" results. Nonetheless, if the aim is to evaluate the quality of life resulting from behavior in environment, it must be understood from the beginning that an aggregate level of research can be used to only a very limited extent to obtain conclusions about how the individuals in that aggregate look upon the quality of the environment and how it affects them. For example, in studies of relations between pollution and health, an aggregate level in the research design might be quite useful because of the clear criteria of quality that can be established. At least in the introductory stages of medical environmental research, it is hard to conceive that it can be done in another way. The eventual effect of some suspect environmental condition is often so small that it can be calculated only as a tiny "percentage" difference in a population of several thousand individuals. Surveys, participant observation, or other methods that give individual-level data on less than great masses of people will of course completely fail to detect such effects.

The approach may also be applicable for studies of certain social pathologies, such as criminal behavior, but then it is at once much more difficult to determine the man–environment relations. Also, the criteria of quality are not as clear as they seem to be in the medical example. In other areas it can become still harder to determine nonspurious relations and to make the results applicable for planning or policy from aggregative data.

Another consideration is that a *combined* aggregate-level and individual-level research approach can be extremely useful, perhaps especially for the field that we are discussing here. Even if ecological (i.e., aggregate-level) correlations cannot be used directly for making conclusions at the level of individuals, they may give clues to relations between behavior and environment that never will be detected in research that is exclusively on the individual level. Variables like minority status – majority status cannot be formed without reference to the collective, and the same is true for many other attributes with a high potential for explaining behavior. The renewed interest in contextual analysis that has been evinced lately in social science (see Lazarsfeld et al., 1972) is very promising also for environmental research.

So the point regarding this second pair of options is that the choice made will have an impact not only on the design of the research, which is self-evident, but also on the kind of conclusions that can be reached. The researcher had better decide on his goals and choose accordingly.

Man as an Abstract or Concrete Being

The third pair of options regards the choice between an abstract, partial look at man and an attempt to see him as a concrete person of flesh and blood. In principle, it should not be difficult to arrive at a decison in this respect. In seems quite natural that the more concrete viewpoint is to be preferred in connection with research about man and the built environment. But a complication is that a great deal of effort in social science, especially in sociology, has for many years been placed in the opposite direction.

What is found in social theories is most often man liberated from the fetter of his body and without spatial, physical, and biological dimensions. Thus the educational background of a social scientist often tempts him to abstract the spatial, physical, and biological dimensions of man's existence right from the beginning of his research. But if we do, we shall probably find that, in the end, there will be considerable difficulties in relating the findings to real people in real settings. It is probably not merely a coincidence that the most interesting developments in the field during recent years have come from persons with an educational background in anthropology, biology, and architecture, rather than from "pure" sociologists. Especially unfavorable for the field has been the postwar vogue among Western sociologists of trying to define everything in terms of Parsons' abstract system building. This has led many sociologists to look upon society as a structure of roles rather than as consisting of real persons. Another questionable practice (perhaps committed more by geographers than by sociologists) is the concrete but nonetheless one-dimensional and partial conception of man. To regard man only as a commuter, a suburbanite, or a consumer may perhaps appeal to an equally single-minded planner, but we can have reasonable doubts if any planning device that can be called human will ever result from such research.

By now there is probably no misunderstanding regarding the standpoint taken here on this pair of options. As social scientists interested in the field of man and environment, we think we should forget most of what we have learned from "structuralist functionalism." We have much more to offer if we make our own fresh connections to our founding fathers, such as Simmel, Durkheim, Weber, and others.

Bureaucracies or Men as Prime Clients

The fourth pair of options can be reformulated as the choice between seeing man himself or the bureaucracy for which most of us directly or indirectly work as the prime client. By bureaucracy, we mean all the organizations that have been set up to administer our society in some aspect or sector. Directly or indirectly, most social research today is sponsored by such bureaucracies. Research about man and the built environment is no exception.

Many people might regard the choice as unproblematical. The credo of Western democracy is that bureaucracies automatically mirror the interests of the citizens. But as many critics have pointed out (Gouldner, 1971), we have to face the fact that it is not that simple, even in stable democracies like Sweden or Canada. Bureaucracies are made up of employees and elected officials, who certainly are human beings as well as the servants of the people. They have their own private goals, such as a career, reelection, power, and so on. We do not want to overstress this, as too much open concern might lead us to avoid doing any research whatever. Still, we should not disregard the question; we should let it have an impact on how we formulate our research questions. At the least, we should have the strength to avoid research whose main object is to keep a bureaucracy in power. Thus we should be specially careful when we design research about people's values, attitudes, or opinions, and how these relate to environmental issues. Probably no other area of social research lends itself more easily to manipulation by a bureaucracy.

A clear-cut example of research that would be manipulative in the bad sense of the word is easy to provide. Assume an investigation of a "grass-root" protest movement against some environmental change (i.e., a proposed inner-city highway). If such an investigation does not deal with the fundamental problem of how real the environmental threat is for the involved individuals, but rather has the aim of mapping what kind of people are the leaders of the protest, it is easy to see how the data and the analysis can be and probably will be misused by the authorities.

Environmental Data as Aggregative or Nonaggregative

Environmental Data as Objectively Recorded or as Experienced

The fifth and sixth pairs of options have to do with how the environment should be brought into analyses of behavior in the environment. Behavioral scientists who are new to this special field of enquiry are likely to underestimate the importance of this question. If trained in sociology or psychology, they are usually well aware of various behavioral or attitudinal survey and testing techniques; but normally they are less aware of the means of collecting and analyzing environmental data. They will then often assume that there are well-established techniques in this latter regard and that it is only a matter of bringing in some geographer to assist with this side of the analysis. In geography and elsewhere there are certainly quite a few methods dealing with spatial phenomena. But what many do not realize is that these techniques, and the features of environment measured by them, are only occasionally immediately useful for studies of behavioral phenomena in environment. Consider, for example, the difficulties that are likely to be attached to a combined analysis of survey data on punch cards and environmental data on maps.

Spatial behavior, such as movements or selection of roads when making trips, may of course be depicted as lines on maps. But difficulties arise when the researcher tries to analyze the spatial behavior against the motives or other attributes of the road-selecting individuals. He will soon find that almost any kind of multivariate analysis will be extremely tedious to perform because of the clumsy way the data are represented. Most existing cartographic and other spatial techniques are adapted to the description and analysis of the objective structures of the physical world. These are not directly identical with the environment as it appears to people, which is what matters for most behavior, even if, indeed, we have reasons to assume that there are strong relations between the one and the other.

The term *experienced environment* is used here to denote the kind of environment relevant for behavior. There is no reason to argue that experienced environments are less real than what is seen conventionally as the objective structures of the physical world. But the concept of experienced environment underlines at least two types of characteristics that are not usually given much thought when speaking about the objective structure of the physical world. One can be called *relational* characteristics. An environment always has a focal spot or space from which the surrounding world is seen; that is, an environment is an environment to something. Theoretically, two spots or spaces cannot have identical environments because at least some spatial relations to the surrounding world will be different when we move from one spot to the other. Furthermore, they differ because obviously spot 1 has spot 2 included in its environment and spot 2 has spot 1 in its environment, but each spot is excluded from its own environment. In practice, of course, it can often be said that nearby spots have similar environments, even if they are not identical. The nature of the phenomena under study determine how specific we should be in discriminating between two or more similar environments.

We are aware of several studies, especially in the field of user-needs surveys, that are characterized by fruitless trials to relate survey data about *individuals* (e.g., time spent in outdoor activities) to physical environmental data at an *aggregate* level (e.g., the total amount of open space in residential areas). Needless to say, such an analysis is not likely to be very illuminating about man – environment relations.

The other type of characteristic not explicitly found in the concept of objective structure is relevant to environments for all living systems, among which human beings certainly are outstanding examples. Man for the most part is not a passive receiver of inputs from his environment. To a large extent the relations between man and environment can be said to be of an informational nature; both man and environment are at the same time receivers, transmitters, and generators of information. Thus the objective structure of the physical world, to some extent, will achieve different attributes, depending upon who is decoding the incoming information. When we say *experienced* environment, we want to stress exactly this informational nature of man's relations to his surroundings. The same physical structure may appear very different for different individuals because of a vast range of factors, such as differences in culture, social position, physiological organization of the senses, intelligence, physical capacity, or previous experiences with the environment in question. Therefore, to make a correct description of experienced environment, it is not sufficient to find a spot from which the surroundings are seen and measured. It is also required that the description be done from the point of view of a specific individual within this environment.

Both types of characteristics that are brought into the picture by the notion of experienced environments will, of course, make the description of

a geographic area more complicated than ordinary mapping. The second characteristic especially appears at first sight almost bewildering to the mind. Ideally, as we are all somehow different from one another, one environmental description should be made for each of us (as well as for each individual location)! In practice this is impossible; compromises must be made.

But if the researcher has decided to do research at the level of the individual, say through questionnaires or participant observation, it is probably a waste of money and effort to treat the environment in an aggregative manner and / or as the "objective structure of the physical world." To have the data make sense, each individual in the sample should be studied in relation to exactly that environment to which he or she individually is exposed. As we have seen, this environment will not be the same for each individual: first, because each person occupies a unique location in it; second, because each individual is a part of the environment of other individuals but not of his own environment; and, finally, because different individuals and cultural groups differ in their informational coding of the same objective structure of the physical world. These facts matter, especially if the aim is to study the relations between environment and behavior on the level of actions. We think, for example, that it was mainly by being very specific about the locations of the different individuals in Westgate that Festinger and his associates was able to demonstrate some interesting relations between environment and behavior (Festinger et al., 1950). They found for this community that the site plan and the ecological distances between the entrances had considerable effects on who became acquainted and later perhaps friends (an important condition being the homogeneity of the population).

To sum up our points regarding the fifth and sixth pairs of options, we think the choice is rather self-evident once it has been decided what kind and level of behavior should be studied. If we have chosen to study behavior as actions and on the level of individuals, it should follow that we also should collect environmental data that are directly relevant to each individual in our sample. In that case, the research design and analysis should be such that each individual is connected to his specific environmental data (as far as this is possible in practice). Unfortunately, most research schemes we know of tend to ignore this.

Direct Versus Indirect Measurement of Environment

The seventh and eighth pairs of options are more technical and practical in substance, but quite critical, we think, for the kinds of results that will come out of our research. By direct measurements of environment, we mean, in this context, measurements made by the researchers themselves, for example, through aerial photos, inventories, direct observations, and similar devices. By indirect measurements we mean measurements that are obtained by asking the persons under study to report the characteristics of their environment. It can be argued that the last method is the cheapest, and also the one that comes closest to what here has been called the experienced environment. But it must be understood that for data to be relevant for physical planning it is not enough merely to have the environment seen through the eyes of the respondents. It is not unusual that one finds "environmental" studies in which the environment only occurs as attitudes of the informants ("How do you feel about the distance to the closest shop?"). Such data taken alone are of course valueless from the physical-planning point of view. It is the relation between the experienced environments and the objective structures of the physical world that is of interest for physical planning, because planning tries to accomplish better experienced environments for people, not by

changing man, but by rearranging the objective structures.

The preceding discussion seems to indicate that the seventh pair of options really does not offer much of a choice. Most often, both direct and indirect measurements are important for the kind of conclusions we want to reach. We put it on our list because too often sociologists and psychologists choose to make only indirect measurements of the environment, presumably because of a combination of poor understanding of the real issue (at least in applied research), lack of resources, and lack of skill in dealing more directly with the environment. But if we make no effort to translate our findings of relations between experienced environment and behavior into how these relate to the objective structure of the physical world, we shall certainly be seen as pure academicians and rather unimportant when it comes to actual planning of the built environment.

Individuals or Environments as the Primary Sampling Units

If we have chosen to make direct measurements of the environment (alongside indirect measurements of it), there is very often not much of a choice in the last pair of options either. To use individuals as the primary sampling units would mean a very costly design for obtaining the wanted measurements of their environments. These individuals would be scattered over a vast geographical area. Furthermore, since interesting variations in the environments are by all means much less common than the number of different individuals, such a design most probably would provide a very weak basis for demonstrating any relationships between man and environment. There are consequently often strong reasons for using the universe of environments as the primary sampling "population" from which a stratified sample is made, according to what is considered to be interesting environmental variations.[1]

One problem of first sampling environments that are stratified according to interesting variations in their characteristics is that often it can be very hard to get the needed data about the total "population" of environments. (Besides this, the most interesting environments are perhaps not yet built.) In practice, one often has to make compromises concerning representativeness and pick out interesting environments by way of intuition. The choice between representative but pointless as opposed to unrepresentative but significant should not be too hard to make. As we think this has been an increasingly common practice recently, we make no further comments on it here. Let us now return to the hypothetical research interest about children's outdoor activities in the built environment put forward in our introduction. Option by option, our ideal research design would look something as follows.

One of the most important decisions has to be made about option 1 (i.e., the option of seeing behavior as actions or as acts). It can be said at once that any qualified research scheme about children's relations to the built environment cannot dismiss either actions or acts. An essential aspect when it comes to children must always be physical safety, and this means that a substantial part of the research can and should be done on the act level. Safety must be a major concern when children are involved because they only obtain experiences and proper concepts of the environment over time. This point is strengthened further by the rapid changes in today's environment caused by technological development (e.g., the introduction of new materials that have unknown effects with reference to slipperyness or toxicity). However, children have the same basic capacity for actions as the grown man, and we think that research that does not proceed to the action level will never succeed in explaining the most important aspects of children's existence and development. One such aspect is the role

that the child's intensive interaction with the environment plays in forming and accumulating his concepts and consciousness of the world around him. This process can hardly be explained by research performed exclusively on the act level. Since the safety aspect and the child's concept building are related sometimes in a contradictory way (e.g., too much concern about safety will diminish the child's chances of forming proper concepts), a research design that specializes in either aspect is questionable.

Option 2 concerns the aggregate versus the individual level of data and analysis. Considering that some part of the research has to be on the level of actions, it is hard to see how we could avoid intense observations of individual children. These should form the basic analytic units. Aggregate-level data may also play a part in the research design: first, by itself in the exploratory stages as sources for the selection of interesting environments (e.g., neighborhood rates of child accidents or of vandalism could be important pieces of information for this); second, as contextual data in the later phases of analysis.

In the case of option 3, the option of seeing man as a whole or as an abstract part of a social system, we already have taken a strong stand in favor of the former view. Considering the child's intense and simultaneous multilevel interactions with the environment, any other view, in our opinion, will lead to absurd and artificial results. Take, for example, the child's trip to school. We can easily imagine what "efficient" but inhuman technical solutions would result from a one-dimensional view of this as just a transit activity.

Option 4, man as the prime client or as an object of investigation, is in our view extremely important to consider seriously in connection with children. Other groups in society often have their own strong organizations, which can press authorities to take proper consideration of their interests. Children are by definition under age and politically powerless. This not only makes the option important, but it is also a very good rationale for research on the environment from the children's standpoint.

Our preferences regarding options 5 and 6 (i.e., aggregative or nonaggregative, objective or experienced environmental data) should be obvious from the previous discussion. Since the emphasis will be on individual-level data when behavior is concerned, it will be necessary as far as possible to treat the environment in the same way; that is, nonaggregative and experienced level data cannot be dismissed. But as we have strongly emphasized, the experienced environment must be related to the objective structure of the environment or at least to what the environment is for the planner or designer. Otherwise we cannot hope to give the people of practical affairs the advice they ask for.

The choice of treating the environment at the experienced level in a way that is relevant to the objective structure makes option 7 theoretically easy, since it means that data on environment have to be obtained both directly by us and indirectly through the children that are to be observed. In practice, neither measurement type is easily performed. Regarding the data on the experienced environment, we cannot use the same interview methods as with adults, and it is also probably much more difficult to employ a subjective method with children. In some way children appear to us as strange people, a situation akin to what a social anthropologist faces when he first meets "his" tribe. We are not for the moment prepared to give any advice as to how this problem should be handled, although other specialists do tackle it. As to the direct measurement of the objective structure and its representation so that it will be possible to relate to the individual-level data on behavior, we think that what we describe later is highly relevant.

Finally, we come to option 8 (whether individuals or the environments should be the primary sampling units). It should be obvious that if we have chosen in the way we suggest on the previous options we actually have no degrees of freedom

left. This means that we first have to look for interesting environments (and uninteresting ones for contrasts) and wait until the second step for the selection of children. In no other way can we be reasonably confident of obtaining the necessary environmental data without spending the rest of our lives on the matter. Such a design will also make it more likely that what we regard as independent variables will vary in our material. The latter aspect is one of the prerequisites for any causal analysis (see Stinchcombe, 1968, pp. 32 – 38).

The last "choice" underlines what we said about theory in the introduction. How should we be able to know what are interesting environments without theories?

The design that in general terms has been suggested is not without problems. Some have already been dealt with superficially in our discussion, and unfortunately the format of this discussion as a single chapter does not permit a more thorough exploration of most of them. It could also be argued that some of the above-discussed methodological questions require no further elaboration here since in one form or another they appear in the well-known handbooks of social science methodology to which we have made occasional reference. Thus problems pertinent to options 1 to 4 and option 8 in our opinion may be fairly well "solved" this way, once the researcher has become conscious of the issues and has decided upon the wanted direction of the research.

In the case of options 5 to 7, the circumstances are different. These options concern how relevant environmental data should be collected and brought into the analysis with behavioral data. As should be obvious from our earlier discussion, the existing know-how in these cases is greatly insufficient, perhaps because the options touch upon areas that up to now have mainly fallen outside the traditional disciplines in the academic world; therefore, to a large extent they have been left unexplored.

Our interest in these problems was aroused some years ago when we tried to design research about issues very similar to the hypothetical research problem that we have discussed here. We came to realize that the major obstacles to achieving what we wanted were the difficulties in describing environment in a nonaggregative manner, relevant to experiential attributes of environments and to individual-level data about behavior. These became the background and research questions for a project that started in 1968 and is continuing. We have now reached a stage where we hope to be able to reap some benefits from our efforts and apply them to larger design problems. The solutions we found to some of the technical problems connected to options 5, 6, and 7 will certainly not be final; but we are quite confident that they at least represent a beginning, and that they are worth reporting to a wider group of researchers looking for relations between human behavior and environment.

Our report will not go deeply into technical details, although some must be presented to make our way of reasoning understandable. The emphasis will be on explaining the main outline of our strategy and on giving the reader an idea of how feasible the methods are, within the framework of future research in the field. Our aim is not to indoctrinate anyone into literal imitation, but rather to stimulate one to innovation and refinement in a problem area that we feel is strategic to the successful development of the field as a whole.

A PRACTICAL STRATEGY FOR DEALING WITH PHYSICAL ENVIRONMENT

Computerized Environmental Descriptions

As we said before, conventional cartographic techniques are not perfectly adapted for environmental problems, and they are especially ill-suited when a combined analysis of behavior and environment is desired. One reason for this is that it is very tedious to measure relational characteristics from ordinary maps. As we recall, each single point in space has in principle its unique spatial relations to the surrounding world. Assume that we wish to study relations between the uses of certain facilities (such as sport arenas, buses, churches, etc.) and people's ecological distances to these facilities. Provided that good maps exist, it is quite possible to obtain measurements of the different ecological distances by means of simple methods, and to code these data as variables among the others obtained for the respondents in the sample. But this procedure will probably be costly, as it must be repeated for each respondent whose dwelling location is unique. The more the researcher is directed to study the microenvironment, the more difficulties will arise in this respect. Conversely, the problems will diminish by increasing the scale of the study. If the aim is to study, for example, the relations between gross distances and commuting to central cities, there is generally no need to complain about conventional maps as data sources and as media from which measurements can be obtained easily.

But our research interest was focused from the beginning on man's everyday, routine behavior in the experienced environment, and we soon found that ordinary maps did not represent suitable media for us, either as sources of data and measurements or as techniques of analysis. On this level of research, conventional cartography has several other deficiencies besides its clumsiness in giving measurements of *relational* characteristics. While the foremost strength of mapping techniques is the direct visual impression that a well-drawn map can give of an environment with respect to simple characteristics and relations, the visual impression given by the map is very deceptive when applied to more complicated environmental characteristics. Different observers of the same map often reach dissimilar interpretations. Furthermore, it is tedious and laborious to make quantitative calculations from a map. The probability of errors is high even with very simple calculations (e.g., counting the number of parking spaces inside an area). Calculations of areas become very time consuming, especially if there are irregular shapes. Such work can be speeded up by using simple instruments, such as planimeters, but the time thus saved will still be marginal.

Another problem is that certain judgments can be extremely difficult to make on the basis of maps. For instance, a comparison of the shortest walking route to somewhere with the route that a respondent actually uses. In a complex road network and in an area with many different kinds of physical and social barriers for movement, establishing the shortest route might be difficult.

Finally, maximum utilization of the mapping technique to give visual impressions of an environment usually depends on the use of different colors and symbols, the dimensions of the mapped area, and scale. Already existing maps are only occasionally ideal in these respects. Thus the researcher often has to expend great effort in producing the desired maps. Both presentation and publication of the analyses will be expensive.

The many shortcomings of the cartographic techniques made us look actively for alternatives for representing environmental data, as well as for more efficient methods of obtaining the necessary basic information about geographical areas. In the former respect, we found that computer technology has provided possibilities that have been utilized only to a very limited extent in environmental research. In the latter respect, we have taken interest above all in the rapidly developing technique of collecting information from aerial photos.

In our work, the techniques of data representation and collection have been very intimately connected with each other, and it is difficult to

describe the one topic without also, now and then, referring to the other. However, we shall first concentrate on the question of computerized representation and save our main points about the photogrammetric technique for the following part.

At the heart of every method of computerized representation of space of which we are aware lies the use of some coordinate system. The most common is the Cartesian coordinate (or rectangular) system. This is the one we are all familiar with from school; by means of this system it is possible to define the location of any point in three-dimensional space by measuring the distances between it and each of the three coordinate planes, usually called the yz plane, zx plane, and xy plane. Each plane is formed by two coordinate axes that travel at a right angle toward each other through a fixed point, the origin. To refresh the memory of those who have had other things to think about since school, Figure 1 shows a Cartesian coordinate system. The main advantage of a rectangular coordinate system is that the simple formulas from plane geometry can be applied to it.

Geodesy is the science that deals with measuring and describing spatial relations between objects on the surface of the earth. To achieve great

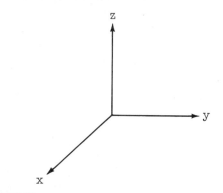

Figure 1
Cartesian coordinate system (the x axis in the figure points toward the reader).

accuracy in such a task, plane geometry is inadequate because of the spherical form of the earth. Spherical coordinate systems offer much more accurate solutions, as was known to navigators long before modern science. However, spherical geometry is more complicated than plane geometry, and it has been found that plane geometry and rectangular coordinate systems are quite acceptable for small areas or when great accuracy of measurement lacks importance. The technique is to make a projection of the geographical area on a plane and then to place a rectangular coordinate system over this plane (for further details, see, e.g., Robinson and Sale, 1969).

Especially in land-use mapping, rectangular coordinate systems are widely employed. Sweden has agreed on a convention for a national rectangular coordinate system where the *x* axis is parallel with the equator and *y* axis is parallel with a meridian that runs close to the east coast of the country. For the altitude, the *z* axis, there is a similar convention.[2] Besides this national system, there are several local nets used on the district level.

It is practical to use an already well established convention for the coordinate system, as this will facilitate connection with spatial information gathered by others. If for some reason this is inconvenient, the researcher should feel free to define his own system. Provided that the coordinates for one point are known in different coordinate systems, transformations of the coordinates of all points to any of the systems can be made easily, especially if the information is computerized.

The slight inexactness of the rectangular coordinate systems when used in geodesy should not worry us, because it is absolutely without meaning on our level of environmental descriptions. For small areas such as residential neighborhoods, this coordinate method will be able to offer representation of spatial relations that, inside the areas, will not deviate more than a few centimeters from the geodetically correct values. Between areas that are geographically apart, the deviations will be slightly larger, but they will be without any significance. Who cares, for example, if his daily half-hour trip to work is calculated to be 2 yards more or less than the absolutely true distance, and what differences will such an error make in empirical studies of human activities? It is quite obvious that a description of spatial attributes with coordinates can never be an exact representation of reality. Besides the small errors that follow from the use of plane geometry, we have to realize that an object occupies space and that there is no finite progression of coordinate points that will be able to fully represent its spatial characteristics. But, as we shall show here, it is possible to achieve sufficient accuracy by choosing one or more coordinate points to represent an object.

In the case of two-dimensional descriptions, we have used, in principle, three methods of spatial representation (Figure 2). The most simple method is to choose *one* characteristic point inside an object to represent the whole object. This method is used in the new official registration system of real estate in Sweden. For each lot, the coordinates for the central point are taken. Added to this piece of information are data about the owner and other relevant matters for deciding the legal status of the property. As every Swede is registered on the lot where he or she is living, it is assumed that this new system, among other advantages, will greatly facilitate future analyses of population movements. On the level of experienced environments, however, spatial representation of an object with only one point is of limited usefulness. The method can be applied only for elements whose shapes or areas are assumed to be of no or minor importance for a certain kind of analysis. Thus, for example, we have represented entrances on houses and in fences as single points. But it is very easy to imagine situa-

Figure 2
Different ways of representing spatial elements with coordinates: examples of elements that are represented by single points [e.g., entrances (1), bus stop (2)], by polygon courses [e.g., footpath (3), hedge (4)], by closed polygons [e.g., parking space (5), playground (6)], and by closed polygons in three dimensions [e.g., residential building (7), grocery shop (8)]. Some of the coordinate points necessary for representing the elements are indicated with crosses. (Courtesy of the Office of the City Surveyor, Lund. Photo by S. Palmkvist and S. Strandberg.)

tions where such a representation would be insufficient.

Another method is to represent an element with two or more coordinate points in a progression, assuming that the points in between those taken consecutively are distributed in accordance with some given function, for example, a straight line or a curve. There are two important subtypes of this. One is to regard the points for an element as an open-polygon course that starts with the first given coordinate point and ends with the last one. This type of representation is applicable when the shapes, but not the areas, of the elements are thought to be relevant for the kind of analysis that is planned. We have used open-polygon courses to represent road nets and certain barriers, such as fences. The other type is to regard the coordinate points as a closed polygon.

In this case, one *also* assumes a line or a curve between the last and first points in the progression. With such a closed polygon that follows the outer contour of an element, it is often possible to describe important facets of its shape as well as the area covered by it. This way of representation has wide applications. We have used it for depicting such elements as buildings, pavements, lawns, squares, outdoor areas designed for specific activities, and so on. In fact, every physical object is eligible for this kind of representation, although it is not always meaningful to be this specific.

So far we have only discussed two-dimensional description, which is a rather gross simplification of the reality around us. If the data source permits it, the third dimension can be represented, too. In a crude way, it can be done by coding the approximate height of the elements when this is assumed to be relevant. When the data source is ordinary maps, perhaps with some complementary information from photos or inventories, this is usually the only possibility available. Thus the number of stories of the buildings can usually be obtained and coded in this way.

But if aerial photos are at hand and instrumented as described in the next section, another and more refined method can be used. It is then possible to obtain the *z* values as well as the *x* and *y* values for any point. This means, first, that the positions of the elements relative to each other will be more accurately represented. If one house stands on a hill and a neighboring house in a valley, this will show up as a difference in the *z* coordinates of the elements. Second, it is now possible to add one or more characteristic points that will help to represent the height and sometimes the volume of an element. For example, instead of representing a tree as a single point, one may choose to take the coordinates for both the foot and head of it. A fence may be represented by two polygon courses, which describe the groundline and the top line, respectively. The

volume of a building can be depicted by taking characteristic points on its connection to the ground (usually the corner points are sufficient for this) and to the roof. In fact, it is also quite feasible to have the shape of the roof represented if this is required.

It is not enough to have the elements described only with coordinates. In ordinary mapping, complementary information is given with colors, figures, names, and other symbols. This is equally possible in the case of computerized environmental descriptions, perhaps with the qualification that it is usually convenient to have the attributes coded numerically. But it is always possible to order outputs from the computer in the form of conventional maps. Besides the points, lines, and

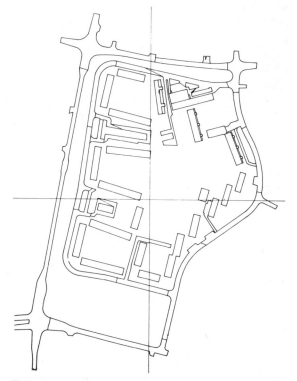

Figure 3
Computer-made map showing roads and buildings.

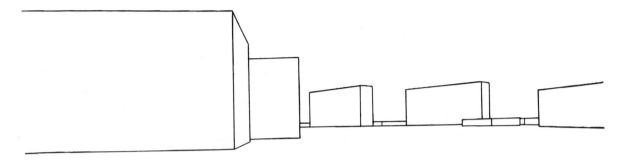

Figure 4
Computer-made perspective of buildings from ground level.

curves given from the coordinates of the elements, these can contain a great choice of symbols. Indeed, with modern equipment, even colors can be used in the symbol making. Figures 3 and 4 are examples of output maps in which, however, only lines have been utilized.

Data of the magnitude necessary for environmental descriptions obviously cannot be heaped into the computer. Even if it could be said that the coordinates of the elements more or less automatically offer a sorting criterion, this is far from enough for the many kinds of analyses that are required. The search procedures would then often be extremely expensive to perform in the computer. But if the input data are given one or a few standardized formats, and if the data are presorted to some system in the computer before being stored somewhere inside it, many search procedures will later be greatly facilitated. It is probably too much to ask for an international standard in these respects, although this would have great advantages. But we should not overstress the importance of a common standard. It is quite feasible that an individual researcher assisted by a sympathetic programmer could design his own system specially tailored for the problems he is interested in. Comparisons and connections with environmental descriptions by others may still be made. In fact, modern com-

puter technology is, from other standpoints, rather frightening in the rapid development of methods for making connections between different data sets.

Our system for ordering the data is thus only one of several possible ways. Nonetheless, a broad outline of its characteristics is not totally out of place, because our sometimes hard-earned experiences may help others to face similar problems.

Our system is quite simple and easily described. It is based on as few and simple rules as possible, the rest being left to the user's own discretion. One rule is that every element shall have a label of identification, which on a phenomenological level tells what kind of element it is. At present, two double-digit codes are used for this. The first code tells the principal category of the element, and the second code is a subclassification. Some examples of principal categories used by us are traffic areas, buildings, vegetation areas, and entrances. Some subclasses to traffic areas are roads and parking spaces. The idea behind the label classification is to offer criteria for presorting the data into categories that we all are likely to use in our everyday confrontation with built environments. Further specification of the elements will then be given by the coordinates and by coded attributes.

Another rule is that every element shall have

an identification number unique within each sub-category. As we shall see in the next section, it is sometimes practical to give this number when collecting the data; on other occasions this is better done automatically by the computer. Besides the above-mentioned information, there is usually a requirement for data to connect the machine coordinates of an element (the system of coordinates that belongs to the machine with which the spatial information has been obtained) to a coordinate base that is general throughout all the material (e.g., to a local, geodetically surveyed coordinate system). This is necessary particularly when many different bases have been used in the data-collection process. There are many ways of arranging for this connection, the most practical generally depending on the kind of input data medium employed.[3] To reduce the need for many special adaptations in the computer, the use of as few different formats of input data as possible is recommended. At least, the identification part of each element should have identical length and form regardless of the kind of element or medium.

To discriminate between different parts of the data about an element and to give special instructions on how a certain data set should be interpreted, special codes can be used instead of highly standardized formats. We have here found it convenient to use negative numbers as such codes, these being easily recognized by the computer and also usually easily assigned when collecting the data.[4]

The requirement of the computer for processing environmental descriptions is first that it should have some kind of direct memory large enough to hold the amount of data needed for an analysis. Since a data set is likely to be rather large in many cases when integrated analyses of environmental data and behavioral data are desired, this means that the computer must be a large one.[5]

A second requirement is for the computer to have some graphical output medium, for example, a curve writer or a screen. Even if most of the analyses will be in the form of quantitative calculations, such a device is necessary for checking and correcting the spatial data. The data relevant

Table 2

Notation of the Data Set	Sources and Nature of the Information	Input Media
Activity data	Coordinates for places actually used by single users and information of the frequency, intensity, length of use, etc. The data may be obtained from surveys or from direct observations.	Punch cards
User data	Information about the user (age, occupation, number of children, income, etc.). Coordinates referring to the dwelling of the user. The data are usually obtained from surveys.	Punch cards
Demo data	Social and demographic compositions of geographical areas. In Sweden, such data can be obtained from official archives.	Magnetic tape
Object data	Physical elements represented by coordinates and numerical codes for their attributes. Data sources are aerial photos, maps, and blueprints; also data from registers and inventories.	Paper tape Punch cards
Road-selection data	Information of how road nodes are linked to each other. Traffic regulations on different road links. Data sources are aerial photos or maps and inventories.	Punch cards

NO.	VARIABLES		EXAMPLE	KEY TO THE EXAMPLE
1	Principal category Subcategory Element number	PC SC ELEMNR	15 2 32	Traffic area Parking space Element 32
2	Number of coordinate points	N	38	
3	Area of the element	A	34527	Area = $345 \text{ m}^2 \cdot 27 \text{ dm}^2$
4	Location of the element	L	11	Element is located in quadrant 11
5	Coordinates that belong to the element. Variable number of drum words.	C	-1225	x coordinate
6		O	-996	y coordinate
7		O	5480	z coordinate
.		R	-1093	x coordinate
.		D	-436	y coordinate
.		I	5481	z coordinate
.		N	.	.
.		A	.	.
.		T	-2225	x coordinate
.		E	-996	y coordinate
.		S	5480	z coordinate
n				
n + 1	Attributes belonging to the element. Variable number of drum words.		1	Marked parking space
n + 2		A	17	Space for 17 cars
.		T		
.		T		
.		R		
.		I		
.		B		
.		U		
.		T		
.		E		
.		S		
.	Indirect addressing to the first item in the attribute part.	I (= n + 1)	119	Attribute part begins in variable 119

Figure 5
Outline of an element field (the standard case).

27

to the kind of analyses we have in mind do not all belong to objects in the physical world. Table 2 is a list of the gross data sets that we have so far tried to bring into an integrated data-processing system. To handle such varied information, once the data fields are inside the computer, it is recommended that they be given a shape that is, as far as possible, general throughout the file. Figure 5 shows the way we normally arrange the data for each element.

It is necessary to organize the data so that they are easily accessed in the computer. As already mentioned, we use mass storage to achieve this. Mass storage can be divided into sectors. Each element is stored with a start in a new sector. The organization in storage is done by bringing together elements belonging to the same principal category and to the same subcategory. These groups of elements are called files. Inside each file, the elements are stored in the order of the numbers of identification.[6]

By giving the elements in the different data sets a general shape and by making them easily accessed in the computer, it is possible to make extensive use of general programs. These are economic from many standpoints. More and more such general programs are published specifically for the purpose of processing spatial data. It is true that these general routines only occasionally are immediately applicable for the problems at hand, but they can very often be rewritten and adapted into a needed program. For example, a recently published book, *Computer Cartography,* contains many routines that may become useful for analyses of behavior in environment (Nordbeck and Rystedt, 1972).

Aerial Photos as Data Sources

To obtain data about outdoor physical environments, many sources, such as maps, inventories, official registers, ordinary photos, and aerial photos, can be used. It would be a mistake to regard these sources as alternatives; in reality they often complement one another. We shall later argue, however, that there are many reasons for referring to aerial photos as a specially interesting data source, which should be used more frequently. To substantiate our arguments, we must first describe what aerial photos are and how they can be used for our purposes.

Aerial photographs in this context can be categorized crudely as either vertical or oblique. A *vertical* aerial photo is taken with the camera axis vertically downward from the aircraft or with a deviance of no more than 5 new degrees from the vertical line. If the deviance is more than 5 new degrees, the picture will be an *oblique* aerial photograph. Here we only describe methods for obtaining data from vertical pictures.

Characteristic of a photographic picture is the *perspective projection*. This means that each detail is projected with a straight line through the center of the camera lens on the plane negative. From this it follows that all details lying along the same line will be depicted on the same place on the photo. Thus higher points in the terrain will be displaced away from the center of the photograph, and lower points will be displaced toward the center (see Robinson and Sale, 1969, pp. 72 –76; or Axelsson, 1964, p. 10). At the point exactly vertical below the lens center, no displacements will occur. It is only when the terrain is perfectly flat that measurements of distances can be made analogically with measurements on ordinary maps. The latter are called *orthogonal projections,* which means that the scale is the same all over the map. But the difficulties of measurements in aerial photos can be overcome by applying certain methods and instruments. The technique is based on man's capacity for stereoscopic vision. If this is intensified with an instrument, a stereoscope or a stereoautograph, it is possible to work with two pictures in a stereo model. The radial displacements in the pictures in that case will neutralize each other, and, provided that the pictures have been orientated in relation to some points that have been geodetically surveyed,

Figure 6
Overlap of photos in aerial photography. (Courtesy of the Office of the City Surveyor, Lund. Photo by S. Palmkvist and S. Strandberg.)

three-dimensional measurements may be made in the model.

The photographs are taken from an aircraft flying in strips over the terrain. The photos are taken so that they overlap each other (Figure 6). Normally about a 60 percent overlap is the standard for achieving a stereo model usuable for measurements. Sometimes it is an advantage to have an 80 percent overlap. If many tracks are required to cover an area, they are flown so that the pictures taken from two parallel strips overlap to at least 25 percent. This is to neutralize instability in the course of the aircraft. The photographing may be done from different altitudes; on a negative of 23 by 23 centimeters, for example, the scales may vary from 1 : 3,000 at the lowest practical altitude of 450 meters to 1 : 30,000 from a flight at 4,600 meters, which is the highest regularly practiced in Sweden. The season for aerial photography is short in our latitude and occurs between the melting of the snow and the leafing of the trees, with accompanying displacements between south and north latitudes. This is specially valid when the aim is to obtain maps in large scales of densely settled areas.

In our experience, environmental descriptions of areas that cover 12 to 25 hectares will require work in three to six stereo models for which five to eight photographs will normally be required. The photographing can be done in color or in black and white. Work on the stereo model requires diapositives in the sizes of the originals (23 by 23 centimeters) and one print without enlargement of each photo.

It occurs more and more often that aerial photos are already taken for the areas that interest the researcher. Where to find such photos naturally varies in different countries. In Sweden, it is rather easy to find whether photos exist, as an official agency (The Geographical Survey Office) has a monopoly of all aerial photographing for map construction. Consequently, this agency has to be approached when ordering aerial photographs covering an area for which no, or only obsolete, pictures exist.

To orientate the photos to a stereo model, there must be *fulcrums* (some kind of control points) that can be seen on the photographs and which have been geodetically surveyed on the ground. Normally, the fulcrums are arranged by professionals trained in geodesy. But this procedure is sometimes unnecessary if there are landmarks whose geodetical positions can be more easily determined. The fulcrums should be spread as evenly as possible over the area, and at least three such points are required in each stereo model.

When stereo models are employed for map constructions or numerical transformations, they are usually arranged in an instrument called a *stereoautograph*, to which various other units can be connected. We have used an instrument made by Wild: type A8. The following units have been connected to this machine: one coordinate autograph with a drawing table; one automatic device for registration of coordinates (Wild type EK 5); one paper tape punch (Facit 6020, 8 channels); and one IBM input – output typewriter. Figure 7 shows all these units.

Registration work in a stereoautograph is a matter of routine for those trained in it. There is no reason for the researcher to learn this. But it is necessary for the researcher to know how to handle a mirror-type stereoscope, which is essential for the preparatory work; he should also be able to interpret aerial photos with respect to phenomena that occur inside his field of interest. For economic reasons, it is important that the work in the stereoautograph be minimized. Preparations and clear instructions from the researcher to the operator will considerably facilitate the procedure. To a great extent, the results will depend on the researcher knowing what possibilities the operator has and on his work being formulated within the limits of these possibilities.

We here report some of our experiences while

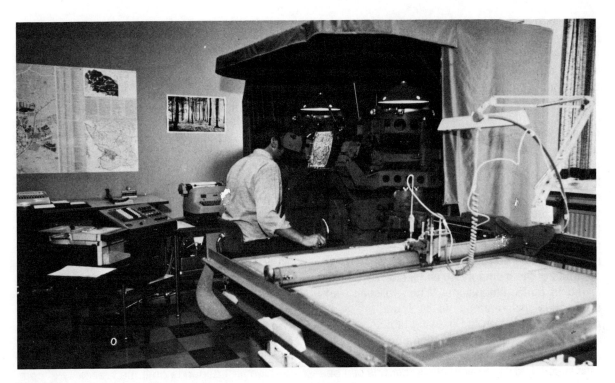

Figure 7
Stereoautograph (Wild type A8) connected to units for automatic registration of coordinates. (Courtesy of VIAK AB, Consulting Engineers and Surveyors.)

working with five residential areas. The areas were built during the 1950s and consist of self-contained houses and blocks of flats. The latter may have 2 to 10 stories and be grouped in different ways. On the basis of the variations in the density of the areas, we think that our procedures are applicable, regardless of land use, to most Swedish urban areas outside the city cores, but do not know to what extent the dense downtown areas might be studied through aerial photos.

The work in the stereoautograph starts with the operator orientating the photos so that a stereo model results. This procedure takes an average of 1½ hours for each model. Thereafter the registration in the model can begin.

The first step is to punch some information about the model. The most important data here are the machine coordinates for the fulcrums and the geodetically decided coordinates for corresponding points. It is through this information that transformation to some convenient coordinate base can be made. We also add data that identify the photos, such as identification numbers, the time of day when the photos were taken, whether the photos are in color or black and white, whether taken before or after the leafing, and whether taken below clouds or in sunshine. When paper tapes are used as registration media, it is not necessary to repeat all this information for the model on each tape. It is sufficient if each tape has some identification number that connects it with the correct model data.

After these preliminaries, spatial elements can begin to be registered according to instructions from the researcher. In our case, the registration is done element by element. The operator begins by assigning codes for the principal category and subcategory to which the element belongs. The element is then given a unique identification number within the subcategory and area. Those attribute codes valid for the element follow, and, finally, those coordinates required to represent the element spatially (see Figure 2). The coordinates are automatically punched on impulses given by the operator after a mechanical pointer has been placed on the location in the stereo model for which the coordinates are wanted. The pointer can be freely moved in the model, and the contours of the element can consequently be followed in three dimensions. When following an element in this manner, its contours are synchronously drawn on the drawing table.[7]

One method of reducing the amount of work is to avoid coordinate registration for an element. This is possible if the relevant coordinates can be obtained by referring to an element in another category that has already been registered. For example, when registering elements in the category of traffic areas, it is often found that they are congruent with some element in the category of surface characteristic. If, for example, a road element has a complicated shape, it is often advantageous not to give the coordinates, but to punch a special negative code and then the identification codes for the corresponding element that has already been registered. The coordinates can be assigned later to the element in the computer.

Some may wonder why we have corresponding elements and why we do not, instead, give one and the same element more attributes to cover several aspects. One answer is that such a procedure would make it very difficult for the operator to define the elements. After all, only occasionally do two or more attributes neatly overlap and form an easily decided area homogeneous with respect to the attributes. The fact is that the more attributes there are connected to the elements, the less meaningful these elements will become. Consequently, there will be many elements as well. Indeed, we may suspect that they will become more numerous than when we use less complicated and larger elements that overlap and sometimes exactly correspond to each other.

Still, this is not the main reason for our strategy. It is more important that the instructions to the operator be less ambiguous and that the interpretations and decisions which have to be made while working in the stereo model be as easy as possible. Another advantage is the possibility our method provides for building up the description system stepwise. Supplements, which on second thought the researcher may need, are easily integrated with the previous information.[8]

But the method chosen by us is not without problems. It depends on it the feasibility of combining elements from different categories to form new elements in the computer. For example, since we register football fields as elements in one file and lawns as elements in another file, it must be possible to combine these files in the computer for obtaining information on pitches that have grass surface. Geometrically, such a problem consists of finding polygons in polygons. General problems for this exist already, as well as for the somewhat less complicated problems of finding points in polygons, and we are just now testing a variant of our own.

Nevertheless, it is possible to be rather sophisticated with respect to the kind and amount of work that is transferred, so to speak, from the operator to the computer. This is particularly valid for most spatial attributes and relations. Even three-dimensional characteristics to a large extent can be deduced by the computer when following our method.

Our method of handling three-dimensional representation will first be demonstrated with respect to topographical conditions. These will often be important in analyses of behavior. The slope of the ground may matter from the point of view of communication, for example, with respect to the requirements of physically disabled persons for a footpath system, or with respect to the advantages of differences in track altitudes for exercise. It may also be a question of how topographical conditions influence the usefulness of elements, for example, a sloping lawn, or how such conditions reduce views and add shadows in an environment.

Our way of representing sloping characteristics depends on registering the physical environment in the form of elements, each described with a number of points in three-dimensional space. These points are chosen when they refer to what we regard as two-dimensional elements, first, to describe the plane picture of the element; but they are supplemented with points that represent differences in altitude when this seems to be important from the user's standpoint.

One example might be a road element, which is straight in the plane. If this is registered only with its two end points, it will be described as a straight line between them. A difference in altitude between the end points, because of a hill that extends over perhaps only one third of the distance, will incorrectly show up with the slope calculated over the whole distance. But if vertical inflexure points are registered also, the description of the slope characteristics of the road will be acceptable, in our opinion.[9]

What we regard as three-dimensional elements, with volumes, are registered according to the following method. First, the relevant coordinates for the ground (bottom) contour are taken as usual. If then the form of the element is approximately regular (with plane, unbroken surfaces), the vertical boundary contour is also registered. But if the shape is irregular, we have

chosen to approximate the description by also registering an adequate number of contours in between the bottom and the top of the element. These contours are usually taken as isoriths of equal altitudes where the element on any side begins to change its form to a significant degree (i.e., at the lines of intersection between different planes). For example, most roofs may be represented fairly well this way. But if the form is very irregular, such as for a natural hill or shrubbery, an approximation has to be made by a number of equidistant isoriths. Also, regular spheric forms are treated in this way, although more accurate methods could be used for them.

The preceding methods illustrate how we have endeavored to routinize and generalize the representation of spatial characteristics without renouncing the realism required for studies at the experienced level of environment.

Our methods demand that a large number of coordinates be registered. The normal procedure is that every time a contour changes direction the coordinates must be obtained. This is feasible as long as the element is bordered by straight lines; the description of it will then be fairly exact. But sometimes the contour is curved; it is then impossible to take the coordinates for each point where a change of direction occurs. One possibility would be to have the coordinates for a reasonable number of points registered and to be content with the approximation this accomplishes (the computer will assume straight lines between consecutive points). Another method, which will sometimes reduce the amount of registration, is to divide the curve into an approximation of arcs. These arcs may be registered by first punching a special negative code and then the coordinates for three points that represent the beginning, middle (exactness is not required), and end of each arc. In the computer, a practical number of points on the arcs will then be generated.[10]

It is inevitable that the operator will make some incorrect registrations. We have found that such errors can be reduced if the researcher first studies the areas in a usual mirror-type stereoscope and then prepares specific instructions concerning difficult elements. These instructions can advantageously be conveyed to the operator through drawings on enlarged aerial photos.

The operator himself will sometimes discover that some element has been incorrectly described. He then has recourse to a number of correction routines; these will not be elaborated on here. But we would like to stress the importance of eliminating as many as possible of the stereo operator errors. It can be much more difficult to make the corrections after the work in the stereoautograph is concluded.

Our general experience in the registration of elements in the physical environment using aerial photos and photogrammetry can be summarized as follows:

The photographs of our five areas were in color, but for one area we also had black and white photos. Unfortunately, the comparison is not altogether valid, as the latter were taken from a somewhat higher altitude. Color photos naturally contain more information that corresponding black and white. For example, blue play apparatus stands out against light brown sand quite differently if both the apparatus and the background are depicted in gray shades. Furthermore, the possibilities of interpreting an object in the shadow of a house, for instance, are much greater if the pictures are in color.

For all color photos, the flying altitude was 600 meters, which gives a scale of about 1 : 4,000. The black and white photos were taken from 930 meters (1 : 6,200). The lower altitude has proved very suitable for our purposes. It has allowed, for example, correct registration of details such as play equipment, carpet-beating racks, and bicycle stands. At the higher altitude, corresponding interpretations were in many cases impossible (but note that we only had black and white pictures from this altitude). With color photos the

limit for interpretation with our requirements for detail is probably an altitude of about 900 meters.

Another factor that influences interpretation is whether the photos are taken in sunshine or below clouds. One area had pictures of the latter kind. The shadows obtained in sun pictures can be an advantage, particularly at the registration of the vertical dimension of smaller objects such as play appliances. The same applies to trees and bushes. Shadows from houses, on the other hand, are a disadvantage; they make it more difficult to interpret the areas close to the houses. Pictures taken below cloudy sky do not have the disadvantage of shadows from houses, but lack the above-mentioned advantages. The perspective projection results in the view at ground level close to elements that have a vertical extension (i.e., houses) being accurate only in the center of the picture. In a stereo model, the operator obtains, parallel with the direction that the airplane has flown, an accurate view at ground level close to such elements over a much wider area. Inside a certain zone, however, viewing is only possible in a single picture (i.e., each picture will show only its side of, for instance, a house). In certain conditions, registration may be made also in these zones; these, however, will be narrower if the photos overlap 80 percent than if they overlap 60 percent.

It is more important that we have been unable to find that the result is worse in those two areas where we have worked with pictures that overlap 60 percent. An explanation for this might be that the operator can deduce, for example, the location of an entrance from some detail of construction or from the form of the house. Furthermore, the mechanical pointer can be moved in a fixed way, for example, to "sound" down a point from the roof to the ground level. Nonetheless, it should be pointed out that an 80 percent overlap gives considerably more options in the choice of stereo models, although the operator will then perhaps choose to work with a stereo pair that consists of every second picture (which gives 60 percent overlap).

The precision of the registration of coordinates in the stereoautograph is so high (0.2 o/oo of the altitude, in this case equal to 12 centimeters in the plane and vertically) that for our purposes we have not had any reason to discuss it. As this is the routine precision of the instrument, no gains can be made from lowering it. The way to make the procedure less expensive has to be through a higher degree of generalization of the elements (i.e., a less realistic description of elements), and must be decided from case to case with the aim of the description system in mind.

The time consumed in stereoautograph work has naturally varied much among the areas because of variations in the amount of information sought, in densities, and in the sizes of the areas. The time spent by the operator in preparation and orientation of the pictures is anything from 2 to 3 hours for each stereo model. The total time for this entry consequently depends on how many stereo models are required for the registration in any given area. This, in turn, depends on the density, topography, and size of the area. In a flat landscape without high elements, registration may be done in a model that with 60 percent overlap covers about 33 hectares. If the overlap is 80 percent, the model will be reduced to a little less than 17 hectares.

The time for registration has varied from 65 hours for an open area (13 hectares) to 116 hours for a densely built up area (28 hectares, three and four stories), but which also had a considerable amount of open space. If a comparison is made of two of our smaller areas (12 to 13 hectares), both of which have an inconsiderable amount of large open spaces but which vary greatly in densities, we find that the time is 5 hours per hectare in the less dense area and just less than 7 hours per hectare in the other. If a similar comparison is made of two areas both of which are rather dense, but which vary in the amount of large open

spaces, the time is found to decrease from 7 to a little more than 4 hours in the area with much open space. These comparisons hint at the variations that can be expected inside most parts of urbanized areas.

The registration of what we have called *surface characteristic*, for example, vegetation areas, has taken the most time of all our categories, or between 40 and 70 percent of the total work. In smaller areas the registration of the surface characteristic has required about 160 elements, and in the largest, 240 elements. Each element consists on average of 22 coordinate points, and the registration time has varied between 7 and 9 minutes. This makes about 20 seconds for each coordinate point.

All entrances have taken 2 hours to register in each area. Trees and street lamps together take 4 hours, irrespective of the size and density of the areas. All play equipment, tables, benches, and bicycle stands were registered in about 90 minutes in each area.

After this outline of our photogrammetric work, we return to the matter of the usefulness of aerial photos as data sources. In our opinion the photogrammetric method has several advantages (at least compared with the use of maps). Our arguments can be summarized as follows:

1. The aerial photo contains a large amount of information that is uniform for all areas where identical technical efforts have been made.
2. The information in the pictures can be used in degrees as needed, and supplements can be made afterward from the pictures.
3. The information refers to a precise time. For areas that have already been photographed, the information is easily available (at least in Sweden).
4. For areas that have not been photographed, the information is easily obtainable, although at considerably increased expense.
5. Aerial photos are easy to handle and file.

6. Aerial photos, provided they are able to form a stereo model, can be used directly for registration of horizontal as well as vertical coordinates.

7. Interpretation, measurement, and registration of physical elements can be made in one single instance and without extensive fieldwork. This must be compared with situations when maps are used. As existing maps are usually made for aims quite different from behavioral studies, the information usually has to be supplemented by very expensive and time-consuming fieldwork in which inventories are made. Then there is usually a work phase, when the new information is correctly represented on the maps; finally, the numerical transformation can be made.

Other Data Sources

In our work we also tried to investigate what methods other than photogrammetry can be employed for environmental description. In particular, we sought for methods that, like the photogrammetric one, can be used for computerized representations and that can supply data which can be integrated with information from aerial photos in a common description system. Another search criterion involved costs. As already existing environmental descriptions are usually on a quite different level and have content other than what is relevant for behavioral problems, it is often extremely difficult to make samples of geographical areas that have interesting variations of environmental characteristics. It is then of great interest to find methods for making quick and relatively inexpensive surveys over many geographical areas, from which the researcher, after preliminary analyses, can make selections of environments for more intensive behavioral studies. We tend to believe that real progress in research about behaior in environment is first possible when such carefully designed studies can be performed.

Relative to the richness of information, aerial photos must be considered an inexpensive data source, and, provided the procedures for obtaining the information from them are routinized, they offer a quick way to scan many geographical areas. But they have certain limitations. One is that only elements visible from above can be interpreted and registered. Elements located within buildings or otherwise shielded must be observed some other way. The same can be said about such attributes as land-use regulations, ownership, traffic regulations, and other norms that apply to different pieces of the land in an area and which in behavioral studies will often be at least as important as the more material aspects of environment. Further examples of what normally cannot be assessed very well, if at all, from the sky are the demographical and socioeconomic composition of an area, the supply of services, and organized activities. There is naturally no single way of obtaining information about these varied aspects; moreover the most convenient methods will differ from country to country.[11]

The methods we have worked out for obtaining coordinate representations from ordinary maps, from blueprints of buildings or from other constructions, and from enlarged photographs are of wider generality. These data sources are specially interesting when the aim is to link information about the inside of buildings to data from aerial photos. The methods require a *coordinate reader* connected to an ordinary output key punch (usually for cards) (Figure 8). In such equipment, the map or equivalent ·is fixed on a special table over which a pointer can be moved freely on the horizontal plane. The horizontal machine coordinates, for the point over which the mark is put, will be calculated automatically by the machine and from an impulse of the operator they will be punched. At the key punch, the operator can also register identification and attribute codes and thus make elements with for-

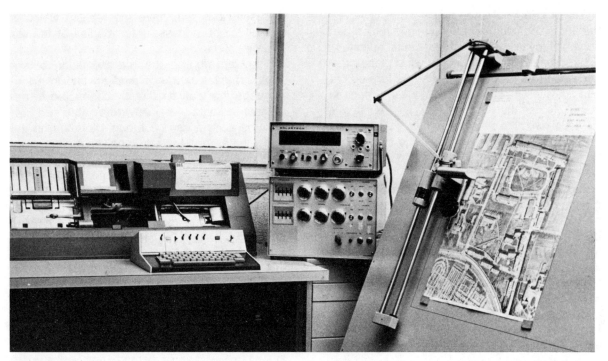

Figure 8
Digitizer table connected to units for automatic registration of coordinates.

mats that are analogous to what we have discussed earlier.

The operator's first step will usually be to ensure that the machine coordinates are transferable to a known coordinate base. There are many possible ways of doing this; we recommend the following. For each map (blueprint, photo) choose three easily observable points (they should not be too close to each other) for which the coordinates in some geodetically decided coordinate system are already known or can be assessed (e.g., from the photogrammetric material). Call these points *base points*, and the machine coordinates for these should be registered on each card containing coordinates of the elements. With the base points it is later possible to make correct transformations in the computer regardless of the position of the map (blueprint, photo) on the table of

the coordinate reader. Errors, such as those caused by distortions of the map due to air humidity, are largely eliminated. The registration of the rest of the information, the coordinates of the elements, and the attributes may in the main be done analogously to what we described earlier in connection with the photogrammetric method.

As mentioned, elements on single photographs also may be registered with a coordinate reader. This presupposes, however, that there are rather low demands on the exactness of the measurements and that considerably more than three base points are known on the photo. This requirement is explained by the earlier-mentioned displacements of details in a photo. But if the coordinates of many points on the photo are known, corrections of this kind of distortion may be made in the computer if the landscape is not too hilly.

The possibility of using single photos is very important in the context of behavioral studies. In a survey study we had our respondents indicate on enlargements of aerial photos what places they had been to and where they had performed certain activities (in some cases we used maps instead). It was then very easy to register this information with the coordinate reader by using the method just described, and later to connect the data with the computerized environmental description. Because we used enlargements of pictures that also had been utilized in the photogrammetric work in the stereoautograph, it was no problem for us to cover the area with many base points (about 50 for each enlargement were regarded as sufficient). These points were registered with the coordinate reader once and for all, together with identification numbers that connected them to corresponding points in the stereoautograph. The registration of the elements could then be made by the same method as earlier described for maps (i.e., only three of the base points had to appear on each element card).

CONCLUDING REMARKS

In this section we describe techniques that might be of use for a researcher performing behavioral studies with environmental references. The methods have the following advantages:

1. They offer a practical alternative to the use of reports of respondents for obtaining environmental data that are directly relevant to specific individuals who are in different locations. Environmental descriptions and measurements may be made from the point of view of any locations in the geographical areas whose attributes are represented in the computer. Such methods offer the possibility of obtaining, without undue costs, environmental descriptions that have the realism which is likely to be necessary for studies at the experienced level.

2. They accomplish the representation of environmental data in a medium and in a language that can be directly connected to behavioral data (i.e., environmental and behavioral data can be brought together in the computer for integrated analyses).

Thus these methods solve some, though by no means all, problems pertinent to what earlier were described as options 5, 6, and 7. Besides this, the techniques promise to be useful in fields other than behavioral studies of built environments where environmental descriptions are required. But that is another story.

NOTES

1. It should be obvious that by primary and secondary units we do not mean anything but an order of the sampling procedure.
2. Here and in what follows we use the mathematical way of denoting the west–east axis as the x axis and the south–north axis as the y axis. For some reason, land surveyors usually have the reverse way of denoting the axes.
3. If punch cards are used, we have found it safest if every card contains its connection code or sometimes even its base coordinates (in machine-coded form). In this way, it will be unnecessary to keep track of the order of the cards reaching the computer. If magnetic tapes or paper tapes are employed as input data media, other and more economical methods can be applied. For the same reason, it is advisable to repeat the label and number of identification on each card when many cards have to be used for describing an element. In fact, since the coordinate description of an element will often require more space than is available on one card, we would advise the use of some other input medium rather than hole cards whenever possible. The system we have designed, however, leaves room for great freedom in the choice of input medium.
4. In the case of paper tape or magnetic tape, for example, we insert a −1 to indicate that no more attributes will be given to an element. This means the following numbers will be coordinate. Likewise, the end of the coordinates will be indicated by −3, which tells the computer that the following number will refer to the identification part of another element. The use of instruction codes gives a well-needed freedom of format, as both the number of

attributes and the number of coordinates are likely to vary considerably between elements. Negative numbers as special instructions are convenient in many other situations, and new ones can be constructed when the need arises. We have negative numbers to indicate, for example, that there is a degree of uncertainty in some of the coordinates for an element (some part of an element may be invisible in the data source), and that a set of coordinates should be interpreted as an isorithm line (such representation is often required in topographical and other three-dimensional descriptions).

5. We have found that the Univac 1103 with a mass storage at the Data Central of Lund University is suitable in this respect. Probably also somewhat smaller computers will do.

6. In the first sector of the mass storage, we store the start-sector number of a content table and the number of words in the table. The content table is placed behind the last element. For each element it contains the element number, start-sector number, and number of words. At processing, the table is read from the mass storage in parts. The parts are searched sequentially. Only those elements required for an analysis are taken from the mass storage. [A complete documentation of the computer routines of our description system (FORTRAN) is found in Dahlgren et al., 1973, Appendix 2.]

7. It is advantageous also to have the fulcrums indicated on the map drawn at the drawing table. These can be used in a procedure of registering complementary information after the work in the stereoautograph. Sometimes, time can be saved by gathering the coordinates for several elements under the same identification and attribute part. The elements are then separated and given unique identification numbers in the computer. This results in less punching, a prerequisite being that the elements belong to the same category and have identical attributes. If the elements are seen as open-polygon courses or as closed polygons and consequently require more than one set of coordinates, these sets have to be separated element by element with a special negative code allotted by the operator.

8. There is one alternative to our method which has sometimes been used in computerized land-use cartography, although not by us. The method consists of first defining a grid net, which is laid over the areas. Each grid in the net is then described with respect to what percentage of its area is covered by each of the attributes. For certain attributes, only occurrence and nonoccurrence are noted. But we would not recommend this method in connection with work in a stereoautograph because it would mean that the operator would spend too much time in estimating and measuring quantities instead of merely registering. We argue that such analytical work is much better done in the computer. Furthermore, even if the grids in principle may be made very small, certain elements, especially those which are narrow and long, such as roads, will present difficulties if the alternative method is used. Rather complicated computer routines would be needed to combine the relevant grids to obtain good representations of such elements. As in practice the grids cannot be made very small because of the increasing time for measurements then involved, the representation will often be poor, regardless of sophisticated computer routines.

9. Very steep slopes, however, have been regarded as elements in themselves and have been categorized as barriers. Pronounced hills, banks, ditches, and ravines have also been treated as single elements with volumes. We have judged that this topographical description will be adequate in our areas, which are all rather flat. For more hilly landscapes, this method is probably not sufficient. Presumably, the solution then is a more general description of the topography, and possibly the methods employed in numerical terrain models might be of interest here.

10. In this context, it should be noted that our method for registering closed polygons does not permit one such polygon to encircle another polygon. In this case, a fictitious borderline has to be put between the outer and the inner contours of the encircling polygon. This line, however, does not really influence the polygon's form, and, provided that it is marked with some negative code, it can be disregarded when, for example, computer-drawn maps are required.

11. Probably specific to Sweden, for example, are the earlier-mentioned coordinate register of real-estate parcels and the population data bank that can be connected to this register. Because of the issue of the integrity of the individual in a "computer society" (which is presently an object of discussion and law making in Sweden), a researcher will in future probably (and hopefully) have to confine himself to obtaining aggregate data from these registers. As the records in the population register contain the address of each individual, it is quite technically feasible to have the data, which are mainly demographical and fiscal, distributed on a very low level of aggregation. For many problems it can be important to have the demographic composition of the residents calculated for each house or each main entrance in blocks of flats. (In areas with single-family houses this is hardly conceivable ethically.) We have set up a routine that makes such a distribution from the alphanumerical street addresses on the records, and transforms the addresses to coordinates. The only technical problem we have had is that the same address is sometime spelled differently on the magnetic tapes of the population register.

REFERENCES

12. Axelsson, H. 1964. *Skoglig fotogrammetri*. (Kungliga Skogsstyrelsen) Stockholm.

13. Dahlgren, R., J. Hellberg, and G. Lindberg. 1973. Byggda omgivningar i bruk: ett förslag till analysinstrument, Bilaga

1: Exempel pä kodscheman och plotterkartor, Bilaga 2: Programdokumentation. Lund: Institutionen för Byggnads-funktionslära, LTH, arbetsrapport nr 2 / 1973.

14. Festinger, L., S. Schachter, and K. Back. 1950. *Social Pressures in Informal Groups*. New York: Harper & Row.

15. Gouldner, A. W. 1971. *The Coming Crisis of Western Sociology*. London: William Heineman.

16. Lazarsfeld, P. F., and H. Menzel. 1961. "On the Relation Between Individual and Collective Properties," in A. Etzioni (ed.), *Complex Organizations: A Sociological Reader*. New York: Holt, Rinehart and Winston.

17. Lazarsfeld, P. F., A. K. Pasanella, and M. Rosenberg. 1972. *Continuities in the Language of Social Research*. New York: Free Press.

18. Lynd, R. S., and H. M. Lynd. 1929. *Middletown*. New York: Harcourt Brace Jovanovich.

19. Lynd, R. S., and H. M. Lynd. 1937. *Middletown in Transition*. New York: Harcourt Brace Jovanovich.

20. Michelson, W. 1970. *Man and His Urban Environment*. Reading, Mass.: Addison-Wesley.

21. Miller, J. G. 1965. "Living Systems: Basic Concepts." *Behavioral Science,* vol. 10, no. 3.

22. Nordbeck, S., and B. Rystedt. 1972. *Computer Cartography*. Lund: Studentlitteratur.

23. Robinson, A. H., and R. D. Sale. 1969. *Elements of Cartography*. New York: Wiley.

24. Robinson, W. S. 1950. "Ecological Correlations and Behavior of Individuals." *American Sociological Review,* vol. 15, pp. 351 – 357.

25. Schutz, A. 1970. *On Phenomenology and Social Relations*. Chicago: University of Chicago Press.

26. Stinchcombe, A. L. 1968. *Constructing Social Theories*. New York: Harcourt Brace Jovanovich.

27. Young, M., and P. Willmott. 1957. *Family and Kinship in East London*. London: Routledge & Kegan Paul.

The Semantic Differential and Other Paper-and-Pencil Tests

Robert B. Bechtel

Robert B. Bechtel received his Ph.D. in social psychology from the University of Kansas in 1967 with his dissertation on the Hodometer under Roger Barker. Since that time, his research has concentrated on behavior-setting methodology in different environments and on adapting behavior-setting techniques to design problems. He is currently working on two books to be published by Dowden, Hutchinson & Ross —Enclosing Behavior, which is a text on the use of behavior-setting surveys, and Typology of Cities, which classifies city environments in the United States. He has worked at the Institute for Community Studies, the Greater Kansas City Mental Health Foundation, and is now Director of Research and an officer of the Board of Environmental Research and Development Foundation. His hobby is investigating haunted houses.

Perhaps no other device has received more use and at the same time more opprobrium than the paper-and-pencil test. In the psychological literature it has been responsible for the bulk of most research. Yet in criticism that has reached the stage of congressional investigation, the paper-and-pencil test has been portrayed as the villain that labels children for life and relentlessly discriminates against minority groups. But because they are so easy to use in a cookbook fashion, and because there are so many of them, paper-and-pencil tests will be around for some time to come. Lest the researcher in architectural and environmental areas be overwhelmed by contradictory results, or by results that are too easily obtained, he had best become familiar at least with the problems involved in the use of paper-and-pencil tests. Above all, it must be remembered that the greatest weakness of the paper-and-pencil test is at the same time its greatest strength—the ease with which it is administered.

SOME GENERAL RULES

What general rules can be developed for the use of paper-and-pencil tests that will help curb some of this temptation? Despite the confusion that may seem to emanate about the use of paper-and-pencil instruments, there are some guidelines that the researcher can use to avoid major pitfalls. Among these are the following:

Size of the Population

When building or designing for a single family, a number of conversations can often remove ambiguities about the client's response to design suggestions or other matters. Hence there is often no need to formalize data. However, when the population is that of a large building or a town or a city, there is no choice but to use some method that will allow an accurate and representative recording of responses on paper.

Of course, a large number of people means that *sampling* is required. No research project has the funds to question every person in a town of 10,000, and the only way to manage the collection of data is by a random sampling of the population according to the characteristics relevant to the project. A school project would not sample an elderly population to ask them about classroom design; it would sample prospective pupils and teachers. In other words, the relevant population are the future users of the design. In public buildings, this often does mean the entire city can be seen as potential users. Sampling techniques are thoroughly discussed in Kish (1965), and the novice researcher is advised to get a consultant on this very critical matter. The national public opinion research organizations generally have the best sampling consultants.

Appropriateness of the Instrument

It is easy enough to say that the researcher must select the right instrument for the questions to be answered. The way to determine whether an instrument is appropriate is *not* just by working over the questions in the instrument, but by reading the literature for examples of just how the questions were intended, used, and interpreted by previous researchers. Buros (1965) contains a representative list of references for many tests and instruments. In the case of many new instruments, the researcher has to resort to a library search for articles in journals like *Environment and Behavior*, to summaries of the literature in Proshansky, Ittelson, and Rivlin (1970), Craik (1970, 1973), Gutman (1972), Michelson (1970), and to the EDRA conferences. There is no substitute for building up a library of these sources.

Generally, from the library sources one can get a feel for the appropriateness of the instrument for the conditions one has in mind. A careful note of how these conditions might differ from past uses should be made *before* the instrument is used.

Overuse and Overreliance

Despite the claims of generality that many authors may make for their instruments, there is always some sense in which every use in unique. Although this is usually not a problem, for persons not expert in the tests and measurements field the results of each instrument should always be accompanied with a certain amount of skepticism. It is always a good practice for the person who will interpret the results of any instrument to go back to a few of the persons who answered questions on the instrument and ask (1) what the respondent thought the question meant, and (2) what the answer meant. It can be a disillusioning experience, but it can, at the same time, introduce the researcher into the wonderfully infinite world of human interpretation.

The inventiveness of human populations in discovering new meaning (or understanding, as you will) in the written word is truly one of the wonders of nature. With this experience in mind, even the novice researcher will have no trouble acquiring an appropriately skeptical outlook on test results.

Another tendency, once an instrument has been used successfully, is to use that same instrument over and over again. This often blinds the researcher to new conditions that clearly call for new instruments. A conscientious effort should be made to assess the needs of each new situation without prejudice to instruments previously used.

The Tendency to Load Up

Once one gets the paper fever of questionnaire administration, there is often a tendency to increase the poundage so that the respondent is loaded up with a series of instruments that take over an hour. The result is that respondents will rebel, become fatigued by the end of the interview, or settle into a compulsive stance just to get the thing over with. One cardinal rule in the use of instruments is to make them as short as possible. If the package must be long, at least the halves should be alternated for every other presentation to determine the fatigue effects.

Plan the Analysis

A common failure is to gather up the instruments one feels will answer his earth-shaking questions without thinking what the analysis of the results will actually yield. Analysis is a field of even more technical proliferation than sampling, and the researcher must be clearly aware of how differing kinds of analyses will influence the amount and quality of the information he seeks.

Will a simple arithmetic mean of results tell the story, or should there be an analysis of variance between potential design users and a control group? This question really relates to how the research itself must be designed. There are many texts illustrating how the questions of research must be put through a rigorous analysis to find answers. These range from the elementary (Underwood, Duncan, Spence, and Cotton, 1954) to the more advanced (Winer, 1971).

Again, it is likely a novice researcher will have to use a consultant if he is not familiar with this area. It is important to be aware that the kind of analysis needed will often preclude the use of certain instruments. Answering merely "yes" or "no" to questions presents analysis problems. Such data cannot be easily treated in factor analysis, for example, the favorite method for dealing with semantic-differential results (see below). Conversely, the use of a chi-square statistic, which tests yes–no types of answers, is not appropriate for a semantic differential because it does not take advantage of the information from the seven-point scale used in that instrument.

It is critically important, then, to have a clear picture of the kinds of statistical results one will have to base decisions on. The shape of these results may be the deciding factor in the use of an instrument.

The author assumes that despite all these cautions the reader either already has or is about to yield to the temptation of paper-and-pencil instruments. There is no recourse then but to plunge ahead into the instruments themselves in the hope that the experience will help provide more valid results in their use.

THE SEMANTIC DIFFERENTIAL

The semantic differential is the most widely used instrument in the study of subject responses to architectural stimuli. Craik (1968), Hershberger

(1972), Collins (1971), and Seaton and Collins (1972) are only a sampling of the more comprehensive studies using this instrument. Because of its popularity, the semantic differential has gained a certain acceptance that has resulted in uses for which it was never intended, and in applications that are misleading.

The original text on the semantic differential (Osgood, Suci, and Tannenbaum, 1957) has now been augmented by a more sophisticated group of studies reported in Snider and Osgood (1969), and recently some very incisive criticisms of semantic-differential methodology have come out in the psychological literature (Heise, 1969; Miron, 1972).

Although there are many methodological cautions that could be made about semantic-differential use, it seems for environmental studies, in which the stimulus is nonverbal and the responses are not often based on language sampling, that there are nine problem areas:

1. A common failure to realize that the semantic differential measures connotative as opposed to denotative meaning, and the sometimes unfortunate confounding of the two.
2. The problem of ambiguity of reference in the presentation of complex stimuli.
3. A lack of representativeness of scales as they naturally appear in the language.
4. Representativeness of the population to be studied.
5. Representativeness of the architectural environments to be studied.
6. Representativeness of media through which environments are shown to subjects.
7. Confusion of response modes among new and habitual modes of behavior.
8. Overemphasis on orthogonality in factors.
9. Ambiguity of derived factors.

Problem 1   Osgood, Suci, and Tannenbaum (1957, p. 290) state: "The semantic differential taps the connotative aspects of meaning more immediately than the highly diversified denotative aspects." But what do connotative and denotative aspects mean? Allport (1955, p. 19) defines denotative meaning as being that with which we can come in contact. Nouns are denotative. They define objects we can touch, smell, taste, and see. Adjectives, on the other hand, are not denotative—they connote objects. Their meaning is secondary to the object, which is primary. But what does this "mean" to a study of the environment? Very simply, it means that the researcher must be sure of the kind of meaning he wants and the use of meaning he has in mind when presenting a stimulus. It is clear that the semantic differential is more likely to measure the emotive reaction to or the feeling about an architectural space than its usual meaning. Given the same architectural stimulus, a subject responding in denotative fashion would say, "That's a house," while a subject responding in connotative fashion might say, "It's warm, soft, small, and cozy." Given that people are usually aware of the differences between houses, churches, and factories, it might seem easy to pass off the importance of denotative meaning. But when the stimuli become highly ambiguous, the unfamiliarity, the inability to place the object into a familiar category result in semantic chaos. This happened when nonartists judged abstract art, for example (Osgood, Suci, and Tannenbaum, 1957, p. 293).

Hence denotative meaning seems to delimit connotative meaning, and this has considerable importance if one wants to present, say, highly unconventional designs whose form and function are not clear to the average subject. And the researcher can never relax in assuming what is clear for the subject. For example, on my own first extensive presentation of stimulus words to subjects for semantic-differential measurement (Bechtel, 1962) there was a denotative confusion that produced a semantic storm. When presented with the stimulus word "China," just enough subjects felt it denoted crockery to conflict with those who felt it denoted a country in Asia to markedly influence results.

And if denotative confusion can arise around a word like China, consider the possible confusions that may accompany the presentation of a total environment. Thus, although the intention of the semantic differential is to measure connotative aspects of a stimulus, unless the denotative aspect is consistently perceived as the same by the subjects, the results will be both unreliable and invalid.

Let us take a common example of semantic-differential rating—the house. A simple design to one subject may denote a vacation house, to another a low-income subsidized house, and to still another a rural house. The semantic-differential ratings of these three interpretations could be quite different—but because of denotative, not connotative, meanings. In short, the researcher must present a stimulus for which there is very high agreement on denotative meaning before he can measure with confidence the connotative meaning it evokes.

Problem 2 Related to, but not the same as, problem 1 is the reference point within the stimulus. When researchers present a stimulus in the design realm, they often assume that the subject responds to the whole stimulus rather than some part of it. This is an assumption that has not been tested, and it is again a likely source for semantic confusion. For example, to return to our house stimulus, it may be quite likely that some subjects react to the amount of window space (or lack of it) while others are intrigued by the slope of the roof, and still others (followers of Wright, perhaps) by the way it fits into the contour of the landscape.

Obviously, as the chances for this kind of confusion are increased, the more complex the presentation stimulus becomes; yet it would also seem extremely important for the designer to know what aspects of the design the subjects are responding to most.

Problem 3 Semantic space, as it has been defined by well over 1,000 studies (Heise, 1969), seems to have three basic dimensions — evaluation, power, activity (EPA). These dimensions are actually a part of the structure of language itself, and they seem to exist in a fixed ratio to one another. Miron (1972, p. 319) states:

Put in terms of meaning, our language (and most interestingly, other languages as well) exhibits more Evaluative than Potency synonyms and, in turn, more Potency than Activity synonyms. Accordingly, the variation observed in natural language qualification predicts the Evaluation, Potency, Activity factor order [but see Osgood's (1971) rebuttal]. But this naturalistic condition may be grossly distorted if equal numbers of scales are used to represent the "normal" factor prominences, especially when the number of concepts being rated is small.

What Miron is saying is that to be truly representative when concepts in language are being rated by semantic differentials, the scales should emulate the E–P–A ratio found in the language structure by having roughly *twice as many evaluative synonyms as power, and twice as many power as activity.*

Of course, when substituting architectural stimuli for language concepts, as Collins (1969) and Hershberger (1972) have recognized, the semantic dimensions must be reestablished. Probably the process should be much like those begun by Tucker (1955) in attempting to establish the semantic dimensions for painting. Osgood, Suci, and Tannenbaum (1957, p. 290) expect that visual stimuli like painting and other forms of art will have far more complex semantic dimensions than language. And, indeed, Hershberger (1972) relates some 16 dimensions derived by seven researchers using architectural stimuli. But we have no assurance that these researchers all tried to obtain *representative* scales as they occur naturally in the language. Furthermore, as in Tucker's (1955) study showing differences between artists and nonartists, where are the naturally occurring scales that separate the way designers react to architectural spaces as opposed to nondesigners? Designers have a highly specific language when referring to design elements, and it is altogether likely that they would be highly polarized and more heavily weighted in the evaluative dimension than nondesigners.

Although the work of Hershberger (1972), Craik (1968), Collins (1971), and Seaton and Collins (1972) provides the beginnings of building a semantic response space to architectural stimuli, their work suffers from a lack of the representativeness of scales. Thus the factors they derived may suffer from the criticism that Miron (1972) gives, that is, failure to use the scales in the same ratio as they occur in the language, and using too few concepts (objects) to be rated.

Problem 4 It was recently pointed out (Higbee and Wells, 1972) that the use of college sophomores as subjects in social psychological experiments has increased through 1969, despite the fact that many authorities (McGuire, 1967; Sears and Abeles, 1969) hoped for and predicted a trend toward more representative populations. In the architectural research world, the tendency to use the available university population is equally compulsive. However, except for university buildings, the students represent building users even less than they represent adequate and relevant populations for social psychological experiments. The elderly, who constitute a population of 28,000,000 in the United States, continue to be vastly underrepresented in these studies; along with other persons who may have handicaps or special requirements in environmental adaptation, they are estimated to total 40,000,000, or 20 percent of the total population (Vash, 1972).

The relevant population for any architectural environment, however, continues to be the user population. Environments are designed with specific users in mind, these may be students, factory workers, or prisoners. Or, as with public

buildings, there may be two populations, the transient public and the resident bureaucrats.[1]

The problem is doubly compounded when the architect wants to be able to tell how people will react to his design without actually building it. The semantic differential seems to be an easy way to get a favorable or nonfavorable response. The design is presented sometimes even to random samples of the population as a whole. But never can the true user population be sampled because they have yet to occupy the building. The result is that user populations are almost never tested and semantic differentials have yet to demonstrate a validity for the prediction of user satisfaction.

Only when a body of information on user population is accumulated will the semantic differential have a chance to be tested for the validity of the purpose for which it is most used.

Problem 5 As Hershberger (1972) states, it would be extremely difficult to obtain a representative sample of architectural environments. Yet if a standardization of semantic space related to architectural environments is ever to be realized, this task must be undertaken someday. Perhaps it need not be so overwhelming if more general architectural principles and architectural styles can be standardized. Collins (1969, 1971) has made a start in attempting to standardize evaluations of architectural environments, but has not dealt with the problem of representativeness. It would seem a fair appraisal of the field to say that most researchers have taken the case-study approach and are waiting for a sufficient accumulation of data before attempting any statements representative of all architectural environments.

Problem 6 Seaton and Collins (1972) compared the presentation of environments through various media, such as models, colored slides, black and white slides, and seeing the real building. Yet this study did not cover (nor was it their purpose) other media, such as television tape or movie film in color and black and white. Hershberger (1972) raises the question of whether any media are really adequate to represent the architectural environment. For although a comparison of the view of a real building with slides and models makes a measurement of the visual contact with the stimulus, actual contact with an architectural environment involves many sensory modalities, such as sound, smell, touch, temperature, and adaptation to all these over time (Helson, 1964).

The question, then, is not which media of all that have been sampled adequately predict the response to the visual contact with the architectural environment, but the prediction of the ultimate response when the architectural environment is experienced in all its sensory modalities.

Problem 7 Barker (1953) pointed out that a new situation is one in which the subject is easily influenced and easily led. Thus in any new situation, such as being asked to rate a stimulus on a semantic differential, the subject is oversensitive to cues around him. For this reason Rosenthal (1966) and others have discovered that subjects are uncannily sensitive to being influenced by researchers. Likewise, when seeing a building for the first time, they are likely to notice aspects that would go unheeded if they went by it every day. The first time a subject enters a building he is experiencing an exploratory mode of behavior. Thereafter, when he regularly uses the building he is experiencing a habitual mode of behavior (Bechtel, 1967). It is the latter mode that is of more importance in evaluating the architectural environment, for it is the habitual use of the building that determines its success or failure. *A building cannot be evaluated before it has acquired its habitual patterns of behavior.* No semantic differentials have as yet been linked to habit patterns. The closest link has been to semantic impressions of persons seeing a building for virtually the first time.

Problem 8 Miron (1972) criticizes semantic-differential studies for their overemphasis on or-

thogonality of factors. It may be, of course, that many factors occur in oblique (i.e., related or correlated) rather than orthogonal (unrelated) relationships. But this, and the next problem, may be an indication that factor analysis itself needs to be reexamined as the sole technique for analyzing semantic-differential data.

Problem 9 When it comes to meaning, the meaning of a factor is as much a problem as the meaning of a stimulus or a response. For example, in his list of preferred factors, Hershberger (1972) places the scale *active* within the factor aesthetic. Of course, no one questions the high loading of the scale on the factor but there is a question of why the factor should be called *aesthetic*. When one sees that *exciting* has an even higher loading than *active*, it begins to look as though we may have really uncovered the *activity* factor of Osgood, Suci, and Tannenbaum (1957). But no; *unique, simple,* and *specialized* are also loading fairly high on the same factor, and perhaps the factor could be called *aesthetic* to encompass these various meanings. But what is this? *Strong,* which clearly belongs in a *potency* factor, is also in *aesthetics* and loading about the same on both! How then can the factors be distinguished?

Of course, some of the reasons why these factors may not be clear is Miron's (1972) admonition to use representative scales. Such failures commonly result in confounding. We have no way of knowing how any of these researchers derive their scales, but few, if any, seem to have attended to representativeness of language.

Possible Solutions to the Problems

The astute observer will notice that solving one or more of the problems may result in resolving one or more of the others. For example, choosing carefully representative scales may also result in orthogonal and/or more clearly labeled factors. An underlying principle beneath all the problems is Brunswik's (1955) probabilistic functionalism. For the semantic differential to tell us something about architectural space, it must approximate the probabilistic occurrences of nature in language, architectural environments, media, and behavior.

The denotative and ambiguous aspects of the stimulus (problems 1 and 2) could probably be ameliorated by Honikman's (1972) suggestion to ask the subject what particular part of the stimulus he is responding to most, and then what part is next most salient, and so on. In this way, it would become clear whether the denotative meanings were similar and whether subjects were responding to different aspects of the stimulus.

Problems 1 and 2, and others like them, tend to cause individual differences to overwhelm the differences between concepts or objects rated. Heise (1969) suggests that the way to help overcome this difficulty is to use means of scales across subjects as data for the correlations rather than raw scores of subjects. Miron (1972) offers the proposition that when means are not used the factors may be confounded, as in Reed's (1972) study. In any case, these are both important admonitions about the use of the semantic differential.

Problems 3, 4, 5, and 6 deal with representativeness. The failure to represent the natural distribution of language as it relates to architectural environments by choosing equal numbers of scales for each dimension can lead to confounded factors. Likewise, the selection of subjects, media, and environments needs to be as representative as possible. The measurement of the habitual mode of behavior is really an admonition to sample the most representative type of behavior in architectural environments.

The last two problems may be solved by trying new methods of cluster analysis. Tryon and Bailey's (1970) methods use pivotal variables to define clusters, rather than depending on the in-

genuity of the researcher to guess underlying dimensions. Furthermore, overlapping variables can be eliminated by preset instructions, producing a much cleaner set of clusters than is obtainable by ordinary factoring. There is the further advantage of being able to classify subjects by their semantic-differential scores to determine if any natural grouping scored significantly differently from any other group. Cluster analysis can be used as a test of control groups or a determination of significant individual variation.

Finally, what is the goal of the use of the semantic differential in architectural research? The ideal would be to produce a semantic index that would tell us the connotative meaning of every conceivable architectural configuration. But even if this were done, would we have anything really useful? The semantic differential is quite similar to many attitudinal measures, and one must bear in mind Wicker's reviews (1969, 1971), which show that there are possibly insurmountable obstacles in predicting human behavior from attitudinal measures. And is that not the true goal of semantic-differential research, to predict human behavior for any architectural setting? It is well to bear in mind Altman's (1971) remarks at the 1971 American Psychological Association convention that self-report methods are probably not going to be the way to unlock the needed information about behavior in architectural environments, and that direct behavioral observation methods need to be developed for this purpose.

Given then that the researcher recognizes the semantic differential will not predict (nor should be confused with) behavior, what is its proper use in architectural research? Probably Tucker's (1955) study is the best example. Tucker demonstrated that artists and laymen have considerably different semantic dimensions in their responses to modern art. Therefore, the semantic differential could be extremely useful in comparing the architect's associations with, say, his clients or with the user population of a building he is designing. By the same token, it could provide a sensitive measure of architectural education, the goal of which must at least involve the increasing ability to discriminate subtle differences in architectural spaces. A carefully validated semantic differential would provide a good measure of both the quantitative and qualitative success of this goal—and compare teachers with pupils as well.

THE REMAINDER OF PAPER-AND-PENCIL INSTRUMENTS

Nearly everyone has heard of such instruments as the Rorschach, or inkblots, test or of intelligence tests. Every schoolchild has been exposed to various kinds of achievement tests. The literature on these tests is voluminous and the listing of their titles and specifics takes a sizable volume (Buros, 1961). However, for the purposes of architectural and environmental research, no instrument has yet been developed that could technically be described as a "test." For a paper-and-pencil instrument to be considered a test, it must pass certain criteria set forth by the American Psychological Association (American Psychological Association, 1966).

The instruments used in architectural research can be classified loosely under six categories, with a seventh being psychological measures used tangentially. The six categories are adjective checklists, sequential-experience notation systems, mapping, standardized questionnaires, nonstandardized questionnaires, and photostimulus techniques.

Before embarking on an exploration of these instruments, it is well to keep in mind the problems encountered in the semantic differential. In addition, one must realize that for an instrument to be useful it must be *standardized* on relevant populations. This means that the items used in the instrument have been demonstrated to be valid and reliable on a representative population. Validity refers to whether the instrument actually measures what it is supposed to measure. Recall that the semantic differential was supposed to measure connotative meaning but that sometimes it was interfered with because denotative aspects of the stimulus crept in. When this occurred, the measurement was invalid.

Reliability is of a different dimension. A measure is reliable if you get the same answer each time the item is presented. To return to the semantic differential, if the semantic profile of a picture of a building is different each time the differential is administered to the same population, it has no reliability. In other words, in selecting instruments one should select those which have been used several times on the same population and shown to be reliable. Naturally, one cannot have validity without reliability, but an instrument can be very reliable without being valid.

It should be further understood that in the burgeoning field of environmental research no listing of instruments can be complete for very long. Too many instruments are tucked away in the Master's theses files of university libraries or in obscure journals which only an exhaustive research project could uncover. The instruments listed here are illustrative only and do not cover special topics dealt with elsewhere in this book, such as daily activity diaries.

Adjective Checklists

Kasmar (1970) provides an excellent example of an adjective checklist for use in describing architectural environments. Her article provides reliability data and shows validity of the scale construction. Another feature of the scale is that it uses adjectives which are understandable to most laymen, rather than words that an architect might feel appropriate for design description.

Adjective checklists, if they are done well, consist of a printed list of words that the respondent can check off as being appropriate or inappropriate to the environment, or which can be arranged very much like the semantic differential with scaled spaces between each dichotomy. Kasmar (1970) uses the latter type with such words as neat–messy, tasteful–tasteless. Her list is shown in Figure 1.

The use of such a list aims toward understanding the essentials of how architectural spaces are perceived by the users. It has many of the same uses as the semantic differential, only it would probably be more relevant to use in the general population since it is composed of laymen's terms. However, as an instrument that depends on purely verbal responses, the adjective checklist is limited to that level of response and does not include many levels of possible response that are nonverbal or which the respondent is not capable of articulating.

Sequential-Experience Notations

A somewhat complex paper-and-pencil technique that is by no means standardized as yet, but which recognizes the very important temporal nature of the response to environment, is the sequential-experience notation scheme. Thiel (1970) has not yet reached finality on his scheme but probably has the most advanced form developed.

The central concept around which the experience notation form is organized is to capture the various experiences of the subject as he walks through and around the architectural stimulus. The reader will note that experience notation has two more dimensions than the previous instruments. For one, the stimulus is a three-dimensional entity such that the subject can walk in and around it. For the second dimension, the subject's responses are expected to change each time he encounters a different aspect of the environment.

Figures 2 to 8 are reproduced from Thiel's 1970 article. They are incomplete and do not do justice to Thiel's more exhaustive attempt at notation. The reader is referred to the full article. It is easy to see from Thiel's attempt at standardized notes that what is most emphasized is the development of a shorthand notation system for recording the architectural stimuli encountered by a subject. As yet, the *human* experience notation is undeveloped and must be written out in longhand. What must be developed is a system for systematically coding the human response to each architectural change. This task would be easier if architects and designers had some notion of what each aspect of design was supposed to evoke. Lacking this, only the prospect of long empirical research can provide an answer.

The most important use of experience notation systems is that, as was mentioned, they provide data on the rarely studied temporal aspect of environment. Some mention should be made of temporal studies conducted without the benefit of notational systems. Lowenthal's (1972) efforts are probably the most comprehensive, consisting of eight separate publications,[2] with (of course) the main instrument being the semantic differential.

If the researcher contemplates the use of an experience notation instrument, it is suggested that he consider the elements of Thiel's system. He then may want to include and develop a method of encoding the behavior associated with each sequence notational symbol.

Figure 1
Example of an adjective checklist. [**From "The Development of a Usable Lexicon of Environmental Descriptors," by Joyce V. Kasmar, from** *Environment and Behavior,* **vol. 2,** **no. 2 (Sept. 1970), pp. 153–169, by permission of the publisher, Sage Publications, Inc.**]

Active-Passive	2a[3]	Depressing-Exhilarating	3e
ADEQUATE SIZE-INADEQUATE SIZE		DIFFUSE LIGHTING-DIRECT LIGHTING	
Affected-Unaffected	2a	Dignified-Undignified	3a,e
Alive-Dead	2a,b	Directed-Undirected	2a,c
APPEALING-UNAPPEALING		DISTINCTIVE-ORDINARY	
Ascending Color-Receding Color	2a	Downward Scale-Upward Scale	2a,c
ATTRACTIVE-UNATTRACTIVE		DRAFTY-STUFFY	
BEAUTIFUL-UGLY		Dry-Humid	3e
BRIGHT-DULL		Dynamic Space-Static Space	2a,c
BRIGHT COLORS-MUTED COLORS		EFFICIENT-INEFFICIENT	
Busy-Calm	3e	ELEGANT-UNADORNED	
Calming-Upsetting	3a,e	EMPTY-FULL	
Changeable-Unchangeable	3e	Encouraging-Discouraging	2a
CHEERFUL-GLOOMY		Euphonious-Diseuphonious	2c
CLEAN-DIRTY		Even Texture-Uneven Texture	2a
Coarse-Smooth	2a	Exciting-Unexciting	3a,e
COLORFUL-DRAB		EXPENSIVE-CHEAP	
COMFORTABLE-UNCOMFORTABLE		Expressive-Unexpressive	3e
COMFORTABLE TEMPERA-TURE-UNCOMFORTABLE TEMPERATURE		Familiar-Unfamiliar	2d
		FASHIONABLE-UNFASHIONABLE	
Complete-Incomplete	3e	Fatiguing-Invigorating	2d
COMPLEX-SIMPLE		Feminine-Masculine	3a,b,e
Confused-Clear	2a	Finished-Unfinished	3e
Consonant-Dissonant	2a,c	FLASHY COLORS-SUBDUED COLORS	
CONTEMPORARY-TRADITIONAL		Flexible-Rigid	2a
Content-Discontent	2a	Formal-Informal	3e
CONVENIENT-INCONVENIENT		Formed-Formless	2a
Coordinated-Uncoordinated	2b	Fragile-Sturdy	2d
Cozy-Monumental	3c,e	FREE SPACE-RESTRICTED SPACE	
Cultured-Uncultured	3a,b,e	FRESH ODOR-STALE ODOR	
Dated-Timeless	2a,b	Friendly-Unfriendly	3a,e
Decorated-Stark	3c	Frilly-Tailored	3a,b,c,e
Deep-Shallow	2a	FUNCTIONAL-NONFUNCTIONAL	
Defined Space-Undefined Space	2a	GAY-DREARY	
Definite Volume-Indefinite Volume	2a		

(continued)

1. Descriptors retained are shown in upper-case lettering
2. The stage in which descriptor was eliminated is indicated: Stage 2 or 3
3. Reason for elimination of descriptor: (a) low median, (b) wide interquartile range, (c) excessive question mark ratings, (d) median sex difference—Stage 2, (e) low Q^1—Stage 3 (see text for more complete explanation).

Gentle-Brutal	2a	LIGHT-DARK	
Glaring-Unglaring	2a	Livable-Unlivable	3a,b,e
Good-Bad	2a	Lively-Dull	3e
GOOD ACOUSTICS-POOR ACOUSTICS		Long-Short	3e
GOOD COLORS-BAD COLORS		Meaningful-Meaningless	2a
GOOD LIGHTING-POOR LIGHTING		Mechanical Space-Nonmechanical Space	2a,c
GOOD LINES-BAD LINES		MODERN-OLD FASHIONED	
Good Odor-Bad Odor	2d	MULTIPLE PURPOSE-SINGLE PURPOSE	
GOOD TEMPERATURE-BAD TEMPERATURE		Mystic-Nonmystic	2a
GOOD VENTILATION-POOR VENTILATION		Natural-Artificial	3a,b,e
		NEAT-MESSY	
Graceful-Clumsy	2b	NEW-OLD	
Happy-Sad	3a,b,e	Nice-Awful	3e
Hard-Soft	2a,b	No Odor-Strong Odor	2b
Hard Texture-Soft Texture	2a	Open-Closed	3e
Harmonious-Discordant	2c	ODERLY-CHAOTIC	
Healthy-Unhealthy	2a	ORGANIZED-DISORGANIZED	
Heavy-Light	2a	ORNATE-PLAIN	
Heterogeneous-Homogeneous	2a,b,c	Orthodox-Unorthodox	2b
		PLEASANT-UNPLEASANT	
High-Low	2a,b	PLEASANT ODOR-UNPLEASANT ODOR	
Honest-Dishonest	2a	Pleasing-Annoying	3e
Horizontal Volume-Vertical Volume	2a,c	Plush-Austere	2c
Hospitable-Inhospitable	3a,e	Polished-Unpolished	2a
Hot-Cold	3b,e	Popular-Unpopular	2a
HUGE-TINY		Positive-Negative	2a
Human Scale-Inhuman Scale	2a,c	Pretentious-Unpretentious	2a,b,c
Imaginative-Unimaginative	3b,e	PRIVATE-PUBLIC	
Impersonal-Personal	3e	Progressive-Conservative	3a,b,e
IMPRESSIVE-UNIMPRESSIVE		Proportional-Unproportional	3e
Inner-directed-Outer-directed	2a,c	QUIET-NOISY	
		Real-Phony	2a
Inspiring-Discouraging	3a,e	Rectilinear-Curvilinear	2a,b,c
Interesting-Uninteresting	3e	Refined-Unrefined	3a,e
		Refreshing-Wearying	3e
INVITING-REPELLING		Regular-Irregular	2a
LARGE-SMALL		Related-Unrelated	2a
Lazy-Energetic	2a,b	Relaxed-Tense	2a,b
		Reputable-Disreputable	2a

Reserved-Uninhibited	2d	Sterile-Filthy	2b
Resonant-Flat	2a,c	Stimulating-	
Restful-Disturbing	3e	Unstimulating	3e
Restrained-Unrestricted	2a	Strong-Weak	2a
Restricted-Unrestricted	2a	Structured-Unstructured	2a
Reverent-Irreverent	2a	STYLISH-UNSTYLISH	
Rhythmic-Unrhythmic	2a	Symmetrical-Asymmetrical	3c,e
Rich-Poor	2b	TASTEFUL-TASTELESS	
Rickety-Stable	2a,b	Temporary-Permanent	2a
Romantic-Unromantic	3a,b,e	Textured-Untextured	2a
ROOMY-CRAMPED		Threatening-	
Scenic-Unscenic	2a,c	Unthreatening	2a
Sectionalized Space-		TIDY-UNTIDY	
Undifferentiated		True-False	2a
Space	2a,c	UNCLUTTERED-CLUTTERED	
Secure-Insecure	2a	UNCROWDED-CROWDED	
Sedate-Flamboyant	2c	UNUSUAL-USUAL	
Sensitive-Insensitive	2a	Urban-Rustic	3a,b,c,e
Sensual-Prim	2a,c	USEFUL-USELESS	
Serene-Disturbed	3e	Valuable-Worthless	2a
Serious-Humorous	2a	Varied-Repetitive	2a
Shaped-Shapeless	2a	Versatile-Nonversatile	3e
Sharp-Blunt	2a	WARM-COOL	
Sincere-Insincere	2a	WELL BALANCED-POORLY	
Sociable-Unsociable	3a,b,e	BALANCED	
SOFT LIGHTING-HARSH		WELL KEPT-RUN DOWN	
LIGHTING		WELL ORGANIZED-POORLY	
Soothing-Distracting	3e	ORGANIZED	
Sophisticated-		WELL PLANNED-POORLY	
Unsophisticated	3a,b,e	PLANNED	
SPARKLING-DINGY		WELL SCALED-POORLY	
Spiritual-Nonspiritual	2a	SCALED	
Stereotyped-Unstereotyped	3c,e	WIDE-NARROW	

Mapping

Another method that attempts to capture the temporal and three-dimensional aspects of the environment is the technique of mapping. There are really two kinds of mapping—cognitive mapping and behavioral mapping. In cognitive mapping the researcher attempts to find out or influence the internal map or orientation a person carries with him about a particular place. In behavioral mapping the researcher plots the places where behavior occurs on a map of the location being studied.

Cognitive maps Cognitive mapping originates from the psychologist Tolman's (1948) hypothesis that every organism has a *cognitive map* of his environment and that learning is acquiring relationships rather than facts. This

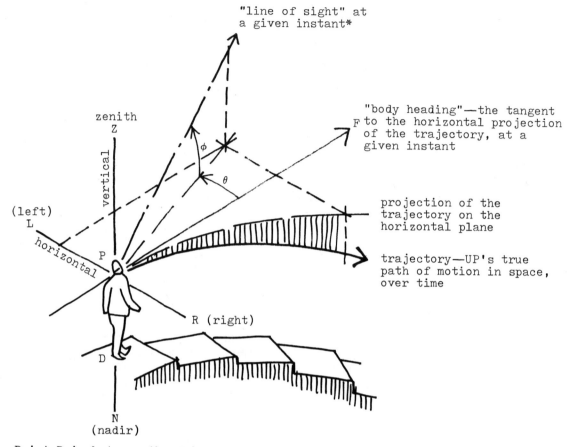

Point P is between the UP's eyes.   PD
   is at eye height.

LR is horizontal and at UP's eye
   height.

ZN is vertical, and intersects LR at P.

Plane LR — ZN is perpendicular to the
   body heading, PF.

θ = bearing ⎫ of the line of sight
⎬ relative to the body
ϕ = elevation ⎭ heading

*Unless otherwise specified,
 $\phi = \theta = 0°$, and the line of sight
 coincides with the body heading.

Figure 2
For a given user-participant (UP), these reference conditions are established at a given moment in a given position in space.

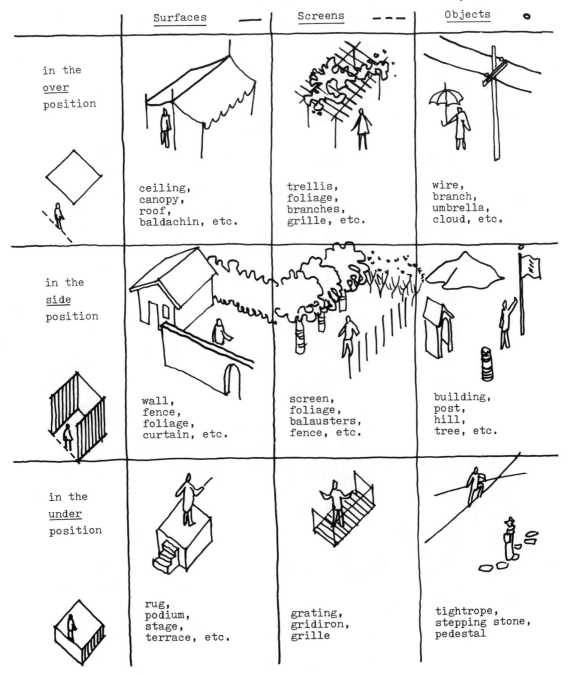

Figure 3
Common space-establishing elements (SEEs) of the three basic types.

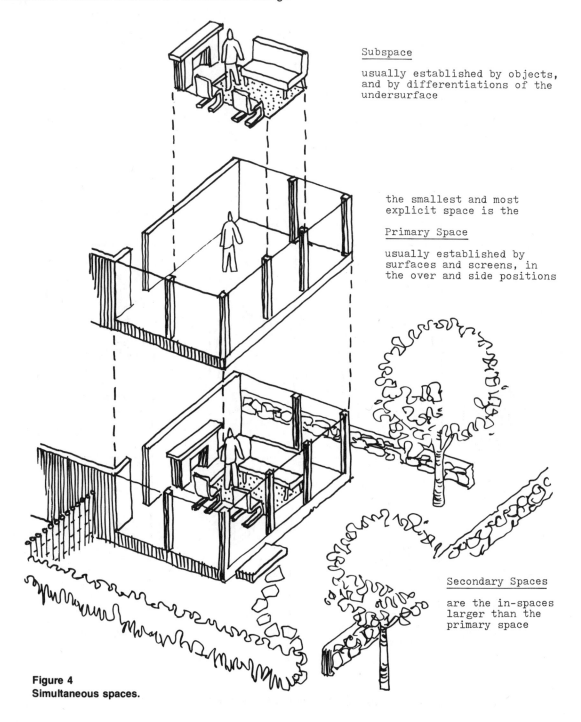

Subspace

usually established by objects, and by differentiations of the undersurface

the smallest and most explicit space is the

Primary Space

usually established by surfaces and screens, in the over and side positions

Secondary Spaces

are the in-spaces larger than the primary space

**Figure 4
Simultaneous spaces.**

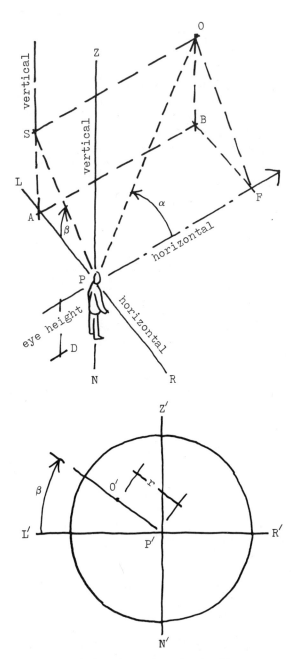

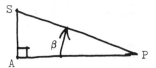

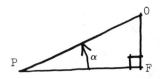

<u>Given</u> any point O in the forward nominal field of view.

PF = line of sight.

Establish plane PSOF through O and PF. This intersects vertical plane LR—ZN in line PS.

β = angle APS. To find β, construct right triangle PAS, using the <u>true</u> lengths of AP and AS.

α = angle FPO and lies in plane PSOF. To find α, construct right triangle PFO, using the <u>true</u> lengths of PF and FO. Note that FO = PS.

To find O′, the hemispherical projection of O, construct a circle of any convenient radius H, with horizontal axis L′ R′, vertical axis Z′ N′, and center P′. On a radius drawn at angle β, lay out distance r from P′, where r = $\frac{\alpha}{90}$H.

Note: When α = 90°, r = H; when α = 0°, r = 0. Lines parallel to PF will lie along a radius in the hemispherical projection.

Hemispherical Projection
radius = H

Figure 5

Let us consider the different ways in which we can represent the concept of "cat." First we may present the actual, live cat itself. Next, we could show a full-color photograph of the cat, then an outline drawing, and finally the letters C A T. In a similar fashion we can set up a scale of abstraction for a spatial situation: starting with the actual scene itself, followed by a full-color fish-eye photograph, then the HP representation, and finally the SEEPI. The SEEPI (Space Establishing Element Position Indicator) is used as a sort of shorthand denotation, roughly analogous to the written word, when the spaces concerned are both rather explicit (in the volume range) and regular in form (in the O-type category). These conditions obtain in most architectural situations, and the use of the SEEPI provides a convenient means for the description of the basic aspects of "architectural" space. Note that both C A T and the SEEPI do not tell the full story: in both cases supplementary notations are necessary to qualify and complete the concept.

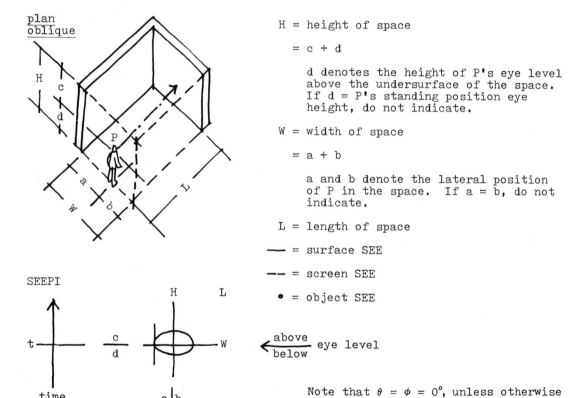

H = height of space

= c + d

d denotes the height of P's eye level above the undersurface of the space. If d = P's standing position eye height, do not indicate.

W = width of space

= a + b

a and b denote the lateral position of P in the space. If a = b, do not indicate.

L = length of space

—— = surface SEE

– – = screen SEE

• = object SEE

above / below ← eye level

Note that $\theta = \phi = 0°$, unless otherwise indicated.

Since there is usually a surface in the underposition in the primary space, it is not necessary to notate this. But when the SEE is not a surface, or when it differs from either the preceding space or the secondary space, it should then be notated.

Figure 6

method was developed for environmental psychology by David Stea and his associates. Stea and Blaut (1970), for example, studied the way children learned their spatial environment. Others (Anderson and Tindall, 1972) studied cognitive maps and territoriality, the use of computer techniques and cognitive mapping (Everitt and Cadwallader, 1972), and cognitive maps for urban areas (Lynch, 1960; Orleans, 1972).

The basic data in a cognitive-map study are acquired by asking the subject to draw a map of the environmental aspect being studied, whether it be home, neighborhood, or city, and to question the respondent about the various details of the map. As an example, Ladd (1970) asked black youths to draw maps of their neighborhoods, hoping to reveal the influence of age on the learning of geographic spaces. In more sophisticated

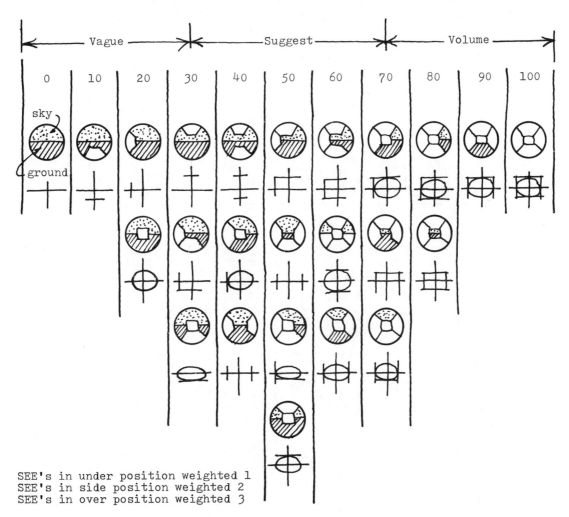

SEE's in under position weighted 1
SEE's in side position weighted 2
SEE's in over position weighted 3

Figure 7
Degree of explicitness represented in HP and SEEPI.

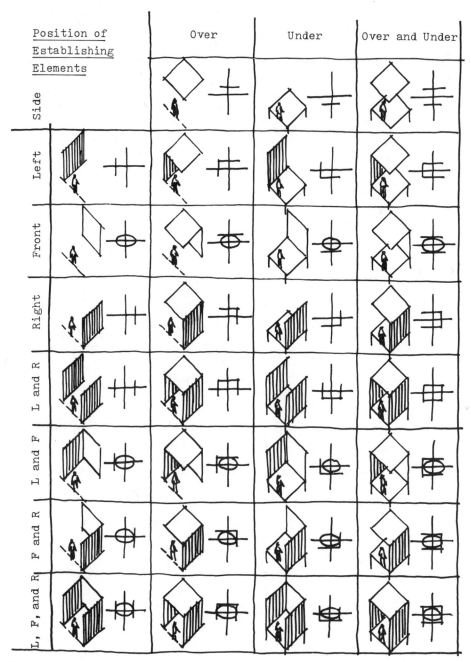

Figure 8
SEEPI: Space-form notation for orthogonal surfaces.

studies, such as several by Stea, the maps are often inferred by the subjects' behavior, and the research is centered around the concept of a cognitive map.

A problem with maps is that they are more often an auxiliary rather than the central measure of study. In any case, the most useful information is obtained from what is asked about the maps rather than the maps themselves.

Wright (1969) has developed a technique whereby the subjects construct their town or neighborhood from toy blocks.

Behavioral mapping In the technique of behavioral mapping, the researcher starts with an actual map of the area being studied and fills in the places where behavior takes place in association with each architectural feature. Srivastava and Good (1968), for example, studied the amount of human interaction across different types of mental hospital ward designs to test out which kind of nursing station resulted in more patient – nurse interaction.

In other studies, *all* behavior is mapped in association with the architectural features (Proshanksy, Ittleson, and Rivlin, 1970). Usually the method involves having observers write down the behavior on a time-sampling basis and then recording the observations on a map.

Standardized Questionnaires

A *standardized* questionnaire is one that has been tested on relevant populations and proved to have validity and reliability. Few, if any, of these exist in the area of environmental research. Part of the reason is that it is difficult to construct a questionnaire that would apply to all environments. A researcher is forced to develop a questionnaire that is specific to the type of environment he is studying. Second, none of the questionnaires deals with the full range of possible responses to the environment. The questionnaire

is constructed around those behaviors suspected or known to already exist in the environment.

Given these limitations, the series of questionnaires developed by Moos and his associates are probably the most exemplary. The Ward Atmosphere Scale (Moos, 1973) is a standardized questionnaire to assess the treatment environment of a psychiatric hospital. The Correctional Institutions Environment Scale, and the Community-Oriented Programs Environment Scales are other examples. These questionnaires are useful to designers who contemplate work in any of these areas. One problem is that these scales are more oriented toward the behavioral aspects rather than the physical aspects of the environment.

A simple questionnaire developed by Shelly (1970) relates satisfaction to environmental locations and environmental variables. For some studies, a questionnaire (Table 1) was used to collect data. In others, the satisfaction sites were located and rated by observation (Table 2). Thus Shelly's work is a form of behavioral mapping, a questionnaire and an observational technique. Shelly finds two kinds of satisfaction sites, those which result in increasing arousal and those which result in decreasing arousal. Shopping centers, and in fact most recreational pursuits, seem to result in increasing arousal up to a point where further arousal is unpleasant or exhausted, and the person leaves. Arousal sites are chiefly characterized as places where social interaction takes place; nonarousal or relaxing sites permit relaxation and decreasing levels of arousal. A third type of site is possible—that where one goes because he has nothing better to do. In Jamaica, Shelley and Adelberg (1969) analyzed 82 sites. Environmental factors include illumination; size in terms of physical space; presence of food, music, noise level, numbers of persons, time spent there; and many others. Surprisingly, the amount of activity across all sites was very low. People were relatively stationary.

Table 1
Pleasant and Unpleasant Experience

For Pleasant Experience

Everyone has some experiences that are much more pleasant than others. We want you to think of one place where you recently had a pleasant experience. This experience may have been at a party, at a club, in your own house, a friend's house, at a lake, etc. It is not important where it occurred. This experience may have taken place when you were alone, with one other person, or with many others. It is not important how many others were present. The only important thing is that you think of one experience which was pleasant for you. We are not interested in what the experience was. We just wish you to answer questions about it. Remember to think only of *one* pleasant time that occurred in *one* place.

1. How many people, not including yourself, were present at the place where you had this experience?
    1. None   4. 3 to 5   7. 21 to 50
    2. One   5. 6 to 10   8. More than 50
    3. Two   6. 11 to 20

2. How many people did you meet for the first time at the place where you had this experience?
    1. None   4. 4 to 6   6. 11 to 15
    2. One   5. 7 to 10   7. More than 15
    3. 2 or 3

3. Was this experience a new experience for you?
    1. No.   2. Somewhat new   3. Yes

4. Did you move around a lot (such as frequently walking from one place to another) at the place you had this experience?
    1. No   2. Somewhat   3. Yes

5. Did this experience involve your work (occupation)?
    1. No   2. Somewhat   3. Yes

6. Did this experience involve your family?
    1. No   2. Somewhat   3. Yes

7. Did this experience involve old friends?
    1. No   2. Somewhat   3. Yes

8. How long did this experience last?
    1. Less than one hour   3. 2 or 3 days   5. Longer than a week
    2. Several hours   4. About a week

9. Did anything unusual happen at this place?
    1. No   2. Somewhat   3. Yes

10. Was this place noisy?
    1. No   2. Somewhat   3. Yes

11. Was there music?
    1. No   2. A little   3. Yes

12. Was there dancing?
    1. No   2. A little   3. Yes

13. Was food available?
    1. No   2. A little   3. Yes

14. Did you engage in (participate in) activities at the place you had the pleasant experience?
    1. No   2. A little   3. Yes

15. Did you talk a great deal?
    1. No   2. Somewhat   3. Yes

16. Did you have something to do with (converse with) people of the opposite sex?
    1. No   2. Somewhat   3. Yes

17. Did the experience involve using something new?
    1. No   2. Somewhat   3. Yes

18. Do you often go to the place where you had the experience?
    1. No   2. Sometimes   3. Yes

Table 1
(continued)

19. Have you had pleasant experiences at this place before?
     1. No   2. A few   3. Yes

20. Were many of your relatives present at the place you had the experience?
     1. No   2. A few   3. Yes

21. Were most of the people present between 16 and 30 years old?
     1. No   2. A few   3. Yes

22. Did the experience involve spending money?
     1. No   2. A little   3. Yes

23. Was there anything to drink available?
     1. No   2. A little   3. Yes

24. Have you had unpleasant experiences at this place before?
     1. No   2. A few   3. Yes

25. Were the others present very active (moving around a lot or talking loudly)?
     1. No   2. A few   3. Yes

For Unpleasant Experience

All of us also have had unpleasant experiences. We are interested in what is an unpleasant experience for you. Just as you were asked to think of a pleasant experience, I want you to think of one recent unpleasant experience. Again, we are not interested in *what* it was but in certain questions about it. Remember to keep thinking about only one unpleasant time that occurred in one place.

1. How many people, not including yourself, were present at the place where you had this experience?
    1. None   4. 3 to 5   7. 21 to 50
    2. One   5. 6 to 10   8. More than 50
    3. Two   6. 11 to 20

2. How many people did you meet for the first time at the place where you had this experience?
    1. None   4. 4 to 6   6. 11 to 15
    2. One   5. 7 to 10   7. More than 15
    3. 2 or 3

3. Was this experience a new experience for you?
     1. No   2. Somewhat new   3. Yes

4. Did you move around a lot (such as frequently walking from one place to another) at the place where you had this experience?
     1. No   2. Somewhat   3. Yes

5. Did this experience involve your work (occupation)?
     1. No   2. Somewhat   3. Yes

6. Did this experience involve your family?
     1. No   2. Somewhat   3. Yes

7. Did this experience involve old friends?
     1. No   2. Somewhat   3. Yes

8. How long did this experience last?
    1. Less than one hour   3. 2 or 3 days   5. Longer than a week
    2. Several hours   4. About a week

9. Did anything unusual happen at this place?
     1. No   2. Somewhat   3. Yes

10. Was this place noisy?
     1. No   2. Somewhat   3. Yes

11. Was there music?
     1. No   2. A little   3. Yes

Table 1 (continued)

12.	Was there dancing?		
	1. No	2. A little	3. Yes
13.	Was food available?		
	1. No	2. A little	3. Yes
14.	Did you engage in (participate in) activities at the place you had the experience?		
	1. No	2. A little	3. Yes
15.	Did you talk a great deal?		
	1. No	2. Somewhat	3. Yes
16.	Did you have something to do with (converse with) people of the opposite sex?		
	1. No	2. Somewhat	3. Yes
17.	Did the experience involve using something new?		
	1. No	2. Somewhat	3. Yes
18.	Do you often go to the place where you had the experience?		
	1. No	2. Somewhat	3. Yes
19.	Have you had pleasant experiences at this place before?		
	1. No	2. A few	3. Yes
20.	Were many of your relatives present at the place you had the experience?		
	1. No	2. A few	3. Yes
21.	Were most of the people present between 16 and 30 years old?		
	1. No	2. A few	3. Yes
22.	Did the experience involve spending money?		
	1. No	2. A little	3. Yes
23.	Was there anything to drink available?		
	1. No	2. A little	3. Yes
24.	Have you had unpleasant experiences at this place before?		
	1. No	2. A few	3. Yes
25.	Were the others present very active (moving around a lot or talking loudly)?		
	1. No	2. Somewhat	3. Yes

Table 2
Satisfaction Site Rating Schedule

1. Part of day
   1. Morning
   2. Afternoon
   3. Early evening (5.00 P.M. to 8:00 P.M.)
   4. Late evening (after 8:00 P.M.)
2. Size of place occupied in square feet
   1. 0-50
   2. 51-100
   3. 101-200
   4. 201-400
   5. 401-800
   6. 801-1600
   7. 1601-3200
   8. Over 3,200
3. Indoors or outdoors
   1. Indoors
   2. Partly indoors
   3. Outdoors

4. Public or private
   1. Public
   2. Semipublic
   3. Private

5. Complexity of visual environment
   1. Simple
   2. Moderate
   3. Complex

6. Level of illumination
   1. Very low
   2. Moderate
   3. Very bright

Table 2 (continued)

7. Relative number of men and women
   1. More men than women
   2. Equal number of men and women
   3. More women than men
8. Median age
   1. 0-10
   2. 11-20
   3. 21-30
   4. 31-40
   5. Over 40
9. Average duration of stay
   1. Less than ¼ hour
   2. ¼ to ¾ hour
   3. ¾ to 1½ hours
   4. 1½ to 2½ hours
   5. Over 2½ hours
10. Cleanliness of site
    1. Unclean
    2. Moderately clean
    3. Very clean
11. Music (percentage of time)
    1. Less than 20%
    2. 20-80%
    3. More thar 80%
12. Food present
    1. Yes
    2. No
13. Drink present (other than water)
    1. Yes
    2. No
14. Level of activity
    1. Little activity
    2. Moderate activity
    3. A great deal of activity
15. Noise level
    1. Almost quiet
    2. Moderate
    3. Very noisy
16. Percentage of people dancing
    1. Less than 10%
    2. 10-60%
    3. More than 60%
17. Crowdedness
    1. Most people far from each other
    2. Most people neither separated nor close
    3. Most people close to each other
18. Average number of people present
    1. 1-3
    2. 4-9
    3. 10-22
    4. 23-46
    5. 47-94
    6. Over 94

19. Clustering of people
    1. Evenly dispersed
    2. Some in clusters
    3. Clustered
20. Modal size of groups
    1. Alone
    2. Pairs
    3. Triplets or more
21. Rate of movement around site
    1. Few or none walking around site
    2. Several walking around site
    3. Many walking around site
22. Percentage of people talking
    1. Less then 5%
    2. 5-40%
    3. More than 40%
23. Percentage of time those who talked engaged in conversation
    1. Less than 20%
    2. 20-80%
    3. More than 80%
24. Physical contact (touching, holding, etc.)
    1. Very little
    2. Moderate
    3. A great deal
25. Gesturing
    1. Very little
    2. Moderate
    3. A great deal
26. Laughing
    1. Very little
    2. Moderate
    3. A great deal
27. Number of people entering per half-hour
    1. 1-3
    2. 4-9
    3. 10-22
    4. 23-46
    5. 47-94
    6. Over 94
28. Number of people leaving per half-hour
    1. 1-3
    2. 4-9
    3. 10-22
    4. 23-46
    5. 47-94
    6. Over 94
29. Focus of attention
    1. Most people focused on several things (no major focus)
    2. About half focused on one thing or most focused on few things
    3. Most people focused on one thing

Case A

Interview: Former Patients at the Royal Victoria Hospital, Belfast[2]

1. Physical conditions of hospital.
   (a) Size of ward. If you were planning a new hospital would you make the ward the same size as the one you were in or would you design it bigger or smaller?
   Have you anything you would like to comment on about—
   (b) The bathrooms
   (c) Ventilation and heating of the wards
   (d) Lighting
   (e) Beds and bedclothes

Case B

Large-Scale Survey: Office Buildings[3]

12. Is there any noise in this office from machines (other than typewriters) being used in other offices?

Yes	226
No	2017
N.A.	47

13. If you find it drafty at all in the office, summer or winter, where in the room do you feel it? Check one or more as applicable:

Throughout room	155
Near windows	603
Near doors	278
Along the floor	334
Cannot really say	201
N.A.	1108

16. Check any of the following statements that apply to your office:

Ventilation is in general satisfactory	1673
There are not enough windows for ventilation in summer	106
The windows can't be opened because of drafts, noise, dirt or rain coming in	640
N.A.	119

17. Is there anything else you would like to say about the ventilation? Answer below.

Case C

Specific Small-Scale Survey: Bank[4]

Part 1. Customer and Public Areas

	Excellent	Good	Satisfactory	Needs Improvement	Suggestions
Lighting					
Temperature					
Building location					
Room sizes					
Ceiling heights					
Colors					
Furniture					
Atmosphere					
Check desks					
Tellers' counter					
Offices					
Director's room					
Quietness					
Pleasantness					
Customers' room					
Coffee room					
Fountain					
Sign					
Parking					
Planting					
Location of drive-ins					
Location of night deposit					
Image to public					

Case H
Self-Survey by Dormitory Residents

How would you rate your present accommodations with regard to each of the following?

	Excellent or Satisfactory	Needs Improvement
Living expenses	11	50
Quiet	13	49
Privacy	28	33
Informal social life	31	30
School spirit	31	25
Study arrangements	18	46
Organized activities	33	24
Student government	39	21
University restrictions	35	26
Amount of living space	21	42
Housework (cleaning, etc.)	37	23
Faculty contacts	51	9
Dining or eating facilities	25	35
Laundry facilities	16	49
Parking facilities	27	34
Lounges	15	44
Bike racks	32	26
Closet space	36	31
Bookcases	15	47
Heating	11	54
Desks	43	19
Sports facilities	29	25
Furnishings	29	33
Soundproofing	3	58
Landscaping	39	20
Lighting (inside)	38	24
Lighting (outside)	52	8
Coed living	24	26
Air conditioning	6	48

Living where you do, do you feel isolated from the rest of the campus? Yes—34; No—20; Don't know—5. Overall, considering everything, how do you rate your present living accommodations? Excellent—1; Good—6; Fair—33; Poor—14; Terrible—7.

Figure 9
Evaluator scales. (From "The New Evaluator Cookbook" by Robert Sommer, in *Design Awareness,* **R. Sommer, ©
1972 by Rinehart Press, a division of Holt, Rinehart and Winston, Inc.; reprinted by permission.)**

Shelly further classified his sites into eight types that ranged from a single person sitting on the hood of his car to a large nightclub. His data support the notion of the two more general types, the arousing and the relaxing.

Shelly's work supports a stimulus reinforcement theory of environment–behavior interaction, and thus probably comes the closest to being a true environmental-behavior theory of any yet presented.

Nonstandardized Questionnaires

Nonstandardized questionnaires are very much like the standardized in appearance, but one does not have supporting data from other populations with which to compare one's own data. Unless the instrument has been used before and reported in the literature, each use is very much like trying it for the first time. However, the example provided as Figure 9, Sommer's Evaluator Cookbook, has actually been used before, but it does not report reliability and validity data. Hence it is better than most nonstandardized questionnaires, but not equal to a standardized form.

These questionnaires, taken from Sommer (1971), provide handy instruments for the evaluation of physical environments and have the added advantage of having been used before. The reader is advised to read Sommer (1971 or 1972) for a full description of how these instruments are to be administered.

Photo-stimulus Techniques

In a photo-stimulus method, the researcher presents the subject with a photograph and asks for his response. Needless to say, this has been the technique for many semantic-differential studies, but many times the researcher will also use other more or less standardized forms of response.

One of these methods, the Instrumental Activities Inventory, was developed by anthropologists (Spindler and Spindler, 1965) to discover normative behavior in acculturating populations. The anthropologist photographs a given behavior (i.e., a person behind a grocery counter) and then asks the respondent to reply to the photograph by naming the role (grocer) of the person and describing in detail what he does.

It would be profitable to adapt this technique to architectural stimuli, but so far only a few have made systematic attempts. Perin (1970)[3] is using photographs in a somewhat different fashion by having respondents photograph their own environments and then describe details in the photographs. Calvin, Dearinger, and Curtin (1972) have used outdoor photographs as stimuli for scaling preferences (Figure 10). Peterson (1967), Sonnenfeld (1969), Canter and Thorne (1972), and Michelson (1966) have also used photographs. Calvin et al. (1972) present a useful scale with results, but unfortunately they used college students as their population.

Use of Personality and Other Measures

Finally, we come to one of the biggest temptations in environmental research—the tendency to link personality variables, attitudes, and other personality-like instruments to architectural and environmental stimuli. Fortunately, very few have as yet attempted to use measures such as the Minnesota Multiphasic Personality Inventory, the Rorschach, or thematic apperception test (TAT) measures. This is fortunate because these measures are fraught with methodological problems. The MMPI has overlapping items (e.g., the same item used for *different* scales), thus creating problems for the use of factor analysis. The Rorschach and all TATs have such problems of validity and reliability that it is best not to consider them for use in environmental research. This judgment may seem harsh, but it is backed up by considerable data (Block, 1968; Entwistle, 1972; Jensen, 1964).

TABLE 2
SCALES

1. Graceful	□	□	□	□	□	□	□	Awkward
2. Wild	□	□	□	□	□	□	□	Tame
3. Boring	□	□	□	□	□	□	□	Exciting
4. Unique	□	□	□	□	□	□	□	Commonplace
5. Full	□	□	□	□	□	□	□	Empty
6. Disturbing	□	□	□	□	□	□	□	Restful
7. Colorful	□	□	□	□	□	□	□	Drab
8. Beautiful	□	□	□	□	□	□	□	Ugly
9. Weak	□	□	□	□	□	□	□	Powerful
10. Active	□	□	□	□	□	□	□	Passive
11. Artificial	□	□	□	□	□	□	□	Natural
12. Hushed	□	□	□	□	□	□	□	Loud
13. Good	□	□	□	□	□	□	□	Bad
14. Primitive	□	□	□	□	□	□	□	Civilized
15. Delicate	□	□	□	□	□	□	□	Rugged
16. Alive	□	□	□	□	□	□	□	Dead
17. Turbulent	□	□	□	□	□	□	□	Tranquil
18. Barren	□	□	□	□	□	□	□	Fertile
19. Simple	□	□	□	□	□	□	□	Complex
20. Cold	□	□	□	□	□	□	□	Warm

HOW MUCH DO YOU LIKE OR DISLIKE THIS SCENE?

21. Like it very much	□	□	□	□	□	□	□	Dislike it very much

Figure 10
Scale of responses to an outdoor photograph. [From "An Attempt at Assessing Preferences for Natural Landscapes," by J. S. Calvin, J. Dearinger, and M. Curtin, reprinted from *Environment and Behavior*, vol. 4, no. 4 (Dec. 1972), pp. 447–470, by permission of the publisher, Sage Publications, Inc.]

Perhaps more successful in their limited way are the micropersonality tests and instruments, those instruments that only attempt to measure a part of the personality. Among those more relevant for environmental research are Rotter's (1966) internal–external (I–E) scale (Figure 11), which measures the extent to which a person feels control over his external environment or, conversely, at its mercy. Rotter's instrument has been used on a variety of populations and in many situations, so there are a great many comparisons that can be made. The basic questions it could be directed to in environmental research are whether those with feelings of low control[4]

Julian B. Rotter is the developer of a forced-choice 29-item scale for measuring an individual's degree of internal control and external control. This I–E test is widely used. The following are sample items taken from an earlier version of the test, but not, of course, in use in the final version. The reader can readily find for himself whether he is inclined toward internal control or external control simply by adding up the choices he makes on each side.

I more strongly believe that:	OR
Promotions are earned through hard work and persistence.	Making a lot of money is largely a matter of getting the right breaks.
In my experience I have noticed that there is usually a direct connection between how hard I study and the grades I get.	Many times the reactions of teachers seem haphazard to me.
The number of divorces indicates that more and more people are not trying to make their marriages work.	Marriage is largely a gamble.
When I am right I can convince others.	It is silly to think that one can really change another person's basic attitudes.
In our society a man's future earning power is dependent upon his ability.	Getting promoted is really a matter of being a little luckier than the next guy.
If one knows how to deal with people, they are really quite easily led.	I have little influence over the way other people behave.
In my case the grades I make are the results of my own efforts; luck has little or nothing to do with it.	Sometimes I feel that I have little to do with the grades I get.
People like me can change the course of world affairs if we make ourselves heard.	It is only wishful thinking to believe that one can really influence what happens in society at large.
I am the master of my fate.	A great deal that happens to me is probably a matter of chance.
Getting along with people is a skill that must be practiced.	It is almost impossible to figure out how to please some people.

Figure 11
Internal–external control: a sampler. (Reprinted from *Psychology Today* **Magazine. June 1971. Copyright ©** **Ziff-Davis Publishing Co.; reprinted by permission.)**

over the environment live better in a more structured environment than those with more feelings of control. Since the persons who score low on external control are usually poor and minority groups, this is a significant question to answer. One could also test whether an environment designed to increase the feeling of control has succeeded.

The Who Am I Test (Table 3) also known as the Twenty Questions Test, developed by Kuhn and McPartland (1954), measures, in effect, how a person relates to his environmental world. The elements measured by the test are largely verbal; but the consequences are definitely related to

Table 3
Who Am I Test

There are 20 numbered spaces on this sheet. Just write 20 different things about yourself in the spaces. Don't worry about how important they are or the order you put them in. Just write the first 20 answers you think of to the question "Who am I?"

1. _____
2. _____
3. _____
4. _____
5. _____
6. _____
7. _____
8. _____
9. _____
10. _____
11. _____
12. _____
13. _____
14. _____
15. _____
16. _____
17. _____
18. _____
19. _____
20. _____

environmental contexts, and the test can be geared to a "what is _____" (environment) format as well. By this technique, Garretson (1962) measured the compatibility of college students with four college environments. The Who Am I Test is an especially critical test for use in environmental psychology because it gets at the roots of how people define objects. A large part of how people react to environmental objects is determined by the social situation in which they are found. The Who Am I Test scores four ways in which people define and anchor themselves to their environments.[5] The "score" on the Who Am I Test is determined by which category classifies the majority of the respondent statements (Table 4). Thus most people are classified as being a C category with socially anchored statements. The second largest group is B category, then D, and then A. The same can be said about environments. In her college study, Garretson (Hartley) used the A, B, C, and D categories for environments and compared these to self-descriptions for a measure of compatibility. In another study, she used four new categories for environments[6] (Table 5). Of course, the researcher is free to discover his own categories, but the ones already used have the advantage of comparison with previous populations.

There are other instructions that might be applicable, the Crowne, Marlowe (1964) test of social desirability in responses, the F Test for authoritarianism (Adorno et al., 1950), and Honikman's (1973) adaptation of Kelly's theory. These are but a few of the many such instruments in the literature. The researcher is cautioned for the final time that such instruments are subject to many methodological problems, and before they are used much careful thought and planning must take place.

AN EXAMPLE

Partly because it is a short instrument to administer and partly because the instrument has wide usage and considerable research behind it, Cantril's (1965) Self-Anchoring Scale was chosen as an example of how a paper-and-pencil test can be used in a design project. The Self-Anchoring Scale has had extensive use cross-culturally and is easy for people of all classes and cultures to understand. In its standard form, it consists of two parts—the ladder scale and the questions on hopes and fears. These are shown in Tables 6, 7, and 8. The instructions shown are used when the researcher wants to know how the respondent feels about himself. The instructions can also be modified to ask about a particular building or a housing project. In the following case, the instructions for both self and a housing project were used.

Background and Purpose

The Self-Anchoring Scale was used at the beginning of a research project in public housing in Cleveland, Ohio. This general project has been described elsewhere (Bechtel, 1972), but the particular data have not been published previously. The research project was intended to provide data on how to modify the exterior of the public-housing buildings to make them more suitable for residents. This part of the public-housing "estate," as it is called in Cleveland, housed 1,716 persons, all black, and consisted of 636 units in 39 buildings on 20 acres. Data were needed from the residents on how they felt about the estate, themselves, and what their needs were. Of course, a considerable amount of information would be collected in the future, once the project got fully under way; but there was no way of estimating representative data without a survey sample.

The Self-Anchoring Scale was chosen because it had relevance to two issues: (1) how should the program be presented, and (2) what psychological resources were needed for handling the program? Previous research (Bechtel, 1970) had shown that high aspirations in rather

Table 4
Four Ways in Which People Define and Anchor Themselves to Their Environments

Category A

Some responses of many respondents (and many responses of some respondents) identify the self in terms of physical attributes and other information of the kind commonly found on identity cards, drivers' licenses, and the like. This kind of statement is illustrated by such examples as "I am blond," "I am five feet, seven inches tall," "I live at 1709 Elm Street," or "I live in Xville." Statements of this kind provide identification without suggesting anything about social behavior, since they refer to a more concrete level than that on which social interaction ordinarily is based. They constitute the A category of response. They contain information about the self that can be validated with a mirror, a yardstick, or a scale, that is, without social interaction. One can determine his telephone number or his home address from a directory without involving another person in the validation procedure. This is not to say, of course, that identifications in these terms do not refer to socially useful categories, but only that they do not imply any particular interactive context or any particular behavior in such contexts.

Category B

The B category used in the analysis of responses to the twenty-statements problem differentiates statements that imply involvement in more or less explicitly structured social situations. This category contains references to statuses that are socially defined and can be socially validated. The identifications of self placed in this positional category are illustrated by such statements as "I am a father," "I am a bricklayer," "I am a college graduate," "I am a home owner," and the like. Statements placed in this category imply an interactive context and refer to positions that depend on performance in defined social contexts for their establishment and maintenance. It also can be said of statements in this category that they imply norms for the behavior of the person who identifies himself in this way, and that they permit rather specific predictions about social behavior.

Category C

The C category of self-identifying statements includes those which are abstract enough to transcend specific social situations. They describe styles of behavior that the respondent attributes to himself. This category of *situation-free* styles of behavior is exemplified by such statements as "I am a happy person," "I am economical," "I like good music," "I like to drink socially," "I dislike hypocrites," and so on. Statements in this category of action responses can also be characterized by the fact that they do not pin the respondent down to specific behaviors, but leave him free to behave in various ways in various situations while maintaining his style. Viewed as a basis for prediction, action statements support predictions about the manner in which a person will behave but not about the contexts in which he will behave.

Category D

The D category of identifications of the self discriminated in this research, and which with the other three categories proves necessary and sufficient to categorize every statement collected in reply to the Twenty-Statements problem, consists of statements which are so comprehensive in their references that they do not lead to socially meaningful differentiation of the person who makes the statement. Said another way, these kinds of statements are so vague that they lead to no reliable expectations about behavior, for example, "I'm a thinking individual," "I am a person who wishes the best for everyone." This category also includes statements that are offered as replies to the Twenty-Statements problem but which, in fact, deny the question. This kind of reply is exemplified by such statements as "People are not trustworthy." The internalized *others* implicit in D statements about the self are transcendental ("the cosmos" or "mankind"), rather than "generalized" in the Meadian sense, and float beyond the possibility of consensual validation or even verifaiable communication.

Although the D category is necessarily defined negatively, since it subsumes statements which by definition transcend consensual validation, it is worth noting that it is *not* a residual category in the sense that statements which do not fall in categories A, B, or C are collected by D.

Viewed together, the four categories of self-identifying statements represent a spectrum that runs from conceptions of the self as a physical structure in time and space (category A), through conceptions of the self as existing in social structures (category B) and as a social interactor somewhat abstracted from social structures (category C), to conceptions of the self abstracted from physical being, from social structure, and from social interaction (category D). The letters used to designate the categories reflect the logical order of successive abstractions that is implicit in this conceptualization, and at the same time avoid any inferences about "goodness" or "badness," which more descriptive designations might invite.

Table 5
Categories for Environments

1. *Social*, which includes the interpersonal and social inter-actional references (learning to give service to others, understanding people, associating with other people, and participating in social activities).
2. *Academic*, which includes statements about scholarly activity and the liberal arts character of the college.
3. *Religious*, which includes both statements with clear references to organized religions, to God, and so on, and statements that refer to problems and standards of ethics.
4. *Material*, which indicates material or physical dimensions of the college. This theme category includes statements of geographical location, of finite size (total number of students, departments, amount of endowment, etc.), and statements about the physical plant, business operation, and activity devoted to maintaining or securing a strong position relative to other institutions.

Table 6
Ladder Scale

1
2
3
4
5
6
7
8
9
10

Instructions

Here is a picture of a ladder. Suppose we say that the top of ladder (*pointing*) represents the best possible life for you and the bottom (*pointing*) represents the worst possible life for you.

A. Where on the ladder (*moving finger rapidly up and down the ladder*) do you feel you personally stand at the present time?
   Step number _____

B. Where on the ladder would you say you stood 5 years ago?
   Step number _____

C. And where do you think you wll be on the ladder 5 years from now?
   Step number _____

poor economic conditions can be self-destructive to any improvement program. Residents with very high aspirations would tend to expect more than the proposed program could provide. The ladder scale would measure the aspiration levels.

It was also important to get from the residents fairly concrete ideas about what they wanted for the project they lived in and for themselves. Relatively unstructured instruments like the hopes and worries questions would permit the residents to respond from any part of their lives or in any area of improvement—such as concerns over safety, health, and other areas as well as physical design.

The Self-Anchoring Scale was part of a general interview on needs that took 25 to 30 minutes to administer.

Procedures

A census was taken of the entire study area of 1,716 persons; 807 were over 18. The over-18 group was chosen because it had the responsibility for dealing with the housing authorities and this would be the group worked with primarily.

Special consideration would be given later to the youth.

A list of 807 names was made and a random selection of 100 was decided upon as sufficient for the resources at hand. In order to end up with 100, it was estimated that there would be about 20 to 25 percent incomplete responses. Therefore, 125 were chosen to ensure 100 complete interviews. This strategy did not work out since a higher percentage were not reached.

The interview in its entirety was pretested on several residents so that they could comment on its clarity and appropriateness. Interviewers were hired from among residents and trained by role

Table 7
Discovering People's Aspirations

Instructions

All of us want certain things out of life. When you think about what really matters in your own life, what are your wishes and hopes for the future? In other words, if you imagine your future in the best possible light, what would your life look like then, if you are to be happy? Take your time in answering; such things aren't easy to put into words.

Permissible probes: What are your hopes for the future? What would your life have to be like for you to be completely happy? What is missing for you to be happy? (Use also, if necessary, the words "dreams" and "desires.")

Obligatory probe: Anything else?

Table 8
Discovering People's Worries

Instructions

Now, taking the other side of the picture, what are your fears and worries about the future? In other words, if you imagine your future in the worst possible light, what would your life look like then? Again, take your time in answering.

Permissible probe: What would make you unhappy? (Stress the words "fears" and "worries.")

Obligatory probe: Anything else?

---

playing among themselves and then by going into the field with experienced interviewers.

Results

As often happens in interviews given to inner-city residents, there were a number of interviews not completed. The number varies with each item. Inner-city residents are often suspicious of questionnaires of any kind, and about 10 percent refused to be interviewed at all.

Ladder scores for self Table 9 shows the mean score for the ladder part of the Self-Anchoring Scale. The "present" scores are lower than the national average for nonwhites found by Cantril (1965) in the early 1960s (5.3), but not lower than the lower-class average of 4.6. This indicates that the residents of the housing estate are probably about average in their view of where they stand now in attaining their life goals.

The "past" scores are lower than the national nonwhite average (5.9) and much lower than the national lower-class average of 6.4. It is normal, and perhaps realistic, for lower-class and non-white minorities to feel that they have slipped in the last 5 years. However, the residents of this housing estate seem to feel the slippage was less for them than the national averages obtained at the time of Cantril's studies.

The "Future" scores of the housing residents indicate that they are near the national nonwhite average of 7.3 (versus 7.2), yet they are considerably above the lower-class average of 5.5. Although these future aspirations may be in tune with nonwhites in the rest of the nation, there is a question as to whether these aspirations are realistic. Put another way, how can these residents of public housing possibly advance as far as they believe they will in the next 5 years?

How does one deal with this unrealistic expectation? One way is to determine further whether there are elements of the population that have higher aspirations than others. A breakdown of the 25-and-over ($N = 46$) and under-25 groups ($N = 20$) shows that the *gap* between present and future for the over-25 groups is only 0.40 on the average, while it is 2.8 for the under-25 group (*t* test is significant, 2.99 below the 0.01 level of probability). Thus we are dealing with a younger population, which accounts for most of the high aspiration level. The rest of the population does not expect to advance even half a rung up the ladder in the next 5 years. These contrasting expectations likely make for some conflict among the older and younger ranks.

Ladder scores for the housing estate itself When asked where they feel their housing estate stands at present on the ladder, residents chose as shown in Table 10. the "present" score of 3.63 for the estate is the lowest present score in any of Cantril's data or in any use of the self-anchoring score in the author's experience. Clearly, the residents place the present position of their housing estate at a very low ebb. Compared to the "past" score of 6.25, they feel the condition of the estate has gone downhill markedly. However, the "future"score shows the aspiration that it will rise to its former position in the future.

Hopes and worries for self When asked to list their hopes and worries, the residents listed the items shown in Table 11. Wanting a home of one's own and the desire to make more money lead the list of self-hopes, while "none" is the leading item for worries. The sparse responses in the worry category reveal a reluctance to discuss negative outlooks. The greatest fear mentioned is being robbed or molested. A significant fact to note is that on any of the self items the major responses have a low percentage.

Hopes and worries for the housing estate Table 12 lists the hopes and worries residents have for their housing estate. The concern for physical improvements is dominant in the hopes, while a fear that there will be no improvement is the dominant strain in worries.

The results of the listing of hopes and worries

Table 9
Self-Anchoring Scores for Self

Past	Present	Future
$N = 70$	$N = 71$	$N = 64$
$\bar{x} = 5.04$	$\bar{x} = 4.92$	$\bar{x} = 7.22$
S.D. = 3.05	S.D. = 2.64	S.D. = 2.99

Table 10
Self-Anchoring Scores for Housing Estate

Past	Present	Future
$N = 63$	$N = 68$	$N = 64$
$\bar{x} = 6.25$	$\bar{x} = 3.63$	$\bar{x} = 6.22$
S.D. = 2.41	S.D. = 2.29	S.D. = 3.18

for self and the estate show more agreement on the physical appearance of the estate than any other item. Therefore, the project to improve that appearance should meet with approval from the residents although there will be difficulty in overcoming a pessimistic view of residents about the estate and themselves.

Used with the other data collected in the research, the Self-Anchoring Scale provided important guidelines in beginning the project. As an instrument directed toward the more global concerns of self and the housing estates, it has limited value for any specific design concerns—but it enabled the researcher to proceed in specific areas of concern to the residents. The next step was to begin discussions with residents with the question: How can we improve the appearance of this estate? Further research then leads to the specific design issues: establishing a laundromat, redesigning the footpaths, reducing the high density of buildings, landscaping the grounds, and providing better play areas. Without the initial lead-in of the Self-Anchoring Scale, the researchers would have been at a loss to know how to tap the concerns of the residents.

With the limited use of this instrument so illustrated, the researcher will no doubt realize that this is a good example of why instruments on more specific design questions need to be developed and standardized, and why most current standardized instruments, tempting as they are, do not satisfy the central needs of environmental research. Nevertheless, with a view in mind of limited application to specific problems, the vast array of paper-and-pencil tests can be a valuable resource in any research project dealing with design issues.

NOTES

1. In fact, most large buildings have at least three populations: residents, visitors, and maintenance personnel. Maintenance personnel are one of the most neglected populations in considering building design.
2. *Environmental Assessment: A Case Study of New York City,* David Lowenthal and Marquita Riel, American Geographical Society (AGS), 1972; *Environmental Assessment: A Case Study of Boston,* David Lowenthal, AGS, 1972; *Environmental Assessment: A Case Study of Cambridge, Massachusetts,* David Lowenthal, AGS, 1972; *Environmental Assessment: A Case Study of Columbus, Ohio,* David Lowenthal, AGS, 1972; *Environmental Assessment: A Comparative Analysis of Four Cities,* David Lowenthal, AGS, 1972; *Structures of Environmental Associations,* David Lowenthal and Marquita Riel, AGS, 1972; *Milieu and Observer Differences in Environmental Associations,* David Lowenthal and Marquita Riel, AGS, 1972; *Environmental Structures: Semantic and Experiential Components,* David Lowenthal and Marquita Riel, AGS, 1972.
3. This reference identifies Perin's earlier work, but her research results are as yet not reported in the literature. See her EDRA 3/AR8 paper for a description of the technique.

Table 11
Self-Anchoring Scale Hopes and Worries
Most Often Mentioned for Self

Hopes	Percent	Worries	Percent
Have a home of my own	17	None	19
Make more money	16	Being robbed or molested	17
Make a relative happy	16	Welfare of a relative	11
Have good health	14	No response	10
Leave the housing estate	12	Don't know	5
Have a better life	7	Lack of education	5

Table 12
Self-Anchoring Scale Hopes and Worries
Most Often Mentioned for Housing Estate

Hopes	Percent	Worries	Percent
Want it to look better	21	Won't get better	35
Have it get better	19	No reply	16
Improve buildings	10	Extinction of estate	9
No reply	10	Won't look better	5
Cleanliness	7		

4. The I–E is scored in reverse: that is, a high score means low control over environment.
5. Descriptions of categories are taken from Hartley's (Garretson's) revision of the manual dated 1965.

REFERENCES

6. Adorno, T., E. Frenkel-Brunswik, D. Levinson, and R. Sanford. 1950. *The Authoritarian Personality*. The American Jewish Committee (Norton Library, 1969).
7. Allport, F. 1955. *Theories of Perception and the Concept of Structure*. New York: Wiley.
8. Altman, I. 1971. Remarks summarizing a symposium on Consumer Behavior and Environmental Design at the American Psychological Association Convention. Washington, D.C., Sept. 4, 1971.
9. American Psychological Association. 1966. "Standards for Educational and Psychological Tests and Manuals."
10. Anderson, J., and M. Tindall. 1972. "The Concept of Home Range: New Data for the Study of Territorial Behavior," in W. Mitchel (ed.), *Environmental Design: Research and Practice*, vol. 1. Proceedings of the EDRA 3/AR8 Conference. University of California at Los Angeles.
11. Barker, R. 1953. "Adjustment to Physical Handicap and Illness: A Survey of the Social Psychology of Physique and Disability." Social Science Research Council.
12. Bechtel, R. 1962. "A Comparison of Manifest Anxiety, Attitude Change, and Cognitive Needs and Styles." Selingsgrove, Pa.: Susquehanna University honors thesis (unpublished).
13. Bechtel, R. 1967. "Human Movement and Architecture." *Transaction*, vol. 4, no. 6, pp. 53–56.
14. Bechtel, R. 1970. "The Discovery of Areas of Potential Social Disturbance in the City." *Sociological Quarterly*, vol. 12, pp. 114–121.
15. Bechtel, R. 1972. "The Public Housing Environment: A Few Surprises," in W. Mitchel (ed.), *Environmental Design: Research and Practice*, vol. 1. Proceedings of the EDRA 3/AR8 Conference. University of California at Los Angeles.
16. Block, J. 1968. "Some Reasons for the Apparent Inconsistency of Personality." *Psychological Bulletin*. vol. 70, pp. 210–212.
17. Brunswik, E. 1955. "Representative Design and Probabilistic Theory in a Functional Psychology." *Psychological Review*, vol. 62, pp. 193–217.
17a. Buros, O. 1961. *Tests in Print*. New York: Gryphon Press.
18. Buros, O. (ed.). 1965. *Sixth Mental Measurements Yearbook*. New York: Gryphon Press.
19. Calvin, J., J. Dearinger, and M. Curtin. 1972. "An Attempt at Assessing Preferences for Natural Landscapes." *Environment and Behavior*, vol. 4, pp. 447–470.
20. Canter, D., and R. Thorne. 1972. "Attitudes to Housing: A Cross Cultural Comparison." *Environment and Behavior*, vol. 4, pp. 3–32.
21. Cantril, H. 1965. *The Pattern of Human Concerns*. New Brunswick, N.J.: Rutgers University Press.
22. Collins, J. 1969. "Perceptual Dimensions of Architectural Space Validated Against Behavioral Criteria." Salt Lake City, Utah: University of Utah Ph.D. thesis.
23. Collins, J. 1971. "Scales for Evaluating the Architectural Environment." Paper presented at the annual convention of the American Psychological Association. Washington, D.C. September.
24. Craik, K. 1968. "The Comprehension of the Everyday Physical Environment." *Journal of the American Institute of Planners*, vol. 34, pp. 29–37.
25. Craik, K. 1970. "Environmental Psychology," pp. 1–122 in T. Newcomb (ed.), *New Directions in Psychology*, vol. 4. New York: Holt, Rinehart and Winston.
26. Craik, K. 1973. "Environmental Psychology." *Annual Review of Psychology*, vol. 24, pp. 403–422.
27. Crowne, D., and D. Marlowe. 1964. *The Approval Motive: Studies in Evaluative Dependence*. New York: Wiley.
28. Entwistle, D. 1972. "To Dispel Fantasies About Fantasy-Based Measures of Achievement Motivation." *Psychological Bulletin*, vol. 77, pp. 377–391.
29. Everitt, J., and M. Cadwallader. 1972. "The Home Area Concept in Urban Analysis: The Use of Cognitive Mapping and Computer Procedures as Methodological Tools," in W. Mitchel (ed.), *Environmental Design: Research and Practice*, vol. 1. Proceedings of the EDRA 3/AR8 Conference. University of California at Los Angeles.
30. Garretson, W. 1962. "Consensual Definition of Social Objects." *Sociological Quarterly*, vol. 3, pp. 107–113.
31. Gutman, R. 1972. *People and Buildings*. New York: Basic Books.
32. Heise, D. 1969. "Some Methodological Issues in Semantic Differential Research." *Psychological Bulletin*, vol. 72, pp. 406–422.
33. Helson, H. 1964. *Adaptation Level Theory*. New York: Harper & Row.
34. Hershberger, R. 1972. "Toward a Set of Semantic Scales to Measure the Meaning of Architectural Environments," in W. Mitchel (ed.), *Environmental Design: Research and Practice*. Proceedings of the EDRA 3/AR8 Conference, vol. 1. University of California at Los Angeles.
35. Higbee, K., and M. Wells. 1972. "Some Research Trends in Social Psychology During the 1960's." *American Psychologist*, vol. 27, pp. 963–966.
36. Honikman, B. 1972. "An Investigation of the Relationship Between Construing of the Environment and Its Physical Form," in W. Mitchel (ed.), *Environmental Design: Research and Practice*. Proceedings of the EDRA 3/AR8 Conference, vol. 1. University of California at Los Angeles.
37. Honikman, B. 1973. "Personal Construct Theory and Environmental Evaluation," in W. Preiser (ed.), *Environmental Design Research*, vol. 1. 4th EDRA Conference.
38. Jensen, A. 1959. "The Rorschach Technique: A Re-

evaluation." *Acta Psychologica,* vol. 16, pp. 108–136.

39. Kasmar, J. 1970. "The Development of a Useful Lexicon of Environmental Descriptors." *Environment and Behavior,* vol. 2, pp. 135–169.

40. Kish, L. 1965. *Survey Sampling.* New York: Wiley.

41. Kuhn, M., and T. McPartland. 1954. "An Empirical Investigation of Self-Attitudes." *American Sociological Review,* vol. 19, pp. 68–76.

42. Ladd, F. 1970. "Black Youths View Their Environment." *Environment and Behavior,* vol. 2, pp. 74–99.

43. Lowenthal, D. 1972. *Environmental Assessment: A Comparative Analysis of Four Cities.* New York: American Geographical Society.

44. Lynch, K. 1960. *The Image of the City.* Cambridge, Mass.: MIT Press.

45. McGuire, W. 1967. "Some Impending Reorientations in Social Psychology: Some Thoughts Provoked by Kenneth Ring." *Journal of Experimental Social Psychology,* vol. 3, pp. 113–123.

46. Michelson, W. 1966. "An Empirical Analysis of Urban Environmental Preferences." *Journal of the American Institute of Planners,* vol. 32, pp. 355–360.

47. Michelson, W. 1970. *Man and His Urban Environment.* Reading, Mass.: Addison-Wesley.

48. Miron, M. 1972. "Universal Semantic Differential Shell Game." *Journal of Personality and Social Psychology,* vol. 24, pp. 314–320.

49. Moos, R. 1973. *Evaluating Treatment Environments: A Social Ecological Approach.* New York: Wiley.

50. Orleans, P. 1972. "Mapping the City: Environmental Cognition of Urban Residents," in W. Mitchel (ed.), *Environmental Design: Research and Practice,* vol. 1. Proceedings of the EDRA 3 / AR8 Conference. University of California at Los Angeles.

51. Osgood, C. 1971. "Commentary on Miron's the Semantic Differential and Mediation Theory." *Linguistics,* vol. 66, pp. 88–96.

52. Osgood, C., G. Suci, and P. Tannenbaum. 1957. *The Measurement of Meaning.* Urbana, Ill.: University of Illinois Press.

53. Perin, C. 1970. *With Man in Mind.* Cambridge, Mass.: MIT Press.

54. Peterson, G. 1967. "A Model for Preference: Quantitative Analysis of the Perception of the Visual Appearance of Neighborhoods." *Journal of Regional Science,* vol. 7, pp. 19–31.

55. Proshansky, H., W. Ittelson, and L. Rivlin. 1970a. "Bedroom Size and Social Interaction of the Psychiatric Ward." *Environment and Behavior,* vol. 2, pp. 255–270.

56. Proshansky, H., W. Ittelson, and L. Rivlin. (eds.). 1970b. *Environmental Psychology: Man and His Physical Setting.* New York: Holt, Rinehart and Winston.

57. Reed, T. 1972. "Connotative Meaning of Social Interaction Concepts: An Investigation of Factor Structure and the Effects of Imagined Contexts." *Journal of Personality and Social Psychology,* vol. 24, pp. 306–312.

58. Rosenthal, R. 1966. *Experimenter Effects in Behavioral Research.* New York: Appleton-Century-Crofts.

59. Rotter, J. 1966. "Internal vs. External Control of Reinforcement." *Psychological Monographs,* vol. 80, no. 1.

60. Sears, O., and R. Abeles. 1969. "Attitudes and Opinions." *Annual Review of Psychology,* vol. 20, pp. 253–288.

61. Seaton, R., and J. Collins. 1972. "Validity and Reliability of Simulated Buildings," in W. Mitchel (ed.), *Environmental Design: Research and Practice.* Proceedings of the EDRA 3/AR8 Conference, vol. 1. University of California at Los Angeles.

62. Shelly, M. W. 1970. "Questionnaires." Fall, 1968, and Spring, 1969. Department of Psychology. University of Kansas. Technical Report 32. April.

63. Shelly, M. W., and T. A. Adelberg. 1968. "Satisfaction Sites in Jamaica: Empirical Analysis." Department of Psychology. University of Kansas. Technical Report 7. December.

64. Shelly, M., and T. A. Adelberg. 1969. "Satisfaction Sites in Jamaica: Empirical Analysis," pp. 221–266 in M. Shelly (ed.), *Analyses of Satisfaction,* vol. 1. New York: MSS Educational Publishing Company.

65. Snider, J., and C. Osgood. 1969. *Semantic Differential Technique.* Chicago: Aldine.

66. Sommer, R. 1971. "The New Evaluator Cookbook." *Design and Environment,* vol. 2, pp. 34–37.

67. Sommer, R. 1972. *Design Awareness.* New York: Holt, Rinehart and Winston.

68. Sonnenfeld, J. 1969. "Equivalence and Distortion of the Perceptual Environment." *Environment and Behavior,* vol. 1, pp. 83–99.

69. Spindler, G., and L. Spindler. 1965. "The Instrumental Activities Inventory: A Technique for the Study of the Psychology of Acculturation." *Southwestern Journal of Anthropology,* vol. 21, pp. 1–23.

70. Srivastava, R. K., and L. R. Good. 1968. "Patterns of Group Interaction in Three Architecturally Different Psychiatric Treatment Environments." Environmental Research Foundation. March.

71. Stea, D., and J. Blaut. 1970. "Notes Toward a Developmental Theory of Spatial Learning." Paper delivered at the EDRA Conference. Pittsburgh.

72. Thiel, P. 1970. "Notes on the Description, Scaling, Notation, and Scoring of Some Perceptual and Cognitive Attributes of Physical Environment," pp. 593–618 in H. Proshansky, W. Ittelson, and L. Rivlin (eds.), *Environmental Psychology.* New York: Holt, Rinehart and Winston.

73. Tolman, E. C. 1948. "Cognitive Maps in Rats and Men." *Psychological Review,* vol. 55, pp. 189–208.

74. Tryon, R. 1955. *Identification of Social Areas by Cluster Analysis: A General Method with an Application to the San Francisco Bay Area.* Berkeley, Calif.: University of California Press.

75. Tryon, R., and D. Bailey. 1970. *Cluster Analysis.* New York: McGraw-Hill.

76. Tucker, W. T. 1955. "Experiments in Aesthetics Com-

munications." Urbana, Ill.: University of Illinois doctoral dissertation.

77. Underwood, B., C. Duncan, J. Spence, and J. Cotton. 1954. *Elementary Statistics*. New York: Appleton-Century-Crofts.

78. Vash, D. 1972. "Discrimination by Design: Mobility Barriers," in W. Mitchel (ed.), *Environmental Design: Research and Practice*. Proceedings of the EDRA 3/AR8 Conference, vol. 1. University of California at Los Angeles.

79. Wicker, A. 1969. "Attitudes vs. Actions: The Relationship of Verbal and Overt Behavioral Responses to Attitude Objects." *Journal of Social Issues,* vol. 25, pp. 41–78.

80. Wicker, A. 1971. "An Examination of the 'Other Variables' Explanation of Attitude–Behavior Inconsistency." *Journal of Personality and Social Psychology,* vol. 19, pp. 18–30.

81. Winer, B. 1971. *Statistical Principles in Experimental Design,* 2nd ed. New York: McGraw-Hill.

82. Wright, H. 1969. "Children's Behavior in Communities Differing in Size, Part Two: The Community Situation and Activity Regimen." Department of Psychology. Lawrence, Kans.: University of Kansas.

Trade-off Games

Ira M. Robinson, William C. Baer,
Tridib K. Banerjee, and
Peter G. Flachsbart

Ira M. Robinson recently joined the Faculty of Environmental Design at The University of Calgary as Professor of Urban Planning after nine years at the University of Southern California. Dr. Robinson has undertaken research on and written extensively in the fields of housing, renewal, new towns, regional development, and planning methods. He was the Principal Co-Investigator for the initial phase of the University of Southern California research project on the residential environment, reported on in this chapter.

William C. Baer is Instructor in Urban and Regional Planning at the University of Southern California. He has previously worked in local government and taught at the University of California at Berkeley. Mr. Baer is completing his doctoral dissertation on housing policy at University of California at Los Angeles; his other interests include the development and use of performance criteria for residential planning.

Tridib K. Banerjee is Assistant Professor of Urban and Regional Planning at the University of Southern California. His research interests are in the areas of behavioral implications and methods of environmental design. Dr. Banerjee will be Principal Investigator of the next phase of the University of Southern California research on the residential environment.

Peter G. Flachsbart is Assistant Professor of Urban and Environmental Management at California State College, Dominguez Hills. In addition to his research on trade-offs, Dr. Flachsbart has investigated the perceptions and preferences of low-income blacks and upper-income whites for housing environments.

The term "trade-offs" has recently been heard more and more often both in the literature and at meetings of the planning and environmental design professions. It is frequently brought up during discussions on identifying community goals, formulating criteria or standards for plans and designs, or evaluating proposed plans, policies, and programs. Current concern for environmental quality has underscored the issue of trade-offs in public decision making at all governmental levels. Policies to encourage population and economic growth appear to be in conflict with concurrent programs to improve the environ-

Parts of an earlier version of this chapter were included in a presentation of Confer-In '73, the 56th Annual Conference of the American Institute of Planners held in Atlanta, Georgia, October, 21–25, 1973.

The research upon which this chapter is based was supported by the Bureau of Community Environment Management, Public Health Service Research Grant 1-RO1 EM 0049-02.

ment, and both appear at odds with resource re-distribution for the poor. It is increasingly clear that compromises must be made in each of these areas without causing undue harm in the others.

THE CONCEPT OF TRADE-OFFS

In general, the concept of trade-offs implies compromises, exchanges, or substitutability between and among multiple, often mutually exclusive goals; it reflects the need to give up something in order to gain something. Trade-offs are made by individuals and families to cope with the constraints of everyday life—finding a place to live, deciding what things to purchase, where to go on a vacation, and so on. Similarly, when faced with sociopolitical and economic-financial constraints, public policy and decision makers are required to make trade-offs in deciding whether to allocate resources to guns or butter, parks or schools, freeways or mass transit, economic growth or environmental improvement, and so on. Usually, the choice is not an either/or situation, but rather one in which a decision must be made as to what portion of each goal or preference can be satisfied; that is, how many guns versus how much butter, how many schools versus how large the parks, and so on.

Although the implicit trade-offs in personal decision making are commonly recognized, this has been less true for public decision making and planning. At one time most public decisions were assumed to be in the public interest unless proved otherwise. Increasing recognition of the plurality of publics has forced planners, designers, and policy makers to face the more unsettling issue of "Who should get what?"; the "who" represents the variety of publics that exist, for example, the poor, the elderly, conservationists, homeowners' associations, and business interests. Furthermore, it is now recognized that the goals of these publics are not always in concert, and often are in competition, if not in conflict.

Thus housing for the poor in suburban areas is perceived as threatening by homeowners' associations, business expansion often threatens conservationists' concerns, and so on.

We know that public policy and decision makers, whether they recognize the term trade-offs or not, commonly allocate resources on the basis of one or several of the following: (1) bureaucratic routine (March and Simon, 1958); (2) conventional wisdom (Galbraith, 1958); (3) precedent (Wildavsky, 1964); (4) fair share (Crecine, 1969); or (5) professional norms and standards (Thompson, 1969).[1] Clearly, such allocative techniques have been less than successful in the past. It is incumbent, therefore, that more reliable and responsible planning and decision-making techniques be developed to reduce the unknown and provide a better basis for planners, designers, and decision makers to exercise their judgment about trade-offs.

Paralleling this awareness has been a related trend: it is now widely recognized that the planner's and designer's conception of community needs and preferences might be at variance with the public's,[2] and that the public must participate in establishing community goals and its preference patterns.[3] This trend, to a large extent, was a reaction to the civil-rights and students' movements, the Office of Economic Opportunity sanctioned community-action programs and their emphasis on "maximum feasible participation," the consumer affairs and citizen environmental protests, and the rise in general of a new brand of participatory democracy among various groups in the population during the past decade. In response, planners and designers are seeking ways and means of discovering what trade-offs or exchanges different population groups are willing to make—what we refer to throughout this paper as *trade-off preferences*—when they have limited resources and are faced with conflicting or incompatible, but equally desirable, goals. Such knowledge should at least make the allocative rationale of public policy and decision makers much more responsive to the needs and preferences of users, even though economic and other constraints make it impossible to satisfy all their "true" desires.

PLANNING STANDARDS

Recent thinking about the development and use of planning or design standards illustrates this heightened concern. Standards, regulatory measures, minimum requirements, and the like, are some of the key public-policy variables that affect the quality of residential environments. Typically, these measures have been based on publications and guides issued by the American Public Health Association (*Planning the Neighborhood*), the Urban Land Institute (I. R. McKeever, editor, *The Community Builder's Handbook*), or the Federal Housing Administration (Minimum Property Standards). Key criticisms leveled at the traditional approach to the development of standards have been: (1) they are usually based upon the needs, wants, and judgments of the planner, designer, supplier, lender, and producer groups with no regard for the experience and evaluation of user groups; typically the users are not consulted directly in the formulation of these standards; (2) these standards usually fail to recognize differences in values and preferences between different user groups (Gans, 1957; Fried and Gleicher, 1961); and (3) the standards have typically ignored the concept of substitutability or trade-offs in their formulation (Blackman, 1968; Webber, 1969; Solow and Ham, 1967; Wheaton, 1965).

The latter criticism is perhaps the most important consideration of all. Normally, standards do not admit of compromises, trade-offs, and exchanges that adjust to existing circumstances. It is now recognized, however, that within certain limits space may be a substitute for accessibility; high income and personal mobility may obviate the need for public transportation; easy access to work may be exchangeable with less polluted air; and age-dependent incapacities, or even ethnic norms, may necessitate the rearrangement of change in location and configuration of facilities. Thus a more relevant system of standards would take cognizance of these distinctions and would define the conditions under which the standard is required, the degree of requirement, the amount of tolerable substitutability, and the trade-off preferences of different population groups (Solow and Ham, 1967; Wheaton, 1965).

Although there is now general agreement about the need to consult users of the environment about their trade-off preferences, little has been said or discussed about *how* such information can be obtained by other than intuitive or inferential means.

Economists have done the most thinking about trade-off preferences in the course of theorizing about consumer choice. To the economist, trade-offs are defined as "marginal rates of substitution between commodities" (Houthakker, 1961) and are conceptually related to the indifference-curve construct, which is in turn a surrogate for measuring "utility" as a way of describing individual preferences. Despite theoretical advances, the number of experimental efforts by economists to derive rates of exchange in the absence of market prices is limited.[4]

One chief problem in applying economic concepts is to use them in such a way that the areas of interest to planners and designers can be fully incorporated into the research. For instance, determining "exchange rates" between apples and oranges is considerably easier than deriving trade-offs between neighborhood residential attributes such as air quality and safety, which are so much more subjectively perceived and evaluated. Moreover, the planner's and designer's universe of concern is not comprised of any single individual but of groups of individuals, each group with (presumably) a different set of preferences; therefore, these professionals are concerned with developing a "community" (or social welfare) trade-off preference function.

TRADITIONAL RESEARCH APPROACHES

Two basic research approaches have traditionally been used to actually operationalize the concept of trade-off preferences and to empirically derive useful data on users' trade-offs; in turn, these are related to different views as to the nature of preferences. One view holds that preferences are expressed in terms of behavior; the other focuses on preferences as expressed in terms of attitudes or opinions.[5] These are not mutually exclusive concepts, although in practice operationalizing the concept of preferences has traditionally meant choosing either one concept or the other as a basis for investigation. Indeed, there are a number of variants to each basic approach; included are different ways of representing the environment to respondents in order to elicit and measure their preferences; that is, the representation may be real, simulated, or hypothetical.

The basic assumption underlying the "preference is expressed as behavior" approach is that the choices users actually make in the real world are the best indicator of preferences and trade-offs; thus what we need is information about what people actually do rather than what they say they will do, which is often quite a different thing. Therefore, it is argued that the only reliable and objective way to find out the trade-off preferences of different population groups is to study their actual behavior, and to observe what choices or trade-offs they have actually made when confronted with a variety of conditions.

Economists have been the most vocal in arguing that preferences and trade-offs can only be inferred by studying market behavior. For example, an introductory textbook on welfare economics states:

How can we find out what the consumer's preferences are? We can hardly question him on the subject and so establish his scale of preferences. This would be a lengthy and clumsy process even if applied to only one person and is obviously impossible to apply to all members of the community. We can, however, infer the consumer's preferences from his market behavior, on the assumption that this is governed by rational choice and is not merely a matter of habit or accident (Scitovsky, 1971, 27–28).

In line with the "preference is expressed as behavior" viewpoint, planners and environmental designers have developed and used such techniques as mathematical simulation models, O–D (origin–destination) traffic surveys, market and consumer surveys, and time–activity budgets, among others, to observe existing behavior and predict future behavior.[6]

The main advantage of these techniques is that they provide information about people's behavior under conditions of constrained choice. For the most part, behavior can be construed as the result of tempering utopian wants with real-world constraints. The disadvantage, however, is the implicit assumption that the world cannot be changed. Such information on behavior fails to take into account current inadequacies in the existing environment; it does not allow for unfulfilled preferences, preferences that might emerge in possible future environments with characteristics and attributes outside the range of current observations. For planners and environmental designers, this is a serious weakness. They are interested in preferences under alternative environmental conditions. Their task is the rearrangement of the environment to better suit user needs and preferences. Thus, as the sole source of information, existing behavior patterns will inevitably provide an oversimplified if not misleading view of user preferences. For this reason, planners have turned to the second basic approach to determining preferences—the use of questionnaires, commonly called *attitude surveys*.

Typically, in an attitude questionnaire about

user preferences, which is either oral or in written form, the respondent is required to answer questions that may be descriptive (Do you own a car?) or evaluative (Do you like to drive?) or projective (Would you ride on a mass-transit system if it were available?)[7] Such questionnaires will often reveal valuable information about the preference orderings of respondents, that is, the basic ranking of desired environmental attributes (e.g., air quality is preferred over schools). However, they reveal little about the trade-offs the respondents are prepared to make between these attributes. Is clean air, no matter how pure, always preferred to better schools? Or is there a certain level of air quality beyond which better schools would be preferred? Moreover, the typical attitude survey rarely attempts to determine the difference in preferences, let alone the trade-off preferences among different population groups. Yet we know that in the real world certain user groups might be willing to sacrifice better schools to achieve higher air quality, whereas under no circumstances would other groups forego their preference for schools even to breathe the purest of Alpine atmosphere.

Furthermore, there may be confusion as to what the preferences mean. At best, a ranking of preferences pertains only to the items ranked. The subsequent introduction of other items to be considered might change the rankings considerably. For instance, to know that among three environmental attributes the person interviewed preferred neighborhood parks to libraries, and preferred both to museums, says nothing at all as to the preferences with respect to access to work, much less various revenue sources to pay for these attributes. The point is that the preferences gathered from the attitude questionnaire pertain only to the items asked about in the survey.

Most important, even if attitude questionnaires addressed themselves to these issues, they would still suffer from a basic weakness: the questions about preferences are typically asked under unconstrained conditions. Yet we know there are always constraints of time and money present in any situation, along with real-world conditions of, say, climate, topography, gravity, and so on. It is now acknowledged that what people want is in part governed by what they think they can get and what sacrifices they must make to get it. For instance, Mueller (1963) found that the public's priorities for federally funded programs were reordered if respondents were told that their list of priorities could be achieved only through a tax increase. In short, even if respondents to a questionnaire answer that they prefer air quality over schools, can we be sure that the public would not sacrifice some clean air for better schools when actually faced with the decision? Since planners and designers are not sure, they are seeking research tools that attempt to identify and measure the trade-off preferences of different populations groups by integrating the two basic approaches, that is, by interrelating attitude measurements with behavior information.

A comparatively new approach to meeting this last objective is the use of trade-off "games." Although the results are mixed and much remains to be done, we feel this approach to identifying and measuring the trade-off preferences of different user–population groups holds out considerable promise and potential for the future. In the remainder of this paper we shall describe and discuss several past efforts along these lines, including a detailed discussion of one such effort with which the authors are involved. We shall then draw conclusions as to the potential value of this approach and its data, along with a discussion of criteria to be followed for devising improved variations to existing trade-off games.

PREVIOUS EFFORTS TO USE "GAMES" TO DETERMINE TRADE-OFF PREFERENCES

The games described in this and the following section might better be termed semiprojective "gaming situations"; they are not "games" in the literal sense of this word as it is generally used in the literature on "gaming." In these games, there is essentially only one player, the respondent being interviewed or playing the game. Moreover, the result of the player's decision does not cause a new situation to which he must respond and make another decision. Each is a game only in the sense that the respondent's decision depends on the interviewer's actions or questions. However, the interviewer's action is independent of the respondent's decision.

In each game trade-offs occur in which the player incurs a loss to achieve a greater gain,

such as one usually associates with such parlor games as Monopoly. The result is that the player, with conflicting goals, makes "moves" or decisions which have him end up winning.[8]

Earlier efforts to develop games to quantitatively identify and measure user trade-off preferences for different environmental attributes were designed and employed by Wilson (1962), Redding and Peterson (1970), and Hoinville and his associates (1970, 1971). These three instruments are briefly reviewed here. (In the following section, a trade-off game recently developed by researchers at the University of Southern California is reviewed in some detail.)

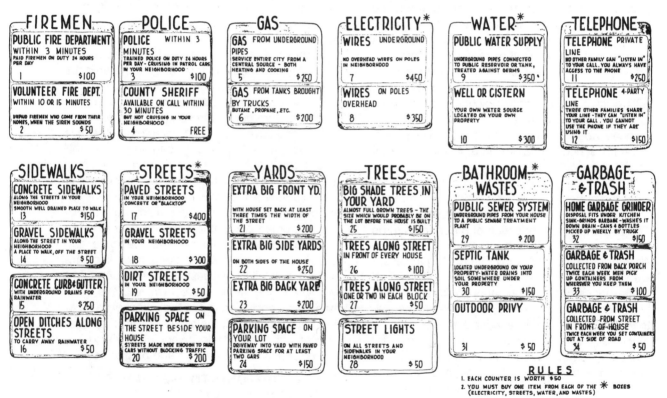

Figure 1
The Wilson Game: game board used to estimate relative importance to respondents of various utilities and services for potential house site.

Wilson's Games

The earliest known attempt to measure user trade-off preferences within a gaming context was devised over a decade ago by Wilson. Wilson actually designed two trade-off instruments (see Figures 1 and 2). In the first game, user preferences were elicited by asking the respondents to pretend that they had won a house on a television program. They were to assume that the house itself met their needs, but they had to de-

termine the kinds of neighborhood facilities and levels of services for the house. Some 34 items of utilities and services were to be chosen from, for example, accessibility and type of fire department (volunteer or public) and police (local or county sheriff); underground or overhead electricity; paved or graveled sidewalks and streets; size of yards; and placement of trees. Each item had a dollar price tag attached (in multiples of $50), the cost rising with the service level. Subjects were given an allotment of play money and told to

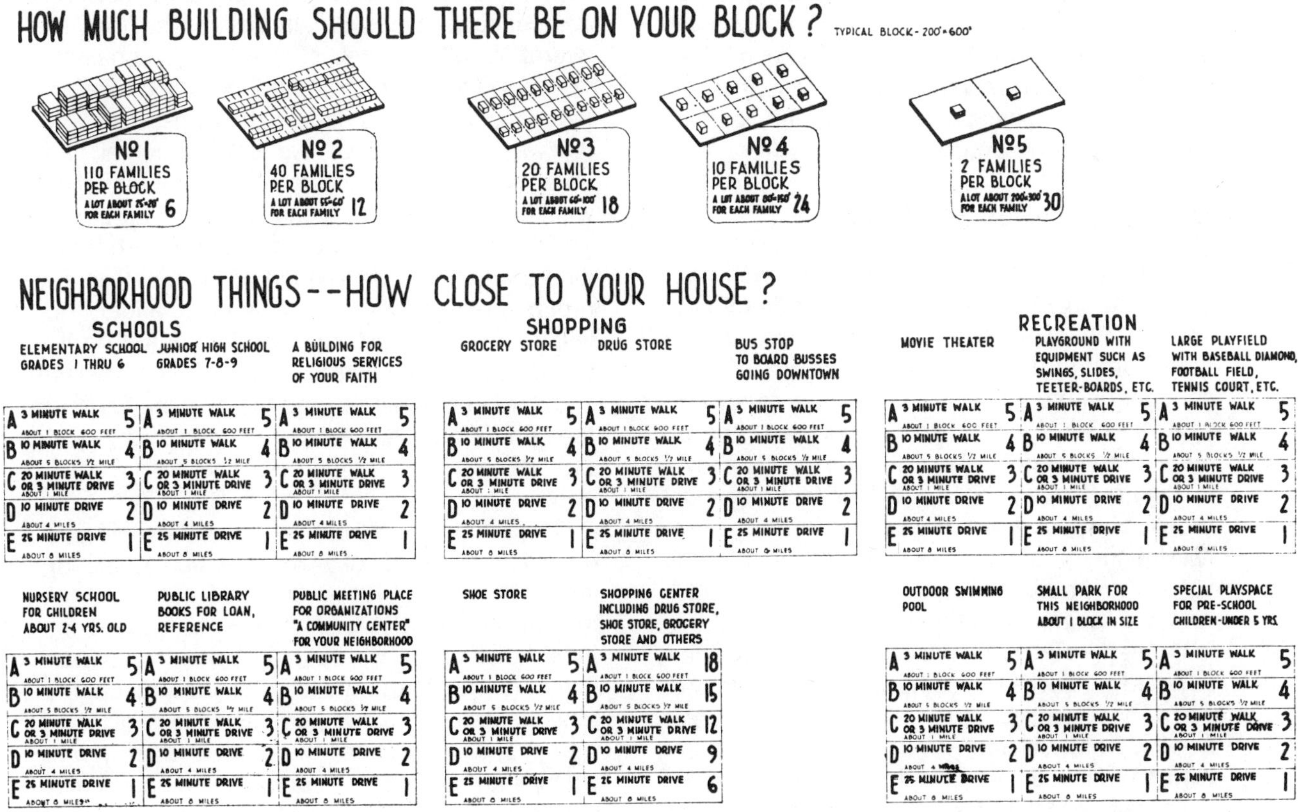

Figure 2
The Wilson Game: game board used to evaluate aspects of neighborhood density and distance relationships. The original, 28 by 45 inches, included five photographs of building types typical of the five densities at the top of the board, to assist in conveying the concept of relative densities.

purchase the quality levels they desired. Since the total sum of money provided was insufficient to purchase the best quality for each environmental attribute, trade-offs were necessary.

The second game measured preferences for five different dwelling-unit densities and five levels of access to 17 neighborhood facilities, for example, schools at a distance of a 3-minute walk, 10-minute walk, 20-minute walk/3-minute drive, and equivalent time distances for shopping, parks, libraries, and the like. Here no price was established for these varying levels of accessibility; rather, a number of points was assigned to each item, while the number of markers allocated to each respondent was less than the total number of points necessary to purchase the highest quality of each item.

Redding and Peterson's Game

Redding and Peterson developed an instrument that quantitatively measured trade-off preferences for alternative levels of access to four neighborhood facilities, for example, a local shopping center, a hospital and emergency service, a children's park and playground, and an elementary school.[9] Their game board is shown in Figure 3. Although these four facilities most likely do not represent the predominant environmental criteria of residential site selection for the user, the prediction of residential preferences was not uppermost in the research design of this instrument. Rather, Redding and Peterson attempted to test the hypothesis that two different consumer groups—the elderly and young families with children—prefer these facilities at different minimum and maximum distances from their residences; that is, the two groups have different perceptions of these facilities as either need-satisfying or nuisance-generating. (This is the only effort to specifically test a hypothesis; the other games tend more to be hypothesis generating.) The measure of trade-offs here was limited

to identifying nearest and farthest thresholds of acceptable distances; in general, however, the academic interest in testing the hypothesis was pursued at the expense of practical information gathering (or prediction).

Hoinville and Associates' Game

Hoinville and his associates designed an electrified game board, which they call a "priority evaluator," a simulation device that permitted respondents to indicate their priorities between competing and costed alternatives so that the overall results of their choices were constantly visible to them. On the board were two overlays that consisted of words and drawings; one overlay was comprised of five environmental variables or attributes and the other overlay dealt with five accessibility variables (see Figures 4 and 5). The rows on each overlay represented a different attribute while each position in that row represented one of three different standards or levels of quality, with the worst standard on the left (also called the "free base line"), the medium standard in the middle, and the best standard on the right. A price tag was attached to each standard, based on a crude estimate of supplier's costs.

Respondents were presented with a fixed sum of "play money" (all of which they had to spend); they were told to allocate and reallocate it among the choices available until they arrived at the most satisfactory or "optimum" mix. Nonallocation of money for a particular attribute meant automatic selection of the free base-line choice. As with the Wilson game, the sum of money provided was insufficient to purchase the best quality level of every attribute, thus forcing the repondent to make trade-offs. To eliminate the need for the respondents to perform the mental arithmetic involved in calculating the mix of attribute quality levels that they could buy, the play money was in the form of pegs (like radio jacks), each worth

£100; when the respondents bought a particular quality level, they inserted the required number of pegs alongside the corresponding picture, which then illuminated. In this way there was no confusion as to when the respondents had spent all their available wealth.

Each of these trade-off games, while advancing the state of the art, nevertheless suffers from some inherent shortcomings. For instance, the Wilson game made only an approximate attempt to establish the "true" cost of the items to be purchased in the first game, and in the second game showed no dollar amounts at all. Hoinville and associates spent considerable time attempting to provide accurate estimates of the "true" cost of the items to be purchased, but confessed

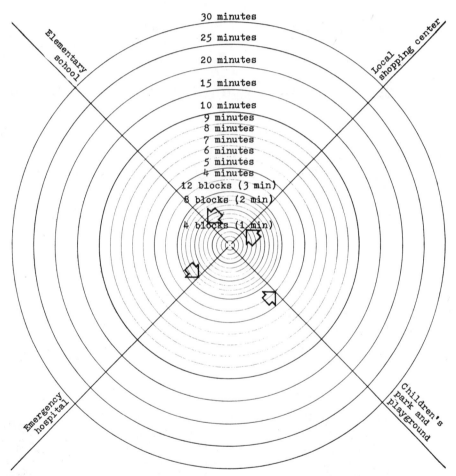

Figure 3
Game board designed by Redding and Peterson to solicit data on people's preferences for locations of activities with respect to their home. Actual size of the board was 20 by 20 inches. Arrows were used by respondent to locate activities. (Adopted and redrawn from the original.)

Noise from traffic	High noise level	Medium noise level	Low noise level
		● ●	● ● ● ●
Traffic in shopping centre	Main road through shopping centre	Local traffic only	Traffic free shopping
		● ● ●	● ● ● ● ● ●
Pedestrian Safety	No pedestrian facilities	Zebra crossings	Pedestrian bridges or subways
		● ●	● ● ● ● ●
Fumes from traffic	Heavy fumes	Medium fumes	Light fumes
		●	● ●
Parked vehicles on street	Continuous heavy parking	Parking mainly on street	Parking mainly off street
		● ●	● ● ● ● ● ● ● ●

Figure 4
Hoinville and Associates' Game: environmental variables.

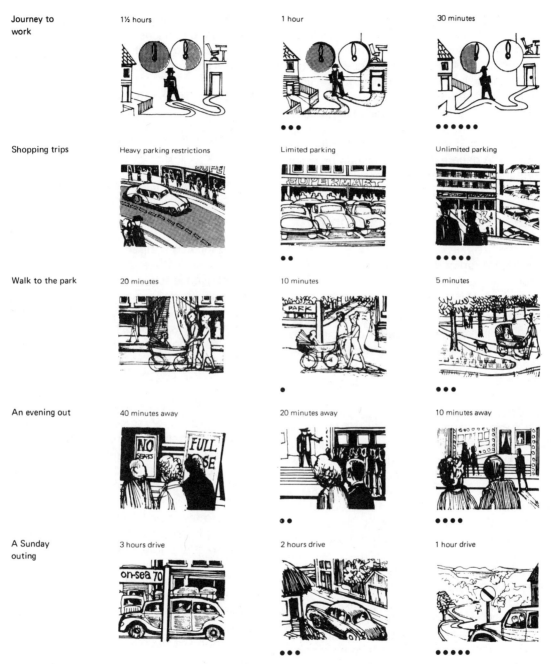

Figure 5
Hoinville and Associates' Game: accessibility variables.

to the difficulty of the task. As will be described in the last section, failure to provide completely accurate costs may invalidate the game results; yet the pricing of publicly provided attributes (those not purchasable on the private market) is a time-consuming and perplexing task.

The University of Southern California game, to be described next, addressed this and other issues in an effort to improve upon trade-off-game techniques. A general list of the criteria by which to judge the games presented here is included in the final section as a guide to future efforts.

UNIVERSITY OF SOUTHERN CALIFORNIA TRADE-OFF GAME

Brief Description of the Research Project

We alluded earlier to two parallel premises that are increasingly being subscribed to by practitioners of environmental design and planning: first, that the concept of substitutability or trade-offs should become an explicit consideration in formulations of design schemes, plans, policies, programs or standards, and, second, that such trade-offs should be based on user choices and needs; in other words, they should reflect the exchanges that different user groups are willing to make under a variety of conditions. These two premises form the basis for the ongoing research on the residential environment in the Graduate Program of Urban and Regional Planning at the University of Southern California (USC) with which the authors of this paper have been associated.[10]

The ultimate objective of this research effort is to develop the performance criteria for the planning and design of residential environments based on concepts of quality of life and the methodologies for eliciting user preferences. An integral element of this research was the design and use of a trade-off game for eliciting user preferences under conditions of constrained choice, the subject of this paper. But before we describe and discuss this game, a brief outline of the design and methodology of the overall research program can be helpful to the reader.

Research Design of the Overall Program

The key element of the research design was an interview survey of selected user groups in the Los Angeles County area. The sampling plan stratified subjects for the study along three dimensions, our major independent variables: (1) race or ethnicity, (2) income, and (3) stage in the life cycle. Accordingly, five population groups— middle-income black, middle-income white, middle-income Spanish surname (brown), upper-income white, and lower-income white — were chosen, each population being broken down into four life-cycle groups: families with young children, families with older children, people (except elderly) without children, and elderly (over 62). This scheme permitted us to hold any two independent variables constant at one time and examine the power of the third variable as a predictor.[11]

The survey instrument comprised a multifaceted approach of standardized and free-form questions of both a descriptive and evaluative nature. Substantively, the questions pertained to (1) perceptions of the residential environment, (2) evaluations and preferences about the residential environment, (3) user activity patterns and exposure to these activities, and (4) trade-off preferences for selected environmental attributes. On the average the total interview took between 2½ and 2¾ hours (respondents were paid $10 for their time); the trade-off portion (which was both descriptive and evaluative in nature) took between 30 to 45 minutes to "play."

Description of the Game

Basically the purpose of the USC trade-off game was to derive constrained choices from the respondent, who was asked to give up a portion of A if he or she desired to obtain a greater amount of B.

The respondents were presented with 11 cards representing various aspects of the residential environment. These aspects we have called *attributes* (see Figure 6). Of these 11 attributes, six were related to accessibility of various places, facilities, and services with respect to one's residence [e.g., work, friends and relatives, schools for children, cultural and entertainment opportunities, shopping, and recreation (parks, beaches, etc.)]. We have called these six *opportunity attributes*. The other five attributes are related to those aspects of one's residential environment that contribute to the overall character of the area (e.g., adequacy of dwelling space, quality of air, number of households per block, personal and property safety, and type of people). We have called these five *ambience attributes*. The number of attributes chosen was based on our estimate of the time necessary to play the game.[12] The choice of specific attributes used in the game was based on our understanding of those facets of the environment that planners and designers can control, a review of existing literature, the identification of variables that appear especially important in the Los Angeles area, and most importantly on our pre-test results.[13]

Each attribute card had a number of statements describing different "amounts" or conditions of that attribute. These descriptions were called *levels;* levels could be specific and quantitative or nonspecific and qualitative, depending on the attribute.[14] The number of quality levels ranged from five to ten. The choice of levels was based on considerations similar to those used in selecting the attributes.

The game itself involved four basic steps. First, the respondent was asked to allocate 25 poker chips among the 11 attribute cards such that the number of chips assigned to each attribute indicated its relative importance. The purpose of this step was to obtain a base-line reading of the respondent's preference ordering before the actual trade-off exercise began. This also served as one of the consistency checks. Also, at this time the subject could indicate (either verbally or by not assigning any chips) which attribute cards were not relevant to his situation. For instance, in the case of a retired person, the "access to work" attribute might not have been relevant, for a single person "access to schools for children" might not have been relevant, and so on. This step permitted the respondent to simplify his subsequent choice process.

The second step established the current *holdings* of the respondent by having him describe and evaluate his present circumstances. Here the respondent took one card at a time, identified the quality level that the attribute presently possessed, if any, in his residential environment, and then indicated how satisfactory that level was by means of a seven-point scale on which the number 1 meant "extremely unsatisfactory" and the number 7 meant "extremely satisfactory."

Before the actual trade-off process began, certain instructions were given. The respondent was told that he would be able to improve three to five attribute quality levels over his present environmental situation; but to obtain an improvement in any one of the selected attribute quality levels, a sacrifice in the quality level of one of the remaining attributes would have to be made. In short, the respondent was told that he would have to *pay* for these desired improvements with cutbacks in quality on the six to eight attributes which he had not selected for improvement. In other words, to gain an improvement in quality for each of the desired-to-be-improved attributes, the respondent would have to decide how much quality he would be willing to surrender in the unimproved attributes. To make these choices, the respondent would have to consider a number

1 ACCESS TO WORK		
A.	Within 5 minutes walk	
B.	Within 15 minutes walk	
C.	Within 10 minutes drive	
D.	Within 20 minutes drive	
E.	Within 30 minutes drive	
F.	Within 45 minutes drive	
G.	Within 1 hour drive	
H.	Within 15 minutes bus ride	
I.	Within 30 minutes bus ride	
J.	Within 1 hour bus ride	

2 ACCESS TO FRIENDS & RELATIVES, ETC		
A.	Within 5 minutes walk	
B.	Within 15 minutes walk	
C.	Within 10 minutes drive	
D.	Within 20 minutes drive	
E.	Within 30 minutes drive	
F.	Within 45 minutes drive	
G.	Within 1 hour drive	
H.	Within 15 minutes bus ride	
I.	Within 30 minutes bus ride	
J.	Within 1 hour bus ride	

3 ADEQUACY OF DWELLING SPACE		
A.	Lots of extra space	
B.	Some extra space	
C.	Just enough space	
D.	Not enough space	
E.	Extremely cramped	

4 AIR QUALITY		
A.	Extremely Clean	
B.	Clean	
C.	Somewhat Clean	
D.	In Between	
E.	Somewhat Smoggy	
F	Smoggy	
G	Extremely Smoggy	

5 ACCESS TO SCHOOLS FOR CHILDREN		
A.	Within 5 minutes walk	
B.	Within 15 minutes walk	
C.	Within 10 minutes drive	
D.	Within 20 minutes drive	
E.	Within 30 minutes drive	
F.	Within 45 minutes drive	
G.	Within 1 hour drive	
H.	Within 15 minutes bus ride	
I.	Within 30 minutes bus ride	
J.	Within 1 hour bus ride	

6 ACCESS TO CULTURAL & ENTERTAINMENT OPPORTUNITIES		
A.	Within 5 minutes walk	
B.	Within 15 minutes walk	
C.	Within 10 minutes drive	
D.	Within 20 minutes drive	
E.	Within 30 minutes drive	
F.	Within 45 minutes drive	
G.	Within 1 hour drive	
H.	Within 15 minutes bus ride	
I.	Within 30 minutes bus ride	
J.	Within 1 hour bus ride	

7 NUMBER OF HOUSEHOLDS ON AN AVERAGE BLOCK		
A.	Less than 10 households per block	
B.	Between	10-25 households per block
C.	Between	25-35 households per block
D.	Between	35-60 households per block
E.	Between	60-100 households per block
F.	Between	100-200 households per block
G.	Over 200 households per block	

8 ACCESS TO SHOPPING	
A.	Within 5 minutes walk
B.	Within 15 minutes walk
C.	Within 10 minutes drive
D.	Within 20 minutes drive
E.	Within 30 minutes drive
F.	Within 45 minutes drive
G.	Within 1 hour drive
H.	Within 15 minutes bus ride
I.	Within 30 minutes bus ride
J.	Within 1 hour bus ride

9 PERSONAL/ PROPERTY SAFETY	
A.	Extremely Safe
B.	Safe
C.	Somewhat Safe
D.	In Between
E.	Somewhat Unsafe
F.	Unsafe
G.	Extremely Unsafe

10 TYPE OF PEOPLE	
A.	Extremely Desirable
B.	Desirable
C.	Somewhat Desirable
D.	In Between
E.	Somewhat Undesirable
F.	Undesirable
G.	Extremely Undesirable

11 ACCESS TO RECREATION (PARKS, BEACHES, ETC)	
A.	Within 5 minutes walk
B.	Within 10 minutes walk
C.	Within 10 minutes drive
D.	Within 20 minutes drive
E.	Within 30 minutes drive
F.	Within 45 minutes drive
G.	Within 1 hour drive
H.	Within 15 minutes bus ride
I.	Within 30 minutes bus ride
J.	Within 1 hour bus ride

Figure 6
Environmental attributes and quality levels used for the University of Southern California trade-off game.

of alternative trade-offs for the particular improvement he desired. Once the subject had identified the "attributes desired for improvement," he or she would be asked to specify the desired levels of such improvements and the corresponding satisfaction scores, using the same scale previously discussed.

In the third step, the respondents actually made the trade-offs according to the instructions: for each desired-to-be-improved attribute they indicated one at a time what quality levels they would sacrifice of the remaining attributes, and the corresponding satisfaction scores of the desired and traded-off levels of quality. This involved a series of pairwise comparisons. If the subject chose to improve three attributes, for example, for each one of them he had to consider giving up some level of one of the remaining eight attributes. In total, then, he had to consider three sets of eight pairwise comparisons. If he had chosen four attributes to be improved, he would have been required to consider four sets of seven pairwise comparisons, and so on.[15] In some cases, however, we anticipated that this exchange would prove difficult, if not impossible, for example, when the respondent had very little to start with, and his existing levels were perceived as minimum thresholds below which he was unwilling to go. Alternatively, we anticipated that wealthy respondents might find themselves in the best of all realistically conceivable worlds, where they were virtually satiated in terms of high-priority items. Hence they would not be able to conceive of an improvement in those attributes, and yet would be unwilling to sacrifice high-priority attributes for improvements in low-priority items; that is, marginal improvement in low-priority attributes would be valued less than marginal sacrifices required in high-priority attributes. Accordingly, respondents were told they need not give up anything, and in such cases we would record that the exchange (transaction) was attempted but not completed.

The fourth and final step required respondents to allocate the 25 poker chips once again among the 11 cards. This last chip distribution was another consistency check and was expected to indicate a more realistic (constrained) preference ordering if the trade-off exercise had sensitized respondents to their implicit orderings.

Findings

Our analysis of the data from the trade-off game, and from other sections of the interview schedule as well, is still in process. Therefore, the findings discussed next are but a sample of the richness of the potential data that may be derived from our game. In any case, since the primary thrust of this paper is to discuss the methods rather than the specific results, the findings we discuss should be adequate for this purpose.

Chip allocation Table 1 shows the mean number of chips allocated to different attributes by different population groups before the trade-off game actually began. The corresponding ranks of various attributes are also shown in this table. It is apparent that all attributes are not equally valued by various population groups, and, as a corollary, the preference orderings of these attributes are not identical for all population groups. This certainly confirms the notion of pluralism in community preferences with which the planner or environmental designer typically deals.

In terms of specific differences, the following points are worth noting. First, we find relative consensus among all population groups in the ranks or relative importance of personal and property safety, type of people, and access to shopping—with ranks higher or equal to the median rank; and of number of households per block, access to friends and relatives, and access to cultural and entertainment opportunities—with ranks less than the median. Second, a more potentially significant finding, is that, although all groups have valued air quality quite high, there

Table 1
Mean Number of Chips Allocated to 11 Attributes by Different Population Groups

| | Population Groups | | | | | | | | | | |
| | Middle Black | | Middle White | | Middle Brown | | Upper White | | Lower White | | All Groups | |
Attributes	$\overline{X}$a	Rb	$\overline{X}$	R	$\overline{X}$	R	$\overline{X}$	R	$\overline{X}$	R	$\overline{X}$	R
Access to work	1.90	7	2.04	6	2.04	8	1.94	6	1.12	11	1.80	8
Access to friends and relatives	1.80	8	1.99	7	1.13	10	1.87	8	1.78	7	1.69	9
Adequacy of dwelling space	2.80	2	2.72	3	2.21	7	2.81	3	2.88	3	2.28	6
Air quality	2.60	5	3.94	1	2.92	3	3.43	1	4.06	1	3.38	1
Access to schools for children	2.50	6	1.88	8	3.58	2	1.92	7	2.32	5	2.43	4
Access to cultural and entertainment facilities	1.53	10	1.40	11	1.46	9	1.68	9	1.22	10	1.26	11
Number of households per block	1.53	10	1.79	9	1.04	11	1.57	10	1.56	9	1.50	10
Access to shopping	2.63	4	2.23	5	2.33	5	2.24	5	2.30	6	2.36	5
Personal and property safety	3.43	1	3.00	2	3.63	1	3.35	2	2.92	2	3.26	2
Type of people	2.73	3	2.27	4	2.25	6	2.68	4	2.54	4	2.49	3
Access to recreational facilities	1.68	9	1.73	10	2.42	4	1.54	11	1.76	8	1.82	7

a $\overline{X}$, mean number of chips.
b R, rank of attributes by population group.

seems to exist a subtle difference between the white and minority groups. All white population groups, regardless of income differences, have identified air quality as the most important attribute; but the middle-income black and the middle-income brown groups have identified personal and property safety as the most important attribute. Air quality ranks fifth for the middle-income blacks and third for the middle-income browns. Third, the middle-income browns have valued three attributes (access to schools for children, adequacy of dwelling space, and access to recreation) differently from the rest of the population groups. Whereas the other groups have generally given access to schools moderate importance, the middle-income browns indicated this attribute as the second most important. Similarly, the other population groups have indicated access to recreation as of low importance and

adequacy of dwelling space as of high importance, but the middle-income browns indicated exactly to the contrary — the former being rated high and the latter rated low. The fact that the middle-income brown group clearly stands apart from the other three groups on these three occasions may be indicative of significant cultural differences that do not exist between blacks and whites.

Finally, the lower-income white group has given access to work much lower importance than the rest. This is somewhat surprising, since with lower income the cost of transportation becomes more significant in the total family budget.

Although it is difficult to speculate on the reasons for these differences without doing additional analysis, it can be pointed out that in general all population groups, with the exception of the middle-income browns, have valued ambience attributes greater than the opportunity attributes, as clearly shown in Table 2. This is also corroborated by the findings of trade-off transactions to be discussed in the following section, where it will be shown that in general opportunity attributes are much more dispensable than ambience attributes.

Transactions   As noted previously, for various reasons certain respondents could not or were not willing to trade off any attribute quality levels in order to improve one of their selected attributes. In these instances, the exchange was recorded as having been uncompleted. The mean numbers of total completed and uncompleted transactions for various population groups are shown in Table 3. Although there are significant differences among various population groups in terms of completed transactions, it is apparent that there are no significant differences among the groups in terms of uncompleted transactions. It is interesting to note, however, that it is the upper-income white and lower-income white groups that had a higher number of uncompleted transactions than the rest; that is, in most instances, they reached points where they refused to trade off attributes. Furthermore, if we look at the ratio of completed and uncompleted transactions, for all groups, except the upper-income white, two out of every three attempted transac-

tions were completed; for the latter it amounted to even less than three out of every five.

This generally indicates that the upper-income white group had more difficulty in giving things up, although one might normally expect that it is the lower-income group who would have difficulty in giving things up, since they presumably have a low level to begin with. In a way, the relatively high number of uncompleted transactions by the lower-income group tends to confirm this notion. But in the case of the upper-income group this difficulty can be attributed to its higher thresholds of acceptability for almost all attributes when compared with that of the middle- and lower-income groups. A typical middle-income respondent from Van Nuys, located in San Fernando Valley, may find "somewhat clean" an acceptable level of air quality, but an upper-income respondent from Palos Verdes Estates, which enjoys the cleanest air in the Los Angeles area because of its location on the coast, may find anything less than "clean" unacceptable (see Figure 6 for descriptions of various levels). It is quite likely that the upper-income respondents who enjoy best or near-best levels of all attributes found themselves more frequently than others in a position where giving up something would involve getting an unacceptable level of that attribute, hence their higher proportion of uncompleted transactions.

Table 2
Attributes with Ranks Higher Than the Median: Initial Chip Allocation

Type of Attribute	Middle Black	Middle White	Middle Brown	Upper White	Lower White
Opportunity attributes with ranks ⟩ median	Shopping	Shopping	Schools Shopping Recreation	Shopping	Schools
Ambience attributes with ranks ⟩ median	Safety Space People Air	Air Safety Space People	Safety Air	Air Safety Space People	Air Safety Space People

It should be noted also in Table 3 that there is a significant difference among the various population groups in the number of improvements that each group sought. If we hold race constant, for example, among the white respondents, the number of improvements desired is clearly a function of the income level; if income is held constant, noticeable differences can be seen between white and nonwhite groups. If the number of improvements desired is seen as an indicator of residential satisfaction, it is clear that income and race have a significant relationship with residential satisfaction, a fact that confirms what is commonly believed.

Trade-off propensities We also looked at the actual patterns of trade-off transactions among different groups. Table 4 shows the frequencies with which changes were sought in various attributes by different population groups, that is, their preference at the margin. Similarly, Table 5 shows the relative dispensability of various attributes in exchange for desired changes.

But none of these tables indicates which attributes were given up in exchange for what, or the propensity of one attribute to be given up in exchange for an improvement in another. To ascertain such propensities, we simply mapped the ratio of completed and total transactions in an 11 by 11 matrix for each population group. These propensity values can be seen as probabilistic in nature on the assumption that the observed ratios are simple estimates of actual probabilities.

Table 6 shows, for illustrative purposes, the transaction patterns for one population group, the middle-income blacks, for the 11 environmental attributes. Only the five most-desired-to-be-improved attributes for this group have been included for simplification in presentation, and these are listed according to their rank order. Arrayed against each of these attributes are trade-off propensity quintiles ranging from high to low. Thus, for middle-income blacks, we see that air quality is most desired, and to achieve a higher level of air quality this group would be willing to forego current levels of the other attributes. The table does not show how much of the level sought and how much of the level foregone is acceptable. Rather, it shows the propensity of the group to select, say, access to work, as an item in which to reduce the quality level in order to achieve a higher level of air quality. Accordingly, we see that middle-income blacks had a high propensity to trade off some quality level of access to work to achieve a higher level of air quality, whereas they had a low propensity to trade off personal and property safety for better air quality.

The trade-off propensity of access to work in

Table 3
Completed, Uncompleted, and Attempted Transactions, and Improvements Desired by Different Population Groups

| Population Groups | Number of Transactions | | | Number of Improvements Desired (mean) |
	Attempted (mean)	Completed (mean)	Uncompleted (mean)	
Middle black (N = 40)	18.68	13.53	5.15	3.78
Middle white (N = 66)	19.95	14.12	5.83	3.29
Middle brown (N = 24)	20.87	14.08	6.79	3.67
Upper white (N = 63)	17.42	10.02	7.30	2.60
Lower white (N = 47)	19.64	12.51	7.13	3.55

Table 4

Frequency and Ranks of Attributes in Which Improvements Were Sought by Five Population Groups

| | Population Groups | | | | | | | | | | |
| | Middle Black (N = 40) | | Middle White (N = 66) | | Middle Brown (N = 24) | | Upper White (N = 63) | | Lower White (N = 47) | | All Groups (N = 240) | |
Attributes	Freq.	Rank	Freq.	Rank	Freq.	Rank	Freq.	Rank	Freq.	Rank	Freq.	Rank
Access to work	11	4	16	6	6	6	12	5	3	10	48	8
Access to friends and relatives	7	6	12	7	3	8	9	7	6	9	37	10
Adequacy of dwelling space	17	3	33	2	11	4	18	3	20	3	91	3
Air quality	26	1	56	1	19	1	43	1	39	1	183	1
Access to schools for children	5	7	0	10	4	7	5	10	7	8	21	10
Access to cultural and entertainment facilities	8	5	16	6	12	3	16	4	15	5	67	4
Number of households per block	11	4	18	5	2	9	7	9	13	6	51	6
Access to shopping	8	5	9	9	2	9	9	7	11	7	39	9
Personal and property safety	25	2	30	3	14	2	27	2	30	2	126	2
Type of people	11	4	11	9	6	6	10	6	19	4	57	5
Access to recreational facilities	7	6	19	4	9	5	8	8	6	9	49	7

Table 5

Frequencies and Ranks of Attributes Traded Off by Different Population Groups

| | Population Groups | | | | | | | | | | |
| | Middle Black (N = 40) | | Middle White (N = 66) | | Middle Brown (N = 24) | | Upper White (N = 63) | | Lower White (N = 47) | | All Groups (N = 240) | |
	Freq.	Rank	Freq.	Rank	Freq.	Rank	Freq.	Rank	Freq.	Rank	Freq.	Rank
Access to work	17	4	34	5	12	4	27	4	18	5	108	5
Access to friends and relatives	20	3	37	3	14	3	36	2	33	1	140	2
Adequacy of dwelling space	8	7	22	9	7	7	27	4	12	8	76	9
Air quality	2	8	1	12	2	8	5	9	2	11	12	11
Access to schools for children	20	3	39	2	16	2	27	4	30	4	132	3
Access to cultural and entertainment facilities	21	2	36	4	7	7	25	5	14	6	103	6
Number of households per block	9	6	25	8	11	5	20	7	13	7	78	8
Access to shopping	28	1	50	1	18	1	38	1	32	2	166	1
Personal and property safety	1	9	16	10	2	8	11	8	4	10	34	10
Type of people	14	5	27	7	12	4	23	6	9	9	85	7
Access to recreational facilities	17	4	33	6	9	6	30	3	31	3	120	4

Table 6
Patterns of Transactions—Middle-Income Black

First Five Attributes for Which an Improved Quality Level is Desired (Rank Order)	Trade-Off Propensities for the 11 Attributes				
	High (81-100)	*Above Average (61-80)*	*Average (41-60)*	*Below Average (21-40)*	*Low (0-20)*
Air quality	Access to work Access to friends and relatives Access to schools Access to culture and entertainment	Density[a]	Dwelling unit space[b] Type of people		Personal and property safety
Personal and property safety	Air quality[c] Access to work Access to friends and relatives Access to culture and entertainment Access to shopping Access to recreation	Access to schools	Dwelling unit space[b] Density[b] Type of people		
Adequacy of dwelling space	Air quality[c] Access to work Access to friends and relatives Access to schools Access to culture and entertainment Access to shopping	Type of people Access to recreation	Density[a]		Personal and property safety
Number of households per block (density)	Air quality[c] Personal and property safety Access to culture and entertainment Access to shopping Access to recreation	Access to schools	Type of people	Dwelling unit space[b]	
Access to work	Access to friends and relatives Access to culture and entertainment Access to shopping Personal and property safety	Access to recreation	Air quality[c]	Access to schools Density[a]	Dwelling unit space[b]

[a] Number of households per block.
[b] Adequacy of dwelling space.
[c] Less than five transactions.

the highest quintile suggests that 81 percent or more of all the persons in this population group who selected, say, access to work to be traded off for air quality completed this transaction. However, only 20 percent or less of all the persons who attempted to trade off personal and property safety for air quality were able to make this exchange. In both cases, the remainder (those who could not complete the transaction) evidently prized the attribute more highly than air quality. And both cases are in accord with the group's marginal attribute ranking. Eighty percent or more of the persons who paired air quality with access to work found that they would be willing to give up some quality level of the latter to gain in the former. However, only 20 percent or less were willing to make such an exchange for personal and property safety, indicating that this latter attribute is relatively highly prized and hence more difficult to trade off for something else, given current circumstances. The rank orderings of desired-to-be-improved attributes as well as the chip allocations for middle-income blacks confirm that this is so.

The attributes of density and adequacy of dwelling unit space fall in between these two extremes for trade-off propensity, and similarly fall in between in the rank order of the five most-desired attributes for improvement of the middle-income black group. Here one rank ordering neatly corresponds to another, and we find that the trade-off mechanism provides a convenient consistency check. But closer inspection of the table reveals that this consistency does not always hold. With respect to the next-most-desired attribute for improvement, personal and property safety, we find that air quality, presumably more highly prized, is nevertheless highly regarded as appropriate to be traded off for increases in personal and property safety. Analysis of the trade-off propensity tables for the other population groups reveals similar sorts of "inconsistencies" in respondents' choices.

Inconsistencies

There are a number of possible explanations for the apparent inconsistencies: (1) they may be an artifact of our trade-off approach, (2) they may reflect actual inconsistencies where the individuals are not entirely clear regarding their preferences, or (3), and most likely, they may be the consequence of aggregating individual preferences where those preferences are not entirely held in common.

Some inconsistency indeed may have been introduced by the approach when the respondent either misunderstood or forgot key aspects of the trade-off game. Debriefing of the interviewers suggests that this probably happened occasionally. As to individual inconsistency, Wallis and Friedman (1942) have implied this possibility in stating that preferences are in part acquired through trial and error of response, which in turn is based on past experience. The uncertainty suggested here would be sufficient cause for individual inconsistency in the course of making some 14 to 30 pairwise comparisons.

But there is another explanation for individual inconsistency as well. In the case of asking a person to rank order his preferences, an assumption is made that such an ordering is possible. In fact, persons may only be able to make partial orderings, or the orderings may be lexicographic,[16] or they may be intransitive. Consequently, unless the respondent challenges the assumption inherent in the question, the response he provides as to preference orderings may be plausible but spurious. There is no way to determine the precise cause of these inconsistencies without tedious consistency checks and exhaustive questioning.

As to the third possible reason for the "inconsistencies," that there are differences *within* groups as well as *among* them, this is also highly probable.

The use to which these revealed inconsistencies can be put by public policy and decision makers is discussed in the final section. Indeed, as we discuss there, we believe that revealing these inconsistencies is one of the strongest assets of our trade-off-game approach.

Substantive The method of sampling we used to enable us to interview sufficient numbers of persons in each of the race–income–life cycle categories severely restricts any generalizations of the findings to the particular areas in which we interviewed. It would be erroneous to generalize the findings to the Los Angeles area, much less to the nation. However, that was not the purpose of the research; and a few comments about the substantive findings might be made as long as it is recognized that they may be speculations rather than fact.

First, with respect to both chip allocation and the designation of attributes chosen for improvement, air quality appeared predominant as a prime concern for all the groups surveyed. This is probably not so surprising given the nature of the air quality in Los Angeles and the constant reference to it in the last few years in the communications media. Personal and property safety was another major concern, although not as strong. This also appears plausible in view of increasing public concern over "safety in the streets" and the growth in house burglaries in urban areas such as Los Angeles. At the other end of the preference scale, access to friends, access to shopping, and, for that matter, almost all other opportunity attributes uniformly appear as very expendable items; that is, there is a high propensity to trade them off for higher levels of other attributes.[17] Given the high level of personal mobility in the Los Angeles area, this does not come as a surprise.

In fact, we might suggest that the finding regarding access to shopping is a tribute to the physical design of the Los Angeles area in this respect. The high level of success in achieving personal mobility has made this normally highly prized attribute relatively dispensable in the Los Angeles region. We believe the finding that access to shopping is one of the most expendable items is implicit proof of the value of measuring user preferences. The location of shopping areas in Los Angeles is dictated by market demand and supplier response. Shopping-center developers, prior to making a development decision, carefully monitor and calculate the shoppers' preferences for shopping services. If the demand warrants the investment, the development decision is made. Thus the private market depends heavily upon consumer or user preferences to influence its decisions, and in this case the data suggest that the decisions were correctly made. It should be noted that this is the only attribute in our trade-off game that is provided primarily by the private sector. If public decision were also to be made after carefully consulting user preferences, we believe these items too would better satisfy environmental users.

CONCLUSIONS

Value of Trade-Off-Game Approach

For planners and environmental designers, an important issue regarding our discussion of trade-off games is their utility. Is this approach more useful to these professions than, say, a questionnaire on community preferences about the environment? Earlier we presented a comparison of different approaches toward eliciting preferences; we stressed the inadequacies of questionnaires that probe unconstrained choices on the one hand, and behavior studies that monitor past or present-day choices on the other. When taken alone, the first approach may provide unrealistic rankings of goals; if solely relied upon, the second approach may endorse the status quo without any indication of preferences with respect to what might be. In short, the former has a tendency to be too utopian, the latter entirely too present-day. What is required is some combination, some in-between ground that is improvement-seeking, yet realistic. For several reasons we believe the trade-off instrument presented here meets these demands.

First, in the earlier discussion the importance of behavior as well as attitude was stressed if preferences were to be learned. The trade-off-game approach attempts to simulate behavior in the face of constraints. On the one hand, since trade-offs involve constrained choice—the respondent must give up something to get something else—they tend to approximate behavior. On the other hand, since trade-off preferences can be elicited through interviews and survey research approaches that can also include simulations of environments, the trade-off choices need not be confined to the present-day world; they can address unfulfilled preferences or preferences for future options.

Second, the trade-off game is a means of permitting respondents (environmental users) to participate more fully in the decision processes that affect their lives and sense of well-being. At an earlier time, planners and environmental designers assumed that they knew what was best for the public: they assumed that they knew what the public's preferences were, what the real-world constraints were, and what the appropriate trade-offs were in the face of these constraints. Accordingly, the public was only minimally involved in the planning and design process. There was no need for their involvement as it was commonly held that the experts knew best. With the widespread recognition of the pluralistic nature of our society and with numerous demands for citizen input, the planner's and environmental designer's response was to conduct surveys of public preferences so as to no longer rely upon what may have been false impressions of the public's interest. With this change the expert now at least knew what the preferences were, but they were unconstrained preferences. When faced

with real-world constraints, the designer still had to modify the original preferences by filtering them through a set of trade-offs to come up with a design solution. Problems still arose, however. It turned out that the public would sometimes have changed their preferences in a fashion different from what the designer had anticipated, if the public had been faced with, or knew about, these same constraints. Thus the design process had improved with citizen participation, but there was still a large chance for error.

The merit of the trade-off-game approach is that it carries citizen participation a step farther along in the design process. It not only permits the different publics to express preferences, but trade-off preferences as well, and in a particularly salient fashion. For instance, in a trade-off-game developed by Jerry Berger, which was played by ghetto residents, it was found that the game achieves

. . . a spontaneous involvement that "addresses itself to the psychological problems of powerlessness and anomie felt by the poor" . . . . The game increases a neighborhood's sense of community and a resident's personal identification with the neighborhood. People have come from a sickbed to take part. The game provides "a convenient structure for accelerated and relevant dialogue between citizens and professionals" (Berkeley, 1968, p. 61).

To be sure, the planner or designer must still contend with any number of constraints that are either too technical in nature to be asked of respondents or too time-consuming to go into detail. Here he will be responsible for the trade-offs. But at least some of the burden of the decision (i.e., some of the trade-offs) has been shifted to the user, so that the designer has a better idea of the trade-offs that should be made.[18] In short, the trade-off-game instrument permits citizens to enter more fully into the decision process and, as a consequence, provides the designer with more complete knowledge as to their desires.

Third, we believe that the USC trade-off-game approach is not only superior to the more traditional approaches to identifying user preferences, but also is applicable and adaptable to a variety of public planning and evaluation situations in addition to the one for which it was primarily developed. For example, it could be used in the goal-formation stage of the planning process, to identify "quality-of-life" indicators, to allocate resources to specific programs, to develop architectural programs, to evaluate alternative plans and their effects on different population groups, and to review environmental-impact statements.

Finally, we believe that the trade-off game provides a learning experience for the respondents. Even though most people believe that they have a fairly good idea of their preferences, when faced with specific trade-offs they are often surprised to discover that what they had believed to be their preferences do not match their past or present behavior, or for that matter their own value system. Thus the cognitive task of considering a series of trade-offs between various attributes provides a unique opportunity that does not otherwise exist to sort things out in one's mind. For, although we have claimed earlier that people do make trade-offs to cope with the constraints of everyday life, the real-world trade-off choices are often redundant, limited, or partial, and certainly nowhere near the range of combinations offered through the trade-off game. At this point, we do not want to exaggerate this claim; rather we would prefer to state it as a hypothesis based on our analysis of preliminary data and pretest findings. We would also like to point out that the sensitizing effect of the game may not be universally true for all respondents; nor for that matter do we believe that the game can drastically alter preferences. Rather, it provides a subject an opportunity to "fine tune" perceptions of his or her own preferences, something that is not likely to happen in standard attitude surveys.

Utility of the Data

Perhaps the most important question for the environmental designer and decision maker is "How can the specific kinds of information derived from our trade-off game be used and in what instances or situations is it most applicable?" Our response is in two parts: first, in terms of the types of data already derived from our analysis to date, especially the propensity-to-trade-off tables; and, second, in terms of possible future extensions of the analysis of the data.

In terms of the types of data currently available, as briefly described previously under Findings, we see their potential use as being related to three specific areas: (1) the pluralistic nature of the public, (2) the realities of most actual decision situations, and (3) the development of planning standards.

Pluralism The USC survey, as previously indicated, grouped persons according to race or ethnicity, income, and age in the life cycle, thereby explicitly recognizing differences in preferences based on these factors. Within these groups, we can provide a simple preference ranking based on the chip-allocation procedure. But such a ranking is expressed in terms of a numerical index score. A trade-off propensity table shows similar information (in terms of the overall import of different attributes), but at a much more disaggregated level, and there is a particular advantage to information disaggregated at this level despite its greater complexity.

The trade-off data are issue-specific; the chip allocation is true "in general" only. Thus, as a general rule, air quality and personal and property safety were rated highly important by both means of rankings. But the chip-allocation device, as with all simple preference rankings, disguises some differences within groups by its summary index number. However, the trade-off propensity tables, which show the importance of each attribute in both an overall sense and in regard to every other attribute as well, permit such internal differences to be revealed in terms of the inconsistencies in the trade-off tables, described earlier.

These inconsistencies may be interpreted in two ways. First, they provide a clue as to the extent of the differences within a particular group. If the planner or designer is faced with making two different kinds of trade-offs, he will select the one that has the least internal differences within a group; that is, he will seek to avoid a controversy. Thus the first important type of information the propensity-to-trade-off tables reveal is the extent of pluralism among certain trade-offs within groups.

Second, the propensity-to-trade-off tables provide an indication of the strength with which these trade-offs are preferred. For instance, Table 6 for middle-income blacks shows that although air quality ranks first and density fourth, in terms of the most-desired-to-be-improved attributes, an above-average number of respondents in this group are willing to trade off the former for the latter. Thus it can be inferred that there exists a minority which prefers density to air quality, and, given their high propensity to exchange some of the latter for the former, this minority may indeed be a highly vocal one; that is, this different order of preferences may be strongly held. If this is so, there is a potential for polarization within this population group if policy and decision makers attempt to make trade-offs without these subgroup differences in preferences in mind. Armed with this kind of trade-off propensity information, an alternative solution can be sought that will be less potentially divisive.[19]

Actual decision situations It is true that the data from our trade-off game cannot be used to produce a neat ratio or interval rank ordering of all 11 attributes used in our trade-off game. Rather, the data, as included in the trade-off propensity tables, only show pairwise comparisons. Considering the reality of most actual decision situations faced by the environmental designer and decision maker, we would argue that the whole set of goal or preference orderings may not be needed.

Frequently, the environmental designer and decision maker are not faced with general issues at the policy level so much as they are with particular issues more narrowly defined. They often do not have the freedom or luxury of allocating resources on the basis, say, of the 10 highest ranked goals or preferences. Many potential considerations are ruled out from the decision arena because they have already been decided and no one is willing to raise the issue again, or another or higher level of jurisdiction has already decided the issue and it is "out of bounds" to the local policy or decision maker, or there is a legal prohibition from considering the larger set of issues, leaving only a small set to be resolved, or other issues have not yet been decided and cannot be made prematurely (e.g., until the legislature next meets or after the next mayoralty election). Even in participatory design or planning situations, it has often been found that, typically, issues that surface are limited in number and very specific in nature. Whatever the reason, the issue arena is circumscribed so that the choice may be in terms of only a few goals, preferences, or attributes. Here the greater specificity of the trade-off propensity tables becomes extremely useful. For example, among 10 goals (or environmental attributes) a user group may rank A higher than E (such as the chip-allocation process might reveal); but when faced with a situation where only A and E are compared, which, as we have been arguing, may be more and more the case, we may find E preferred to A.

Standards Another use of the trade-off information pertains to the formulation and use of standards. Earlier we described some of the shortcomings attributed to the current set of planning standards in use: failure to consider user preferences, to distinguish preferences between user groups, and to acknowledge the need for trade-offs. The formulation of planning standards on the basis of incorporating user preferences could be superior to the current "experts only" input. Such information would permit a variant of citizen participation in much the same way that a doctor will consult with his patient before prescribing treatment, although in doing so he does not shirk his professional responsibilities and obligations. Similarly, the incorporation whenever possible of user preferences information contributes to a more effective development and use of standards, without obviating the professional planner's or environmental designer's obligations.

Most importantly, the presentation of relatively disaggregated trade-off preferences allows the planner to learn which substitutions might be made when developing standards for a variety of environmental attributes. For example, if air quality is shown as both most important in an ordinal ranking and also the item least likely to be traded off against anything else, this suggests that not only is air quality strongly preferred to other attributes, but also that the community is willing to undertake a variety of trade-offs to achieve better air quality. Thus the planner can conclude that air quality is a strong end, but a poor means to achieve other ends. Conversely, if access to shopping is generally accorded a high potential for being traded off to gain an increase in quality for some other attribute, it suggests that, given the current level of access to shopping, the residents have a relatively high propensity to sacrifice it to acquire a better quality level of some other attribute. Access to shopping, therefore, is seen as a weak end in and of itself, but an effective means to other ends, and the standards should reflect this potential substitutability.

The trade-off preferences themselves provide some guidance to the planner or environmental designer as to how to grapple with a situation when the standards are in conflict (if only from an allocation of scarce resources point of view), yet admit of no compromise. Traditional planning standards tell us, for example, that cities, or parts thereof, should have X acres of recreational land per 1,000 population and Y number of schools per 1,000 school-age population. In allocating scarce resources between these attributes, traditional standards say, "Do both." But they give no solution if the planner responds, "I can't." Knowledge of the user groups trade-offs (and present satisfaction levels) provides some clues as to which standard(s) to relax in such a circumstance. Although other criteria may be important in formulating planning standards, such as knowledge of public health and public safety, the trade-off preferences provide some of the necessary information to make the exchange.

At a minimum, recognition of these factors should increase cost effectiveness as greater sensitivity to user needs should permit increased user satisfaction for a given expenditure. For instance, park standards sensitive to the preferences of a particular client group eliminate wasteful expenditures (e.g., swings and sandboxes in parks largely used by the elderly, or a football field in a park patronized by Latins who prefer soccer).

But for these examples, it might be argued that any number of preference-learning devices would suffice; for example, a simple questionnaire asking people what they would like would register preferences and could be aggregated by various characteristics, such as age, sex, race, and ethnicity. Although an improvement as a basis for standards formulation, such data still provide no indication of what to do if two different requirements cannot be satisfied at the same time. No information on exchange rates is provided in a simple listing of preferences. Consequently, in making such exchanges in the process of allocating resources and assigning different environmental attributes to different population groups, the planner must be guided largely by hunch, intuition, and his own (or the politician's) trade-off preferences.

Trade-off data, on the other hand, openly display (albeit at an elementary level) the user-desired trade-offs, which, in turn, can act as guides to the planner in exercising his professional judgment. The trade-off information does not displace the planner's judgment; it merely sharpens it. Furthermore, it gives him additional insight and direction in searching for plan alternatives, and reveals some of the relationships (in terms of choice) among different variables on the part of user groups. Knowledge of these relationships is more valuable than knowledge of a simple preference ranking, which may conceal the nuances in trade-offs. In short, the presentation of trade-offs allows the planner to interpret and to use more effectively and sensitively the planning standards he is faced with.

Extensions of current data analysis To make trade-off data even more useful for planners, designers, and decision makers, such research should be pursued along several different lines; it would appear, however, that our data only permit us to pursue a few of these possibilities.

Ideally, what the planner, designer, and decision maker would like to know are the quantitatitve trade-off relationships between different goals, preferences, and attributes for different population groups, what is referred to as a *trade-off rate* (Friend and Jessop, 1969, Chapter 10; Robinson, 1972). For example, a trade-off rate between noise levels in residential areas and access to schools would show how much additional traveling time to school (measured, say, in minutes) each population group would be willing to accept on behalf of their school-aged children in order to realize a certain decrease in noise level (measured, say,in decibels) in the neighborhood. Suppose, for instance, that the information (from a trade-off game of the kind we have been discussing) showed that, in the case of population group A, for every decrease of 5 to 10

decibels of noise it would be willing to accept (sacrifice) an additional 5 minutes of travel time to school. (Presumably, this trade-off relationship would be different for other groups.) We could then develop the trade-off rate for this group by converting the school travel time in terms of the noise level; that is, we could say that 5 to 10 noise decibels represents 1 "noise unit"; therefore, the trade-off rate between increased travel time and less noise for this population group would be 1 : 5, which says that 1 unit of noise (i.e., 5 to 10 less decibels) equals 5 additional minutes of travel time to school.

Now suppose that the planners or decision makers contemplated introducing a stringent noise ordinance in a neighborhood in which population group A lives (or is likely to live), which would decrease the noise from its current average level of 50 to 70 decibels to the ideal standard of 40 to 50 decibels, that is, a 10- to 20-decibel decrease. But to do this would necessitate that the residents' school-aged children spend an additional 20 minutes more everyday to get to school. This is because achievement of the contemplated standard would require elimination of most vehicle traffic within the neighborhood (a major source of the higher noise level at the present time), and thus curtail drastically the current practice of parents driving their young children to school and / or older students driving their own cars to high school. The upshot of these restrictions is that the school-aged youngsters would be forced to walk or ride their bicycles to school, which, of course, would take longer.

The proposed new noise level would, in effect, represent a trade-off rate of I : 10, which is twice as high as this population group indicated it was prepared to accept as a trade-off. Faced with this situation, the policy and decision makers could either ignore the wishes of this group and "ram" through the ordinance anyway or, following the wishes of the residents, discuss with them a compromise solution. For example, a school-bussing system would at least transport more pupils per vehicle, and although it would not eliminate vehicle traffic altogether, it would decrease the noise level to 45 to 60 decibels, which is still an acceptable standard.

If similar types of quantitative trade-off relationships were available for a variety of goals, preferences, and attributes, and for different population groups, they could be collected in a book or manual of planning trade-off "matrix" tables, and the planner need only look up his particular situation in the appropriate tables to find the solution to his allocation problems. Indeed, the use of high-speed computers would make the various trade-off computations fairly easy to calculate and interpolate.

Friend and Jessop illustrate how trade-off rates can be used in evaluating alternative solutions or "plans" and how different trade-off rates can affect which solution or plan will be selected, that is, how the numerical values determine the solution or plan selected (Friend and Jessop, 1969, pp. 185 – 191). In their illustrations, however, the authors use assumed rates. Their technique would be immeasurably improved if, by using the trade-off instrument we have described, they were able to develop the actual numerical weights for different population groups (and decision makers), rather than assuming them. We do not envision that such a precise approach will be possible in the near future, nor that such a "mechanical" approach is necessarily desirable. Still, such data would assist planners and decision makers in making ultimate trade-off decisions.

The concept of trade-off rate assumes invariance in the rate of substitutability; that is, the rate is constant or linear (see Figure 7). In actuality, we know that this is probably not always true; in many instances, as an individual gets additional increments of a particular good or service, he may be willing to give up diminishing amounts of the second good or service in exchange (and

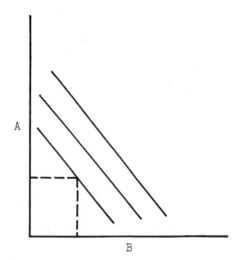

Figure 7
Theoretical construct of trade-off rate.

stay as well off). In the terminology of the economist, increases in many goods and services have diminishing marginal utility. Using the noise versus school location example, this concept means that the second unit, so to speak, of the noise-level decrease may not be as important, relative to the second unit of travel-time increase, as the first unit. In other words, the negative impact of increased travel time for this population group may not increase linearly with the decrease of noise level.

In short, the rates at which an individual or group of individuals are willing to exchange would probably change, as he (or it) gets more of preference B and less of preference A, owing to diminishing marginal utility. Therefore, a better representative of trade-off relationships would be in the form of a trade-off *curve* for any pair of preferences, or a trade-off *function* relating to a number of objectives or preferences (see Figure 8); the idea of the trade-off curve or function is similar in concept to the economist's indifference curve, and the rates of exchange so represented are what the economist calls "marginal rates of substitution."

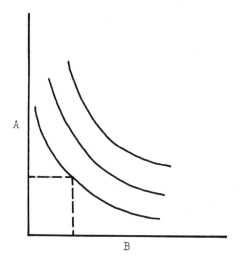

Figure 8
Theoretical construct of trade-off curve.

Our data do not permit development of trade-off rates, curves, or functions. Such a task is probably beyond the current state of the art. Time and expense, the high degree of probable error, the problem of quantifying qualitative objectives (Hill, 1968), and the conceptual issue of aggregating individual preferences (Arrow, 1963; Zeckhauser and Schaefer, 1968) all combine to make determination of an exact rate extremely difficult, if not impossible. The closest we believe we can come to this ideal, using our present approach, is to develop trade-off *domains* or trade-off *bands* for different population groups. Although admittedly a less precise form of aggregation, they are nevertheless still useful for planning, design, and decision-making purposes.

The trade-off domain represents the more rudimentary analysis of the data. At a minimum, it would provide an indication of where not to focus concern, and hence, through the residual, where to focus concern. By plotting the points where individual trade-offs for the group have been made, we learn where trade-offs were *not* made. In other words, even if one is unwilling to aggre-

gate the trade-offs into an index, plotting the trade-off points will reveal two basic areas where no trade-offs occurred. First, there will be some trade-offs ruled out because they will be *unacceptable* to the respondents (these would be at or toward the point of origin in Figure 9), because they fall below some minimum threshold of acceptance. Other points would be ruled out because they are *unfeasible* to the respondents under present circumstances (i.e., insufficient resources), even though they might ideally like to see trade-offs made in this general region (points farthest away from the point of origin in Figure 9). For instance, a respondent might say that a 2-hour drive to work and a high degree of smog at home are unacceptable, while believing that a 5-minute drive and low smog are currently unfeasible; that is, the respondent is too close to the center of town to escape the smog completely. The region remaining after subtracting these two areas becomes the acceptable trading domain within which the policy and decision makers should be considering making trade-offs.

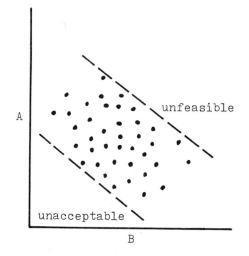

Figure 9
Empirically determined trade-off domain.

Obviously such information, while helpful, is still so sufficiently vague that more precise demarcation is desirable. Here an improvement may result from developing the trade-off band. While the trade-off domain might well appear to be an amoeba-shaped residual after eliminating unacceptable and unfeasible regions, the trade-off band is a compromise between the trade-off curve and the trade-off domain (see Figure 10). Here the area of trade-offs resembles a line (curved or straight), but precision is lacking; so at best we can only say that the middle of the band has a higher probability of being "correct" then either of the edges, but that the data available are such that this band can only be expressed in terms of probabilities. Nevertheless, the decision maker and policy maker are provided with better, but still not exact, data.

With further analysis we hope to reach a point of developing trade-off domains, and ultimately, bands. To do this, of course, requires some common unit of measurement (Hill, 1968; Ackoff, 1962), and here we expect to use satisfaction scores as a means of doing this.

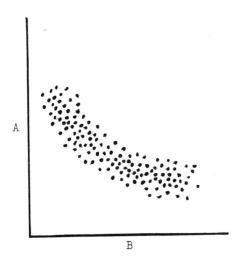

Figure 10
Empirically determined trade-off band.

Designing a Trade-Off Game

A step-by-step procedure for designing a trade-off instrument cannot be given here, since the final product can be achieved from any number of starting points. In general, the designer proceeds through a trial-and-error process to his ultimate goal. In this respect the design of a trade-off game is both an art and a science.

Nevertheless, from the instruments reviewed earlier and from experience gained from the design of the USC instrument, there are some lessons to be learned about the design of a trade-off instrument. These lessons are discussed as they pertain to five different areas of concern: (1) theoretical concerns regarding preferences and trade-offs, (2) environmental attributes to be traded off, (3) research design, (4) response format, and (5) media for presentation. In each of these areas we present criteria to be used to evaluate past and future work.

Theoretical concerns Underlying the notion of trade-offs are a number of assumptions with respect to how people develop and effectuate their preferences. We have touched upon a number of these in an earlier section. Any effort at developing a trade-off game will be organized around these assumptions, implicitly if not explicitly. But these assumptions, if not thought through systematically, may be logically contradictory or inconsistent; hence the results generated from the game will be ambiguous in their interpretation. Theory, at a minimum, places basic assumptions into a consistent framework. A first step then in developing a game is to familiarize oneself with the pertinent literature and the theory and concepts therein so as to at least avoid glaring mistakes that others have noted in the past. One need not be in agreement with the existing theory, but at least it provides a clarification of pertinent issues that must be addressed.

But a review of the literature and familiarization with pertinent theory and concepts are just starting points. Ultimately, one must wrestle with the very real problems of designing a game. The literature and theory serve another purpose, however, after the initial design has begun — they serve as potential criteria by which to evaluate and modify the instrument in the process of its formulation. The following criteria stem largely from the theory developed in the microeconomics and welfare economics literature.

If the "cost" of the item to be "purchased" in the game is given, it should be a "true" (not hypothetical) cost, for the trade-offs derived are always a function of the prices stated. People have a different ranking of preferences depending upon the cost of achieving them. If the costs change, the preference ordering is likely to change as well. Since the true "cost" of many of the attributes that planners and environmental designers work with is very hard to estimate, this can be a source for considerable concern. For example, how does one assess the "cost" of improving air quality, of providing better accessibility to schools, or of providing personal and property safety? There are many alternative methods for achieving these goals, each with a different price, yet there may be preferences with respect to the methods as well; for example, for school accessibility one can either compute the cost of relocating school sites or the cost of bussing. Yet we know that people may not be indifferent between these alternatives within a wide range of different costs. Wilson's game had approximate costs (in multiples of $50) that are suspect in certain instances, insofar as they failed to reflect realistic pricing. For example, within the category of streets, dirt streets were priced at $50, gravel streets at $300, and paved streets at $400. The $250 difference between dirt and gravel streets versus only a $100 difference between gravel and paved streets appears questionable.

The USC game attempts to surmount this difficulty by requesting that the subject measure his gains and losses in quality in terms of degrees on a seven-point scale of satisfaction. Hence personal satisfaction was the common measure of utility, rather than dollars, and the amount of satisfaction was assigned by the subject, rather than fixed a priori, as in the case of the Wilson and Hoinville games.

Similarly, if budgets are given to participants, they should be realistic, because the exchange rate indicated by respondents is also a function of the budget they possess. The principal issue here is the same in criterion 1, although here we are interested in the resources possessed. If a person is provided with a "minimum" budget (in much the sense that "poverty" level is defined), his resultant priorities for purchases will be different than if the budget amount were lavish. Wilson seems not to have recognized this point, nor did he address himself to it explicitly, whereas Hoinville did. Again, the USC game attempted to avoid this problem through the use of satisfaction scores and a feedback process in the overall research design (not described here).

The price assigned to an attribute should not be interpreted as necessarily being an infallible indicator of quality. In general, the higher the price, the higher the quality of the attribute, but there may be exceptions to this rule. Different groups may place a different valuation on an attribute, regardless of the price. For instance, in the Wilson game, graveled streets "cost" less than paved ones. There is the likelihood, therefore, that an implicit assumption will be made that the paved streets are of higher quality. Hence anyone who opts for the gravel streets does so to save money to buy a more expensive quality in another attribute; that is, graveled streets are not rated very high overall by the respondent. Quite the converse may be true, however. Some persons may prefer the rustic quality of nonpaved streets, and find to their delight that they cost less as well. In other words, for any given attribute the perceived quality level may or may not be directly proportional to the cost (see also criterion 6 under Response Format).

Trade-off preferences should be transitive. The transitive criterion requires that if attribute A is preferred to attribute B, and B is preferred to C, then A is preferred to C. If this situation obtains, rigorous analysis can follow. If it does not, only limited analysis is possible. Preferences may be intrinsically transitive, but not elicited in that fashion owing to difficulties in operationalizing the means of elicitation. Or preferences may not be even intrinsically transitive in every instance; that is, they may be probabilistic (Wallis and Friedman, 1942), only partially ordered, or lexicographically ordered. To determine whether the subject's preferences are transitive, the very time-consuming procedure of comparing each item with various combinations of other items, as described by Churchman, Ackoff, and Arnoff (1957), may be necessary. Only the Redding-Peterson instrument followed this procedure, which may explain why they considered only four environmental attributes.

Environmental attributes The selection of attributes to include in the trade-off game usually starts with a review of the literature to determine which are important to the population groups under study. Once determined, the list of attributes can be supplemented through open-ended pilot surveys of the population groups. When it is not possible to undertake a pilot survey, owing to lack of time or resources, then expert opinion, brainstorming, or even simplified versions of the Delphi technique (Helmer, 1966) can serve as reasonable surrogates for generating the list of attributes. Since the initial list of attributes is likely to be too long, judicious cutting must be done while retaining a maximum amount of variance of the different attributes across the subject groupings. In addition, the designer must guard against overselecting attributes that can be easily quantified. He must include subjective attributes as well. Finally, the selected attributes should be

mutually exclusive to prevent the respondent from making choices that are logical absurdities.

The choice of items to be traded off should be constrained. Unrealistic or nonsensical exchanges should be avoided. If the respondent is asked, for example, "What would you give up to get better accessibility to the downtown area?" and he replies, "Higher density," in most instances this is no real trade-off at all. Density is normally associated with accessibility; hence his trade-off is providing the best of both worlds, superior access (downtown living) and lower (suburban, say) densities. None of the games permitted the respondent completely free choice in picking what to trade. The USC game, perhaps because of the variety of choices, comes closest to potentially violating this criterion.

Environmental attributes should be selected on the basis of their functional independence. The issue here is a variant on criterion 1, since interdependencies exist in the preceding example. In the Wilson instrument, for instance, it was possible to buy the best fire and police protection *without* buying any telephone service; it was possible to buy dirt streets *and* a concrete curb and gutter. In a related case, it was possible to buy an "extra big front yard" and "big shade trees in your yard" in the first game, whereas in the second game it was nevertheless possible to purchase a high-density neighborhood (110 families per block), which would preclude ownership of the yard and trees. Here it was the games that presumed independence, yet the results taken together would be confounding. To rectify this problem, an attempt could have been made to formulate a bundling of the attributes so that respondents had to buy prerequisite goods if these goods are in fact the basis for other goods.

There should be a sufficient number of environmental attributes to approach the complexity of multichoice reality. Of the four instruments reviewed, the one designed by Redding and Peterson had the fewest environmental attributes with only four; the one designed by Wilson had the greatest number with 34. Unfortunately, the greater the number of environmental attributes, the more difficult the game may be to explain, and certainly the more difficult and time-consuming the game is to play. Nevertheless, within these constraints an effort should be made to include the maximum number of environmental attributes in the game.

The ratio of the number of different environmental attributes to the number of different subject groupings should be maximized. This criterion reflects the assumption that not all environmental attributes will be equally important to each subject grouping under consideration. For example, the attribute journey to work may have little significance for the retired elderly; access to schools may have little relevance to single persons without children. The instrument should have sufficient numbers of attributes so that important attributes are represented for the major population groupings to be investigated.

Both quantitative and qualitative environmental attributes should be included. The easiest attributes to include in an instrument are those which represent access to facilities, as they readily lend themselves to quantification in terms of either distance or time. Indeed, Wilson's second instrument consists entirely of quantitative attributes — 17 access attributes and one density attribute. Redding and Peterson also restrict themselves to attributes of access to facilities.

In the Hoinville and USC instruments attempts were made to include qualitative attributes. Specifically, the Hoinville instrument included such attributes as noise from traffic, pedestrian safety, and fumes from traffic. These attributes were quantified using a ratio scale, since Hoinville attached prices to the quality levels of these attributes. The USC instrument included four qualitative attributes: adequacy of dwelling space, air quality, personal and property safety, and type of

people. These attributes were quantified using an ordinal scale.

Research design Good research design encompasses several things. One, obviously, is the set of hypotheses entailing the proposed relationship between the independent and dependent variables. A second is the degree of congruence between the conceptual and operational definitions of the variables; the closer the congruence, the better the design. To achieve this the designer should employ several operational definitions for each conceptual variable. A third is validity, both internal and external. Internal validity, which is more important than external validity, is concerned with whether or not confirmation of a hypothesis can be explained away as an artifact of the way the measurement was taken. The standard remedy for this problem is to measure the same thing in several ways, the triangulation-of-data technique. External validity concerns the problem of generalizing from the sample to a larger population when interpreting the results. Here the standard remedy is to randomly choose a sample from the larger population. A fourth item is reliability: can the results be repeated over time? It should be sufficient to repeat the experiment several months later to ensure reliability. The overall goal of good research design is to rule out plausible rival hypotheses that make results ambiguous and tentative.

The instrument should have internal checks on the consistency of the subject's responses. Whereas the "validity" of the responses can only be checked ultimately by observing the behavior of the respondents if they were confronted with the actual situation,[20] the consistency of the responses provides some limited measure of validity. The less consistent, the less likely the validity. Of the four instruments, the USC game satisfied this criterion to the extent that two different ways were used for eliciting preferences. Chip allocation (the first part of the game) provided one means for determining trade-offs (if one can have confidence in the interval scale so derived), whereas the propensity to trade-off provided the other method.

There should be comparability of data across subjects. For data to be aggregated across subjects, each subject should receive the same instructions, media of presentation, and set of environmental attributes so that it can be said that each subject received the same stimulus. All four games reviewed satisfied this criterion.

Response format Among other purposes, a trade-off instrument is designed to ascertain the exchange rate between environmental attributes, as discussed in the previous part. A number of such approaches use the indifference construct — a special case of preferences in general — as a means of determining this exchange rate. But the designer of the game must use words and phrases that his respondents will understand, not technical jargon such as "exchange rate" or "indifference," in preparing the rules for the game.

Two techniques of ascertaining the exchange rate between attributes were employed in the instruments reviewed earlier. The first employed the allocation of a scarce resource in the form of play money or a finite number of points or pegs. In the case of prepriced quality levels, the resource amount was limited so that the subject could not purchase the best quality of every environmental attribute under consideration. The second technique employed some form of direct trading in which the subject was asked to indicate how much gain in quality for one attribute equaled how much loss in quality for another.

The concept of indifference, if it is used in the game, may have to be explicitly taught to the respondent. The use of indifference as a special case of preference has potential utility in the conduct of such trade-off games. As a practical matter, however, it may be a foreign notion to most respondents, who might ask, "Why should someone go through an exchange procedure that leaves him in precisely the same overall state of satisfaction as before? What about the costs of the exchange? Why are they not counted?" Since the indifference concept has technical rather than practical value, this special case may have to be explained to the respondent carefully to ensure that he does not begin to assume he will benefit from his imaginary exchange.

An understandable fiction should be presented to the respondent so that he understands that the interview merely represents a hypothetical situation. When dealing with changes in the environment, the respondent may become suspicious that these changes will involve him in urban renewal, freeway routes, or some other real physical and programmatic change in his environment as planned by "city hall." Consequently, the questions should avoid any association with negative images, and instead should portray some believable "let's pretend" situation, such as winning a house on a television quiz show (Wilson) or being shown a house by a real estate broker (Hoinville et al.).

The instructions of the instrument should be simple enough to be readily understood. Only the Wilson and Hoinville instruments completely satisfied this criterion, as their basic instruction required "buying" different attributes, which so closely parallels the purchases commonly made in stores. The instructions for the USC game were much more elaborate and, in the end, tedious for some, particularly the old and the illiterate. Since there was only an abstract exchange between quality levels of different goods, the game had no immediate counterpart in reality in the way that the "purchase" games of Wilson and Hoinville did. In a related vein, the Redding – Peterson test for transitivity required numerous pairwise comparisons, which respondents are apt to find tedious and frustrating.

Existing as well as preferred levels of quality should be ascertained to determine the direction and magnitude of desired change. This criterion refers to preferences at the margin. What people want next is based on what they have now. Thus, to ask persons in the abstract what they most desire might provide quite a different ranking than to inquire what their preferences are in terms of improving their existing situation. The benefits of knowing the benchmark from which to measure desired change are the direction and magnitude of change, the latter being the difference between the preferred and existing quality levels. Only the Wilson instrument failed to determine the respondent's existing quality level for each attribute.

The listing in the response format of quality levels for each attribute should not a priori appear to prejudice the desirability of the ordering. In designing the response format it is important to keep in mind that the order in which the levels are presented may inadvertently influence the respondent's perception of what is desirable. This is particularly true if more than one dimension or mode is involved in the description of levels. For instance, in the case of the six opportunity attributes used in the USC game, the quality levels were ordered into three categories according to mode of transit: pedestrian, automobile, or bus. The pedestrian mode appeared at the top of the list, followed by the automobile and bus modes. Within each category, the least amount of time appeared at the top of the list, followed by successively increasing travel times. Hence placing the 45-minute automobile drive higher than the 15-minute bus ride may have been perceived to be a cue that the automobile drive was "better," and the farther the respondent dropped down the list the greater the quality he was forfeiting.

Similarly, in determining a "price" for an attribute, the cost established should not prejudge the quality of the attribute in the eyes of the respondent. The point here is similar to criterion 3 under Theoretical Concerns, except here it is the respondent who should not prejudge the quality. In other words, the respondent should be warned that the cost established need not be an indicator of quality so far as the respondent is concerned. Neither the Hoinville nor the Wilson games appeared aware of the need for this caveat.

Media for presentation Basically, there are two modes of presenting the environment to the subject: (1) direct presentations and (2) representation (simulation). A direct presentation involves a site visit by all subjects. If a number of different environments are contemplated in the study, the logistical problem of arranging visits and the expense of these visits can make this mode of presentation prohibitive. The representation mode can be achieved in one of three ways: (1) sketches, drawings, maps, models, and replicas; (2) photography, cinema, and television; and (3) imaginal presentation, that is, words and phrases. Simulation of the environment often involves combinations of two or more of these.

Environmental attributes and quality levels should be presented in a concrete manner to the respondents. Hoinville et al. used symbolic drawings to depict each quality level for each attribute.[21] Ostensibly, the drawings made the different levels of quality more concrete. Unfortunately, different respondents still could have held different interpretations of the drawings. For example, what one respondent judged as "heavy fumes from traffic" another respondent could conceivably judge as "medium fumes from traffic," even though both respondents came from the same environment.

The USC instrument attempted to eliminate misinterpretations with an instruction to respondents that they give a verbal description of that quality level which described their present environment. Descriptions were required for the four qualitative attributes only. The descriptions, which were recorded in longhand by the interviewer, seemingly made the qualitative attributes more concrete. However, the descriptions also added time to the analytical phase of the study, as they had to be content analyzed.

Some of the opportunity attributes used in the USC instrument turned out to be not sufficiently concrete. For example, with respect to access to recreation and access to shopping, the question arises as to what kinds of recreation and shopping, there being in reality a diversity of both. Again, with respect to number of households on an average block, it is not clear as to what constitutes an average block. In any event, an average block would be different for different subjects, for the subjects in the USC study came from 16 different sites in Los Angeles County.

Environmental attributes and quality levels should be unbiased in presentation. Wilson's second game suggests that if the subject selected higher densities, it would enable him to purchase better access to neighborhood amenities. This may have introduced a bias in presentation that can be contested. For, although "better" access may mean having amenities within walking distance, it is not clear that residents living in low-density areas necessarily mind driving 10 to 15 minutes to various neighborhood amenities. As we have discussed earlier, high levels of personal mobility may obviate the need to have neighborhood amenities within walking distance. Second, higher-density neighborhoods may in fact have fewer amenities, as witnessed in our high-density ghettos, and may involve longer travel times to get to such amenities as large parks, playgrounds, shopping centers, and discount stores. Thus particular care should be given to avoid inadvertently introduced biases in presenting environmental attributes and quality levels.

Summary Comment

The preceding statements represent the important criteria we would recommend for designing a trade-off game. As the research and development of such instruments continues, no doubt other criteria will be formulated.

It should be pointed out that many of the criteria governing the design of a trade-off instrument exist themselves in a trade-off relationship, thus making the design of these instruments an art as well as a science. For example, scientific rigor must be traded off against operationality, the range of attributes included must be traded off against the accompanying complexity, comprehensive scope must be traded off against time and money constraints, and so on. Each of the instruments presented here is an example of such trade-offs, for each has its strengths and weaknesses. This is not to say, however, that improvement is impossible. Clearly, some criteria are more important than others, so that the choice among characteristics desired is obvious. Similarly, there are different purposes to which such trade-off games can be put; hence these purposes will dictate the kinds of trade-offs made as well. Overall, however, we believe this is a fruitful area for considerable research.

NOTES

1. Cyert and March (1963) have proposed "bargaining" as another resource-allocation approach. In effect, bargaining resembles trade-offs, although trade-offs are derived from *inter*personal negotiations, not *intra*personal negotiations, in the sense that we mean trade-offs here. In a related vein, Lindblom (1965) has posed the model of "partisan mutual adjustment" as a means of allocating resources, since it both reveals preferences (to others as well as to oneself) and formulates them in the first place. We do not deal with this additional constraint of "others."

2. For example, a study of neighborhood quality in Detroit showed that the planners' evaluations differed significantly from those of the residents themselves (Lansing and Marans, 1969).

3. For example, to establish planning goals, elaborate public participation programs have been carried out (and there are many underway or contemplated) in many cities and metropolitan areas by involving a wide variety of business, professional, religious, and other citizen groups. (See, as examples, Graduate Research Center of the Southwest, *Goals for Dallas,* 1967; Environmental Goals Committee, Los Angeles Region Goals, *Environmental Goals for the Los Angeles Region,* 1967; and City of Chicago, *Comprehensive Plan of Chicago,* 1966.)

4. Thurstone (1931) was able to construct an individual's indifference curve from his explicit choices in comparing various combinations of hats, coats, and shoes. Rousseau and Hart (1951) derived a composite indifference map for 67 persons, pertaining to their choices of various combinations of bacon and eggs. More recently, MacCrimmon and Toda (1969) determined individual indifference maps for different amounts of money and ball-point pens, and for varying amounts of money and numbers of pastries. This last effort is perhaps the most convincing in that it overcomes some of the shortcomings of the earlier efforts, for example, hypothetical choices, dubious assumptions to achieve operationality, and so on.

5. In a related context, Peterson (1968) calls this distinction "operative values" as compared with "conceived values," whereas Michelson (1968) explains the related research dilemma in terms of "experiential congruence" on the one hand and "mental congruence" on the other.

6. Some researchers urge the construction of experimental situations (e.g., New Towns) and then the monitoring of people's behavior to determine their use of new kinds of environments. For example, Webber (1973) argues that we should encourage imaginative experimentation with new environments and new systems and then put them "out to consumer test." Needless to say, this approach to determining user preferences is very costly.

7. These categories are roughly equivalent to the typology of attitude questionnaires suggested by Upshaw for determining an individual's stand on controversial issues: (1) cognitive, (2) affective, and (3) behavioral (Upshaw, 1960, pp. 6–11).

8. Technically speaking, it might be preferable to say that the person cannot lose, although he may not maximize his "winnings" if he makes incorrect (from his subjective point of view) choices. In this respect these instruments might be thought of as similar to the notion of non-zero sum games.

9. The theoretical basis for this instrument was first presented in Peterson and Worrall (1970).

10. The research was first initiated in 1968 under a grant from the Bureau of Community and Environmental Management of the U.S. Public Health Service.

11. Tentative survey areas were picked after first determining relatively homogeneous areas from preliminary returns of the 1970 Census, and, where necessary, after discussions with persons knowledgeable about Los Angeles County. Following this tentative identification, a field check was made and the final survey areas determined. Altogether there were 16 interview areas, and for each of the five population groups we selected a minimum of two or a maximum of four different, widely separated geographic areas in Los Angeles County. This allowed us to partially "randomize" the effect of a fourth, postulated independent variable — environmental experience. Potential households in the survey areas were picked at random from street address lists and screened as to eligibility. If determined as eligible, the member of the household interviewed (those members over 16 years old) was selected by using a set of randomly generated numbers. Some 400 subjects were selected for the survey, but financial limitations have restricted us thus far to 244 interviews.

12. Important criteria used in developing this game were that it should not take too long (not more than 30 minutes or so) and it should be relatively easy to play. It was also apparent from our experience with trial versions that any game that included more than 10 to 12 variables was likely to get highly unwieldy, tedious, and perhaps boring.

13. Initially, a long list of attributes was considered. At one point there were as many as 35. Some of the residential attributes considered initially were difficult to operationalize, some of them were not mutually exclusive, and others were not considered important enough. Finally, from staff discussions, comments from consultants, and review of current literature, we managed to develop a "gestalt" of attributes that were considered important. Although admittedly not exhaustive, they became the basis for the final list.

14. All access-related attributes and the density attribute could be operationalized in terms of quantitative levels — driving time, number of households per block, and so on. It was felt best to leave the levels of the remaining attributes nonspecific, but in such cases the respondents were asked to describe what the levels they checked meant.

15. Thus the possible number of transactions was anticipated to range between 24 and 30.

16. Lexicographic refers to the ordering found in a dictionary where among words beginning with, say, the letter "M," the second letter of each word is compared; if they also are the same, then the third letters are compared until an ordering can be found for the words beginning with letter "M." For attributes with a bundle of characteristics, the same process may be invoked. For further discussion on lexicographic concepts, see Morgenstern (1972).

17. Similar findings have been found in other recent studies. See Chapter 4.

18. It is not at all clear that this view will be wholly subscribed to by professionals, but we submit the following quote as evidence of the dangers if it is not:

Reaction to TRADEOFF [Berger's game] is mixed. Ghetto residents are enthusiastic about the game, and serious about it, playing with sophistication. But most planners, according to Berger, do not see its value. In fact, almost everyone "looks at it strangely," he [Berger] says, except for very conservative Establishment people, who see the problem of priorities as a basic one, and militants, who see the essence of reality in the game. Although ghetto residents use the game as part of their continuing participation in planning, planners seem to prefer having it used as a single day's novelty for the ghetto, a way of leaving residents with the thought: "Now you can see how hard it is to make decisions. We will go off and make them for you." This, obviously, is the opposite of what the game designers had in mind (Berkeley, 1968, p. 61).

19. There are no doubt other ways that these inconsistencies and intensities of preferences could be determined, for example, through rank-order correlations. The point here is that this kind of information is presented in the trade-off propensity tables as a matter of course without the need for specialized analysis.

20. One experiment, covering planning issues, successfully tested the hypothesis that when hypothetical offers are presented in a questionnaire the results will give an accurate picture of what people will do when actual offers are made (Dolven, 1968). The researcher in charge of the experiment concluded that, although it may be difficult to generalize from the results of this test, "reactions to hypothetical offers can be regarded as reliable when the offers are precisely described and concern matters with which people in general are intensely preoccupied."

21. The drawings used were tested for comprehension, by traditional methods, before they were adopted. Some of the variables, it was recognized, were extremely complex to represent pictorially. In the case of noise, for example, the drawings were reinforced by a tape recording incorporating three noise levels. Even so, there were difficulties in playing a tape recording of the "low-noise" level to respondents if their home happened to be on a busy main road (Hoinville, 1971).

REFERENCES

22. Ackoff, R. L. 1962. *Scientific Method: Optimizing Applied Research Decisions*. New York: Wiley.

23. American Public Health Association. 1960. *Planning the Neighborhood*. Chicago: Public Administration Service.

24. Arrow, K. J. 1963. *Social Choice and Individual Values*. New York: Wiley.

25. Berkeley, E. P. 1968. "The New Gamesmanship." *The Architectural Forum*, vol. 129, no. 5 (Dec.), pp. 58–62.

26. Blackman, Allan. 1968. "The Meaning and Use of Standards," pp. 432–441 in Hendrix Blum and Associates, *Notes on Comprehensive Planning for Health*. Berkeley, Calif.: School of Public Health, University of California.

27. Cassel, J. C. 1972. "Health Consequences of Population Density and Crowding." Paper presented at the American Medical Association's Congress on Environmental Health. Apr. 24–25, Los Angeles.

28. Churchman, C. W., R. L. Ackoff, and L. E. Arnoff. 1957. *Introduction to Operations Research*. New York: Wiley, pp. 136–153.

29. City of Chicago, 1966. *The Comprehensive Plan of Chicago*. Chicago: Department of City Planning (Dec.).

30. Crecine, J. P. 1969. *Governmental Problem-Solving: A Computer Simulation of Municipal Budgeting*. Skokie, Ill.: Rand McNally.

31. Cyert, R. M., and J. G. March. 1963. *A Behavioral Theory of the Firm*. Englewood Cliffs, N.J.: Prentice-Hall.

32. Dahir, James. 1947. *The Neighborhood Unit Plan, Its Spread and Acceptance: A Selected Bibliography with Interpretative Comments*. New York: Russell Sage Foundation.

33. DeChiara, Joseph, and Lee Koppelman. 1969. *Planning Design Criteria*. New York: Van Nostrand Reinhold.

34. Dolven, A. S. 1968. "Reactions to Hypothetical and Actual Job and House Lot Choice." *Journal of the American Institute of Planners*, vol. 34 (May) pp. 189–191.

35. Environmental Goals Committee, Los Angeles Region Goals. 1967. *Environmental Goals for the Los Angeles Region*. Los Angeles: City of Los Angeles. (July).

36. Fried, Marc, and Peggy Gleicher. 1961. "Some Sources of Residential Satisfaction in an Urban Slum." *Journal of the American Institute of Planners*, vol. 27 (Nov.) pp. 305–315.

37. Friend, J. K., and W. N. Jessop. 1969. *Local Government and Strategic Choice*. Beverly Hills, Calif.: Sage Publications.

38. Galbraith, J. K. 1958. *The Affluent Society*. Boston: Houghton Mifflin.

39. Gans, Herbert. 1957. "Recreation Planning for Leisure Behavior: A Goal Oriented Approach." Philadelphia: University of Pennsylvania unpublished Ph.D. dissertation.

40. Gold, Seymour. 1972. "Nonuse of Neighborhood Parks." *Journal of the American Institute of Planners*, vol. 38 (Nov.), pp. 369–378.

41. Graduate Research Center of the Southwest. 1966. *Goals for Dallas*. Dallas, Tex.: Southern Methodist University.

42. Hall, Edward. 1966. *The Hidden Dimension*. New York: Doubleday.

43. Hartman, C. W. 1966. "The Consequences of Relocation for Housing," pp. 293–335 in J. Q. Wilson (ed.), *Urban Renewal: The Record and the Controversy*. Cambridge, Mass.: MIT Press.

44. Helmer, Olaf. 1966. *Social Technology*. New York: Basic Books.

45. Hill, Morris. 1968. "A Goals-Achievement Matrix for Evaluating Alternative Plans." *Journal of the American Institute of Planners*, vol. 34 (Jan.) pp. 19–29.

46. Hoinville, Gerald. 1971. "Evaluating Community Preferences." *Environment and Planning*, vol. 3, pp. 33–50.

47. Hoinville, Gerald, and Richard Berthoud. 1970. *Identifying and Evaluating Trade-Off Preferences: An Analysis of Environmental / Accessibility Priorities*. London: Social & Community Planning Research. Mimeographed.

48. Houthakker, H. S. 1961. "The Present State of Consumption Theory: A Survey Article." *Econometrica* vol. 29 (Oct.), pp. 704–740.

49. Lansing, J. B., and R. W. Marans. 1969. "Evaluation of Neighborhood Quality." *Journal of the American Institute of Planners*, vol. 35 (May), pp. 195–199.

50. Lindblom, C. E. 1965. *The Intelligence of Democracy*. New York: Free Press.

51. MacCrimmon, K. R., and M. Toda. 1969. "The Experimental Determination of Indifference Curves." *Review of Economic Studies,* vol. 36 (Oct.), pp. 433–451.
52. March, J. G., and H. A. Simon. 1958. *Organizations.* New York: Wiley.
53. McKeever, I. R. (ed.) 1968. *The Community Builder's Handbook.* Washington, D.C.: Urban Land Institute.
54. Michelson, William. 1968. "Urban Sociology as an Aid to Urban Physical Development: Some Research Strategies." *Journal of the American Institute of Planners,* vol. 34 (Mar.), pp. 105–108.
55. Morgenstern, Oskar. 1972. "Thirteen Critical Points in Contemporary Economic Theory: An Interpretation." *Journal of Economic Literature,* vol. 10 (Dec.), 1163–1189.
56. Mueller, Eva. 1963. "Public Attitudes Toward Fiscal Programs." *Quarterly Journal of Economics,* vol. 77 (May), pp. 210–235.
57. Orleans, Peter. 1967. "Urban Experimentation and Urban Sociology," pp. 103–117 in *Science Engineering and the City.* Washington, D.C.: National Academy of Sciences.
58. Peterson, George. 1968. "Values and Goals for Urban Development," in *Guidelines for New Systems of Urban Transportation,* vol. II, A Collection of Papers. Chicago: Barton-Aschman Associates, Inc.
59. Peterson, G. L., and R. D. Worrall. 1970. "An Analysis of Individual Preferences for Accessibility to Selected Neighborhood Services." Paper presented at the 49th Annual Meeting of the Highway Research Board, Washington, D.C. (Jan.), pp. 12–16. Evanston, Ill: Northwestern University Department of Civil Engineering.
60. Redding, M. J., and G. L. Peterson. 1970. "The Quality of the Environment: Quantitative Analysis of Preferences for Accessibility to Selected Neighborhood Services." Evanston, Ill.: Northwestern University Department of Civil Engineering (unpublished).
61. Research Center for Urban and Environmental Planning. 1969. *Planning and Design Workbook for Community Participation.* Princeton, N.J.: Princeton, University.
62. Robinson, I. M. 1972. "A Note on the Determination of Community 'Trade-Off' Preferences." *ITCC Review,* Tel Aviv, Israel, vol. 1 (Oct.), pp. 36–42.
63. Rousseau, S. W., and A. G. Hart. 1951. "Experimental Verification of a Composite Indifference Map." *Journal of Political Economy,* vol. 59 (Aug.), pp. 288–318.
64. Scitovsky, Tibor. 1971. *Welfare and Competition,* rev. ed. Homewood, Ill.: Irwin, pp. 27–28.
65. Solow, Anatole, and Clifford Ham. 1967. *Residential Environmental Health. A New Look at the Document Planning the Neighborhood.* Pittsburgh: University of Pittsburgh Graduate School of Public and International Affairs.
66. Sommer, Robert. 1969. *Personal Space: The Behavioral Basis of Design.* Englewood Cliffs, N.J.: Prentice-Hall.
67. Thompson, V. A. 1969. *Bureaucracy and Innovation.* University, Ala.: University of Alabama Press.
68. Thurstone, L. L. 1931. "The Indifference Function." *Journal of Social Psychology,* vol. 2 (May), pp. 139–167.
69. U.S. Department of Housing and Urban Development, Federal Housing Administration. 1963. *Minimum Property Standards.* FHA No. 2600. Washington, D.C.
70. Upshaw, H. 1960. "Attitude Measurement," pp. 6–11 in H. M. Blalock, Jr. and A. B. Blalock (eds.), *Methodology in Social Research.* New York: McGraw-Hill.
71. Wallis, W. A., and M. Friedman. 1942. "The Empirical Derivation of Indifference Functions," pp. 175–189 in O. Lange, F. McIntyre, and T. Yntema (eds.), *Studies in Mathematical Economics and Econometrics: In Memory of Henry Schultz.* Chicago: University of Chicago Press.
72. Webber, M. M. 1969. "Planning in an Environment of Change — Part II: Permissive Planning." *The Town Planning Review,* vol. 39 (Jan.) pp. 277–295.
73. Webber, M. M. 1973. "Alternative Styles for Citizen Participation in Transport Planning." *DMG – DRS Journal: Design Research and Methods,* 7 (Jan.–Mar.), pp. 60–64.
74. Wheaton, W. L. C. 1965. "Report on Housing and Health, Part I: The Possibility of Codes Embodying Neighborhood Standards." Berkeley, Calif.: University of California Institute of Urban and Regional Development (Sept.) (unpublished).
75. Wildavsky, A. B. 1964. *The Politics of the Budgetary Process.* Boston: Little, Brown.
76. Wilson, R. L. 1962. "Liveability of the City: Attitudes and Urban Development," pp. 359–399 in F. S. Chapin and S. F. Weiss, (eds.), *Urban Growth Dynamics.* New York: Wiley.
77. Zeckhauser, Richard, and Elmer Shaefer. 1968. "Public Policy and Normative Economic Theory," pp. 27–101 in R. A. Bauer and K. J. Gergen (eds.), *The Study of Policy Formation.* New York: Free Press.

Survey Research

Robert W. Marans

Robert W. Marans is a Senior Study Director at the Institute for Social Research, The University of Michigan, and Associate Professor of Architecture. Prior to his affiliation with Michigan he worked as an architect and planner in Providence, Rhode Island, Detroit, Michigan, and Tel Aviv, Israel, and he has taught at the Technion: Israel Institute of Technology, Michigan State University, Wayne State University, and Florida State University. He has also been a consultant to numerous practicing architects and planning agencies, including the Tennessee Valley Authority. Currently, Dr. Marans is directing an environmental research program on the quality of life in urban and urbanizing areas for the Institute's Survey Research Center.

There is basic agreement that the environmental design professions are in a state of rapid change. Technological advancements with respect to building materials, energy sources, construction techniques, new legislation, and changes in individual values and life styles have all contributed to the tumultuous state within which the professions must now work. To further complicate matters, a number of behavioral scientists, many of whom deal with the environment, have taken an active interest in public policy matters. Many have become intrigued by the potential influence of environmental phenomena on a variety of behaviors, perceptions, preferences, and attitudes of people.

In order to pursue their interests, economists, sociologists, and psychologists have developed research programs and projects aimed in part at determining the role played by environmental phenomena with respect to human performance. In doing so they have brought to bear techniques and tools developed and used by their respective disciplines. Recently, the appropriateness of using these research techniques and tools when addressing the kinds of problems and issues faced by the environmental design professions has been questioned by a number of social scientists (Gump, 1971; Bechtel, 1972; Proshansky, 1972; Patterson, 1973). By raising such questions, further debate has been generated among the potential users of the research—the architects, environmental planners, and others who formulate policies which, directly or indirectly, deal with the environment. To help clarify the issues centered around this methodological debate, it is important that those who use research findings understand the vaule of each approach, the basic differences between approaches, and how they can be used in conjunction with one another.

One approach that can be useful in providig information for architects, environmental planners, and policy makers is the survey—a technique used widely in social science research and with increasing regularity by people from the design professions (Committee on Housing Research and Development, 1972; Sanoff, 1972; Levin and Sachs, 1972). Within the context of this paper, *survey* refers to the systematic collection of data from populations or samples of populations through the use of personal interviews or other data-gathering techniques that involve direct contact with people. The entire survey procedure, however, involves considerably more than the systematic collection of data. It incorporates sampling procedures developed by statisticians and agricultural economists; the experiences of social psychologists, sociologists, and anthropologists in choosing and designing data-collection instruments; the scaling and measurement techniques of psychologists; and the statistical skills of all quantitative researchers in the social sciences.

Although it would hasten our understanding of man–environmcnt relationships if environmental designers were proficient (or at least conversant) about every phase of the survey process, the likelihood of this occurring in the near future is not great. Moreover, a single chapter in a methodological primer cannot hope to cover each phase with any degree of completeness. Rather, the strategy that has been adopted for this chapter is to present an overview of some issues concerning the appropriateness of survey research for the environmental design and planning professions. This is done in several ways. First, some appropriate uses and limitations of survey research are considered. Next, because environmental designers and planners operate at several scales ranging from individual buildings to large regions, a discussion of the geographic scope of surveys is presented. To give the reader an expanded version of the potential of surveys, several basic types of survey designs are considered in the following section. We then discuss two important components of the survey process that tend to mystify environmental designers or planners embarking on a survey: sampling and data collection. Finally, in an effort to demonstrate the applicability of survey results, we conclude with a description of a study of planned communities, including the approach and some of the major findings.

USES AND LIMITATIONS OF SURVEYS

There is an inherent danger in any new tool or technique; when introduced to it without guidance or instruction, one may tend to use it indiscriminately. For example, a young boy who is given a penknife often discovers that there are many things to carve, including the family furniture. Similarly, for the environmental designer who wants to understand his client, using surveys too freely could be a costly and painful experience. As two notable social researchers have suggested, it will require continued resistance to use surveys only where they are most appropriate (Lansing and Morgan, 1971).

Appropriate Uses of Surveys

What then are some appropriate uses of survey research for the environmental design professions? For designers or other groups seeking information, survey research can be used to describe, explain, evaluate, and predict how people respond to a phenomenon in the world around them. When the phenomena involve attributes of the physical and social environments that are subject to manipulation, the information becomes especially useful to environmental designers. Such information can become input into discussions of policy revolving around an existing or anticipated problem or issue. Information in the form of survey results, however, cannot determine policy directly. Yet survey results *can* sensitize those who make policy to the thoughts and activities of people who are likely to be affected by policy. In a very real sense, the activities of architects, urban designers, and planners involve policy making.

What types of information can surveys provide for the person in a policy-making role? Unlike many other methodological approaches, surveys can provide information on "who," "how," and "why." Specifically, this involves questioning people about their socioeconomic and personal characteristics, their levels of understanding, their attitudes, opinions, expectations, and motives. Questions about age, sex, occupation, educational attainment, marital status and family income are often asked as part of surveys. Additional socioeconomic questions of interest to environmental planners could deal with housing payments, utility costs, assets, and the like, and could be analyzed in relation to objective housing conditions, satisfactions, or preferences. At the same time, questions aimed at assessing personality traits or other psychological attributes

have been developed (Robinson and Shaver, 1969) and could be used to describe additional charcteristics of the respondent.

With respect to levels of understanding, paper-and-pencil tests, such as those described in Chapter 2, could be incorporated in an interview. Care should be taken, however, in the proportion of time devoted to knowledge testing relative to other aspects of the data collection. Overburdening the respondent with a tedious battery of questions to test his factual knowledge could reduce the degree of cooperation in other parts of the questionnaire. In an effort to determine the extent to which young people in the Youth Conservation Corps learned about ecological concepts and environmental issues, questionnaires that incorporated several items dealing with specific concepts and issues were administered to the youths at the beginning and end of their corps experience. Levels of understanding were determined at the two points in time and changes-in-knowledge scores were analyzed in relation to corps-member characteristics and to organizational and environmental conditions (Marans, Driver, and Scott, 1972; and Scott, Driver, and Marans, 1973).

Attitudes and opinions deal with people's feeling about people, places, things, or events. For the most part, they are expressions of approval or disapproval and can be considered in relation to other attitudes, behaviors, or objective environmental conditions. In the past, analysis of survey data has primarily dealt with attitudes as they relate to each other. However, as more environmental designers and planners become sophisticated in the use of the survey technique, attitudes vis-à-vis the physical environment and individual or group behavior will become the principal form of analysis in the future. Nevertheless, attitudes as they relate to each other can be useful to planners. In a study of the quality of life based on a national sample, respondents were asked to express their overall level of satisfaction with the community in which they lived (Marans and Rodgers, 1974). They were also asked to assess several attributes of that community. Besides indicating how people feel about their communities, the attribute assessments were considered in relation to overall community satisfaction.

Table 1 shows that people tended to rate attributes of their local community highly, with garbage collection rated most favorably and parks and playgrounds for children least favorably. In Table 2, the evaluations are considered in relation to overall community satisfaction. The first column in the table shows that, among all attributes rated, evaluation of public schools is most strongly related to community satisfaction. The table also presents the results of considering the

entire set of nine assessments in predicting community satisfaction. Together they explain 19 percent of the variation in responses to the community-satisfaction question; that is, if we know how a respondent evaluates each of the nine aspects of his community, it reduces the uncertainty about how he evaluates his community by 19 percent. Finally, for each assessment Table 2 shows beta coefficients reflecting the relative importance of each item in predicting overall satisfaction.

Had objective measures been available for each respondent's community to cover the tax rate, frequency of garbage collection, availability of parks and playgrounds, and so on, an analysis of these measures vis-à-vis the corresponding

Table 1

Assessments of Specific Community Attributes (Percentage Distributions of Respondents in the Quality-of-Life Study)

Attributes	Very Good	Fairly Good	Neither Good Nor Bad	Not Very Good	Not Good At All	Total	Number of Respondents
Garbage collection[a]	56	28	5	6	5	100	1,703[b]
Public schools[a]	38	42	6	8	6	100	1,678
Police-community relations[a]	36	43	9	9	3	100	1,904
Climate[c]	36	42	11	8	3	100	2,152
Police protection[a]	33	40	11	10	6	100	2,007
Parks and playgrounds[a]	30	33	7	14	16	100	1,476[b]
Public transportation[a]	30	38	10	15	7	100	884[d]
Streets and roads[a]	22	51	7	15	5	100	2,152
	Very Low	Low	Moderate	High	Very High	Total	Number of Respondents
Local taxes[e]	1	4	36	39	20	100	1,921

[a] Respondents were asked to evaluate the way streets and roads are kept up, the quality of public schools, garbage collection, parks and playgrounds, police protection, police-community relations, and public transportation in their neighborhood or in the area "around here."

[b] Residents in rural areas were not asked questions about neighborhood garbage collection and parks and playgrounds.

[c] The question was, "Another way people judge a place to live is what the weather throughout the year is like; as far as you are concerned, how good is the climate here?

[d] If no local public transportation was available, respondents were not asked to make this evaluation.

[e] The question was: "Would you say that the local taxes in (*name city or county*) are very low, low, moderate, high, or very high?"

assessment would indicate the level of service that elicits positive or negative responses.

Similarly, questions dealing with behaviors such as the use of leisure time, public transportation, and parks and playgrounds could have been asked and considered in relation to attribute assessments. A move to a new residence could be analyzed in relation to overall satisfaction with the present and prior residential setting.

Expectations about future behavior can also be explored in a survey. In nationwide studies, data have been gathered on people's plans to buy a car, take a trip, and move to a new dwelling. When a survey is one of several being conducted as part of a reinterview study (see Types of Survey Designs) it is possible to determine the extent to which these expectations have been fulfilled. Expectations can also be explored in relation to attitudes. For instance, a group of people living in a residential environment considered to be favorable by outsiders may express less satisfaction with it than another group living in a less favorable environment. One possible explanation is that the first group has higher expectations than the second group and therefore views its situation less favorably. Data on expectation levels could be used in connection with satisfaction measures and objective data to test this hypothesis.

Closely related to expectations are motivations that underlie different forms of behavior. In an exploratory effort, researchers at the University of Michigan are developing scales using survey instruments that aim at understanding forces behind people's choices in recreational pursuits. By understanding people's motives for participating in different types of outdoor activities, it is anticipated that environmental and recreational planners will be better able to design and plan facilities and programs aimed at satisfying specific human needs.

At another level, questions about individual or group behavior can be asked as part of a survey. As examples, we have already mentioned moving to a new dwelling, the use of local public transportation, and attendance at a local park or playground. Questions could also be asked about other forms of travel, visits to a shopping center, attendance at meetings, or the use of a balcony or courtyard of a dwelling. Although these questions are likely to be addressed to an individual respondent, the behavior could apply to a group with which that respondent is familiar—his children, business colleagues, or entire family.

It should be apparent that these questions cover relatively major forms of behavior to which the respondent can give reasonably accurate responses. At a more finite level of behavior (e.g., activities performed around the house or in sequence) the survey may not be the most appropriate method of obtaining behavioral data. Although frequency of engagement in an activity is generally a reliable bit of information obtained through interviews, surveys cannot determine the qualitative aspects of the behavior or its dimen-

Table 2

Multivariate Analysis of Community Satisfaction Using Ratings of Specific Community Attributes (Multiple Classification Analysis on 1,253 Respondents in the Quality-of-Life Study)

Attributes	Correlation Ratio	Beta Coefficient
Public schools	0.27	0.17
Climate	0.23	0.17
Streets and roads	0.22	0.13
Parks and playgrounds	0.19	0.13
Police-community relations	0.25	0.12
Local taxes	0.17	0.10
Garbage collection	0.18	0.08
Public transportation	0.15	0.08
Police protection	0.21	0.07
Adjusted multiple R^2 (explained variance)		19%

Source: Marans and Rodgers (1973).

sionality. For example, we can use a survey to find out how many times during the past week a person went swimming at the local pool, but it would be difficult to ascertain directly what prompted the individual to swim on each occasion, who he went with, or the nature of his entire recreational experience, including other activities he may have performed simultaneously. To capture the entire experience would require a battery of questions far exceeding the time limitations of a normal interview, assuming that an individual could recall and articulate each dimension of the experience. In recent years, time budgets within the context of surveys have been used to obtain data on sequences of events that occur through space.[1] We suspect that as greater skill is acquired in handling time-budget data, more survey researchers interested in behavior vis-à-vis the environment will use this technique in their work.

Finally, and of importance to environmental designers, information about the objective environment could be collected in survey work and analyzed in conjunction with attitudinal and behavioral data. The objective environment refers to the environment as it actually is, and may be defined in physical, social, organizational, or economic terms. For example, it is possible to quantify several dimensions of a respondent's physical environment, such as the size of his dwelling or yard, the degree to which the latter is enclosed, the amounts and kinds of open space in his neighborhood, the layout of structures, and the dwelling-unit density at which he lives. Three factors enable us to obtain this information at relatively little cost. First, aerial photographs, site plans, and large-scale maps are available and reveal much information about the physical environment. Second, we can train interviewers to make assessments of certain quantitative aspects of the environment. Interviewers, for instance, have estimated distances between structures with a high degree of accuracy. Finally, in a probability sample where a cluster of contiguous

households is selected, the objective environmental characteristics of the neighborhood can be identified, measured, and assigned to respondents in each sample household in the cluster. For instance, if a sample of 100 people in a community is scattered, each respondent would have his own set of environmental characteristics associated with his neighborhood. By clustering resondents in, say, household units of four, each cluster would have its own set of environmental characteristics. Therefore, only one fourth as much information would have to be collected.

At the present time, experience with identifying and measuring the salient objective attributes of a respondent's home or other environments is limited. As our capabilities for identifying and measuring objective attributres increase and as these attributes are analyzed in relation to attitudes and behaviors, survey research will become a more potent tool for understanding man-environment relationships.

Limitations of Surveys

Implicit in our discussion of the uses and kinds of information generated by surveys is the fact that surveys, to the extent that they deal with man –environment interrelations and interactions, do so through the final outcome of the study. That is, the process for those interrelations and interactions is inferred from the statistical analysis of the survey data. Therefore, a major limitation in using surveys is that one cannot directly observe, measure, and analyze ongoing processes. If an architect needed information on the sequence of activities of a group of elderly citizens as a basis for redesigning a retirement home, a survey could not convey what is happening while it is happening. That is, it could not provide a natural or detailed picture of the interactions that take place among people and between them and their environmental setting. Similarly, it could not be used to determine how aged persons with sensory decrements experience the environment.[2]

If a researcher needs to know about man –environment interactions and interrelations that took place at a previous point in time, it is possible to obtain such information as part of a survey. However, as the processes under investigation become more complex and if high degrees of precision and accuracy are required in the data, the survey would present severe limitations, since it relies on the respondent's memory. Similarly, there are limitations in collecting attitudinal data about environments when there is a strong probability that attitudes toward a particular environment are not fully formulated by the respondent.

Surveys are also not very useful in providing information on client needs when the client is unknown. In planning a new town or building to be occupied at some future time, a designer can only turn to past research covering people's attitudes and behaviors vis-à-vis similar types of environments. Once the initial occupants move in, however, it is possible to use surveys to determine their particular feelings and requirements and to design subsequent stages of the environment accordingly. Indeed, the process of surveying occupants could take place on a regular basis.[3]

Another limitation of surveys is in dealing with the feelings and behaviors of very young children. There are pitfalls associated with asking questions of parents about their children as well as asking questions of the children themselves. The validity of a mother's responses to questions about her child's attitudes toward a park or wherever the child is playing presently is questionable. Similarly, there may be problems in interpretation when asking a child why he plays where he does.

Surveys are also not useful for studying illegal or illegitimate activities, such as vandalizing a housing project or picking flowers in a park. It would be unusual to find respondents who would be sufficiently certain of the confidentiality of their answers.

We mentioned earlier that surveys are inappropriate for obtaining behavioral data when those behaviors involve a sequence of finite activities. The activities of a housewife as she moves from room to room or the movements of people at a cocktail party are examples of behavioral data more appropriately gathered by other techniques.

Finally, there are the costs associated with doing survey research. The high cost of surveys relative to other methodologies has been a significant factor in restricting their use in man –environment studies. Moreover, budget constraints associated with many private planning and design activities may continue to limit their use. Nevertheless, the growing awareness among governmental funding agencies that survey research has potentially high payoffs for policy makers who operate on environmental matters suggests that more money may be allocated for survey work in the future.

Undoubtedly, there are other pitfalls in using survey research as the principal means of obtaining data on a wide range of issues and problems associated with the environment. As specific problems or issues are addressed, the environmental designer and planner should explore the limitations as well as the advantages of surveys and other techniques prior to launching the research effort.

Possibilities for the Future

In man–environment studies there are numerous possibilities for conducting surveys in conjunction with other methodologies. Field studies of small areas (office buildings, housing projects, transportation terminals) for which an in-depth understanding of the ongoing interactions and interrelations among individuals and between individuals and the environmental setting is required can use surveys to complement and/or validate information obtained through observation techniques. While the latter approach may provide insights as to how some occupants of a small housing development or office building behave, a survey can be used to systematically determine if the behavioral pattern is really characteristic of all occupants. Furthermore, it can be used to ascertain a range of attitudes and expectations, which can then be assessed in relation to specific behaviors. The survey can provide information to those interested in determining the influence of past experiences on present forms of observed behavior as well as information on other aspects of the background of individuals or groups.

The work of Michelson reported in Chapter 5 illustrates the use of surveys with time diaries. As another example, the University of Michigan's Survey Research Center is conducting a methodological study focusing on the time families spend in child-rearing practices. In addition to interviews, the methodology involves the use of personal diaries complemented with an experimental beeper system used for validation purposes. The substantive data that will eventually be analyzed, however, will be derived from both the survey and the time budgets.

Planners and architects, by the nature of their training, are generally adept at observation techniques. Such techniques are often used when conducting an inventory of existing conditions in an area for which a plan is to be made. Information on land and building use, housing conditions, the amount of litter in the streets, and so on, is collected, mapped, synthesized, digested, and used in the planning and design process. Besides telling planners something about the physical environment, the information can sometimes tell them about the behavior of the people living in the environment: whether they are rich or poor, neat or messy, outgoing or reclusive, and so forth. Similarly, planners are accustomed to working with secondary source data, such as government-sponsored census, aerial photographs, maps, and records. But the information obtained through observation techniques and secondary source data provide little insight as to the human meaning attached to the conditions reflected by statistics

and designers' perceptions. What is accepted as good or bad by those who do the observing or use the information to make policy or designs may appear different to various segments of the population whose lives are affected by such policies and designs. To obtain a more balanced picture of the conditions that really exist in, say, a neighborhood, surveys can be used to complement information derived from observation and other sources.

Finally, surveys conducted at the national level can provide a basis for comparing findings derived from studies of smaller geographic areas, such as neighborhoods or entire communities. These small-area studies could be based on one or more surveys and/or on other methodologies. At the same time, surveys or other methodologies used to investigate man–environment relations in small areas may generate hypotheses that can be tested with survey data collected at the national level. For instance, a small-area study may show a relationship between a specific environmental setting and a behavior of a specific population in that setting. Through a national survey designed to measure key behavioral and environmental variables, the hypothesis could be tested that different populations in similar environmental settings behave in a different manner. Similarly, it would be possible to determine the behaviors of the same population group in totally different environments. Further discussion of small-area and national-sample surveys is presented in the next section.

Undoubtedly, there are numerous situations in which survey methods alone are not appropriate for discovering the links between behavior and environment. Yet the strength of the survey as a technique for learning about man cannot be overlooked by the environmental design and planning professions. The survey's potential for aiding architects and planners will be more fully realized when the creative talents of these groups are combined with those of social scientists working with environmental variables.

GEOGRAPHIC SCOPE OF SURVEYS

Although surveys can vary greatly in geographic scope, architects and planners are most familiar with those that focus on small geographic areas, such as an individual building, a housing project, or a single neighborhood. These surveys are usually designed to learn something about the residents, such as who they are, what their attitudes are toward particular environmental or social attributes, and what their uses of space are within dwellings or within the neighborhood as a whole. Ideally, surveys conducted in single neighborhoods or other special environmental settings should be performed within the context of a more comprehensive field study. The field study, as we suggested earlier, enables the social scientist or planner to study a single community or group in terms of its social structure, that is, the interrelations and interactions of the structural parts, including behavior and the physical environment (Katz, 1953). Specifically, the field study attempts to observe and measure directly the ongoing processes that are taking place within the community or group setting. Thus the field study either attempts observations of behaviors such as social interaction or thoroughly investigates the reciprocal perceptions and attitudes of people who play interdependent roles in that setting. This thorough investigation would include carefully planned surveys or interviews with all or a sample of the people involved. Therefore, to have its full impact as a device for learning about the residents of a specific geographic area, the survey should be viewed as one of several possible data-gathering techniques. The study of married-student housing by Festinger, Schachter, and Back (1950) and the work of Gans (1962, 1967) best typify the use of surveys in more comprehensive field investigations.

Field studies that cover single geographic areas are, unfortunately, all too rare. We noted earlier that the types of insights obtained from such in-depth studies cannot be expected from a survey alone. Nor does a single survey represent more than the responses of a single group of people in one geographic area at a single point in time. For instance, it may be useful for the planners in Boston to know how a working-class population responds to forced relocation, but it would be unwise if from this information these and other planners were to infer the reactions of other segments of the population to a relocation proposal. Small-area surveys, certainly, can provide useful feedback to designers of that area or of a new environment to which these people are expected to move. But the results of such surveys are not always generalizable to other people in other environmental settings, nor do they provide the in-depth knowledge necessary for developing a theory on the impact of the physical environment on man.

At the other end of the geographic spectrum are surveys that are national in scope. The most widely known surveys of this type are conducted by the Harris and Gallup organizations. Less known but perhaps of greater interest and importance to planners and policy makers are the national studies of the Survey Research Center at the University of Michigan. For more than 25 years, the Survey Research Center has maintained a national sample of the population of the United States and a well-trained staff of interviewers. Since the sample is representative of the population as a whole, the respondents selected in such surveys are distributed throughout the country and include people who vary widely in their socioeconomic and demographic characteristics. They also vary with respect to the types of dwellings and residential environments in which they live.

Perhaps the best known of the Survey Research Center's national studies are the annual

Surveys of Consumer Finances. Among the topics covered by these studies is consumer behavior with respect to the housing market. A wealth of information on housing transactions, including the distribution of and attitudes toward home ownership, have been collected over the years for different age, income, and family life-cycle groups. The potential use of such data for planners and policy makers is great. For instance, one can tell for any age, income, or family life-cycle group their attitudes, expectations, and behaviors with respect to purchasing or renting a home. Furthermore, this information is available for different regions of the country, thus providing a basis for comparison of responses from studies of small geographic areas such as communities or neighborhoods.

When such studies attempt to elicit responses on the physical characteristics of housing and the environment and to relate these responses to objective measures of the characteristics, the findings can become useful to architects and urban designers as well as planners. Just as data are now available that enable us to explain how different segments of the population in different regions respond as consumers to the housing market, new environmental data dealing with specific features of dwellings and neighborhoods, ranging from the amount of private outdoor space to the frequency of rubbish collection, could contribute to architects' and urban designers' understanding of how different population groups respond to environmental conditions.

One major advantage of national surveys is their ability to differentiate between subgroups of the population in their responses to different residential environmental settings. As we noted earlier, such comparisons are rarely possible in samples of single geographic areas where population compositions and the components of the physical and social environment do not vary greatly.

We have already mentioned that surveys which deal with specific issues or specific populations can use data from national surveys as a basis for comparision. Does the population being studied differ from the population of the United States as a whole or differ comparably with similar subgroups in other parts of the country? Are environmental conditions in the location under study different than conditions existing elsewhere? If such conditions are similar to conditions elsewhere, to what extent does the local population perceive them differently and why? These and similar questions illustrate the potential value of national surveys for researchers involved in specific area studies.

Thus far our discussion of the scope of surveys has focused on two ends of the geographic spectrum. It is obvious that surveys can be designed to cover populations living in areas larger than a housing project and smaller than the nation as a whole. But it is less obvious that surveys can be designed to deal with populations which are distinguished by some common behavior, experience, or other characteristic. There have been surveys of college graduates, recent home buyers, people who ride public transit, visitors to wilderness areas, and other equally specialized kinds of people. Samples of these groups are selected because these people have special significance in relation to the objectives of a study. For instance, a current study at the Survey Research Center deals with the past, existing, and anticipated living arrangements of elderly persons and those approaching retirement, and uses as its respondents (1) those people in the national sample who are over 55 years old, (2) people in the national sample between 35 and 55, and (3) the living parents of the people in the 35 to 55 age group. In this way, we can focus on a preretirement group as well as a substantially larger group of people over 55. Part of our analysis will compare, retrospectively, the living arrangements of the over-55 group with those living arrangements as perceived by their children who fall in the sample.

Although most surveys conducted in the past have been based on samples of large heterogeneous populations, there has been an increase in recent years in the number of surveys of populations of a more restricted character, either in terms of who they are or where they live. To an extent, this has resulted from a desire to learn about population groups who have special problems or live under relatively unique conditions (e.g., the poor, the elderly, ghetto residents, people living in high-rise buildings, and new-town residents). In the Western world today the number of people in many of these groups is increasing, as is an awareness of the magnitude of the problems facing them. It is likely that as efforts are made to deal with these problems, particularly those associated with housing, research will be needed on the interrelationships of people in special circumstances and their residential environments.

TYPES OF SURVEY DESIGNS

Whenever survey data are to be collected, a decision must be made as to the specific design that the sampling and data collection will follow. This decision is based on a variety of factors, which range from the hypotheses to be tested and the relationships to be explored to the size of the research budget. In this section we discuss three basic types of designs: cross-section surveys, longitudinal surveys, and surveys based on contrasting samples.

Cross-Section Surveys

Cross-section surveys are the most widely used because they are relatively simple in design and low in cost. This survey method is the best way to determine the characteristics, attitudes, and behavior of a population or subgroups of that population at a single point in time.[4] Furthermore, much of the data derived from such surveys are presented in the form of distributions and can be used by planners and designers. For instance, the contention of many planners that neighborhood parks are not being used by the majority of children living around them has been supported in part by distributive information from a recent national recreation study (Mandell and Marans, 1972). The study showed that over two thirds of all children between 2 and 9 years old play in the yards of their homes. An additional 15 percent play in the street or sidewalk area near home, and only 5 percent play in a local or neighborhood park. When the distance to the nearest park was considered, the situation improved somewhat but not as much as some park planners would lead us to believe. In those households located within 2 minutes of a local park, one out of four young children play there, and nearly two thirds play in their yards or on the street or sidewalk near their homes. The implications of such findings pose a number of important questions for planners and researchers with respect to the future of urban parks and the recreational needs of young people.

In a cross-section survey, relationships can be identified among different groups and specific attitudes, expectations, or behaviors; relationships can also be established between background characteristics and the amount of time a group devotes to various activities. However, the establishment of relationships does not reveal whether these relationships are stronger or weaker than they had been at an earlier period. Nor does the allocation of time as determined by a single survey suggest which activities are gaining or losing in importance or popularity. For example, a 1965 national study of outdoor recreation showed that participation in bicycling for people over 12 years of age was low relative to other forms of recreation. When rates were compared with data from a similar study conducted 4 years earlier, however, it was noted that participation in bicycling grew faster than any other activity over the 4-year period. This illustration suggests that repeated cross-section surveys at successive points in time offer one approach to investigating changing events, attitudes, or behaviors.

As part of our current social indicator work, we are identifying a number of residential environmental conditions and people's assessments of them. We are also measuring people's satisfaction with their housing, neighborhood, and community (Marans and Rodgers, 1974). Repeated measures in subsequent cross-section surveys will enable us to assess changes in objective environmental conditions and people's responses to them in terms of their expressions of satisfaction and residential mobility. Furthermore, it will be possible to analyze these data in relation to the timing of governmental economic and social policies, such as those dealing with housing or income subsidies for low-income families. As modeling techniques improve, this information can be used to understand and predict how segments of the population will respond in the future to programs and environmental designs for housing.

Although the respondents in these successive surveys will be different, the population from which the samples are drawn will be identical. Thus, by using probability sampling techniques, we shall be able to discern from the data trends over time. Moreover, the systematic use of fixed questions, open-answer techniques, and identical procedures for measuring objective environmental conditions will be essential if comparisons are to be made from these repeated cross-section surveys.

Longitudinal Surveys

Repeated cross-section surveys are not the only way of capturing the changing experiences and attitudes of a population. Another way is through reinterview panels (longitudinal surveys) in which the experiences and behaviors of a select group or groups are traced in repeated interviews. This approach has been advocated by planners and designers who seek information on how certain environmental configurations alter people's behaviors. However, whether in small areas or national studies, high costs relative to sample size are a major problem of panel interviewers. There are the costs of following, finding and interviewing people who are no longer clustered geographically as they were when first surveyed. There are also costs associated with paying respondents who are being asked for repeated cooperation and for allowing their names and other identifications to be kept on tap for a period of time. Finally, there are additional costs in dealing with the complex problems of editing, data management, and maintaining elaborate record files.

Despite higher costs and budgetary and manpower limitations, there are obvious advantages to collecting data from the same individuals over, say, a 5-year period. First, surveys are often criticized on the grounds that certain types of variables cannot be measured retrospectively. In part, this criticism is justified with respect to variables that are subject to change over time and which can only be ascertained by objective measurement (or subjective judgment) by someone other than the respondent. For example, it is impossible to determine the condition of the dwelling that the respondent lived in 3 years earlier, unless someone has assessed that dwelling as part of a survey conducted at that time. Similarly, although it is conceptually possible to measure attitudes retrospectively—"How satisfied were you with your neighborhood 3 years ago?"—it is clearly inappropriate to do so if such attitudes are to be used as a basis for explaining subsequent behavior, such as moving.

Second, compared to single retrospective surveys, longitudinal surveys have the advantage of reducing errors in response that may be attributable to faulty memory. This is especially true if one is interested in analyzing changes in transportation, recreation, or other forms of behavior appropriately determined by the survey method. Other advantages of longitudinal studies are associated with the study of developmental processes that an individual or family goes through over a period of time and with the study of causation (see Parnes, 1972).

A proposed Survey Research Center study that aims at capturing the advantages of the longitudinal survey will investigate people's preferences for housing and community in terms of what they pay for and get when purchasing a housing package. Presumably, the results of this study would help elected representatives and planners decide how scarce resources would be allocated. Such survey information would also be useful to architects and urban designers who are interested in how segments of the population respond to various environmental configurations and change.

We propose to do several things as part of the study. First, we would interview people about their past and present environments and detail the things they like and dislike about them. Then we would return several years later to the same dwellings and talk to the people who live there. If the people have moved, we would follow them to their new dwelling. For each dwelling and neighborhood we would collect data on a number of objective attributes, ranging from things potentially manipulable by architects and urban designers to local public services, such as the quality of schools, parks, and rubbish collection.

The analysis can provide much useful information. For those who have not moved but whose neighborhoods have changed, we can find out how they currently assess their environment before and after the change and, in the second interview, what they think about the

changes that have taken place. Those who have moved are even more interesting, because their descriptions of the former neighborhood can serve as a check on their previous responses and as part of the explanation as to why they moved. Moreover, in the original dwellings from which the first people moved we will have new residents whose attitudes can be ascertained and compared to the original residents of the dwellings. In this way we can develop information in both changing and unchanging environments about the responses of different groups to the same situation. Finally, we will be in a position to identify those environmental attributes and the changes in them that influence people's decisions to move from one neighborhood to another.

Contrasting Samples

If we are interested in studying the effect of a particular variable on a population, it may be efficient to draw samples from groups which contrast with respect to that variable. For example, a hypothetical study might want to find out whether the introduction of supersonic aircraft would tend to produce anxiety in communities that surround airports scheduled to receive such aircraft. To test this question, samples could be interviewed in several cities located within, say, 10 miles of the airports; similar samples could be interviewed in cities paired with the airport cities in geographical, industrial, racial, socioeconomic, and other characteristics, but located at some distance from a major airport.

The rationale for such designs is that the effects of a variable thought to be important can be most clearly seen if situations are studied which provide the greatest extremes in the presence of that variable. As we shall see in the study presented in the last section of this chapter, contrasting communities were selected that differed in a number of environmental attributes associated with high and low levels of planning.

Fundamentals of Sampling

In our definition of a survey we mentioned that data were collected from *populations or samples of populations.* By populations, we mean the totality of units for which the survey results are to apply. In sampling literature, the totality of units is sometimes referred to as the universe. The units could include persons, households, businesses, city blocks, and so on. In a study of the behavior of selected members of a particular commune, for example, data might be collected from each member of that commune's adult population. If the specific behavior of adult members of communes in New Mexico were under investigation, a sample of all communes might be selected and, within each sample commune, a sample of adult members could be chosen for study. Thus the decision as to whether data were to be collected from a population or from a sample of that population rests, to a large extent, on the size of the population being studied. That decision is also influenced by the funds available for the survey and by the nature of the information being sought.

Unless the population under investigation is very small, as in a housing project containing, say, 30 dwellings, or unless unlimited funds are available for data gathering, surveys will likely be based on a sample of the population. The prime advantage then of sampling as against complete coverage should be obvious; it saves money.

Other advantages of sampling are in the saving of labor and time. The staff needed would be smaller, not only for fieldwork but for coding and tabulating the data as well. For example, the time saved in collecting answers from a sample of 300 families rather than from all 3,000 families in a neighborhood would undoubtedly determine when the results are available. In cases where these results are needed to make an impending decision affecting the neighborhood, a sample of families is highly advantageous.

Finally, observations or measurements can frequently be made more accurately on a sample of cases than on an entire population. If information were needed about businesses forced to relocate because of freeway construction, the universe of such businesses in a single city could number in the tens of thousands. Even if the information were abstracted from records, total coverage would entail constant supervision and painstaking verification. Undetected clerical errors and failure to locate records temporarily missing from the files could result in biases greater than those associated with estimates derived from a sample of cases.

When a sample of the population under investigation is to be selected, a decision must be made as to the most appropriate type of sampling procedure to be used. Although there are numerous possible sampling designs for any particular study, there are two basic categories within which all sample designs fall: probability (or random samples) and nonprobability samples.

Probability Sampling

Probability samples are based on a method of selection whereby every member of a specified population has a known nonzero chance of being chosen as part of the sample. In this way, estimates of the population characteristics can be made from the sample results; at the same time, the precision of these estimates can be gauged from the sample results themselves. For example, in a survey of Columbia, Maryland, where a probability sample of 200 respondents was used, we estimated that 21 percent of the adult population in the community rode a bicycle for other than recreational purposes. Based on the sample design, we could also measure the precision of this estimate. This precision was determined by the *sampling error,* a measure of the chance deviation of the sample statistic from the corresponding true population value. For the estimated proportion of adult bicycle riders, the chances are 95 out of 100 that the true proportion of adult bicycle riders was within a range of 21 percent plus or minus 6.5 percent, or between 14.5 percent and 27.5 percent. Had the sample size been larger, say 800 respondents, the sampling error would have been reduced to 3.3 percent, assuming all other factors remained constant, and the range for the true population value would be between 17.6 percent and 24.4 percent. On the other hand, with a smaller sample size, say 50, the sampling error would increase to 13 percent and the range for the true proportion of adult bicycle riders would be between 7 percent and 34 percent. We can see from this example and Figure 1 that, as the sample size increases, the precision of the estimate as measured by the sampling error will improve. But a point is reached where increased precision of estimates is numerically small in comparison with the cost of collecting data from a large number of respondents. The researcher is always faced with this dilemma and must make his decision based on the resources he has at his disposal and the purposes for which his results will be used.

Another important characteristic of probability sampling is that the researcher first creates a list of all units in the population, a *sampling frame,* and then makes his selection from that list. As we suggested, the population may be broad (e.g., all families in a nation) or it may be narrow (e.g., all adult males in a neighborhood or all businesses of a specific size in a central business district).

The selection of a sample from a sampling frame is generally performed in the office and then the selected units are either assigned to an interviewer, telephoned, or mailed a questionnaire. Prior to the data-collection effort, every member of the population has a calculable chance of being included in the sample. This selection procedure enables the researcher to specify in advance just how much sampling error he is willing to tolerate in the estimates and, with the help of a sampling statistician, to so choose an approach that the error falls within tolerable limits.

The choice of an appropriate sampling design depends on the research objectives, time, resources, and skill of the researcher. Sampling designs vary from simple to complex, and the reader who wishes to investigate the range of design thoroughly is referred to one of several excellent references, or he may seek expert assistance in choosing one for his particular re-

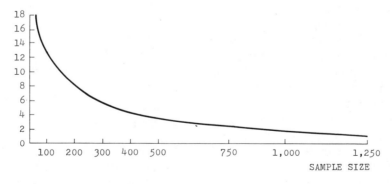

Figure 1
Approximate sampling error.

search problem (Kish, 1953, 1965; Moser and Kalton, 1971; Lansing and Morgan, 1971). The following designs, nevertheless, should be familiar to the environmental designer or planner interested in behavioral research.[5]

Simple random sampling In a simple random sampling design, every unit in the population has an equal and independent chance of being selected. Suppose that an organization needs additional space and hires an architect to study space requirements and the needs of individuals in the organization who will occupy the space. The architect decides to select and interview a sample of 100 employees from 1,200 members of the organization. The mechanics of the selection would be the following:

1. Using a complete list of all employees, each name would be numbered consecutively from 1 to 1,200.
2. Using a table of random numbers, 100 different numbers in the range 1 to 1,200 would be drawn, ignoring duplicates of those that have already been drawn.
3. The names associated with the 100 drawn numbers would represent the sample of employees to be interviewed.

A problem in simple random sampling occurs when the list is incomplete or if some people are listed more than once (e.g., they may be reported by more than one department). Prior to making selections, one could go through the list to eliminate all repetitions or add missing employees. This task, however, would not guarantee a complete list free from duplication and would be painstaking and costly to undertake. One way of reducing the magnitude of this work, and at the same time ensuring that selected cases are spread throughout the organization, is to divide the employees by some foreknown characteristic, such as primary departmental affiliation. This technique is called stratification.

Stratified sampling As the name implies, stratified sampling consists of dividing the population into homogeneous groups (strata) according to some characteristic, such as department within an organization, type of function (secretarial, managerial, etc.), neighborhoods within a city, or family life-cycle types within a neighborhood (married with young children, elderly couples, etc.). A separate sample is selected then within each stratum. Each person (or household) is placed within one and only one stratum before sampling. If measurements are made on an adequate sample of each stratum, separate estimates may be computed by stratum; when combined the strata form estimates of the population. An important objective in stratification is to minimize differences in a variable under study within a stratum while maximizing such differences among strata.

The main advantages of stratification are the following:

1. More power to compare subgroups whose numbers are too small to be adequately covered in a random sample of the entire population.
2. Greater precision in the sample estimates can be gained through the reduction of the variances of the sample results.
3. Opportunities to use different selection procedures with each stratum, if desired, can be obtained.
4. Estimates of some stated precision can be constructed separately for each subpopulation of stratum, as well as for the entire population.

Disadvantages associated with stratification are the following:

1. The practical difficulties of simple random sampling are still present, since this technique is used in the sample selection of each stratum.

2. Prior knowledge is necessary of the relationship of the variable of interest and those available for stratification.

3. Unless there are large differences among the strata with respect to the variable under investigation, gains in precision by using stratified sampling rather than simple random sampling are slight.

4. A stratified sample constructed to estimate one variable with increased precision may result in less precise estimates for other variables in the study.

Systematic sampling Simple random sampling and stratified random sampling both involve considerable clerical work in the selection procedure. Using the preceding example, an alternative to numbering each employee in the organization and then choosing random numbers to designate the sample is to take an interval or systematic sample. This design involves selecting every kth individual from the list of employees after a random start equal to or less than k, but greater than zero. When we want a sample of 100 people from a total population of 1,200, the sampling interval k would be $1,200/100 = 120$. A random number from 1 to 120 would be selected, as would every kth individual thereafter. For example, if the random number chosen initially were 30, the sampled employees would be those numbered 30, 150, 270, 390, 510, and so on. The apparent advantage of systematic sampling is that only one random number need be selected. However, there is a disadvantage when the list of the population is ordered in such a way that a systematic bias in the sample is created. For instance, if the list of employees is ordered by room numbers and by floors in a building, and each floor has an equal number of rooms, it is conceivable that the systematic sample will result in the selection of employees that occupy offices at one corner of the building. If this were

likely to occur, the selection procedure should be altered by, say, making a random selection within each interval. This is accomplished by dividing the population into groups that correspond to the size of the interval and choosing a different random number within each.

If the length of the list is extremely long (e.g. all households in a city), it should be obvious that a systematic selection will be time-consuming and costly. A sampling design developed to reduce these and other costs associated with survey research is that of cluster sampling.

Cluster sampling As we suggested earlier in our discussion of objective environmental measures, this sampling procedure involves selecting population elements in groups or clusters. For example, instead of counting through all households in a city to select a systematic sample of families, one can select first a sample of city blocks and then include all or a fraction of households located on the sample blocks. The households selected from a block comprise one cluster, and the number of sample clusters would equal the number of sample blocks.

Under certain conditions, cluster sample designs yield the desired sampling estimates at less cost than would be entitled with other sampling methods. Other advantages of cluster sampling are that (1) the clusters can be easily and uniquely defined and identified; and (2) once a sample element is located, data-collection costs are relatively low for additional, nearby elements. These conditions were met in the study of planned communities presented in the concluding section of this chapter.

Nonprobability Sampling

We noted earlier that in probability sampling techniques every member of the population has a calculable chance of being included in the sample, a condition necessary for estimating the precision of the sample estimates. In nonprobability samples this condition is not met. Such samples provide no means within themselves to measure the precision of sample estimates. Furthermore, there is often no definable universe characterized by the estimates.

Nonprobability samples vary widely in their complexity—from a subjective selection of people passing through a main entrance to a shopping center to an objective selection of shoppers who are judged by the researchers to reproduce the universe of all shoppers using the facility.

There are several types of nonprobability samples. *Judgment sampling* involves some judgment on the part of a researcher, presumed to be "good" in the selection procedure. *Purposive samples* are chosen to satisfy some predetermined criteria. In attempts to be "representative" of the population, quota samples are often used. *Quota sampling* occurs when the investigator is instructed to collect information from an assigned number of individuals (the quota) with the selection of individuals left to his or her personal choice. For instance, in a pilot study of recreation vehicle owners in Michigan, the procedure was first to select a sample of state parks and campgrounds where such vehicles could be found. This selection was made randomly and did not differ from a probability sample in that respect. But once the sites were selected within which interviewers were assigned to collect data, the selection of the recreation vehicle owners was left to the personal choice of the interviewer. This choice involved the day of the week and the time of day that he entered the park and the people he approached. As a result of this element of personal choice on the part of the interviewer, there was an inherent tendency toward ambiguity and uncertainty as to exactly what was to be done, and hence a great likelihood of biasing the sample selection. Furthermore, the recreation vehicle owners selected

may not have been representative of all recreation vehicle owners in the state of Michigan.

If there is no great disadvantage to biased estimates, or if the objective of the study is to obtain interviews without concern as to how and from whom they are obtained, quota and other nonprobability samples may be used. They are generally economical because they reduce travel costs and the need for making call-backs for a predetermined respondent. They are often easy to administer since they involve little record keeping, clerical, and statistical work. Finally, they can be done relatively quickly. But the value of the results is highly questionable. It should be realized by anyone contemplating the use of nonprobability methods that they lack the precision of probability sampling techniques and sometimes yield seriously misleading results. As behavioral science research related to the environment matures and as environmental designers become more sophisticated in probability sampling techniques, the use of nonprobability samples will become less justifiable.

METHODS OF DATA COLLECTION

In our definition of a survey, we mentioned that data were collected through the use personal interviews or other techniques involving direct contact with people. The specific technique or techniques used in a survey, of course, derive from the objectives of the research and the uses to which the survey is put. In the examples of surveys discussed so far, the personal interview has been the principal means of data collection. To present a more complete picture of the data-gathering techniques associated with survey research, we present in this section a brief overview of the advantages and disadvantages of telephone interviews, mail questionnaires, and personal interviews. At the same time, we shall discuss a number of factors that should be considered when designing questions.

Telephone Interviews

Telephone interviews have been gaining in importance in recent years, partly because of their low cost relative to personal interviews and partly because the proportion of households with telephones is gradually increasing in the United States. The cost factor becomes particularly advantageous if the number of questions to be asked is not too great and the sample is spread over a wide geographic area.

The major disadvantage of this method of data collection is the possible bias that results from probability sampling in areas where there are households without telephones and/or unlisted telephones are known to exist. Often, this disadvantage can be overcome when personal interviewers, mail questionnaires, or letters asking respondents to call collect are used to contact sample respondents not having a telephone or listed number. Also, the problem of unlisted telephones has been circumvented by random-dialing techniques (see Scott and Chanlett, 1973).

Mail Questionnaires

Mail questionnaires are often cheaper than telephone interviews, a major advantage when the population to be covered is widely dispersed and when the funds and time available are severely limited. Besides the cost savings, mail questionnaires also avoid the problems of interviewer's errors of interpretation—a major source of unreliable data.

Mail questionnaires are advantageous when information is required concerning several members of the same family. For example, if the researcher wants to know about swimming pool usage in a community or, more specifically, the total number of times members of each family used that facility, mail questionnaries afford the opportunity for discussion or consultation among family members prior to completion and return of the questionnaire.

Finally, there is the potential advantage that certain questions—perhaps those of a personal or potentially embarassing nature—will be more willingly and accurately answered in an anonymous mail questionnaire than when asked in a face-to-face situation by an interviewer.

Despite these advantages, numerous disadvantages of mail questionnaires can be cited, the most crucial being nonresponse. As might be expected, the response rate when using mail questionnaires in a survey tends to be much lower than when interviewers are used. Response rates using personal interviews generally run around 80 percent, but response rates with mail questionnaires tend to be between 20 and 40 percent. The critical problem is not so much that the number of responses is usually a small proportion of the original sample, but that the nonrespondents are likely to differ significantly from the respondents in their characteristics, attitudes, behaviors, and so forth; so the estimates based on the latter group may be biased. Three factors can influence the response rate of mail questionnaires and it is left to the researcher to determine how each will influence the return on his questionnaire. They are the organization sponsoring the research, the topics being covered, including the number of questions asked, and the population that is being investigated.

Questionnaires prepared under the sponsorship of well-known and respected organizations are likely to yield a higher rate of return than those originating from an obscure or distrusted sponsor. The most favorable situation occurs when the organization conducting the survey has some direct link with the population—the American Institute of Planners conducting a survey of urban planners, a travel club investigating the vacation preferences of its members, and so forth. If the topic is of sufficient interest and importance to the respondents, the response rate is likely to be higher than if it is viewed as uninteresting or irrelevant. A questionnaire asking how residents feel about a proposed freeway adjacent to their neighborhood will certainly generate more interest and, concomitantly, more returns than will one asking for people's views on foreign aid.

Mail questionnaires that are complex or lengthy often result in lower response rates than simple short questionnaires. Similarly, surveys of uneducated respondents yield few returns, since this group is likely to have difficulty in question interpretation and in understanding the value of the research.

Other disadvantages associated with mail questionnaires include the inability to collect observational data about the respondent's dwelling or residential environment, the requirement that questions be relatively simple and straightforward, the inability to secure spontaneous answers, and the lack of an opportunity to probe when more information or clarification is desired.

Personal Interviews

As might be expected, several of the above-mentioned limitations can be overcome by combining mail questionnaires with other data-gathering techniques, that is, visits by trained interviewers. It would be possible, for instance, to send questionnaires to respondents and have them picked up by interviewers who could then clarify difficulties, check answers, ask additional, more complex questions, and collect observational data. Or, conversely, visits could be made to drop off questionnaires with instructions for completing them and to ask that they be returned by mail at a later time. During this initial visit, complex questions could be asked and observations made and recorded. Despite the relatively high costs, the personal interview is the most commonly used data-gathering technique in survey research. It is usually conducted in the confines of the respondent's home, although it may take place in an office, at a campground, on the street, or in other places where the interviewer and respondent can interact with minimal interference.

Unlike mail questionnaires or telephone interviews, the mere presence of an interviewer leads to a high level of cooperation (Scott and Chanlett, 1973). This cooperation may occur despite the complexity of the question sequence that can be asked in a personal interview—a major advantage of interviewing. And unlike other forms of gathering information from respondents, the personal interview enables independent information to be collected about the respondent's environment, the interior and exterior of his dwelling, or its immediate surroundings. Thus, when subjective responses are to be analyzed with objective environmental conditions and when those conditions are to be identified on the site, personal interviews are highly advantageous.

Finally, if responses to visual stimuli, such as photographs or drawings, are required, the personal interview situation offers obvious advantages over mail questionnaires or telephone interviews.

Question Design

In the design of questionnaires to be used in surveys, too often the wording and sequence of questions receive little attention. Failure to do so may result in responses that are not very useful in fulfilling the objectives of the study. There are a number of extensive and excellent references on question and questionnaire design, and attention should be given to this task at an early stage in the survey process (Cannell and Kahn, 1953; Moser and Kalton, 1971; Selltiz et al., 1959). The designer who is about to launch a survey is advised to consult one of these references or, at the very least, pretest the questionnaire to determine whether it is providing the kinds of data necessary to serve his purposes. In the meantime, the following discussion is intended to give the reader a basic understanding of certain topics associated with questionnaires.

Question wording The primary criterion for choosing the wording of questionnaires is that the vocabulary and syntax should offer maximum opportunity for accurate and thorough communication between the interviewer and respondents. The words chosen should be understandable to the population being studied; that is, the language of the question should approximate the language of the respondent. Technical terms should be avoided in a survey of the general population but may be appropriate in a survey of a professional group. For all groups, however, efforts should be made to simplify the language as much as possible. Questions like "What elements in this courtyard do you think define the space?" should be avoided. The words "elements" and "space" are ambiguous to most people, and the space in question may not be generally referred to as a courtyard. Similarly, it is more natural to ask "Do you think . . . ?" than "Is it your opinion . . . ?" or "What is your attitude with regard to . . . ?".

Single idea Questions should be limited to a single idea. Answers to the question "Do you favor or oppose public housing and housing allowances?" would not permit the researcher to determine whether the respondent is answering one or both of the items mentioned in the question. If it were the intent of the researcher to learn about people's feelings toward both public housing and housing allowances, two questions should be asked. However, if it were of interest to the researcher to know how people feel about government assistance to the poor, the question might be asked in a modified form: "Do you favor or oppose government programs such as public housing, housing allowances, and the like?" The interpretation of this type of question must be very conservative. In other words, a positive response to a global question must be taken to indicate favorableness in the general area and cannot be interpreted as indicating respondent support for any of the examples cited.

Question sequence Besides the wording of individual questions, the researcher must give considerable thought to the arrangement of questions in the questionnaire. The sequence of questions should be determined by the inteview process rather than by the analysis that eventually will be performed. The well-planned interview usually takes the respondent through a logical sequence of ideas so that he often can anticipate the next question. The sequence of questions for any single topic may be determined by a *funneling* approach. That is, the more general or most unrestricted questions are asked before more restricted questions. The funnel sequence prevents early questions from conditioning those which come later and can be used to learn from the opening questions something about the respondent's frame of reference. The early questions should also motivate the respondent to participate more thoroughly and can serve an orienting or educational purpose, informing him about the substance of the research.

Leading questions It should be obvious that questions phrased to suggest a particular response should be avoided. But one sometimes finds biased questions, such as "You wouldn't say that you were in favor of the elderly housing project, would you?" or "Would you say that you are in favor of the elderly housing project?" The biased wording found in the second question is less obvious than the first example and makes it easier for the respondent to answer "yes" than "no." A better question would be "How do you feel about the elderly housing project? Do you approve of it, disapprove of it, or what?"

Open and precoded questions The form of the response to questions should be considered in the process of designing them. Open or unrestricted questions are those to which the respondent can reply in his own words. Precoded, closed, or restricted questions have a series of prearranged categories to which the respondent selects the one coming closest to his opinion, preference, or behavior.

The open question has the advantage of allowing the respondent to structure his answer as he wishes and, at the same time, of giving the researcher the opportunity to learn about the respondent's knowledge of a subject and frame of reference. For instance, a precoded question asked respondents how they felt about their communities as a place to live by giving categories of excellent, good, average, below average, and poor. The open question, "In what ways?," allowed the respondent to mention things that came to his mind when making the rating. The researcher was able to identify attributes that were deemed important to community satisfaction but which he had not considered beforehand.

Precoded questions are generally easier for the respondent to answer since he has the list of choices specified for him. A disadvantge exists when the respondent is asked about an issue that he has not previously considered and is forced to make a choice among those answers given to him.

Usually, questionnaires are designed with both open and precoded questions. The proportion of each type is determined by the objectives of the research and the budget. As might be expected, open questions are more costly to administer both in terms of interviewer time and the coding of responses. Nevertheless, in exploratory research such as much of that now occurring

in the man–environment area, the use of open questions may readily justify the expense.

A SURVEY OF PLANNED-COMMUNITY RESIDENTS

A few years ago we conducted a study of new towns and other less-planned communities that used surveys as the principal source of data. Based on the number of requests for the report, it is safe to say that the study has generated considerable interest on the part of the academic community and the environmental design professions. The nature of this interest, however, is difficult to determine. We suspect that it is a combination of methodological rigor and substantive data, which architects, planners, and community builders find both interesting and useful. Rather than attempt to describe the entire study, we will present an overview of our approach to the research and discuss the potential applicability of some of its findings for architects and planners.

Background

In the late 1960s the Bureau of Public Roads of the U.S. Department of Transportation began to explore the potential impact on transportation planning of emerging new-towns movement. Although the predominant means of meeting housing demand had been suburbanization of vacant land at or near the edge of metropolitan areas, the prospects were promising that more housing would be built as part of new towns and planned unit developments. A desire to know about the transportation behavior and other responses of residents in such environments led to the study of planned residential environments (Lansing, Marans, and Zehner, 1970). Past research on transportation prepared by Lansing for the Bureau suggested that the Survey Research

Center was the most suitable organization to do the work (Lansing, Mueller, and Barth, 1964; Lansing, 1966; Lansing and Hendricks, 1967).

Following the establishment of a set of conditions that distinguished between planned and less-planned residential environments, we began the task of selecting areas in which surveys would be conducted. Initially, we realized that it would not be enough to simply study planned communities themselves. Comparisons based on similar measurements undertaken at the same time using the same procedures in other communities offered better bases for generalization. The communities selected had to be similar in every respect except the physical environments. Differences in physical environments were to be a reflection of the degree of planning that was used prior to actual development.[6] Budget limitations determined that a total of 1,200 interviews could be taken in the study. Similarly, an estimation of the sampling error we would tolerate in our results led to a decision to conduct 200 interviews in two highly planned environments (new towns) and 100 interviews in each of the other selected environments. To take into account the dimensions of time and regional location, it was decided that older communities and new communities in central locations would be included among the other types of environments. The survey design that resulted is summarized in Table 3.

This design enabled us to make a number of comparisons: highly planned peripheral locations and central locations; highly planned old environments and highly planned new environments; highly planned and less-planned new environments; highly planned and less-planned old environments; and less-planned new and old environments. We could also make comparisons within any single classification containing more than one area. Finally, the selection of environments within three regions of the country (Baltimore–Washington, Detroit, and northern

Table 3

	Number of Areas	Interviews per Area	Interviews
Highly planned environments			
Peripheral locations in metropolitan areas, new	2	200	400
New environments in central locations	2	100	200
Older planned environment	1	100	100
Less-planned environments			
Peripheral locations, new	4	100	400
Older less planned environment	1	100	100
	10		1,200

New Jersey) enabled us to compare responses within the same regions.

Since a fundamental objective of the study was to determine if differences in the physical environment were related to attitudes and behaviors of residents, the selection of specific areas was made from places where population characteristics were thought to be similar. We did not want differences in family characteristics (income, life-cycle stage, age of household head) to influence significantly attitudes and behaviors.[7]

Within each of the designated communities, a probability sample was selected to represent a cross section of people living in single-family houses and townhouses.[8] The interviews were taken in November and December 1969 and lasted about 1 hour. The person interviewed in each family was either the head or the spouse of the head; the choice between them was randomly determined beforehand with no discretion left to the interviewer. In addition to interviews, data on the environments were collected from maps, aerial photographs, and visits to the communities.

The interview schedule reprinted in its entirety on pages 151–179, was designed to identify a number of attitudes and behaviors of the respondent and his or her family; specifically, respondents were asked to assess their community, their immediate neighborhood, and specific attributes of each environment. They were also asked what attracted them to the community they chose to live in. With respect to behavior, respondents were asked about participation in outdoor recreation, neighboring, organizational involvement, and travel. Travel behavior considered journey to work, weekend and other trips, and walking and bicycling for recreational and other purposes.

Overview of Major Findings

Among the major findings were that the levels of satisfaction with the community were highest in the new towns would reduce the driving residents was not confirmed. Similarly, our expecrated their communities as excellent. Lower levels of satisfaction were identified in the less-planned suburban environments of similar age where an average of 34 percent of the respondents gave their community excellent ratings. When asked why they gave positive evaluations, residents of Columbia and Reston were likely to mention the availability of facilities, the planning of the town, and the proximity of open space. In the more traditional suburban communities, having neighbors who were "friendly" and "desirable" and having good schools were mentioned most often by their residents.

Similarly, when asked what attracted them to the community they chose to live in, Columbia and Reston residents said the natural environment and the philosophy or image of the new town were primary motivating factors. For those people living in the more traditionally built communities, characteristics of the individual dwellings and lot and good schools were mentioned most often.[9]

It was also found that residents' ratings of their immediate neighborhoods were somewhat higher in the new towns than in other places. Furthermore, density of development was found to underlie many factors important to neighborhood satisfaction.[10] Important factors included privacy within the yard, the level of noise in the neighborhood, and the adequacy of outdoor space for family activities. The most important single factor related to neighborhood satisfaction in all communities was how well the neighborhood was kept up.

With respect to participation in outdoor recreation, the study found that people in the new towns tended to be considerably more active than residents in other communities. Indeed, facilities for walking, hiking, swimming, tennis, and golf were more available and accessible. The distances between where people live and different kinds of recreational faciities influenced the extent to which these facilities were used. However, the distance–use relationship differed considerably for the activities considered in the study (Marans, 1971).

As a background to travel behavior, we found that the proportion of families owning two or more cars was related to the level of planning in the six suburban communities under study. Multiple-car ownership was about 20 percent higher in the less-planned communities than in the highly planned new towns.

At the time of our study, the extent to which the suburban communities were planned made little or no difference in the total annual mileage driven by residents. Indeed, our suspicion that the availability of a range of community facilities in the new towns would reduce the driving of residents was not confirmed. Similarly, our expectations were not met that people in highly planned peripheral locations would take fewer weekend trips of 10 miles or more than would people in the less-planned communities. In fact, weekend-trip reporting was greater in Columbia and Reston than in the other suburban areas.

Specific Findings and Applications

Although many of the preceding findings are of general interest to environmental designers and planners, the direct applicability of these results may be questioned. If we were to consider the study a first attempt at evaluating planned communities from the residents' point of view, the use of the study becomes clearer. First, the fact that new-town residents expressed more satisfaction with their community than residents of less-planned environments suggests that, from at least one perspective, new towns are a success. Furthermore, the facilities that builders and planners provide are important to that success and are a major factor in attracting residents, more so in many cases than the quality and price of the dwelling itself.

Also important to community satisfaction is one's feelings about the immediate neighborhood. The analysis of neighborhood satisfaction, moreover, indicated the importance of several attributes, many of which are amenable to design consideration. For example, Table 4 shows a partial set of attribute assessments and their relationships to neighborhood satisfaction.[11] Not surprisingly, residents who reported hearing their neighbors often and those who reported living in a "noisy" neighborhood evaluated their neighborhoods less favorably than those who "almost never" heard their neighbors and those who said their neighborhood was "quiet." Similarly, people who had no privacy in their yard from neighbors and those who had too little outdoor space for family activities were less inclined to assess their neighborhood favorably than people who had privacy and adequate outdoor space near their home. Among other items evaluated, how well the neighborhood was main-

Table 4

Neighborhood Satisfaction for Responses Related to Select Environmental Attributes

	Percentage Giving Area Highest Rating on Neighborhood Satisfaction Scale	Number of Respondents
Frequency of:		
Hearing neighbors		
Very often	36	44
Occasionally	41	191
Almost never	54	1,013
Noise level		
Noisy	23	31
	20	54
	34	198
	37	337
Quiet	67	615
Privacy in yard from neighbors		
Yes	57	646
No	44	602
Adequacy of outdoor space for family activities		
More than needed	54	158
Right amount	54	861
Too little	35	224
Neighborhood maintenance level		
Well kept up	71	705
	28	398
	12	97
	4	24
Poorly kept up	18	11
The neighbors are		
Friendly people	70	640
	37	343
	21	266
	29	38
Unfriendly people	9	11
People similar to me	81	298
	43	306
	46	433
	24	119
People dissimilar to me	29	68

Source: Lansing, Marans, and Zehner (1970).

tained was strongly related to satisfaction, as were the perceptions of neighbors as being friendly people and as being similar to the respondents.

When several attribute assessments were considered simultaneously, how well the environment is maintained was the most important predictor of overall neighborhood satisfaction. To the extent that a planner–developer either designs neighborhoods to favor ease of maintenance and/or provides for regular upkeep of the building and grounds, he can influence, if not fully determine, the residents' subsequent reports of satisfaction (Zehner, 1970). Similarly, in high-density neighborhoods, residents mentioned that adequate outdoor space for family activities was important. In these areas, people who said they had too little space referred specifically to space for children to play, space for outdoor cooking, games, pets, and various hobbies. Such findings suggest that whenever possible provisions should be made for outdoor space in high-density areas for these activities.

We have mentioned that density was found to underlie many factors important to neighborhood satisfaction. Certainly, residential density is subject to manipulation by designers and planners, particularly at the level of a small cluster of dwellings. But how important is density in influencing the responses of residents to their environment?

In a subsequent analysis of density and density-related variables, using data from a national survey, we found that density indeed was related to a number of assessments of neighborhood attributes (Marans and Rodgers, 1973). In Table 5 we see that at densities of 6.5 dwelling units per acre or greater, about two thirds of the people interviewed were likely to report hearing their neighbors. Furthermore, about one third are likely to describe their neighbors as "noisy."

Table 5 also shows that the feeling that one has private outdoor space decreases regularly with increasing density as does the probability of having any outdoor space associated with one's dwelling. Perceptions of too much traffic and dangerous streets also increase regularly with rising density up to 11.49 dwelling units per acre, at which time they remain constant until densities above 20 dwellings per acre are reached.

One of the strongest relationships is shown in the last panel of Table 5, where people's perceptions of the level of crowding in the neighborhood increase precipitously with rising densities. This is not surprising since one's feeings of crowding are a good subjective indicator of the objective density measure.

In a multivariate analysis of neighborhood satisfaction, the five density-related responses (along with respondent characteristics) accounted for 59 percent of the variation in responses to the neighborhood satisfacton question. When the objective density measure was added to the analysis, the amount of variance explained remained at 59 percent. Thus it is not density per se that influences feelings of overall satisfaction with one's neighborhood, but rather it is the perceptions that one has which strongly determine such feelings. The designer would do well to consider ways in which the environment could be planned to elicit positive responses to neighborhood attributes such as those we have considered. There is little reason to believe that this could not be accomplished at relatively high as well as low densities.

Another example of the potential applicability of the results of the planned residential environments study is shown by data compiled on the use of internal walkway systems in the highly planned environments. Planners and designers often claim that walkway systems located away from roads will be used for recreational walking and bicycling more often than walkways paralleling roads. In our study, we were able to see if this was, in fact, the case.

Among the sampled communities, five highly

Table 5

Neighborhood Responses Related to Density, by Dwelling-Unit Density

	Dwelling Units per Acre						
	Less Than 1.0	1.00-3.49	3.50-6.49	6.50-11.49	11.50-19.49	19.50-39.49	39.50 or more
Frequency of hearing neighbors							
Very often	2	6	8	38	19	35	22
Occasionally	10	20	26	28	44	36	43
Almost never	88	74	66	34	37	29	35
	100	100	100	100	100	100	100
Noise level in neighborhood							
Noisy	4	7	9	21	11	22	25
	2	5	8	8	17	19	11
	6	19	20	32	22	24	33
	15	23	23	21	24	16	9
Quiet	73	46	40	18	26	19	22
	100	100	100	100	100	100	100
Available outdoor space							
No	1	1	6	14	29	35	62
Yes—without privacy	8	30	34	52	40	47	27
Yes—with privacy	91	69	60	34	31	18	11
	100	100	100	100	100	100	100
Traffic level in neighborhood							
Too much traffic	12	14	19	26	18	28	39
	8	13	14	11	20	20	22
	22	23	22	25	21	32	17
	16	17	22	18	16	15	3
Not much traffic	42	33	23	20	15	5	19
	100	100	100	100	100	100	100
Dangerous streets	13	12	12	20	14	34	28
	7	12	11	15	16	16	19
	17	19	20	25	32	25	20
	17	20	22	18	23	19	11
Safe streets	46	37	35	22	15	6	22
	100	100	100	100	100	100	100
Level of crowding							
Crowded	1	5	6	9	12	28	31
	2	7	9	18	21	21	30
	7	21	25	31	50	32	3
	8	23	22	11	10	11	8
Uncrowded	82	44	38	21	17	8	28
	100	100	100	100	100	100	100
Number of respondents	285	415	258	132	85	80	36

Source: Marans and Rodgers (1973).

planned environments had internal walkway systems; the remaining five less-planned environments did not have systems available. The first column in Table 6 shows that in each of the 10 communities a least half the adult population went walking or hiking for recreational purposes during the preceding year. However, there are slightly more active walkers and hikers found in Reston, Columbia, and Radburn than in the remaining communities. Among the adults who went hiking or walking and who did so within 2 miles of home, a significantly higher proportion is found in these three highly planned suburban communities; in the two highly planned central-city communities, however, the proportion of hikers or walkers is no different than that found in places where internal walkway systems are not available.

Comparable analysis with respect to bicycle riding shows that the availability of internal

walkway systems has virtually no influence on the number of frequent bicyclers nor on the places where bicyclers usually ride, the exception being the central-city locations where the proportion of bicyclers who ride on walkway systems is significantly lower.[12]

Given these findings, what are some of the implicatons for designers and planners, particularly with respect to the planning of in-town residential environments? One factor worthy of consideraton is the extent and quality of an internal walkway system, including the environment through which it passes. Although both central-city communities under study had internal walkways, the extent of each of the systems was either incomplete or interrupted by busy streets. In one community (Lafayette–Elmwood), not all walkways were built at the time of the interviewing. Furthermore, there were few places to which residents could walk, such as parks,

Table 6

Relationship Between Availability of Internal Walkway Systems and Where People Walk and Bicycle

	Percentage of Adults Who Went Hiking or Walking Five Times or More in the Last Year	Percentage of Adults Who Went Hiking or Walking and Who Did So Within 2 Miles	Percentage of Adults Who Went Bicycling Five Times or More in the Last Year	Percentage of Adults Who Went Bicycling and Who Did So Within 2 Miles
Internal walkway system available				
Reston	75	90	32	99
Columbia	65	91	21	98
Radburn	65	89	28	95
Lafayette-Elmwood	48	77	15	71
Southwest Washington	49	71	14	57
Internal walkway system not available				
Crofton	60	65	32	94
Montpelier	54	66	28	95
Southfield	47	68	42	98
Norbeck	44	66	17	90
Glen Rock	44	65	12	90

Source: Lansing, Marans, and Zehner (1970).

playgrounds, and shops. In Southwest Washington, walkways existed within each block of residential development; but the walkways connecting blocks were interrupted by streets, driveways, and parking lots. The blocks themselves were not very large, thereby limiting the area a pedestrian or bicycle rider could cover within the immediate environs. In the suburban locations, communities with internal walkways contained systems that covered extended areas and were seldom interrupted by streets carrying heavy automobile traffic. Where such crossing did occur, the separation of pedestrian and vehicular movements was accommodated by grade separations, allowing the pedestrians to move freely under roads (Radburn and Reston).

Another difference between the suburban and central-city locations with internal walkway sytems was the quality of the environment in which walkways were located. In the suburban locations, walkways largely passed through wooded areas or other "natural" conditions. In contrast, walkways in the in-town locations passed through "man-made" areas of buildings, parks, streets, and the like. To the extent that the central-city walkways penetrated the surrounding environment, they often passed through densely built-up areas in varying stages of decay. There is evidence emerging that these are the qualities that prompt people to escape the central city for recreational purposes.

A second factor that may have influenced walking and bicycling in central-city locations was crime. The existence or perception of crime may have contributed to lower participation rates for walking and bicycling in the central-city locations than in suburban locations. A cursory investigation of crime statistics in the central-city location indicated that crime rates were high. Had we asked attitudinal questions about crime and related them to responses on participation, we suspect that perception of crime would have adversely influenced active walking and bicycle riding.

The implicatons of these findings are clearer for suburban locations than they are for central-city locations. As many planners and architects have suspected, the availability of an internal walkway system influences the extent to which people walk or bicycle for recreational purposes. Indeed, the planned residential environments study showed that internal walkways also influence the extent to which people walk for other purposes, such as shopping and visiting friends. The extent of the system and the quality of the environment through which the system passes are also important factors for the designer. Should planners wish to increase the extent to which people in central-city locations walk for recreation and other purposes, future redevelopment plans might consider more extensive walkway systems that penetrate the surrounding environment, are clearly illuminated, and are better policed. Where walkways must cross major thoroughfares, grade separations should be provided whenever possible. And when development of a large area is to take place over time, complete walkway systems might be constructed after the initial dwellings have been occupied and linkages to surrounding walkway systems made. We do not know if such efforts would influence the amount of bicycling of residents. We suspect that environmental factors, such as flat terrain and local streets free from traffic, are more important to bicycle riding than the availability of an internal walkway system. Data on bicycling from the less-planned communities would suggest that this hypothesis may be correct.

The researchers have identified a number of other specific findings from the planned-communities data, which potentially would be helpful to planners and environmental designers (Lansing, Marans, and Zehner, 1970; Zehner, 1971; Marans, 1971). Undoubtedly other results have been used by practitioners and other researchers in developing their own work. The reader who wishes to examine the full range of findings and explore their applicability is referred to one of the original references.

SUMMARY

This chapter began with the observation that survey research and other techniques used widely in the social sciences were being subjected to considerable criticism as to their appropriateness for man–environment research. The thrust of the chapter has been to demonstrate that surveys can play an active part in enriching our understanding of relationships between various environmental settings and a number of human responses. We have done this in several ways. First, we considered the uses and limitations of survey research for the environmental design and planning professions. At the same time, several possibilities were identified for using surveys in conjunction with those methodologies appropriate to the needs of designers and planners. We then presented an overview of the scope of the surveys that might be conducted, including those covering small areas such as buildings and neighborhoods, and the nation as a whole. Although the geographic unit will continue to be the focus of many surveys, we suggested that studies of identifiable groups of the population will increase in the future, irrespective of geographic setting. Such studies will create opportunities for investigating the responses of unique population groups to a range of environmental conditions. Following a description of three types of survey design, we discussed sampling and data-collection procedures used in the survey process. The chapter concluded with an overview of the planned-communities study, which used surveys as the principal form of data collection and which produced results that are applicable to environmental planners and designers.

Throughout the chapter the cost associated with surveys has been mentioned as a factor re-

stricting their use or limiting the scope of the research effort. Yet the number of surveys conducted in recent years that have taken environmental variables into account suggests that the cost of survey research may not be as much of an inhibiting factor for architects and planners as it is for social scientists. In part, this has resulted from a growing awareness on the part of funding agencies that survey research can provide information for policy makers concerned with environmental matters. Indications are that these informational needs are likely to increase and that survey research will find new uses in the future.

NOTES

1. See, for example, Michelson and Reed's "The Time Budget" in this volume, and Chapin and Logan (1969).
2. An innovative research approach to simulating environmental experiences has been developed by the Institute of Gerontology in collaboration with the Department of Architecture at the University of Michigan. For an overview of the approach, see Pastalan, Mantz, and Merrill (1973).
3. This procedure, in fact, has been operationalized (Marans, 1970).
4. For a thorough discussion of cross-section surveys, see Morgan (1972).
5. The following draws heavily from Hess, Riedel, and Fitzpatrick (1961).
6. The assumption was made that every contemporary residential environment was built according to a plan. The differences between communities was in the extent to which they were planned. Therefore, the major difference in community selection was between highly planned environments and less-planned environments.
7. The communities selected were the new towns of Columbia and Reston (highly planned peripheral environments); Southwest Washington and Lafayette Park–Elmwood Park in Detroit (highly planned environments); and Crofton, Maryland, Montpelier, Maryland, Norbeck, Maryland, and Southfield, Michigan (less-planned peripheral environments).
8. The decision to exclude residents of high-rise and garden apartments was made in an effort to minimize the number of respondents at the two ends of the family life cycle. That is, we wanted to have mostly as respondents families with parents in their late twenties or early thirties and with children living at home.

9. For a more thorough discussion of community satisfaction, see Lansing, Marans, and Zehner (1970), and Zehner and Marans (1973).

10. For a detailed discussion of the effects of density for this sample of communities, see Marans and Zehner (1972), and Zehner and Marans (1973).

11. A complete set of items used in the study and their relationships to neighborhood satisfaction are shown in Tables 32, 33, 37, and 38 of Lansing, Marans, and Zehner (1970).

12. These relationships between the availability of an internal walkway system and hiking, walking, and bicycling remained the same in a multivariate context when characteristics of the respondents were also considered.

REFERENCES

13. Bechtel, R. B. 1972. "Social Goals Through Design: A Half Process Made Whole." Paper delivered at the American Institute of Planners Conference, Boston.

14. Cannell, Charles, and R. L. Kahn. 1953. "The Collection of Data by Interviewing," in L. Festinger and D. Katz (eds.), *Research Methods in the Behavioral Sciences.* New York: Dryden Press.

15. Chapin, F. S., and T. H. Logen. 1969. "Patterns of Time and Space Use," in H. S. Perloff (ed.), *The Quality of the Urban Environment.* Washington, D.C.: Resources for the Future, Inc.

16. Committee on Housing Research and Development. 1972. "Families in Public Housing: An Evaluation of Three Residential Environments in Rockford, Illinois." Urbana–Champaign, Ill.: University of Illinois.

17. Festinger, Leon, S. Schachter, and K. Back. 1950. *Social Pressures in Informal Groups.* New York: Harper & Row.

18. Gans, H. J. 1962. *The Urban Villagers.* New York: Free Press.

19. Gans, H. J. 1967. *The Levittowners.* New York: Random House.

20. Gump, P. V. 1971. "The Behavioral Setting: A Promising Unit for Environmental Designers." *Landscape Architecture,* vol. 61, no. 2.

21. Hess, I., D. C. Riedel, and T. B. Fitzpatrick. 1961. *Probability Sampling of Hospitals and Patients.* Ann Arbor, Mich.: Bureau of Hospital Administration, University of Michigan.

22. Katz, Daniel. 1953. "Field Studies," in L. Festinger and D. Katz (eds.), *Research Methods in the Behavioral Sciences.* New York: Dryden Press.

23. Kish, Leslie. 1953. "Selection of a Sample," in L. Festinger and D. Katz (eds.), *Research Methods in the Behavioral Sciences.* New York: Dryden Press.

24. Kish, Leslie. 1965. *Survey Sampling.* New York: Wiley.

25. Lansing, J. B., Eva Mueller, and Nancy Barth. 1964. *Residential Location and Urban Mobility: A Multivariate Analysis.* Ann Arbor, Mich.: Institute for Social Research, University of Michigan.

26. Lansing, J. B. 1966. *Residential Location and Urban Mobility: The Second Wave of Interviews.* Ann Arbor, Mich.: Institute for Social Research, University of Michigan.

27. Lansing, J. B., and G. Hendricks. 1967. *Automobile Ownership and Residential Density.* Ann Arbor, Mich.: Institute for Social Research, University of Michigan.

28. Lansing, J. B., R. W. Marans, and R. B. Zehner. 1970. *Planned Residential Environment.* Ann Arbor, Mich.: Institute for Social Research, University of Michigan.

29. Lansing, J. B., and J. N. Morgan. 1971. *Economic Survey Methods.* Ann Arbor, Mich.: Institute for Social Research, University of Michigan.

30. Levin, M. S., and S. Sachs. 1972. "Some First Returns on Planned Unit Development." Paper presented at the American Institute of Planners Conference, Boston.

31. Mandell, Lewis, and R. W. Marans. 1972. *Participation in Outdoor Recreation: A National Perspective.* Ann Arbor, Mich.: Institute for Social Research, University of Michigan.

32. Marans, R. W. 1970. "Social and Cultural Influences in New Town Planning: An Israeli Experiment." *Journal of the Town Planning Institute,* vol. 57, no. 2, pp. 60–65.

33. Marans, R. W. 1971. "Determinants of Outdoor Recreation Behavior in Planned Residential Environments," Ann Arbor, Mich.: University of Michigan unpublished doctoral dissertation.

34. Marans, R. W., B. L. Driver, and J. C. Scott. 1972. *Youth and the Environment.* Ann Arbor, Mich.: Institute for Social Research, University of Michigan.

35. Marans, R. W., and R. B. Zehner. 1972. "Some Observed Patterns of Residential Density and Social Interaction," in K. Bernhardt (ed.), *Housing: New Trends and Concepts.* Ann Arbor, Mich.: Institute of Science and Technology, University of Michigan.

36. Marans, R. W., and Willard Rodgers. 1974. "Toward an Understanding of Community Satisfaction," in A. Hawley and V. Rock (eds.), *Urbanization–The State of Knowledge.* Washington, D.C.: National Academy of Science.

37. Morgan, J. N. 1972. "How Useful Is the Cross-Section Sample Survey?", *Monthly Labor Review,* reprint 2787.

38. Moser, C. A., and G. Kalton. 1971. *Survey Methods in Social Investigation.* London: Heinemann Educational Books.

39. Parnes, Herbert. 1972. "Longitudinal Surveys: Prospects and Problems." *Monthly Labor Review,* reprint 2787.

40. Pastalan, Lee, R. K. Mantz, and John Merrill. 1973. "The Simulation of Age-Related Sensory Losses: A New Approach to the Study of Environmental Barriers," in W. Prieser (ed.), *Environmental Design Research,* vol. I. Stroudsburg, Pa.: Dowden, Hutchinson & Ross.

41. Patterson, A. H. 1974. "Unobtrusive Measures: Their Nature and Utility for Architects," in J. Lang et al. (eds.),

Designing for Human Behavior. Stroudsburg, Pa.: Dowden, Hutchinson & Ross.

42. Proshansky, Harold. 1972. "Methodology in Environmental Psychology: Problems and Issues." *Human Factors,* 14(5).

43. Robinson, John, and Phillip Shaver. 1969. *Measures of Social Psychological Attitudes*. Ann Arbor, Mich.: Institute for Social Research, University of Michigan.

44. Sanoff, Henry. 1972. "Housing Research and Development." Paper presented at a symposium on Housing and Mental Health, School of Architecture, University of Maryland.

45. Scott, J. C., and Eliska Chanlett. 1973. *Planning the Research Interview*, Chapel Hill, N.C.: Laboratories for Population Statistics, University of North Carolina.

46. Scott, J. C., B. L. Driver, and R. W. Marans. 1973. *Toward Environmental Understanding*. Ann Arbor, Mich.: Institute for Social Research, University of Michigan.

47. Sellitz, C., M. Jahoda, M. Deutch, and S. Cook. 1959. *Research Methods in Social Relations*. New York: Holt, Rinehart and Winston.

48. Zehner, R. B., and R. W. Marans. 1973. "Residential Density, Planning Objectives and Life in Planned Communities." *Journal of the American Institute of Planners,* vol. 39, no. 5.

Project 45789
Fall, 1969

A STUDY OF RESIDENTIAL ENVIRONMENTS

Form Approved
Bureau of the Budget
No. 04-S69003

SURVEY RESEARCH CENTER
INSTITUTE FOR SOCIAL RESEARCH
THE UNIVERSITY OF MICHIGAN

(Do not write in above spaces.)

Interviewer's Label

A. Segment Number____________________
B. Your Interview Number______________
C. Date______________________________
D. Length of Interview__________(Min.)

1. INTERVIEWER: LIST ALL PERSONS, INCLUDING CHILDREN, NOW LIVING IN THE DWELLING UNIT BY THEIR RELATION TO THE HEAD. CONSULT ITEM 5 ON THE COVER SHEET AND INDICATE RESPONDENT BY A CHECK (✓) IN RIGHT COLUMN BELOW. THE RESPONDENT MUST BE THE HEAD OF HOUSEHOLD OR HIS WIFE. MAKE NO SUBSTITUTIONS.

FOR ADULTS' AGE (CARD 1):
A. 18-24
B. 25-34
C. 35-44
D. 45-54
E. 55-64
F. 65-74
G. 75 OR OVER

FOR CHILDREN UNDER 18: ASK AGE IN YEARS.

a. All persons, by relation to head	b. Sex	c. Age (See above: for adults age 18+, enter letter)	d. Family Unit Number	e. Indicate R by "✓"
1. HEAD OF HOUSEHOLD				
2.				
3.				
4.				
5.				
6.				
7.				
8.				

Figure 2

Note: The cards referred to in the questionnaire are reproduced on pages 178 and 179.

2. Where did you live most of the time while you were growing up -- in the country, in a small town, in a suburb, or in a city?

☐1 COUNTRY   ☐2 SMALL TOWN   ☐3 SUBURB   ☐4 CITY

3. During that time did you usually live in a single family house or an apartment, or what?

☐1 SINGLE FAMILY   ☐3 APARTMENT

☐ OTHER (SPECIFY)_____

4. Could you tell me when the house you are living in now was built?

☐1 1939 OR BEFORE   ☐5 1965   ☐9 1969
☐2 1940-1949   ☐6 1966
☐3 1950-1959   ☐7 1967   ☐0 DON'T KNOW
☐4 1960-1964   ☐8 1968

5. And when did you move into it?

☐1 1939 OR BEFORE   ☐5 1965   ☐9 1969
☐2 1940-1949   ☐6 1966   │
☐3 1950-1959   ☐7 1967   ▼
☐4 1960-1964   ☐8 1968

┌───┐
│ 5a. What month did you move in?   │
│   │
│   ☐1 JAN.   ☐2 FEB.   ☐3 MARCH   ☐4 APRIL   ☐5 MAY   │
│   │
│   ☐6 JUNE   (IF LATER, DO NOT INTERVIEW)   │
└───┘

6. Just before you moved to your present home were you living in a single family house or an apartment or what?

☐1 SINGLE FAMILY HOUSE   ☐3 APARTMENT

☐ OTHER (SPECIFY)_____

7. Was that in the country, in a small town, in a suburb, or in a city?

☐1 COUNTRY   ☐2 SMALL TOWN   ☐3 SUBURB   ☐4 CITY

8. When you were looking for a place to live what especially appealed to you about coming here?

_____

_____

8a. Anything else?_____

_____

|1| MOVED HERE IN 1964 OR EARLIER (SEE Q. 5) → GO TO Q. 10

|5| MOVED HERE IN 1965-1969

↓

9. Would you say that living here has worked out about as you expected, or better than you expected, or not as well?

|1| BETTER THAN EXPECTED |2| ABOUT AS EXPECTED

|4| BETTER IN SOME WAYS, NOT IN OTHERS |5| NOT AS WELL AS EXPECTED

9a. Why do you say that? _____

_____

9b. Anything else?_____

_____

_____

10. TYPE OF DWELLING - BY OBSERVATION:

|1| R LIVES IN A SINGLE FAMILY HOUSE ON A SEPARATE LOT → GO TO Q. 12

|5| R LIVES IN A TOWNHOUSE

↓

11. If you could do as you pleased, would you prefer to live in a single family house, a townhouse, or an apartment?

|1| SINGLE FAMILY HOUSE |2| TOWNHOUSE |3| APARTMENT

11a. Why do you say so?_____

_____

12. I'd like to ask you how you feel about this area as a place to live - I mean the area outlined on the map (SHOW MAP). From your own personal point of view, would you rate this area as a place to live as excellent, good, average, below average, or poor?

[1] EXCELLENT　　[2] GOOD　　[3] AVERAGE　　[4] BELOW AVERAGE　　[5] POOR

12a.　In what ways?_____

_____

_____

_____

INTERVIEWER:　IF R MAKES ANY VOLUNTARY COMMENTS ABOUT THE APPROPRIATENESS OF THE MAPPED AREA PLEASE NOTE THEM.

[1] MAPPED AREA TOO SMALL

[2] MAPPED AREA TOO LARGE　　　　[7] OTHER_____

[3] MAPPED AREA WRONG SHAPE

[4] DON'T UNDERSTAND IT　　　　　_____

　　　　　　　　　　　　　　　　　_____

---

[1] HOUSEHOLD CONTAINS NOBODY AGED 55 AND OVER ➔ GO TO Q. 14

[5] HOUSEHOLD INCLUDES SOMEONE AGED 55 AND OVER

---

13. For retired people how would you rate this area as a place to live? Would you say it was excellent, good, average, below average, or poor?

[1] EXCELLENT　　[2] GOOD　　[3] AVERAGE　　[4] BELOW AVERAGE　　[5] POOR

13a.　In what ways?_____

_____

_____

154

⊡ HOUSEHOLD CONTAINS NOBODY 12-17 → GO TO Q. 15

⊡ HOUSEHOLD CONTAINS SOMEONE 12-17

14. From teenagers' point of view how would you expect them to rate this area as a place to live - would you say it was excellent, good, average, below average, or poor for them?

⊡ EXCELLENT　　⊡ GOOD　　⊡ AVERAGE　　⊡ BELOW AVERAGE　　⊡ POOR

14a. In what ways?_____

_____

_____

⊡ HOUSEHOLD CONTAINS NO CHILDREN AGED UNDER 12 → GO TO Q. 17

⊡ HOUSEHOLD CONTAINS ONE OR MORE CHILDREN UNDER 12

15. As a place to raise children under 12 how would you rate this area - would you say it was excellent, good, average, below average, or poor?

⊡ EXCELLENT　　⊡ GOOD　　⊡ AVERAGE　　⊡ BELOW AVERAGE　　⊡ POOR

15a. In what ways?_____

_____

_____

16. How do you feel about the places right near your home for children under 12 to play out of doors - would you say they are excellent, good, average, below average, or poor?

⊡ EXCELLENT　　⊡ GOOD　　⊡ AVERAGE　　⊡ BELOW AVERAGE　　⊡ POOR

16a. Why do you say so?_____

_____

17. How many times in the last week have you yourself spent an afternoon or evening with friends or gone to a meeting or social event or something like that?

☐0 NOT AT ALL

☐1 ONCE

☐2 TWICE

☐3 THREE OR FOUR TIMES

☐5 FIVE OR SIX TIMES

☐7 SEVEN OR MORE TIMES

18. Now I'd like to ask you just about your close neighbors - I mean the half dozen families living nearest to you. How many of the adults in these families would you know by name if you met them on the street - all of them, nearly all, half of them, just a few of them, or none of them?

☐4 ALL

☐3 NEARLY ALL

☐2 HALF OF THEM

☐1 JUST A FEW OF THEM

☐0 NONE OF THEM → SKIP TO Q. 20

19. How often do you talk to any of the half dozen families who live closest
    to you just to chat or for a social visit - would it be every day, several
    times a week, once a week, 2-3 times a month, once a month, a few times a
    year, or never? (HAND R CARD A)

    6 EVERY DAY

    5 SEVERAL TIMES A WEEK

    4 ONCE A WEEK

    3 2-3 TIMES A MONTH

    2 ONCE A MONTH

    1 A FEW TIMES A YEAR; RARELY

    0 NEVER

20. Do you people have a place where you can be out in your yard and feel that you can
    really have privacy from your neighbors if you want it?

    1 YES   5 NO

    20a. Why do you say so?_____

    _____

    _____

21. Some homes are close enough together so that even when people are indoors they
    hear their neighbors and their neighbors hear them. Do you and your neighbors
    hear each other very often, occasionally, or almost never?

    1 VERY OFTEN   2 OCCASIONALLY   3 ALMOST NEVER

22. How much do you care whether you hear each other - a great deal, somewhat, or don't you care?

   ☐*1* A GREAT DEAL   ☐*2* SOMEWHAT   ☐*3* DON'T CARE

23. How do you feel about the amount of outdoor space near your home which members of your family can use for their different activities - do you people have more space than you need, or about the right amount, or too little space?

   ☐*1* MORE THAN NEED   ☐*2* RIGHT AMOUNT   ☐*3* TOO LITTLE

24. Why do you say so?_____

   _____

   _____

25. Now here is a list of clubs and organizations that many people belong to. Please look at this list (SHOW R CARD B), and tell me which of these kinds of organizations you yourself belong to. (PAUSE) Are there any others you're in that are not on this list? (<u>CHECK AT LEFT</u> EACH KIND OF ORGANIZATION R BELONGS TO, <u>THEN</u> ASK Q. 26 FOR EACH KIND OF ORGANIZATION MENTIONED.)

26. Would you say you are very involved, somewhat involved, or not very involved in _____? (CHECK RESPONSE IN "INVOLVEMENT" COLUMN BELOW.)

25. ORGANIZATION	26. INVOLVEMENT		
	-1-	-2-	-3-
a. ☐ Church or synagogue	a. /Very/	/Somewhat/	/Not very/
b. ☐ Church-connected groups (but not the church itself)	b. /Very/	/Somewhat/	/Not very/
c. ☐ Hobby clubs	c. /Very/	/Somewhat/	/Not very/
d. ☐ College alumni (alumnae) associations	d. /Very/	/Somewhat/	/Not very/
e. ☐ Fraternal lodges or organizations	e. /Very/	/Somewhat/	/Not very/
f. ☐ Business or civic groups	f. /Very/	/Somewhat/	/Not very/
g. ☐ Parent-teachers associations	g. /Very/	/Somewhat/	/Not very/
h. ☐ Community centers	h. /Very/	/Somewhat/	/Not very/
i. ☐ Regular card playing group	i. /Very/	/Somewhat/	/Not very/
j. ☐ Sport teams	j. /Very/	/Somewhat/	/Not very/
k. ☐ Country clubs	k. /Very/	/Somewhat/	/Not very/
l. ☐ Youth groups (Girl Scout Leaders, Little League Managers, etc.)	l. /Very/	/Somewhat/	/Not very/
m. ☐ Professional groups	m. /Very/	/Somewhat/	/Not very/
n. ☐ Local political clubs or organizations	n. /Very/	/Somewhat/	/Not very/
o. ☐ State or national political clubs or organizations	o. /Very/	/Somewhat/	/Not very/
p. ☐ Neighborhood improvement associations	p. /Very/	/Somewhat/	/Not very/
q. ☐ Charity or welfare organizations	q. /Very/	/Somewhat/	/Not very/
r. ☐ Other (Specify)_____	r. /Very/	/Somewhat/	/Not very/
s. ☐ Other (Specify)_____	s. /Very/	/Somewhat/	/Not very/

☐ NONE (IF NONE, CONTINUE WITH QUESTION 27.)

27. Thinking of your involvement in clubs and community organizations in the past 2 years - would you say you are more involved now, or less involved now than you were 2 years ago?

☐1 MORE INVOLVED NOW   ☐2 SAME AS BEFORE   ☐3 LESS INVOLVED NOW

28. Some people would like to be more involved in clubs and community activities than they are while others would like to be less involved. How about you, would you like to be more involved, less involved, or about as involved as you are now?

☐1 MORE INVOLVED   ☐2 SAME AS NOW   ☐3 LESS INVOLVED

28a. Why do you say so?_____

_____

_____

29. Here is a list of outdoor activities. (HAND R CARD C) I'd like to know which of these you yourself have taken part in within the last year , not counting when you were away from here on vacation. (COMPLETE Q. 29 FOR ALL ACTIVITIES, THEN ASK Q. 30-31 SEQUENCE FOR EACH ACTIVITY R MENTIONS.)

☐ NO LISTED ACTIVITIES PARTICIPATED IN ➙ GO TO Q. 32

29. ACTIVITIES PARTICIPATED IN	30. How often did you _____ in the last year not counting when you were on vacation? (READ ALTERNATIVES)	31. Where did you go (most often)? Was it within 10 miles of here?
A. Outdoor swimming at a pool ☐ Participated	☐1 Once or twice ☐3 Three or four times ☐5 Five to ten times ☐7 More often	☐1 More than 10 miles ☐2 Within 10 miles ↓ Where?_____ _____ (NEAREST INTERSECTION OR EQUIVALENT)
B. Tennis ☐ Participated	☐1 Once or twice ☐3 Three or four times ☐5 Five to ten times ☐7 More often	☐1 More than 10 miles ☐2 Within 10 miles ↓ Where?_____ _____ (NEAREST INTERSECTION OR EQUIVALENT)
C. Hiking or walking ☐ Participated	☐1 Once or twice ☐3 Three or four times ☐5 Five to ten times ☐7 More often	☐1 More than 10 miles ☐2 Within 10 miles ↓ Where?_____ _____ (NEAREST INTERSECTION OR EQUIVALENT)

(CONTINUED ON NEXT PAGE) ⟶

160

29. ACTIVITIES PARTICIPATED IN	30. How often did you _____ in the last year not counting when you were on vacation? (READ ALTERNATIVES)	31. Where did you go (most often)? Was it within 10 miles of here?
D. Picnicking ☐ Participated	⑴ Once or twice ⑶ Three or four times ⑸ Five to ten times ⑺ More often	⑴ More than 10 miles ⑵ Within 10 miles Where?_____ _____ (NEAREST INTERSECTION OR EQUIVALENT)
E. Golfing ☐ Participated	⑴ Once or twice ⑶ Three or four times ⑸ Five to ten times ⑺ More often	⑴ More than 10 miles ⑵ Within 10 miles Where?_____ _____ (NEAREST INTERSECTION OR EQUIVALENT)
F. Boating ☐ Participated	⑴ Once or twice ⑶ Three or four times ⑸ Five to ten times ⑺ More often	⑴ More than 10 miles ⑵ Within 10 miles Where?_____ _____ (NEAREST INTERSECTION OR EQUIVALENT)
G. Bicycling ☐ Participated	⑴ Once or twice ⑶ Three or four times ⑸ Five to ten times ⑺ More often	⑴ More than 10 miles ⑵ Within 10 miles Where?_____ _____ (NEAREST INTERSECTION OR EQUIVALENT)

⑴ MOVED HERE IN 1964 OR EARLIER (SEE Q. 5) ➤ GO TO Q. 33

⑸ MOVED HERE IN 1965-1969

32. Since you came to live here have you participated in outdoor activities like these more than you did before, or less, or about the same?

⑴ MORE NOW   ⑵ ABOUT THE SAME   ⑶ LESS NOW

33. How often in the last week have you walked from your home to any of these places?
    (SHOW R CARD D)

	Not at all in last week	Once or twice	3-4 times	5+ times
a. Picnic area	0	1	3	5
b. Grocery store	0	1	3	5
c. Other stores	0	1	3	5
d. Friend's house	0	1	3	5

34. Do you ever use a bicycle to get somewhere from your home?

   5 NO, NEVER → GO TO Q. 35

   1 YES

   ┌───┐
   │ 34a. In the last week have you ridden a bicycle from your home to any │
   │   of these places? (SHOW R CARD D) (CHECK EACH PLACE BICYCLED TO) │
   │   │
   │   ☐ a. Picnic area   ☐ c. Other stores   │
   │   │
   │   ☐ b. Grocery store   ☐ d. Friend's house   │
   └───┘

35. How important to you is it to have sidewalks or footpaths going by your
    home - is it very important, fairly important, or not important at all?

    1 VERY IMPORTANT   2 FAIRLY IMPORTANT   3 NOT IMPORTANT AT ALL

    35a. Why do you say so?_____

    _____

    _____

36. <u>Last weekend</u> did you go on any trips ten miles or more away from here other than on your vacation?

☐1 YES   ☐5 NO → (GO TO S-SERIES)   ☐6 NO - WAS AWAY ON VACATION → (GO TO S-SERIES)

36a. How many miles away from here did you go? (LONGEST TRIP)

☐1 10-19 miles   ☐3 20-39 miles   ☐5 40-59 miles   ☐7 60 or more

36b. What was the main reason for the trip?

_____

_____

****

S-SERIES:

Thank you. This next section goes better if you fill it out yourself. Here are some statements that some people agree with and others disagree with. Please mark each one according to whether you agree or disagree, and how strongly. (EXPLAIN BY USING FIRST ONE AS AN EXAMPLE, IF NECESSARY.)

****

37. How many cars or trucks do you people have for family use?

_____ (NUMBER)   ☐ NONE → GO TO Q. 41

ASK ABOUT EACH CAR OR TRUCK OWNED OR USED

		First	Second	Third
38.	What year was the car bought?			
39.	Altogether about how many miles has it been driven since you bought it?			
40.	In the last twelve months about how many miles has the car been driven?			

163

41. Is there a bus stop within a 10 minute walk of your home?

　1 YES　　　　　5 NO → GO TO Q. 43　　　8 DON'T KNOW → GO TO Q. 43

42. How often do you yourself use the bus?

　☐ 1. Daily or almost every day (5-7 days a week)
　☐ 2. 1-4 days a week
　☐ 3. 2-3 days a month
　☐ 4. One day a month or less
　☐ 5. Never

43. How important is it to you whether there is a bus stop near your home?

　1 VERY IMPORTANT　　2 FAIRLY IMPORTANT　　3 NOT IMPORTANT AT ALL

44. Where is most of the grocery shopping done for your family these days?

NAME OF STORE OR SHOPPING CENTER:_____

LOCATION (E.G., STREET INTERSECTION:_____

TOWN:_____

45. How long does it usually take to get there from here? (ONE WAY)

　1 Less than 5 minutes
　2 5-9 minutes
　3 10-14 minutes
　4 15-19 minutes
　5 20-29 minutes
　6 30-39 minutes
　7 40+ minutes

46. Now I'd like to know about all of the trips taken by people in this family yesterday. By a trip I mean one way - driving to a store and back would be <u>two</u> trips.

47. Did (FAMILY MEMBER) go to work or go anywhere by car or public transportation yesterday?

☐ YES ➔ GO TO Q. 48   ☐ NO ➔ REPEAT Q. 47 FOR NEXT FAMILY MEMBER

☐ NO FAMILY MEMBER TOOK ANY TRIP YESTERDAY ➔ SKIP TO Q. 52

```
*******************************************************************************
*                                                                             *
*  IMPORTANT:  QUESTION 47 MUST BE ASKED FOR ALL FAMILY MEMBERS LISTED. BEGIN WITH *
*              HEAD.  IF OTHER FAMILY MEMBERS WENT ALONG ON A TRIP, INDICATE WHO AT *
*              THE TOP OF COLUMN FOR THAT TRIP.                                *
*                                                                             *
*******************************************************************************
```

WHO IS THIS TRIP FOR? ENTER EACH PERSON BY RELATIONSHIP TO HEAD →	Family Member(s) Who Went: _____	Family Member(s) Who Went: _____
48. Where did (you) begin (your) (next) trip?	① Work (Priority) ② Home ③ Friend's or Relative's Home ④ Store, Restaurant, Bank ⑤ Doctor's Office, Hospital ⑥ School ⑦ Other	① Work (Priority) ② Home ③ Friend's or Relative's Home ④ Store, Restaurant, Bank ⑤ Doctor's Office, Hospital ⑥ School ⑦ Other
49. What was the purpose of this trip? (CHECK TWO BOXES IF NECESSARY)	① Go home ② Get to work } (GO TO Q. 51) ③ Shopping ④ Attend school ⑤ Social or recreational ⑥ To take someone somewhere (serve a passenger)-(CHECK ALSO THE PURPOSE OF HIS TRIP) ⑦ To change mode of travel ⑧ Personal business, medical, dental ⑨ Eat meal　⓪ Other	① Go home ② Get to work } (GO TO Q. 51) ③ Shopping ④ Attend school ⑤ Social or recreational ⑥ To take someone somewhere (serve a passenger)-(CHECK ALSO THE PURPOSE OF HIS TRIP) ⑦ To change mode of travel ⑧ Personal business, medical, dental ⑨ Eat meal　⓪ Other
50. Where did (you) go?	① Home ② School ③ Friend's or Relative's Home ④ Store, Bank, Restaurant ⑤ Doctor's Office, Hospital ⑥ Other	① Home ② School ③ Friend's or Relative's Home ④ Store, Bank, Restaurant ⑤ Doctor's Office, Hospital ⑥ Other
51. How did (you) travel? (IF BY CAR): Did (you) drive? (CHECK TWO BOXES IF ONE FAMILY MEMBER DROVE ANOTHER)	① Auto driver-WHICH FAMILY MEMBER DROVE? _____ ① Auto passenger ② Suburban Railroad ③ Bus ④ Rapid Transit ⑤ Walk to work ⑥ Taxi ⑦ Other	① Auto driver-WHICH FAMILY MEMBER DROVE? _____ ① Auto passenger ② Suburban Railroad ③ Bus ④ Rapid Transit ⑤ Walk to work ⑥ Taxi ⑦ Other

INTERVIEWER: REPEAT QUESTIONS 46-51 FOR EACH TRIP. INCLUDE TRIPS BY ANY FAMILY MEMBER AGED 5 AND OVER. LIST THE FAMILY MEMBERS AGED 5 AND OVER BELOW. (SEE Q. 1)

1. _____　　4. _____　　7. _____

2. _____　　5. _____　　8. _____

3. _____　　6. _____　　9. _____

166

Family Member(s) Who Went:	Family Member(s) Who Went:	Family Member(s) Who Went:
1 Work (Priority) 2 Home 3 Friend's or Relative's Home 4 Store, Restaurant, Bank 5 Doctor's Office, Hospital 6 School 7 Other	1 Work (Priority) 2 Home 3 Friend's or Relative's Home 4 Store, Restaurant, Bank 5 Doctor's Office, Hospital 6 School 7 Other	1 Work (Priority) 2 Home 3 Friend's or Relative's Home 4 Store, Restaurant, Bank 5 Doctor's Office, Hospital 6 School 7 Other
1 Go home 2 Get to work } (GO TO Q. 51) 3 Shopping 4 Attend school 5 Social or recreational 6 To take someone somewhere (serve a passenger)-(CHECK ALSO THE PURPOSE OF HIS TRIP) 7 To change mode of travel 8 Personal business, medical, dental 9 Eat meal 0 Other	1 Go home 2 Get to work } (GO TO Q. 51) 3 Shopping 4 Attend school 5 Social or recreational 6 To take someone somewhere (serve a passenger)-(CHECK ALSO THE PURPOSE OF HIS TRIP) 7 To change mode of travel 8 Personal business, medical, dental 9 Eat meal 0 Other	1 Go home 2 Get to work } (GO TO Q. 51) 3 Shopping 4 Attend school 5 Social or recreational 6 To take someone somewhere (serve a passenger)-(CHECK ALSO THE PURPOSE OF HIS TRIP) 7 To change mode of travel 8 Personal business, medical, dental 9 Eat meal 0 Other
1 Home 2 School 3 Friend's or Relative's Home 4 Store, Bank, Restaurant 5 Doctor's Office, Hospital 6 Other	1 Home 2 School 3 Friend's or Relative's Home 4 Store, Bank, Restaurant 5 Doctor's Office, Hospital 6 Other	1 Home 2 School 3 Friend's or Relative's Home 4 Store, Bank, Restaurant 5 Doctor's Office, Hospital 6 Other
1 Auto driver-WHICH FAMILY MEMBER DROVE?	1 Auto driver-WHICH FAMILY MEMBER DROVE?	1 Auto driver-WHICH FAMILY MEMBER DROVE?
1 Auto passenger 2 Suburban Railroad 3 Bus 4 Rapid Transit 5 Walk to work 6 Taxi 7 Other	1 Auto passenger 2 Suburban Railroad 3 Bus 4 Rapid Transit 5 Walk to work 6 Taxi 7 Other	1 Auto passenger 2 Suburban Railroad 3 Bus 4 Rapid Transit 5 Walk to work 6 Taxi 7 Other

INTERVIEWER: REPEAT QUESTIONS 46-51 FOR EACH TRIP.   INCLUDE TRIPS BY ANY
FAMILY MEMBER AGED 5 AND OVER.

WHO IS THIS TRIP FOR? ENTER EACH PERSON BY RELATIONSHIP TO HEAD →	Family Member(s) Who Went:	Family Member(s) Who Went:
48. Where did (you) begin (your) (next) trip?	1 Work (Priority) 2 Home 3 Friend's or Relative's Home 4 Store, Restaurant, Bank 5 Doctor's Office, Hospital 6 School 7 Other	1 Work (Priority) 2 Home 3 Friend's or Relative's Home 4 Store, Restaurant, Bank 5 Doctor's Office, Hospital 6 School 7 Other
49. What was the purpose of this trip? (CHECK TWO BOXES IF NECESSARY)	1 Go home 2 Get to work } (GO TO Q. 51) 3 Shopping 4 Attend school 5 Social or recreational 6 To take someone somewhere (serve a passenger)-(CHECK ALSO THE PURPOSE OF HIS TRIP) 7 To change mode of travel 8 Personal business, medical, dental 9 Eat meal 0 Other	1 Go home 2 Get to work } (GO TO Q. 51) 3 Shopping 4 Attend school 5 Social or recreational 6 To take someone somewhere (serve a passenger)-(CHECK ALSO THE PURPOSE OF HIS TRIP) 7 To change mode of travel 8 Personal business, medical, dental 9 Eat meal 0 Other
50. Where did (you) go?	1 Home 2 School 3 Friend's or Relative's Home 4 Store, Bank, Restaurant 5 Doctor's Office, Hospital 6 Other	1 Home 2 School 3 Friend's or Relative's Home 4 Store, Bank, Restaurant 5 Doctor's Office, Hospital 6 Other
51. How did (you) travel? (IF BY CAR): Did (you) drive? (CHECK TWO BOXES IF ONE FAMILY MEMBER DROVE ANOTHER)	1 Auto driver-WHICH FAMILY MEMBER DROVE? _____ 1 Auto passenger 2 Suburban Railroad 3 Bus 4 Rapid Transit 5 Walk to work 6 Taxi 7 Other	1 Auto driver-WHICH FAMILY MEMBER DROVE? _____ 1 Auto passenger 2 Suburban Railroad 3 Bus 4 Rapid Transit 5 Walk to work 6 Taxi 7 Other

INTERVIEWER: REPEAT QUESTIONS 46-51 FOR EACH TRIP. INCLUDE TRIPS BY ANY FAMILY MEMBER AGED 5 AND OVER. LIST THE FAMILY MEMBERS AGED 5 AND OVER BELOW. (SEE Q. 1)

1. _____   4. _____   7. _____

2. _____   5. _____   8. _____

3. _____   6. _____   9. _____

168

Family Member(s) Who Went:	Family Member(s) Who Went:	Family Member(s) Who Went:
[1] Work (Priority) [2] Home [3] Friend's or Relative's Home [4] Store, Restaurant, Bank [5] Doctor's Office, Hospital [6] School [7] Other	[1] Work (Priority) [2] Home [3] Friend's or Relative's Home [4] Store, Restaurant, Bank [5] Doctor's Office, Hospital [6] School [7] Other	[1] Work (Priority) [2] Home [3] Friend's or Relative's Home [4] Store, Restaurant, Bank [5] Doctor's Office, Hospital [6] School [7] Other
[1] Go home [2] Get to work } (GO TO Q. 51) [3] Shopping [4] Attend school [5] Social or recreational [6] To take someone somewhere (serve a passenger)-(CHECK ALSO THE PURPOSE OF HIS TRIP) [7] To change mode of travel [8] Personal business, medical, dental [9] Eat meal [0] Other	[1] Go home [2] Get to work } (GO TO Q. 51) [3] Shopping [4] Attend school [5] Social or recreational [6] To take someone somewhere (serve a passenger)-(CHECK ALSO THE PURPOSE OF HIS TRIP) [7] To change mode of travel [8] Personal business, medical, dental [9] Eat meal [0] Other	[1] Go home [2] Get to work } (GO TO Q. 51) [3] Shopping [4] Attend school [5] Social or recreational [6] To take someone somewhere (serve a passenger)-(CHECK ALSO THE PURPOSE OF HIS TRIP) [7] To change mode of travel [8] Personal business, medical, dental [9] Eat meal [0] Other
[1] Home [2] School [3] Friend's or Relative's Home [4] Store, Bank, Restaurant [5] Doctor's Office, Hospital [6] Other	[1] Home [2] School [3] Friend's or Relative's Home [4] Store, Bank, Restaurant [5] Doctor's Office, Hospital [6] Other	[1] Home [2] School [3] Friend's or Relative's Home [4] Store, Bank, Restaurant [5] Doctor's Office, Hospital [6] Other
[1] Auto driver-WHICH FAMILY MEMBER DROVE?	[1] Auto driver-WHICH FAMILY MEMBER DROVE?	[1] Auto driver-WHICH FAMILY MEMBER DROVE?
[1] Auto passenger [2] Suburban Railroad [3] Bus [4] Rapid Transit [5] Walk to work [6] Taxi [7] Other	[1] Auto passenger [2] Suburban Railroad [3] Bus [4] Rapid Transit [5] Walk to work [6] Taxi [7] Other	[1] Auto passenger [2] Suburban Railroad [3] Bus [4] Rapid Transit [5] Walk to work [6] Taxi [7] Other

INTERVIEWER: REPEAT QUESTIONS 46-51 FOR EACH TRIP. INCLUDE TRIPS BY ANY FAMILY MEMBER AGED 5 AND OVER.

52. Does that include all the trips made anytime yesterday by anybody in the family?

  ☐1 YES → GO TO Q. 53

  ☐5 NO → ADD THESE TRIPS ON THE TRIP RECORD FORM

53. Do you own this home, pay rent, or what?

  ☐1 OWNS OR   ☐2 RENTS   ☐3 NEITHER OWNS NOR RENTS
      IS BUYING

  ┌───┐
  │ 53b. How is that?_____   │
  │   _____│
  │   GO TO Q. 56   │
  └───┘

  ┌───┐
  │ 53a. (HAND R CARD E-1) Could you tell me the letter of the group │
  │   on this card that would indicate about how much rent you pay │
  │   a month, not including utilities?   │
  │   │
  │   A. ☐1 Under $100   E. ☐5 $250-$299   │
  │   B. ☐2 $100-$149   F. ☐6 $300-$349   │
  │   C. ☐3 $150-$199   G. ☐7 $350-$399   │
  │   D. ☐4 $200-$249   H. ☐8 $400 and over   GO TO Q. 56 │
  └───┘

┌───┐
│ 54. (HAND R CARD E-2) Could you tell me the letter of the group on this card that │
│   would indicate about what the present value of this home is? What would it bring │
│   if you sold it today?   │
│   A. ☐1 Under $20,000   F. ☐6 $44,000-$49,999   │
│   B. ☐2 $20,000-$25,999   G. ☐7 $50,000-$61,999   │
│   C. ☐3 $26,000-$31,999   H. ☐8 $62,000-$73,999   │
│   D. ☐4 $32,000-$37,999   I. ☐9 $74,000 and over   │
│   E. ☐5 $38,000-$43,999   │
│   │
│ 55. Compared to other homes you considered at the time you were buying do you think │
│   that this home will be a better financial investment, a worse investment, or │
│   about the same?   │
│   ☐1 BETTER   ☐2 SAME   ☐3 WORSE   │
│   │
│   55a. Why do you feel that way?_____ │
│   │
│   _____ │
│   │
│   _____ │
└───┘

56. As far as you're concerned, do you think it's a good idea for neighborhoods -- and here again I'm thinking of clusters of five or six homes -- to have people of different religious backgrounds or the same religious backgrounds, or doesn't it matter?

    [1] Good if different   [2] Doesn't matter   [3] Good if the same

57. And as far as you're concerned, do you think it's a good idea for neighborhoods to have people of different racial backgrounds or the same racial background or doesn't it matter?

    [1] Good if different   [2] Doesn't matter   [3] Good if same

58. What is (HEAD'S) (your) main job at the present time? What kind of work (does HEAD) (do you) do? (IF RETIRED OR UNEMPLOYED, GET LAST MAIN JOB. PROBE CAREFULLY FOR SPECIFIC JOB. E.G., BANK TELLER, VICE-PRESIDENT IN CHARGE OF RESEARCH AND DEVELOPMENT, ETC.)

    HEAD IS: (CHECK)

    [1] EMPLOYED   [2] UNEMPLOYED   [3] RETIRED;DISABLED   [4] HOUSEWIFE → GO TO
                                                                                Q.65

    | JOB DESCRIPTION FOR HEAD: _____ |
    | |
    | |
    | |

59. What kind of business is (was) that in? (MAIN JOB) _____

    _____

60. Does (HEAD) work for himself or someone else?

    [1] SELF-EMPLOYED   [5] SOMEONE ELSE

5 HEAD IS <u>NOT</u> NOW WORKING ➤ GO TO Q. 65

1 HEAD IS NOW WORKING

61. What are the names of the two streets at the intersection nearest (HEAD'S) place of work?

a. _____

b. _____

☐ HEAD DOES NOT HAVE ONE REGULAR PLACE OF WORK ➤ GO TO Q. 65

62. (Just a few minutes ago you told me how (HEAD) got to work yesterday. Now I'd like you to tell me if this is how (HEAD) usually makes the trip to work.)

Does (HEAD) always go by car, sometimes by car and sometimes by public transportation, always by public transportation, or some other way?

1 Always car

2 Sometimes car, sometimes public

3 Always public ➤ GO TO Q. 64

7 Other:_____

_____
(GO TO Q. 64)

63. When (HEAD) does go by car, does (HEAD) usually drive to work alone or do other people ride in the same car with (HEAD)?

☐ Shares trip   1 Goes alone ➤ GO TO Q.64

63a. (IF SHARES:) How many people other than (HEAD) ride in the same car?

2 One other   3 Two others   4 Three or more others

64. What time does (HEAD) usually leave home to go to work?   _____

64a. And what time does (HEAD) usually get to work?   _____

64b. Then it takes about   _____ minutes, is that right?

INTERVIEWER: CALCULATE NUMBER OF MINUTES, CHECK WITH R, RECORD ANY CORRECTIONS IN MARGIN AT RIGHT.

172

5 HEAD HAS NO WIFE LIVING AT HOME → GO TO Q. 66

I WIFE LIVING AT HOME

65. Is (WIFE) doing any work for pay at this time (too)?

    I YES   5 NO → GO TO Q. 66

    65a. On the average about how many hours a week does (WIFE) work?

        I Less than 10   2 10-19   3 20-29   4 30-39   5 40 or more

66. Please tell me the letter of the group on this card (HAND R CARD F) that would indicate about what the total income for you and your family was last year -- 1968 -- before taxes, that is.

    A. ☐ Under $5000   F. ☐ $17,500-$19,999

    B. ☐ $5000-$9999   G. ☐ $20,000-$24,999

    C. ☐ $10,000-$12,499   H. ☐ $25,000-$29,999

    D. ☐ $12,500-$14,999   I. ☐ $30,000 and over

    E. ☐ $15,000-$17,499

    66a. Does that include the income of everyone in the family?

        I YES   5 NO -- ASK FOR "EVERYONE'S" INCOME, MAKE CORRECTION ABOVE.

67. What was (HEAD'S) father's usual occupation while (HEAD) was in grade school?

    _____

    67a. What kind of business was that in?_____

    _____

    67b. Was he self-employed? *I* YES   5 NO

68. How many years of school or college did you complete?

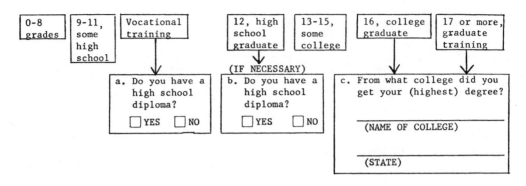

69. (IF MARRIED) How many years of school or college did your (SPOUSE) complete?

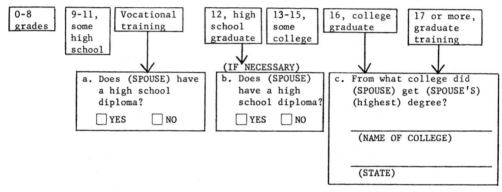

BY OBSERVATION:

70. RACE: 1 WHITE   2 BLACK   3 OTHER:_____

71. Is there a sidewalk along the street in front of this home?

   1 SIDEWALK EXISTS ALONG THE STREET

   5 NO SIDEWALK

   ☐ HARD TO TELL - EXPLAIN:_____

   _____

174

```
┌─────────────────────────────────┐
│                                 │
│   INTERVIEWER'S LABEL           │
│                                 │
│                                 │
└─────────────────────────────────┘
```

Your Int. No. _____

Please indicate for each of the following sentences whether you agree or disagree
with it and how much. Do this by placing an (X) over the appropriate alternative
under the sentence.

1. When I go outside and look around me at the street and the neighbors' homes
    I like what I see.

1. AGREE STRONGLY	2. AGREE SOMEWHAT	3. DISAGREE SOMEWHAT	4. DISAGREE STRONGLY

2. A modern style of architecture is more attractive for a new home than a
    colonial style.

1. AGREE STRONGLY	2. AGREE SOMEWHAT	3. DISAGREE SOMEWHAT	4. DISAGREE STRONGLY

3. Whenever an opportunity arises I like to try doing things in new ways.

1. AGREE STRONGLY	2. AGREE SOMEWHAT	3. DISAGREE SOMEWHAT	4. DISAGREE STRONGLY

4. The raising of one's social position is one of the more important goals
    in life.

1. AGREE STRONGLY	2. AGREE SOMEWHAT	3. DISAGREE SOMEWHAT	4. DISAGREE STRONGLY

5. I would enjoy living for a year or two in a foreign country.

1. AGREE STRONGLY	2. AGREE SOMEWHAT	3. DISAGREE SOMEWHAT	4. DISAGREE STRONGLY

6. Most people in this community really care what happens to it.

1. AGREE STRONGLY	2. AGREE SOMEWHAT	3. DISAGREE SOMEWHAT	4. DISAGREE STRONGLY

7. We need a lot more freeways in and around our big cities.

1. AGREE STRONGLY	2. AGREE SOMEWHAT	3. DISAGREE SOMEWHAT	4. DISAGREE STRONGLY

8. I don't like to belong to clubs that get new members all the time.

1. AGREE STRONGLY	2. AGREE SOMEWHAT	3. DISAGREE SOMEWHAT	4. DISAGREE STRONGLY

9. As a rule you can tell quite a bit about a person by the way he dresses.

| 1. AGREE STRONGLY | 2. AGREE SOMEWHAT | 3. DISAGREE SOMEWHAT | 4. DISAGREE STRONGLY |

10. I have as many friends as I want.

| 1. AGREE STRONGLY | 2. AGREE SOMEWHAT | 3. DISAGREE SOMEWHAT | 4. DISAGREE STRONGLY |

11. I enjoy working on a project with people I don't know.

| 1. AGREE STRONGLY | 2. AGREE SOMEWHAT | 3. DISAGREE SOMEWHAT | 4. DISAGREE STRONGLY |

12. It is worth considerable effort to assure one's self of a good name with important people.

| 1. AGREE STRONGLY | 2. AGREE SOMEWHAT | 3. DISAGREE SOMEWHAT | 4. DISAGREE STRONGLY |

13. Most people around here would like to spend more time with their neighbors.

| 1. AGREE STRONGLY | 2. AGREE SOMEWHAT | 3. DISAGREE SOMEWHAT | 4. DISAGREE STRONGLY |

14. In general, how satisfying do you find the way you're spending your life these days? Would you call it completely satisfying, pretty satisfying, not very satisfying, or not at all satisfying?

| 1. COMPLETELY SATISFYING | 2. PRETTY SATISFYING | 3. NOT VERY SATISFYING | 4. NOT AT ALL SATISFYING |

15. Here are some words and phrases which we would like you to use to describe this <u>neighborhood</u> as it seems to you. By neighborhood we mean just what you can see from your front door, that is, the five or six homes nearest to yours around here. For example, if you think the neighborhood is "noisy," please put a check right next to the word "noisy." If you think it is "quiet," please put a check right next to the word "quiet," and if you think it is somewhere in between, please put a check where you think it belongs.

Noisy	: ___	: ___	: ___	: ___	: ___	: Quiet
Attractive	: ___	: ___	: ___	: ___	: ___	: Unattractive
Unfriendly people	: ___	: ___	: ___	: ___	: ___	: Friendly people
Poorly kept up	: ___	: ___	: ___	: ___	: ___	: Well kept up
People similar to me	: ___	: ___	: ___	: ___	: ___	: People dissimilar to me
Pleasant	: ___	: ___	: ___	: ___	: ___	: Unpleasant
Very poor place to live	: ___	: ___	: ___	: ___	: ___	: Very good place to live

```
CARD 1

AGES OF ADULTS

        A.   18-24

        B.   25-34

        C.   35-44

        D.   45-54

        E.   55-64

        F.   65-74

        G.   75 OR OVER


P. 45789, Q. 1
```

```
CARD A

A.   EVERY DAY

B.   SEVERAL TIMES A WEEK

C.   ONCE A WEEK

D.   2-3 TIMES A MONTH

E.   ONCE A MONTH

F.   A FEW TIMES A YEAR; RARELY

G.   NEVER


P. 45789, Q. 19
```

```
CARD B

CLUBS AND ORGANIZATIONS

a.  Church or synagogue              j.  Sport team
b.  Church-connected group (but not  k.  Country club
    the church itself)               l.  Youth group (Girl Scout Leader,
c.  Hobby club                           Little League Manager, etc.)
d.  College alumni (alumnae)         m.  Professional group
    association                      n.  Local political club or
e.  Fraternal lodge or organization      organization
f.  Business or civic group          o.  State or national political
g.  Parent-teachers association          club or organization
h.  Community center                 p.  Neighborhood improvement
i.  Regular card playing group           association
                                     q.  Charity or welfare organization


        Are there others that are not on this list?
```

CARD C
OUTDOOR ACTIVITIES

a. Outdoor swimming at a pool
b. Tennis
c. Hiking or walking
d. Picnicking
e. Golfing
f. Boating
g. Bicycling

P. 45789, Q. 29

CARD D
PLACES PEOPLE WALK TO FROM HOME

a. Picnic area
b. Grocery store
c. Other stores
d. Friend's house

P. 45789, Q. 33

CARD E-1
MONTHLY RENT

A. ☐ Under $100
B. ☐ $100-$149
C. ☐ $150-$199
D. ☐ $200-$249
E. ☐ $250-$299
F. ☐ $300-$349
G. ☐ $350-$399
H. ☐ $400 and over

P. 45789, Q. 53a

CARD E-2
PRESENT HOME VALUE

A. ☐ Under $20,000
B. ☐ $20,000-$25,999
C. ☐ $26,000-$31,999
D. ☐ $32,000-$37,999
E. ☐ $38,000-$43,999
F. ☐ $44,000-$49,999
G. ☐ $50,000-$61,999
H. ☐ $62,000-$73,999
I. ☐ $74,000 and over

P. 45789, Q 53a

CARD F

A. Under $5,000
B. $5,000-$9,999
C. $10,000-$12,499
D. $12,500-$14,999
E. $15,000-$17,499
F. $17,500-$19,999
G. $20,000-$24,999
H. $25,000-$29,999
I. $30,000 and over

P. 45789, Q. 66

The Time Budget

William Michelson and Paul Reed

William Michelson is Professor of Sociology and Associate Director of the Centre for Urban and Community Studies at the University of Toronto. He is the author of Man and His Urban Environment: A Sociological Approach (Reading, Mass.: Addison-Wesley, 1970). His recent research has been concerned with the social implications and consequences of the built environment. He has also contributed to the planning of several new communities and to design work within existing cities.

Paul Reed is currently conducting social statistics research in the Canadian government. He is completing doctoral work at the University of Toronto through an exploration of the concept "life style" and its applications to mobility and design.

As professionals, most of us should have a well-developed sense of curiosity when it comes to the behavior of people. In this paper we outline one effective and old but under-used technique for satisfying that curiosity—the time budget. This research technique provides information in unequaled detail about nearly everything people do in the course of their everyday life.

Fortunately or otherwise, the time budget produces a great amount of rather *dry* but highly detailed information that people offer freely. Far from *mis*using time-budget data, most researchers have had to face the problem of just how to cope with its richness. With the increasing sophistication of researchers, however, this is less and less of a problem, and today some of the most fruitful applications for this kind of data are in the area of design, at both micro and macro levels of environment.

Although it might be pedagogically advisable to start by enumerating how the time budget is useful for design purposes, such a discussion requires prior information on what, in fact, the label "time budget" means. Hence we shall begin with a description of the time budget and its alternative forms. Then we shall turn our attention to its design application, as well as to other applications of potential interest. After this, we shall briefly explore its history and development, expand on the technical aspects of its use, and discuss some major pitfalls to avoid in the process. We conclude with an example from our own work, together with a bibliography on time-budget usage intended both to support our assertions and to assist the reader who wishes to probe the field further.

WHAT IS A TIME BUDGET?

A time budget is very simply a record of what a person has done during a specified period of time—usually a 24-hour day or a multiple thereof. This record is detailed; it lists in chronological order a person's activities during the period and states either when each activity began and terminated or simply the amount of time spent on each activity.

The function of a time budget is to show how an individual's time is "consumed" or utilized. This information has a number of components and correlates:

1. The total *amount* of time allocated to specified activities, with variations by the time of day, day of the week, or season.
2. The *frequency* with which activities and types of activities are engaged in.
3. *Patterns* or *clusters* of "typical" activities.

Depending on the purpose of the study, additional information may be requested, such as if any other persons were present and active in the situation, and the location (and/or site characteristics).

Such data have two main applications in general. First, time allocation constitutes choice-making behavior; it thus provides a basis for inferring attitudes, values, and value hierarchies of individuals and populations. This is premised on the assumption that preferred or valued activities will be engaged in more frequently or with greater duration (especially during discretionary or "free" time)—an assumption whose validity is situation specific, but applicable in enough areas to justify use. Second, activity choosing and time allocating provide information about the use of and, less directly, demand for facilities and services, particularly in the areas of transportation, land-use planning, and recreation.

METHODS

Time budgets are typically generated in one of two ways: by means of a self-completed diary or by means of an interview schedule. The format of both could be identical; their difference lies in *when* and *where* they are completed. Each has distinct advantages and disadvantages.

With the diary method, each respondent is given a form as physically compact and portable as possible on which to record the day's activities and the time when each was begun and ended. The respondent may be instructed to record this information either with every change in activity or at natural break-points in the day, such as coffee and meal breaks and immediately before retiring.

The claimed advantages of this mode of data acquisition are that (1) the short time span between activities and recording them results in higher accuracy and reliability, and (2) it is the *only* way to acquire *accurate* time-use data for periods of time longer than one full day.

The disadvantage of this method is that "keeping a diary" while engaging in activities can affect what and how activities are carried out. Respondents are also less likely to complete the task than when in an interview context.

With the interview schedule, the respondent is asked to provide details about activities, with times, places, and coparticipants, for the preceding day. The problem of detailed, accurate recall is the liability of questionnaire-generated time budgets; the noninterference in ongoing activity is a relative asset.

Formats

Whether for use in diary or in an interview schedule, there are two general types of time-budget format—precoded and open-ended. The precoded format has a set of alternative answers from which the respondent must choose his replies. This format limits the range or variety of answers and makes the task somewhat easier for the respondent; however, the alternative answers must be simple, relevant, inclusive of nearly all possibilities, and clearly different from one another; this may both oversimplify and prejudge the results. An open-ended format allows full freedom for response and is almost always used in interviews, as the interviewer can in any case monitor the answers to ensure that they are on target.

Figure 1 shows a partially precoded time diary (self-administered). Table 1 shows the first of the many pages needed in a thorough time-budget interview schedule that is open-ended.

The format in Table 1 is sometimes used without specifying time points (6:00 A.M., 6:15, 6:30, etc.), allowing (theoretically, at least) the respondent to fill in his own recollection of the exact time of beginning and ending each activity, as in Figure 1. This usually fosters a false sense of precision. By displaying specific time points 10 to 15 minutes apart, recall of activities is assisted; that is, respondents may be able to recall activities better when they think first about the time at which they took place.

Additionally, the format in Table 1 avoids the redundancy of asking both when each activity was begun and when completed, since the time when any activity begins almost always implies termination of the previous activity.

Since no evaluative research has been done on the various formats, choosing between them now depends more on the ultimate purpose to which the data will be put. More detailed discussion on this, as well as on the diary–interview dilemma, will follow later in the paper. One thing is certain, however; regardless of format type, time-use questionnaires and diaries are more accurate than simple questions that ask for "summed time" (e.g., "How much time do you spend traveling to and from work each day?"). And they may probe other dimensions of human activity than time use.

The Time Budget in Design Research

In the introduction to this volume we deal at some length with the place of behavior in design research. The time budget deals with a wide range of behaviors or activities. Whichever word is applied, the crucial focus is primarily on what people *do,* and secondarily, if at all, on what they *think*. As the previous section should indicate, the time budget, whether done by interview or self-completed diary, is always a report to the time-budget investigator and not something that he witnesses.

When contemplating design, those creating a relatively small scale, single-use space (e.g., residential dwellings) may be inclined to wonder whether the time budget provides information that is overly elaborate and indirect. Why not just observe directly what people do in a particular place or, better yet, join in and do it yourself? In Chapter 7, Aas indicates that under some circumstances this approach is very well taken and

Please complete this activity record for your activities during waking hours on

_____   _____   _____   _____
(day of week)   (month)   (day)   (year)

NOTE: Any time spent working at your job (or jobs) should simply be recorded as "At work".
However, please rember to include any lunch or coffee breaks.

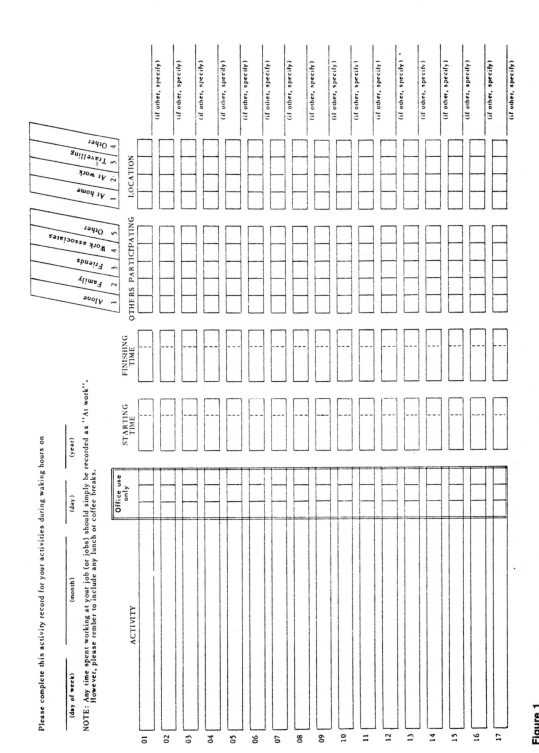

Figure 1
Time diary. (Courtesy of the Department of Secretary of State, Ottawa.)

183

that there are systematic procedures to follow for optimum results.

Nonetheless, for many design purposes, particularly as they merge at the macroscopic level, first-hand observation becomes impractical. Although direct observation may be sufficient to record the interplay of different persons in a given place, it is not particularly helpful in understanding the *pattern* of movement of a person from one place to another, let alone the habits of large numbers of persons over a large number of places. When considering institutional complexes, neighborhoods, and metropolitan or even larger designs, one must understand the impact on individuals and particular groups of the juxtaposition of spaces and land uses. It is helpful for this type of problem to have information on what many people do, how long and in what sequence they do it, where this takes place, and what other people are involved in the process. Observation may handle well questions dealing with the microscopic environment, but it fails to provide sufficiently detailed information for higher levels of complexity; on the contrary, the time budget is an extremely parsimonious

and efficient instrument for tackling questions of design at the macroscopic level.

Furthermore, design must accommodate not just those isolated or sensational forms of behavior that might prove especially interesting to a designer or to an aroused public, but rather common, ordinary, everyday activities. Many of the social sciences were intensely interested at the time of their inception with the gravest social and psychological problems. Urban sociology, for example, was concerned with the crime and personal "disorganization" seen as accompanying the large-scale growth of cities in the early part of this century. For years, one sociologist after another studied the various forms of deviance abounding in urban areas, placing much less stress in the process on the normal metabolism of the very same places. Some people studied crime, others juvenile delinquency, mental illness, or unusual sexual practices.

Single-minded fads are no stranger to the design professions either. Where is the design product which even attempts to embrace the full spectrum of behaviors that occur within it? There

Table 1
Time-Budget Interview

Now I'd like to get some idea of what an average day for you might include. Let's take yesterday. (Last weekday) *Use respondent's own words as much as possible.*

    At what time did you get up? (*circle time*)

    Then what did you do? How long did it take you?

    Was anyone else with you?

    Where did you do it?

    Were you doing anything else at the same time?

Begin by asking the respondent the time he (she) got up that morning and what he did first. Ask how long this activity took and then record it on the sheet at the appropriate times. Ask whether or not anyone was with the person when he did it; determine whether the presence of the other individual (s) was incidental or whether he was asked to accompany the respondent such that it was really an interaction process. Ask where the activity took place and whether or not the respondent was doing anything else at the time. If a person goes to a store or somewhere, be sure to check the time to store, shopping and home again. Finally, ask the respondent what he did next and then repeat the above line of questioning. *Do not attempt to record what was being done at each time given on the sheet*; rather, use the sheet simply as a method of calendaring the day's activities.

The minimum time span to be considered for an activity is 15 minutes. Record start and stop time to the nearest quarter-hour. Do not record for any activity that is less than a quarter-hour.

Time spent traveling to *or* from an activity *is a separate activity and should not be included with that activity.*

are very many practices, from "ville radieuse" to "neighborhood unit plan," to new town, to modern high rise, let alone hospitals, airports, and downtown renewal, that have been plagued by the faddish insistence on building to achieve certain utopian goals or to eradicate evils which usually have a larger social than physical basis; not surprisingly, life goes on much as always among inhabitants, in reality providing the basis for the success or failure of these projects.

The time budget is one of the few instruments explicitly concerned not with just a single aspect of life but with the various basic component parts of daily life. For this reason, its relevance to the design process, which must accommodate this very same complex, is paramount. This is particularly true since the time budget handles not only daily behavior in *given* places but across the entire spectrum of locations where daily behavior can be found.

Although the design profession covers a large range from the subjective and inexact to the hard-nosed and exact, it quite properly prefers to base its decisions on information as exact as possible. Over the last number of years, considerable credence has been given to the results of

Time	What did you do? How long did it take you?	Was anyone else with you?	Where did you do it?	Were you doing anything else at the same time?	Typical activity
6:00 A.M.					
6:15 A.M.					
6:30 A.M.					
6:45 A.M.					
7:00 A.M.					
7:15 A.M.					
7:30 A.M.					
7:45 A.M.					
8:00 A.M.					
8:15 A.M.					
8:30 A.M.					
8:45 A.M.					

economic analyses, however incredible the assumptions on which they were based, because results were expressed in terms of exact figures. While we do not at all advise the abandonment of more subjective information, particularly representing people's feelings, strivings, and frustrations, because it might be inexact, we do find that one advantage of the time budget is that it produces information which is quantitative and analyzable. For example, the extent of the difference between two groups of people who live under different physical conditions can be expressed in terms of numbers that have a definite magnitude and clear-cut meaning, and which are subject to many forms of computation. This does not necessarily mean that such answers are readily transferable into design; it does mean, however, that the answers do not rely on idiosyncratic interpretation or sympathetic understanding on the part of the user.

These properties, then, make the time budget ideal as a technique to monitor what happens in given physical settings, with particular emphasis on complex settings not open to assessment as easily by other methods. As the previous paragraph suggests, one form of monitoring is to assess whether a particular product or design innovation induces an expected or desired set of daily behaviors that do not appear in its absence. This type of monitoring, therefore, pertains to variations between places.

A second form of monitoring, instead of or in addition to the first, is from time to time. It traces "before" and "after" patterns vis-à-vis the introduction of a new design stimulus; this often happens, for example, when industries or offices change premises to a supposedly improved site or interior space. It happens when poor or ill people move to supposedly therapeutic surroundings. And it happens when ordinary people make ordinary moves to ordinary new housing. Monitoring over time can also be more than a before and after, yes or no proposition. When applied at regular intervals during a given design process, monitoring can detail the adjustment pattern encountered, which may be of considerable interest and indeed importance when separating short-term versus long-term reactions and efficiencies.

As the introduction suggests, social techniques, particularly those having to do with behavior, are of relevance at various stages in the design process. For example, time-budget studies performed elsewhere in situations analogous to those for which a design may be currently concerned may have an effect on design decisions; designers are frequently in a hurry, and new research may be dysfunctional to the total effort, particularly if appropriate findings have been made available from the work of others. However, when one is designing for a client with known and fruitful patterns of behavior and activity to be accommodated exactly in a new setting, it is not at all dysfunctional to perform specific studies pinpointing what must be accommodated by the design.

Another point in the process of design where time budgets are relevant, which was suggested by the earlier discussion on the monitoring process of the time-budget metric, is the area of project evaluation. Sometimes it is very difficult to know, even in the rare instance when a designer conscientiously tries to find out, whether his decisions have been correct and for what reasons. If a series of decisions has been made on the basis of behavioral considerations, the evaluation as to whether or not the expected has occurred can sometimes be done by use of the time budget. This can take the form of place-to-place or time-to-time monitoring, or indeed combinations of the two. The point, however, is that in at least one area of concern the time budget may take the place of ambiguously worded protests, maintenance-cost figures, mobility rates (which may actually reflect something totally different), or other very indirect and often obscure measures of the success or failure of a design project.

The time budget is relevant to various *levels* of design decision. On a very micro level, for example, the home or office, a detailed record of who does what for how long, in what sequence, and with whom is very helpful in arranging internal space for optimal flow and function. At this level much of the same information, though, can be provided by systematic observation, particularly of the kind discussed in Chapter 6, but the time budget can nonetheless be utilized, especially if a quantitative record is desirable.

This work becomes considerably more meaningful if the usual time-budget questions are supplemented by others that ask how satisfactorily the existing spaces facilitate the intended activities, or how happy the individual is with the duration or some other aspect of the activity itself. Although the usual time budget does not include such evaluative queries, appending these other questions permits documentation of group attitudes toward spatial arrangements, as well as toward such concepts as privacy, and can contribute information on user needs within the constraints of an existing situation.

At a somewhat more macro level, time budgets are useful in the design of land-use mixtures and facilities within neighborhoods. They can be used to provide information about the actual use of facilities compared to one another, to document the time that people spend in and out of their homes, to illustrate what recreational activities are participated in by what combinations of persons, and a whole host of other questions. At this level the time budget enables some merger of the considerations of both physical and social planners. In Chapter 1, Lindberg and Hellberg gave illustrations of some types of information with which one can learn about neighborhoods and their function, even though their work was not linked to any on-line planning activities.

And at a still more macro level, time budgets may be used as an input to planning that is concerned with the overall form of cities and metropolitan areas. F. Stuart Chapin, Jr., and his colleagues at Chapel Hill, for example, have done considerable work on the relationship of land uses to one another in terms of people's proclivities to visit them in particular orders and combinations. This stochastic linkage of land-use-specific activities is quite relevant here as people are not inclined to rationally make all their stops in a logical order; instead, their own home has been shown to be a major part of most trips, which indicates the relevance of facility location to residential location and the importance of what *consumers* view as convenience, as compared to, for example, downtown businessmen or wholesalers.

At the same level, one can use the time budget to compare the uses of different social milieux within a metropolitan area, indicating the possibility that different sections of town may have different physical requirements, designs, and land-use mixtures. But even at the most macroscopic level, there is no necessity that all cities have the same form or the same combinations of interior neighborhood forms, and hence the documentation of the ways in which the behavior of residents in one metropolitan area differ from residents in others is an important input to overall conceptual planning.

Physical planning, of course, is not just a matter of levels and designs. Among the many other relevant components is management. The kind of information produced by time budgets is of considerable relevance to management practices as well. One illustration may make this clear. A group of Swedish researchers proposed a large-scale time-budget study for the Stockholm area for the purpose of readjusting the opening and closing hours of the public facilities and services. (Swedener et al., 1967). When one considers the proportion of the day people devote to their work and to sleeping, along with the necessity for them to perform other self-maintenance, recreational and civic activities, the logic of the optimal time of day for certain establishments to be open and available certainly lies somewhere between the extremes of complete simultaneity and complete randomness. Time-budget information is one way of documenting the logic that underlies sensible management practice.

In sum, we have attempted to indicate some of the ways in which the time budget can be used to further the aims of the design profession. The time budget, however, was not originated for the purpose of aiding in the creation of design. Since it is a relatively basic research tool, its potential is free to be applied in many other directions, some of which deserve mention, inasmuch as what is relevant to design (particularly on a preplanning basis) does not necessarily have to have an overt spatial dimension.

Although time budgets have been put to many uses outside the design field (e.g., to assess the age at which children acquire independence; the social impact of commuting patterns; the effect of full-time employment in the lives of women), we shall discuss only one in detail; how changing patterns in the use of time are indicative of broader and deeper changes in the nature of society. As pointed out by Robinson and Converse (1972), time budgets used in this context serve not only a generally informative purpose, but also have very practical, concrete *policy* applications. For some time now in a number of socialist countries, time budgets have been collected frequently and on a large scale for use in national economic and social planning. Robinson and Converse cite a major finding from a USSR study done first in 1924 and replicated in 1959: Soviet urban workers, in spite of substantial reductions in the amount of time spent at work, had gained little or no more discretionary or leisure time. The reason was that the time gained from work was lost to longer commuting, shopping, and line-up waiting time. This pointed up how gains in the production system were being offset by flaws in the distribution and service sectors of Soviet society and the need for remedial action.

This pattern is not peculiar to the USSR; it holds true in most industrialized, urbanized societies (see de Grazia, 1962). Robinson and Converse report also that, on the basis of massive time-budget studies (consisting of over 100 billion annual man-hours) of "primitive housework" in the USSR, it has been estimated that a significant fraction of this time could be "saved" or allocated to other activities with the use of labor-saving devices.

With specific reference to the United States, Robinson and Converse report findings from a number of studies conducted over a 30-year period. Most visible is the drastic change in leisure activities with the advent of television; while reading, socializing, and radio listening have been displaced, there has been a substantial increase in the amount of time devoted to the mass media (as high as 41 percent more, one study shows). (Neither the change itself, nor its magnitude, are universally the same; they vary with major socioeconomic characteristics of individuals and groups.)

The work week has declined for virtually all types of paid workers (e.g., from 45.5 to 38.0 hours, for production workers); similarly, the time spent by women on housework has declined. Changes in travel time are interesting: whereas there has been a slight decrease in time spent traveling to and from work, the time going to and from school, as well as that spent in going to and from shopping and other personal business, has nearly doubled—undoubtedly partially a consequence of the large and rising number of multiple-car families.

These changes and others visible only with more complex analysis are the effects of technology and innovation (television, public transit systems), affluence and economic growth (more cars, highways, leisure facilities), and other fundamental structural changes in various sectors of U.S. society (family structure, patterns of urbanization, and modes of education, to name several), as well as explicit government policy (e.g., transportation policies and the introduction of Medicare).

HOW DO YOU USE A TIME BUDGET?

An initial practical question of use focuses on whether the time budget should be administered as part of an interview (i.e., *orally*) or as a time diary. The method selected is largely a function of the time period that you wish to cover, as well as the return that you expect to get. At least one study has shown that when you are concerned only about the activities of the immediately preceding day, it does not matter whether one uses interview or diary approaches. However, if you wish to gather information on more than a single day, the diary is far superior. The usual practice is to leave a diary with a respondent, outline the period for which the diary should be completed by the respondent, and then arrange a time for study personnel to pick up the completed time diary; on the last occasion, he or she looks through the time diary and tries to obtain any pieces of information apparently missing.

The use of an interviewer to pick up a self-administered questionnaire doubtless adds to what would otherwise be a relatively low cost compared with the use of a questionnaire alone. However, the time budget is a sufficiently detailed instrument that a personal visit is often required to explain sufficiently how the time budget should be filled out, as well as to provide some *incentive* for the person to actually do it. It is very easy for a respondent to throw out a questionnaire that looks the least bit complicated or threatening. Similarly, the call-back after completion prompts the respondent to realize that someone does have expectations of his or her performance, and it similarly allows the interviewer to have the opportunity of checking the completeness and quality of the finished record before it is too late to do anything about it. Al-

though this does take the time of interviewers, which could have been utilized equally well to take a record of the previous day's time budget by interview techniques, it is reasonable to utilize this procedure when the period to be covered is more than just a previous day. Accounts of activities for periods of a week are not uncommon.

The trouble with the time diary, however, is that in spite of their best intentions and promises many people do not follow through and complete the diary. There is also little chance to question or to discuss their categorization of activities; whoever picks up the diaries may spot questionable responses, but it is normally only blanks that draw strong attention at that time.

An interview relies on a respondent's memory of the period involved; therefore, a valid reconstruction is generally possible only for the previous day. Nonetheless, the level of cooperation by respondents is considerably higher for this mode of data acquisition. The oral time budget, however, takes a great degree of interviewer time, and frequently interviewers discover that they have at least as much difficulty as their respondent, since quite some strain is involved in ensuring that all levels of detail are completed for as complex a matter as a person's day.

Interviewers normally ask less complex questions than those of the time-budget series, such as people's preferred brand of orange juice or their opinions on the actions of political leaders. Hence interviewers feel that they may be straining the attention of their respondents when going through the necessary details of the time budget, and this frequently interferes with their perseverence. This problem is avoided by sufficient interviewer orientation before the actual interviews. In fact, as long as the interviewer is not on edge, people seem to enjoy reconstructing their day's events.

Time budgets are normally coded and placed on data cards and/or tape for future analysis. Coding a time budget following open-ended responses is generally extremely time-consuming and, hence, expensive. Furthermore, analysis can be extremely aggravating. Individual researchers have worked up computer programs to facilitate time-budget analysis, which they are in the process of making available to other interested researchers (e.g., Kranz, 1970). Nonetheless, there is as yet no standardization of programs nor any regular arrangement for program distribution. Needless to say, with great amounts of information on large numbers of persons, great amounts of computer time are taken simply by reading the information already on tape, let alone analyzing it.

There is no single agreed-upon set of activity categories or codes (e.g., see Swedener and Yague, 1970). One set of 99 categories was devised and utilized in the Multinational Comparative Time-Budget Research Project (Szalai, 1966b; Szalai, 1972), and it has been utilized by others subsequently. This set of codes is reproduced in Table 2 in the form utilized in the study described in the last section of this chapter. In places several "blank" codes were replaced by "extra" activities that we found relevant.

Other researchers find, however, that even such an international set of codes does not provide a level of subtle detail sufficient to distinguish among certain kinds of activities in which they have a special interest. That is, what is intended to cover the entire spectrum of activities in a variety of cultures, but yet remain relatively parsimonious, may not be sufficient to differentiate among forms of behavior relevant to a particular problem.

In addition, there is a tension between the creation of a large number of codes to describe behavior, so as to be complete and accurate, and the desire to have as few codes as possible, so that analysis can be efficient and relatively uniform. If there is a large number of codes, many of them will not apply to most people (or to none at all), and the results of the analysis may

be extremely uneven and difficult to comprehend. The use of only small numbers of categories, however, may mean that they are too general to differentiate sensitively enough among the groups being compared.

In the process of coding, intercoder reliability is extremely important, and the validity of what is later reported depends on accurate understanding by coders of how the categories of the code differ from one another, so that they may accurately assign them. Considerable training and practice are necessary before a coder is either accurate or fast.

A very specific problem in coding has to do with the recording of points of time. For accuracy and simplicity, the 24-hour clock is optimal. However, coders are not commonly accustomed to it, and errors may creep into the data set without extensive checking as to the accuracy of the figures. Dinner, for example, from 7 (implied P.M.) to 20.00 can seriously distort a body of data.

More difficult to solve are the problems of accurately recording time spent sleeping and the length of a day. Some time budgets begin with midnight and continue through the following midnight. Others start at the time the person gets up at the beginning of the day and continue until he goes to bed. Absolutely accurate construction of a person's day, including his sleep time, requires either the assumption that a person has the same rising habits on two consecutive days or that the time budget be continued from the time a person gets up until the time that his sleep ends the following day. There are, almost inevitably, logical difficulties in analysis, however accurate the information given the investigator.

The coding process can be greatly simplified by the use of precoded questionnaires or diaries, as suggested earlier. This would be an ideal solution, except that with a *general* population prior studies have shown that time-budget analysis is relatively fruitless unless a wide variety of categories is utilized (*about 100*). This is too large a number for most respondents to use accurately. Researchers have found it possible to precode with a smaller number of categories in specific contexts where expected behaviors (or at least the only behaviors in which the researchers were primarily interested) were much more limited in number. One study in Belgium, for example, precoded the professional activities of physicians successfully (Bachy, 1972).

Information is usually placed on tape in the form of a large number of identical "fields," each one of which deals with one episode during the day, that is, an activity, the times involved, the

Table 2
Nomenclature of the Activities

Working Time and Time Connected to It (00-09)

00 Normal professional work (outside home)
01 Normal professional work at home or brought home
02 Overtime if it can be specifically isolated from 00
03 Displacements during work if they can be specifically isolated from 00
04 Any waiting or interruption during working time if it can be specifically isolated from work (e.g., due to supply shortage, breakdown of machines, etc.)
05 Undeclared, auxiliary, etc., work, wives-children, unpaid members to assist family
06 Meal at the workplace
07 Time spent at the workplace before starting or after ending work
08 Regular breaks and prescribed nonworking periods, etc., during work time
09 Travel to (return from) workplace, including waiting for means of transport

Domestic Work (10-19)

10 Preparation and cooking of food, putting away groceries
11 Washing up and putting away the dishes
12 Indoor cleaning (sweeping, washing, bedmaking), general nonspecific housework
13 Outdoor cleaning (sidewalk, disposal of garbage)
14 Laundry, ironing
15 Repair or upkeep of clothes, shoes, underwear, etc.
16 Other repairs and home operations, packing and unpacking, washing or repairing car
17 Gardening, animal care, walking dog[a]
18 Heat and water supplies—upkeep
19 Others (e.g., dealing with bills and various other papers, usual care to household members, etc.)

Care of Children (20-29)

20 Care of babies, feeding baby
21 Care of older children
22 Supervision of school work (exercises and lessons)
23 Reading of tales or other nonschool books to children, conversations with children
24 Indoor games and manual instruction
25 Outdoor games and walks
26 Medical care (visiting the children's doctor or dentist, or other activities related to the health of children)
27 Others
28 Not to be used
29 Travel to accompany children, including waiting for means of transport

Table 2 (continued)

Purchasing of Goods and Services (30-39)

30 Purchasing of everyday consumer goods and products, shopping
31 Purchasing of durable consumer goods
32 Personal care outside home (e.g., hairdresser)
33 Medical care outside home
34 Administrative services, offices, bank, employment agency, customs, etc.
35 Repair and other services (e.g., laundry, electricity, mechanics, car wash)
36 Waiting, queuing for the purchase of goods and services, house or apartment hunting
37 Others, signing lease or contract to buy
38 Selling house or house contents; showing own house
39 Traveling connected to the above-mentioned activities, including waiting for means of transport

Private and Nondescribed Activities (40-49)

40 Personal hygiene, dressing (getting up, going to bed, etc.)
41 Personal medical care at home
42 Care given to adults, if not included in household work
43 Meals and snacks at home
44 Meals outside home or the canteen, essential other than 70-79[b]
45 Night sleep (essential)
46 Daytime sleep (incidental), long time, e.g., 1 hour or more
47 Nap or rest, 1 hour or less
48 Private activities, nondescribed, others (using sauna alone)
49 Traveling connected to the above-mentioned activities, including waiting for means of transport

Adult Education and Professional Training (50-59)

50 Full-time attendance to classes (undergraduate or postgraduate student), studies being the principal activity
51 Reduced programs of professional or special training courses, driving lessons (including after-work classes organized by the plant or enterprise in question)
52 Attendance to lectures (occasionally)
53 Programs of political or union training courses
54 Homework prepared for different courses and lectures (including related research work and self-instruction)
55 Reading of scientific reviews of books for personal instruction, specific to own profession
56 Others
57 No response, no further activity
58 No secondary activity
59 Traveling connected to the above-mentioned activities, including waiting for means of transport

Civic and Collective Participation Activities (60-69)

60 Participation as a member of a party, union, etc.
61 Voluntary activity as an elected official of a social or political organization
62 Participation in meetings other than those covered by 60 and 61
63 Nonpaid collective civic activity (e.g., volunteers)
64 Participation in religious organizations
65 Religious practice and attending religious ceremonies
66 Participation in various factory councils (committees, commissions)

Table 2 (continued)

67 Participation in other associations (family, parent, military, etc.)
68 Others
69 Traveling connected to the above-mentioned activities, including waiting for means of transport

Spectacles, Entertainment, Social Life (70-79)

70 Attending a sports event
71 Circus, music hall, dancing, show, nightclub (including a meal in entertainment local), parade
72 Movies
73 Theater, concert opera
74 Museum, exhibition, library (educational purposes)
75 Receiving visit of friends or visiting friends, relatives at airport
76 Party or reception with meal or snack offered to or offered by friends, relatives
77 Cafe, bar tearoom
78 Attending receptions (other than those mentioned above)
79 Traveling connected to the above-mentioned activities, including waiting for means of transport

Sports and Active Leisure (80-89)

80 Practice a sport and physical exercise
81 Excursions or drive, hunting, fishing
82 Walks, browsing, window shopping
83 Technical hobbies, photography and developing, collections
84 Ladies' work (confection, needlework, dressmaking, knitting, etc.)
85 Artistic creations (sculpture, painting, pottery, literature, writing poetry, etc.)
86 Playing a musical instrument, singing
87 Society games (cards, etc.), crosswords, board games, chess
88 Others
89 Traveling connected to the above-mentioned activities, including waiting for means of transport

Passive Leisure (90-99)

90 Listening to the radio, piped music
91 Watching television
92 Listening to records, tape recording
93 Reading books
94 Reading reviews, periodicals, magazines, pamphlets, etc., including proofreading done at home
95 Reading newspapers
96 Conversations, including telephone conversations
97 Writing private correspondence, reading mail, writing in diary
98 Relaxing, reflecting, thinking, planning, doing nothing, no visible activity (arrive home, use on Sunday if long interval between activities)
99 Travel connected to the above-mentioned activities, including waiting for means of transport

---

a Gardening and animal care are to be recorded as Domestic Work only if not part of professional work or gainful employment.

b A number of special types of meals outside home and the canteen have special codes, different from 44 (see Spectacles, Entertainment, Social Life, 70-79).

people involved, and the location. Standard social science analysis programs may be used with time-budget data to a greater extent if one episode is placed on one card; the problem with this, however, is that it usually creates an unmanageable number of cards in the data file, which further prolongs the machine reading process. One major difficulty in conducting analysis is that the number of episodes a day will vary greatly by respondent.

Results may be produced in a variety of forms. Each of these is available not just for a whole aggregate of people who were subjected to time-budget procedures but also for different subgroups being compared (from place to place or from time to time or both, as discussed earlier). One may, for example, report the *average time* devoted to each of the activities coded by members of the whole aggregate or by persons in each of the relevant subgroups.

One can report not just averages, but also *extremes* in time usage that might apply to one subcategory as opposed to another; this is indicated by such measures of dispersion as standard deviations, deciles or quartiles, interquartile ranges, or other such measures.

One can measure not only how much time was devoted to what activity, but also how much time was devoted to certain activities by particular kinds of people, or to what activities in what places, or what activities with which other people, in what places with which other people, and so on. Two-way and three-way analyses involving the type of activity, the location, and the persons present, all with respect to the amount of time spent, are both possible and fruitful with this technique. It is these analyses that are most useful for design purposes.

Of certain relevance in this context is the fact that one can portray the spatial components of activity *graphically*. The CalComp plotter, a widely distributed machine, is particularly helpful in this respect. Hence, if one wants to see the spatial distribution of particular activities or indeed of the whole spectrum of life activity, one can easily do so. One can also ascertain the relationship of residential locations to other locations frequented. Some examples of this technique are presented later in this paper.

One can also use time-budget data as input to larger analytic techniques. If one wants to look for certain regularities or alternatives in behavior within a given population, the quantitative statistical properties of time-budget data make them ideal for use with such techniques as factor analysis.

WHAT ARE SOME OF THE PITFALLS?

We have so far discussed only the merits and applications of time budgets. Their weaknesses require mention, however, since some are not readily apparent.

When we ask people for information, we usually try to select people so that they reflect or represent a much larger group; we then assume that their responses are typical or representative of both the individuals who give them and the larger group. There is some question, though, as to whether a time budget for 1 or 2 days in an individual's life provides accurate, representative evidence of typical activity patterns, since these shift with the day of the week, season, physical and social locale, and so on. It is commonplace to request from respondents time-use profiles of at least 1 weekday (i.e., work day) and 1 weekend day. To ask for more usually results in the completion time for the questionnaire becoming unacceptably long, with rapidly diminishing accuracy.

Length is a chronic problem; time-use questionnaires or interviews are almost always time-consuming because of the detail and recall effort required. The accuracy and reliability of this kind of data diminish rapidly in proportion to increased completion time.

Another aspect of the issue of representiveness is underenumeration of certain kinds of activity. It is a documented fact that *all* questionnaires and interviews evoke responses significantly affected by the respondent's acquiescence and perceptions of social desirability; hence time-use questionnaires are very unlikely to contain any record of body function activity, sexual activity, or any other behavior regarded as very private, generally disapproved of (whether mildly or totally), or deviant, no matter how "normal" or commonplace any of these activities may be. Furthermore, simultaneously executed activities (e.g., watching television while eating, talking, or working) usually result in only one being recorded. Mental activity or purposeful nonactivity (such as relaxing or contemplating) are unlikely to be reported very frequently. And most activities of shorter duration than 10 to 15 minutes are likely to be forgotten and unrecorded.

We think time budgets are useful because they tell us something important about the respondent. But the meaning and intent of activity are never self-evident; they must be inferred. The duration or frequency of activities are not certain indicators of importance to the respondent. For example, 20 minutes spent reading the newspaper may be more important (or "less replaceable") than 3 hours spent watching television. In addition, activities may have both manifest and latent functions; eating or walking may be done for their own sake or as a means of achieving a particular objective. Hence inferences of some kinds can be made only with extensive analysis of data and additional qualifying information from respondents.

We mentioned earlier that some degree of evaluation of the component parts of the time-budget data are possible by the addition of supplementary questions as an integral part of the time-budget schedule. Hence, as part of the regular time-budget exercise, one can ask a person to evaluate whether or not he likes the amount of time he devotes to an activity or whether a given location is adequate for the performance of that activity. This is not commonly done; but, although it adds to the time, expense, and trouble of the time-budget interview, it also adds an entirely new, useful dimension of practical importance. A diary that adds this dimension is illustrated in Figure 2.

If one is interested in activities that do not occur everyday or at any great length, one should base the time budget on more than just a single day in the life of a person. Otherwise, it is a matter of real chance as to whether this use of time will emerge. This is particularly relevant in comparisons from time to time. If the period of time sampled is insufficient for very many people to have exhibited an activity of interest to the researcher, then whether a person has increased or decreased in the amount of time devoted to the activity over time is not easily determined. An analysis would show, for example, that on an average day most people did not do the activity and only small numbers showed an increase or decrease in their patterns. If one sampled a larger period of time, the analysis would be more easily done. However, another way of finding out such information on times of rare occurrence is to ask directly about them and not utilize the time budget as a vehicle.

The coding of activities is often rather problematic; controversy occurs over precoded questionnaries and *ex post facto* coding of responses, whether from questionnaires and diaries or interviews. The issue is whether it is best for respondents to describe their activities from an inventory of activity types provided in the questionnaire or interview, or whether they should describe their time use entirely in their own words, with the coding being done by the investigator after the fact. Many current users of time-use data appear to favor the latter alternative.

Another problem is that the tabular presenta-

TIME BEGAN	TIME ENDED	WHAT DID YOU DO?	WERE YOU DOING ANYTHING ELSE AT THE SAME TIME? (specify activity)	CHECK ONE — WHEN YOU WERE DOING THIS HOW DID YOU FEEL?					WERE YOU WITH YOUR CHILDREN
				1 pleased or delighted	2 mostly satisfied	3 mixed or neutral	4 mostly dis- satisfied	5 unhappy or terrible	
									☐ YES ☐ NO
									☐ YES ☐ NO
									☐ YES ☐ NO
									☐ YES ☐ NO
									☐ YES ☐ NO
									☐ YES ☐ NO
									☐ YES ☐ NO
									☐ YES ☐ NO
									☐ YES ☐ NO
									☐ YES ☐ NO
									☐ YES ☐ NO
									☐ YES ☐ NO
									☐ YES ☐ NO
									☐ YES ☐ NO
									☐ YES ☐ NO
									☐ YES ☐ NO
									☐ YES ☐ NO

Figure 2
Supplementary diary for time-budget data. (Courtesy of Survey Research Center, University of Michigan.)

tion of results is almost always detailed and difficult for the inexperienced reader to decipher. Although these results can be parceled out into a great number of simple tables, summary measures of general time-budget results are not well developed.

A final pitfall worth mentioning is related to the interpretation of time-budget data. It is inherently a measure of what exists now under current conditions, and not necessarily what might be under other conditions. It is ideal for use in evaluation. Under other circumstances, however, the researcher must always be aware of the range of constraints above and beyond those constraints that he wishes to measure, which may be accounting for the behavior observed. In other words, what you see people doing is not always a measure of what people might want to do in the best of all worlds. How they might change under realistic alternative conditions is something not intrinsic to time-budget data, but a consideration that must be used in their interpretation. Under certain circumstances, time expenditure may be fruitfully analyzed in a manner analogous to the analysis of marginal utility in economics; but such interpretation must be undertaken carefully.

HISTORY AND DEVELOPMENT OF TIME-BUDGET RESEARCH[1]

Scientific interest in how people use time arose in the first third of this century in two diametrically different situations. With the advent of Taylorism and the extension of the idea of efficiency to the use of time (in addition to efficiency of money and machinery), the time budgets of factory workers were examined in the form of time-and-motion studies. At the other extreme, research into leisure behavior (Lundberg et al., 1934) was based on time-budget data. The few time-budget studies carried out during this period suffered numerous methodological weaknesses and consequently failed to ignite much interest in the time budget as a worthwhile information-producing instrument.

In North America, more enduring interest in time-use data arose in the late 1950s and 1960s, again in the contexts of leisure and work, but this time with a more unified perspective. Time came to be viewed as either a commodity that could be bought with money or as a resource to be consumed like money. [Recent work, most notably by Becker (1965) and Linder (1970)—both economists, has attempted to describe in some detail the interchangeability of time and money.] Growing interest in leisure activities and consumption behavior has led to considerable use of time budgets in market research in both the private and public domains. The allocation of individuals' time to certain kinds of activity may be used by companies as an indicator of likely demand for certain kinds of products. Similarly, in the public domain, certain kinds of time use are indicative of existing or latent demand for facilities and services—most typically in the areas of transportation, recreation, and housing.

In the case of work, the absence of any clear measures of economic output by housewives prompted the use of time-use data to ascertain the economic equivalence of their housework. Leibowitz (1972) and Walker (1969) have done recent and detailed studies in this field, adding to the general work of Becker and Linder.

Interestingly enough, the largest portion of recent time-budget research has been done *outside* North America. In addition to extensive work in France, Japan, and the Soviet Union, perhaps the most notable study of all is the Multinational Comparative Time-Budget Research Project. This project initially involved collaboration by social scientists from 12 countries in carrying out 30,000 time-budget interviews, under the general auspices of the European Coordination Center for Research and Documentation in the Social Sciences. The initial surveys were done in 1965 and 1966, in 13 locations in nine countries, with additional surveys being conducted later in three more countries. All surveys, across every phase, were coordinated; sampling, interviewing, coding, and analysis were thoroughly standardized.

The natural result of all these time-use studies is a very sizable body of data. These studies have been helpful, perhaps necessary, in strengthening the methodological foundations of time-budget research, but the usefulness of these data is seriously impaired by the noncomparability of many of the studies due to variation in their population and time samples, activity categories, and analytic procedures.

A sizable percentage of the recent studies has had a physical or social planning orientation because of the growing recognition of the need for behavioral data for these contexts.

AN EXAMPLE OF THE TIME-BUDGET METHOD IN ENVIRONMENTAL DESIGN

Let us now provide an example of how we utilized a time budget in a research project with explicit design intentions.

The Theoretical Question

A classic question in the field of housing and urban development is whether people translate into long-term experience that which was in their minds when they chose their housing. Specifically, people may choose housing and/or location because they want or expect something, but what remains is whether or not they find it subsequently.

This question is particularly relevant because the housing literature suggests strongly that there is a rational *social* element in people's choice of housing, in addition to the real economic constraints which affect most people.

Housing research has gone through a number of theoretical stages. In earlier days, a number

of different determinants were felt to affect where people lived and what happened to them once they were there. The human ecologists, for example, generally treated housing choice as a subsidiary element to people's socioeconomic and ethnic identification. "Birds of a feather" would "flock together," and the physical nature of where they flocked together was a function of the economic strength of this group relative to others in the community (Park, Burgess, and McKenzie, 1925). However, those interested in housing per se felt that the nature of housing itself had a dramatic effect, on the mental health and functioning of people, quite independent of their own characteristics and expectations or neighborhood characteristics (Riis, 1890).

Somewhat later, housing was seen as a symbol reflecting a person's status. Consequently, housing choice was not simply a reaction to spatial needs but rather an active mechanism for consciously improving one's own status. Again, housing was not viewed functionally, but rather for extrinsic purposes (Warner and Lunt, 1941; Warner et al., 1957).

Rossi's classic study (1955) on residential mobility added the dimension that moving is a response to demographic pressures within the family relative to the characteristics of the housing unit already occupied. This viewpoint treated housing as a functional unit with respect to a narrow range of demands put on it by its users. Matters of storage and bedroom count are vital in Rossi's work, but not such wider considerations as what people might be doing with their daily lives and activities when living in such units and neighborhoods. Considerations of life style did not appear until later studies.

Just after Rossi's work, a number of statistical studies began to indicate the importance of broader facets of people's lives in housing choice. This work indicated that the educational component of status was frequently more relevant than the more strictly economic components in determining who would live with what neighbors in what neighborhood. Thus it was not exclusively purchasing power that led people to certain residences, but broader considerations covering who their neighbors would be (Duncan and Duncan, 1957; Feldman and Tilly, 1960; Tilly, 1961; Wheeler, 1968). This led to a period signaled by Bell's work (1958, 1968) on "self-selection," which made explicit the notion of choosing a location and a housing type at least partially on the basis of desired behavior. One moved not to improve one's own status, but rather to be with others like oneself and to emphasize that life style most fruitfully practiced under the spatial arrangements chosen. Bell himself confined his suggestions to the substantive aspects of behavior that were involved in a tripartite typology centering on familism, careerism, and consumerism. These three categories, of course, represent only certain aspects of the wide range of potential behavior, and he left it somewhat unclear as to the specific elements of the residential setting that called forth the behaviors, as well as the specific behaviors to be expected within these suggested categories.

Others, however, suggest certain ways in which neighborhoods could help fulfill certain behavioral goals. Several writers, for example, talk about the prevalence of neighboring in suburban locations (Fava, 1956; Tomeh, 1969). Beshers (1962) discussed neighborhood as a spatial field that provided a pool of potential spouses during the years when boy meets girl; he advanced this notion as a possible explanation for people's efforts to obtain social homogeneity within neighborhoods (particularly among the upper classes). Gans (1967), for example, discusses a new suburb in terms of its potential in providing outlets for social participation through service clubs and voluntary organizations.

So far, however, researchers have focused mainly on specific areas of interest concerning behavior, rather than treating the home environment as a general opportunity structure—a spatial field that contains a greater or lesser number of specific social, recreational, and commercial opportunities (to say the least), depending upon its design and provision. Although the environment may not determine to any extent what people do, certain pursuits may be made easier or more difficult depending on the access provided to them. Hence different residential settings imply different degrees of opportunity vis-à-vis specific activity. Our research aims were to find out from people who had had first-hand experience with polar design and planning alternatives, which are directly encouraged or discouraged by government policy or its absence, (1) what they wanted at the start of their residence in these specific environments, (2) what they experienced as a consequence of exposure to them, and (3) how they differed from each other beforehand so as to influence differential selection. In short, we wished to assess the social implications of these differing environments: high-rise apartments, single-family detached homes, central-city locations, and far-suburban locations.

Our Approach

Our own study[2] is a longitudinal analysis of self-selection and adaptation among families in the child-bearing years who moved either to high-rise apartments or to single-family houses in either the central city or the far suburbs in the greater Toronto area. Sampling was conducted on a 100 percent basis from as complete an inventory as could be gathered of persons signing agreements to buy or leases to rent appropriate units of relatively comparable monthly costs; this cost was intentionally moderately high so as to select families whose financial resources permitted some degree of choice within the housing market. The median income at the time of moving was about $13,000, with about 40 percent over $15,000 (although only 16 percent over $20,000) and only about 12 percent under $9,000. Thus, family income data indicate the relative success of this attempt at stratification through indirect means.

Families were interviewed after they had selected their new housing, but before effecting the move (phase I). They were interviewed again approximately 2 months after they moved (phase II) and 1 year followng the second interview (phase III, 1 year and 2 months following the move). At each of these points, the main interview was with the female head of the household, although every attempt was made to secure a complementary interview with the male head of the household and with one child, if there was one, between the ages of 10 and 17.

There has been approximately a 10 percent loss in the sample with each succeeding phase of interviewing. This is due partly to moves outside the Toronto area (which were not of interest concerning the local housing market) and partly to refusals; no systematic bias by category of environment is evident with respect to the refusal rate. Cross-sectional analyses of these data are based on the respective numbers of respondents within each phase of the study; trend analyses are based on the 591 families interviewed at each of the three stages in the study.

A number of the same questions were asked at each of the three phases in the interviewing process, and to both husband and wife. The major constant instrument was the time budget. This technique was considered ideal for the project's purposes because it provided simultaneous data on what people do (weighted by the length of time devoted to it), where this takes place, and with whom it takes place. It is not seen as an explicitly value-laden inquiry into specific activities that have varying degrees of social approval attached to them; the investigator can yet manipulate his file of information to explore those specific uses of time of interest to himself and his hypotheses. Hence, the time budget is an ideal potential instrument to assess what people do within the spatial parameters of their daily lives, as well as how these behaviors change under specific conditions, such as residential mobility.

Typical Time-Budget Results

We present some examples from this study to indicate typical time-budget results in this context. The reader is referred to other publications for more substantive reports from this project (Michelson, Belgue, and Stewart, 1973; Michelson, 1973a, 1973b, 1973c, 1973d).

Table 3 is a typical and complete time-budget table; in this case, it compares the time usage of female heads of households who are about to move to one of five combinations of housing and location: high-rise apartments downtown, single-family houses downtown (all resale houses), high-rise apartments in the suburbs, newly built single-family houses in the suburbs, and resale single-family homes in the suburbs. All the information concerns the time-usage pattern characteristic of these people before they moved, so as to understand what these people were like (albeit under constraints that were also taken into account) as a possible predisposing factor in the choice of the above-mentioned types of new housing.

Such a table enables comparison among categories of movers with respect to each type of activity considered. Nonetheless, an inspection of each box in this cross-classification indicates that there are many ways in which even this information can be conceived. Let us just look, for a start, at the very first activity, normal work for pay (as compared to nonremunerative types of work effort, such as housekeeping).

Table 3

Average time (minutes) spent pursuing activities by housing type and location—phase 1: wife weekday

Within each box in table: N1 N2 / MEAN 1 / MEAN 2 / STDEV 1 / COL% MN1 / %±SIDEV1 — ACTIVITY CODE	1 APRTMENT DOWNTOWN	2 HOUSE DOWNTOWN	3 APRTMENT SUBURB	4 NEW HOUSE SUBURB	5 RESALE HOUSE SUBURB
	108 79	94 25	283 116	208 51	62 11
	265.7	87.3	142.7	83.3	66.0
0 NORMAL PROF WORK	363.2	328.1	348.1	339.7	372.3
	182.9	161.3	189.0	162.6	145.8
	13.1	4.5	6.9	4.1	3.1
	50.9	17.0	26.1	14.9	12.9
	108 2	94 1	283 6	208 5	62 1
	2.1	0.8	2.3	4.2	6.3
1 PROF WORK – HOME	112.5	75.0	110.0	174.0	390.0
	18.9	7.7	18.9	30.7	49.1
	0.1	0.0	0.1	0.2	0.3
	1.9	1.1	2.1	1.9	1.6
	108 2	94 0	283 1	208 1	62 0
	2.4	0.0	0.2	0.4	0.0
2 OVERTIME WORK	127.5	0.0	45.0	75.0	0.0
	17.2	0.0	2.7	5.2	0.0
	0.1	0.0	0.0	0.0	0.0
	1.9	0.0	0.4	0.5	0.0
	108 3	94 0	283 4	208 5	62 0
	2.8	0.0	0.9	1.9	0.0
3 WORK DISPLCEMNTS	100.0	0.0	63.8	78.0	0.0
	17.6	0.0	10.3	15.7	0.0
	0.1	0.0	0.0	0.1	0.0
	2.8	0.0	1.4	2.4	0.0
	108 0	94 1	283 0	208 0	62 0
	0.0	0.1	0.0	0.0	0.0
4 WORK INTERRUPTNS	0.0	14.0	0.0	0.0	0.0
	0.0	1.4	0.0	0.0	0.0
	0.0	0.0	0.0	0.0	0.0
	0.0	1.1	0.0	0.0	0.0
	108 0	94 1	283 4	208 4	62 0
	0.0	1.9	3.0	2.2	0.0
5 AUXILIARY WORK	0.0	180.0	210.0	112.5	0.0
	0.0	18.5	30.2	18.3	0.0
	0.0	0.1	0.1	0.1	0.0
	0.0	1.1	1.4	1.4	0.0
	108 46	94 15	283 72	208 30	62 7
	21.5	7.3	11.7	10.4	5.8
6 WORKPLACE MEALS	50.5	46.0	46.0	72.0	51.4
	40.1	18.7	25.6	39.1	22.8
	1.1	0.4	0.6	0.5	0.3
	21.3	8.5	14.1	7.7	4.8
	108 30	94 4	283 48	208 21	62 1
	9.0	1.0	6.8	3.5	0.2
7 BEFORE-AFTER WRK	32.5	22.5	40.3	35.0	15.0
	21.9	5.3	27.1	13.9	1.9
	0.4	0.0	0.3	0.2	0.0
	11.1	1.1	6.7	6.3	0.0

For key to table, see page 213

Within each box in table:	N1 N2 MEAN 1 MEAN 2 STDEV 1 COL% MN1 %±STDEV1	1 APRTMENT DOWNTOWN	2 HOUSE DOWNTOWN	3 APRTMENT SUBURB	4 NEW HOUSE SUBURB	5 RESALE HOUSE SUBURB
ACTIVITY CODE						
		108 42	94 12	283 61	208 23	62 5
		25.0	5.9	18.3	8.0	5.6
8		64.3	46.2	85.1	72.4	69.0
REGULAR WRK BRKS		52.7	25.5	51.2	32.0	27.5
		1.2	0.3	0.9	0.4	0.3
		11.1	2.1	9.5	5.3	1.6
		108 80	94 23	283 116	208 53	62 12
		54.6	16.1	26.7	16.2	12.5
9		73.6	65.9	65.1	63.7	64.8
WORKPLACE TRAVEL		55.2	39.0	40.9	35.1	32.0
		2.7	0.8	1.3	0.8	0.6
		36.1	7.4	18.0	8.2	4.8
		108 77	94 81	283 249	208 188	62 58
		38.5	69.7	66.9	80.5	82.5
10		53.9	80.9	76.0	89.1	88.1
FOOD PREPARATION		37.4	61.2	54.0	64.5	56.1
		1.9	3.6	3.3	3.9	3.9
		3.7	14.9	13.1	17.8	19.4
		108 58	94 59	283 190	208 155	62 45
		17.1	26.5	30.6	37.6	39.7
11		31.8	42.2	45.6	50.4	54.6
WASHING DISHES		31.3	32.3	34.9	41.1	40.8
		0.8	1.4	1.5	1.8	1.9
		1.9	9.6	14.1	17.3	24.2
		108 41	94 65	283 197	208 157	62 43
		27.6	60.5	68.7	81.1	63.4
12		72.8	87.5	98.7	107.5	91.3
INDOOR CLEANING		57.2	80.1	79.4	89.5	63.3
		1.4	3.1	3.3	4.0	3.0
		6.5	13.8	16.3	18.3	12.9
		108 0	94 3	283 4	208 2	62 3
		0.0	1.3	0.8	0.6	1.2
13		0.0	40.0	60.0	60.0	25.0
OUTDOOR CLEANING		0.0	7.5	8.3	6.6	5.6
		0.0	0.1	0.0	0.0	0.1
		0.0	3.2	1.4	1.0	4.8
		108 18	94 33	283 112	208 98	62 26
		11.8	29.5	38.0	41.6	31.9
14		70.8	84.1	96.1	88.3	76.2
LAUNDRY+IRONING		40.9	57.2	62.6	60.3	54.7
		0.6	1.5	1.9	2.0	1.5
		2.8	9.6	17.3	19.2	11.3
		108 0	94 2	283 5	208 8	62 4
		0.0	1.0	1.5	2.2	7.5
15		0.0	45.0	84.0	58.1	116.3
CLOTHES REPAIR		0.0	6.9	13.4	14.0	30.2
		0.0	0.0	0.1	0.1	0.4
		0.0	2.1	1.4	2.9	6.5

Within each box in table:	N1 N2 MEAN 1 MEAN 2 STDEV 1 COL% MN1 %±STDEV1	1 APRTMENT DOWNTOWN	2 HOUSE DOWNTOWN	3 APRTMENT SUBURB	4 NEW HOUSE SUBURB	5 RESALE HOUSE SUBURB
ACTIVITY CODE						
		108 16	94 20	283 48	208 42	62 12
		18.2	35.4	21.6	31.1	25.2
16		122.8	166.4	127.5	153.9	130.0
HOME REPAIRS		52.6	110.4	66.1	87.2	62.6
		0.9	1.8	1.1	1.5	1.2
		6.5	8.5	7.4	11.1	9.7
		108 0	94 16	283 11	208 18	62 8
		0.0	9.3	2.1	5.7	6.5
17		0.0	54.4	54.5	65.8	50.6
GARDEN-ANIMALS		0.0	29.1	13.7	25.5	19.4
		0.0	0.5	0.1	0.3	0.3
		0.0	11.7	3.2	6.3	11.3
		108 0	94 0	283 0	208 0	62 0
		0.0	0.0	0.0	0.0	0.0
18		0.0	0.0	0.0	0.0	0.0
HEAT+WATER CARE		0.0	0.0	0.0	0.0	0.0
		0.0	0.0	0.0	0.0	0.0
		0.0	0.0	0.0	0.0	0.0
		108 2	94 2	283 6	208 2	62 2
		0.3	1.1	1.3	0.4	1.7
19		15.0	52.5	62.5	45.0	52.5
OTHER HSHLD CARE		2.0	9.3	11.0	4.6	10.1
		0.0	0.1	0.1	0.0	0.1
		1.9	2.1	2.1	1.0	3.2
		108 6	94 31	283 73	208 46	62 24
		8.1	34.0	29.9	22.9	50.1
20		145.0	103.0	116.0	103.7	129.4
BABY CARE		36.7	81.8	69.9	59.5	102.9
		0.4	1.7	1.5	1.1	2.3
		3.7	12.8	11.3	8.7	16.1
		108 5	94 40	283 119	208 133	62 34
		1.7	34.1	28.5	44.4	32.6
21		36.0	80.2	67.8	69.4	59.5
OLDER CHILD CARE		8.5	65.9	47.3	55.1	43.0
		0.1	1.7	1.4	2.2	1.5
		0.0	11.7	14.1	17.8	9.7
		108 1	94 5	283 3	208 11	62 0
		0.6	2.6	0.6	2.0	0.0
22		60.0	48.0	55.0	38.2	0.0
SCHOOL WORK SUPR		5.7	11.7	6.2	9.9	0.0
		0.0	0.1	0.0	0.1	0.0
		0.9	5.3	1.1	5.3	0.0
		108 1	94 6	283 8	208 14	62 7
		0.6	3.8	2.1	2.8	3.4
23		60.0	60.0	75.0	41.8	30.0
CHILD READG+TALK		5.7	17.8	16.6	13.1	10.9
		0.0	0.2	0.1	0.1	0.2
		0.9	5.3	2.1	4.3	6.5

Within each box in table:		1 APRTMENT DOWNTOWN	2 HOUSE DOWNTOWN	3 APRTMENT SUBURB	4 NEW HOUSE SUBURB	5 RESALE HOUSE SUBURB
N1 N2						
MEAN 1						
MEAN 2						
STDEV 1						
COL% MN1						
%±STDEV1						

ACTIVITY CODE

24 INDOOR GAMES	1 APRTMENT DOWNTOWN	2 HOUSE DOWNTOWN	3 APRTMENT SUBURB	4 NEW HOUSE SUBURB	5 RESALE HOUSE SUBURB
N1 N2	108 2	94 10	283 23	208 11	62 7
MEAN 1	0.7	4.1	5.1	3.9	10.6
MEAN 2	37.5	39.0	62.6	73.6	94.3
STDEV 1	5.9	13.6	20.3	18.0	36.4
COL% MN1	0.0	0.2	0.2	0.2	0.5
%±STDEV1	0.9	8.5	7.1	5.3	9.7

25 OUTDOR GAMES+WALK	1	2	3	4	5
N1 N2	108 1	94 12	283 23	208 23	62 9
MEAN 1	0.4	7.8	5.8	10.5	12.3
MEAN 2	44.0	61.3	71.1	95.2	85.0
STDEV 1	4.2	26.0	23.2	35.0	32.9
COL% MN1	0.0	0.4	0.3	0.5	0.6
%±STDEV1	0.9	8.5	6.7	9.6	12.9

26 MEDICAL CARE	1	2	3	4	5
N1 N2	108 1	94 6	283 1	208 12	62 0
MEAN 1	0.3	3.8	0.1	2.2	0.0
MEAN 2	30.0	60.0	30.0	37.5	0.0
STDEV 1	2.9	17.2	1.8	9.8	0.0
COL% MN1	0.0	0.2	0.0	0.1	0.0
%±STDEV1	0.9	6.4	0.4	5.8	0.0

27 OTHER CHILD CARE	1	2	3	4	5
N1 N2	108 0	94 5	283 6	208 12	62 4
MEAN 1	0.0	1.8	1.0	2.0	3.4
MEAN 2	0.0	33.0	44.8	35.0	52.3
STDEV 1	0.0	9.0	7.2	10.0	13.5
COL% MN1	0.0	0.1	0.0	0.1	0.2
%±STDEV1	0.0	5.3	2.1	5.8	6.5

28	1	2	3	4	5
N1 N2	108 0	94 0	283 0	208 1	62 0
MEAN 1	0.0	0.0	0.0	0.1	0.0
MEAN 2	0.0	0.0	0.0	15.0	0.0
STDEV 1	0.0	0.0	0.0	1.0	0.0
COL% MN1	0.0	0.0	0.0	0.0	0.0
%±STDEV1	0.0	0.0	0.0	0.5	0.0

29 ACCOMPANY CHILD	1	2	3	4	5
N1 N2	108 1	94 13	283 25	208 43	62 5
MEAN 1	0.1	7.2	2.7	7.7	1.9
MEAN 2	15.0	51.9	30.5	37.3	24.0
STDEV 1	1.4	24.7	10.2	20.9	6.9
COL% MN1	0.0	0.4	0.1	0.4	0.1
%±STDEV1	0.0	8.5	5.7	12.0	4.8

30 EVERYDAY PURCHSE	1	2	3	4	5
N1 N2	108 36	94 34	283 76	208 64	62 16
MEAN 1	17.6	18.6	15.2	21.0	13.5
MEAN 2	52.9	51.6	56.6	68.2	52.4
STDEV 1	35.7	33.1	33.1	43.7	26.5
COL% MN1	0.9	1.0	0.7	1.0	0.6
%±STDEV1	12.0	13.8	10.6	16.3	12.9

31 DURABLE PURCHASE	1	2	3	4	5
N1 N2	108 9	94 5	283 13	208 18	62 10
MEAN 1	4.7	2.7	4.5	9.1	16.7
MEAN 2	56.7	51.0	96.9	105.0	103.4
STDEV 1	20.9	12.8	25.5	35.6	47.2
COL% MN1	0.2	0.1	0.2	0.4	0.8
%±STDEV1	4.6	3.2	3.2	7.2	11.3

Within each box in table:	N1 N2 MEAN 1 MEAN 2 STDEV 1 COL% MN1 %±STDEV1	1 APRTMENT DOWNTOWN	2 HOUSE DOWNTOWN	3 APRTMENT SUBURB	4 NEW HOUSE SUBURB	5 RESALE HOUSE SUBURB
ACTIVITY CODE						
		108 1	94 1	283 4	208 9	62 0
		0.7	0.3	1.5	4.3	0.0
32		75.0	30.0	108.8	100.0	0.0
OUT PERSONL CARE		7.2	3.1	13.3	21.7	0.0
		0.0	0.0	0.1	0.2	0.0
		2.9	1.1	1.4	4.3	0.0
		108 3	94 3	283 12	208 6	62 2
		1.5	2.4	2.4	1.3	2.7
33		55.0	75.0	57.5	45.0	82.5
OUT MEDICAL CARE		10.4	16.3	13.8	9.4	15.1
		0.1	0.1	0.1	0.1	0.1
		2.8	3.2	4.2	2.9	3.2
		108 5	94 4	283 12	208 10	62 0
		1.9	1.0	1.3	1.3	0.0
34		42.0	22.5	31.3	26.9	0.0
ADMIN SERVICES		14.6	4.8	8.6	6.3	0.0
		0.1	0.0	0.1	0.1	0.0
		4.6	4.3	4.2	4.8	0.0
		108 3	94 1	283 8	208 7	62 1
		1.1	0.3	1.5	2.3	0.5
35		40.0	30.0	54.4	68.6	30.0
REPAIR+SERVICES		6.7	3.1	12.0	14.1	3.8
		0.1	0.0	0.1	0.1	0.0
		2.8	1.1	2.8	3.4	1.6
		108 1	94 1	283 3	208 8	62 3
		0.1	0.6	0.3	1.9	1.7
36		15.0	60.0	30.0	50.6	35.0
PURCHASE WAITING		1.4	6.2	3.8	12.6	8.6
		0.0	0.0	0.0	0.1	0.1
		0.9	1.1	1.1	3.8	4.8
		108 5	94 5	283 4	208 15	62 2
		3.2	5.1	0.3	4.8	1.5
37		69.0	95.8	22.5	66.9	45.0
OTHERS+CONTRACTS		16.1	31.0	2.8	19.3	8.0
		0.2	0.3	0.0	0.2	0.1
		4.6	4.3	0.7	6.7	3.2
		108 0	94 0	283 2	208 3	62 2
		0.0	0.0	0.7	1.3	6.5
38		0.0	0.0	97.5	90.0	202.0
SELL+SHOW HOUSE		0.0	0.0	8.2	12.0	37.7
		0.0	0.0	0.0	0.1	0.3
		0.0	0.0	0.7	1.4	3.2
		108 44	94 36	283 105	208 94	62 25
		24.0	16.7	22.0	25.2	25.1
39		59.0	43.7	59.4	55.8	62.2
TRAVEL FOR GOODS		49.8	28.5	47.1	42.4	47.9
		1.2	0.9	1.1	1.2	1.2
		8.3	8.5	9.2	11.1	16.1

Within each box in table:	N1 N2 MEAN 1 MEAN 2 STDEV 1 COL% MN1 3 ±SIDEV1	1 APRTMENT DOWNTOWN	2 HOUSE DOWNTOWN	3 APRTMENT SUBURB	4 NEW HOUSE SUBURB	5 RESALE HOUSE SUBURB
ACTIVITY CODE						
40 PERSONAL HYGIENE		108 106 52.1 53.1 32.2 2.6 2.8	94 86 36.7 40.1 35.2 1.9 2.1	283 242 46.9 54.9 126.9 2.3 3.9	208 175 38.7 46.0 35.1 1.9 1.4	62 50 30.5 37.8 25.1 1.4 0.0
41 HOME MEDICARE		108 1 0.6 60.0 5.7 0.0 0.9	94 1 6.2 585.0 60.0 0.3 1.1	283 0 0.0 0.0 0.0 0.0 0.0	208 2 0.9 97.5 11.6 0.0 1.0	62 0 0.0 0.0 0.0 0.0 0.0
42 CARE TO ADULTS		108 4 1.7 45.0 12.0 0.1 1.9	94 3 1.3 40.0 7.5 0.1 3.2	283 14 3.3 67.3 31.4 0.2 2.8	208 13 1.5 24.2 6.8 0.1 2.4	62 2 1.0 30.0 5.3 0.0 3.2
43 HOME MEALS+SNACKS		108 103 64.0 67.1 64.0 3.1 5.6	94 90 94.0 98.2 59.4 4.8 17.0	283 273 79.9 82.8 49.4 3.9 10.6	208 203 84.8 86.9 51.0 4.1 13.0	62 59 85.6 89.9 50.2 4.0 11.3
44 OUTSIDE MEALS		108 33 19.9 65.0 37.5 1.0 22.1	94 15 13.4 84.0 42.1 0.7 10.6	283 31 7.7 70.2 32.7 0.4 6.7	208 17 5.7 69.7 23.9 0.3 6.3	62 6 8.0 82.3 27.3 0.4 9.7
45 NIGHT SLEEP		108 108 1097.5 1097.5 316.7 53.9 17.6	94 94 1027.8 1027.8 292.8 52.7 11.7	283 283 1101.7 1101.7 318.6 53.6 17.0	208 208 1114.0 1114.0 420.5 54.2 20.2	62 62 1217.4 1217.4 660.7 56.9 24.2
46 DAY SLEEP HOUR+		108 4 3.2 86.3 16.6 0.2 3.7	94 2 1.0 45.0 6.9 0.0 1.1	283 5 4.4 249.0 45.3 0.2 1.8	208 5 4.3 177.0 31.0 0.2 2.4	62 0 0.0 0.0 0.0 0.0 0.0
47 NAP OR REST		108 12 13.9 125.0 63.1 0.7 9.3	94 17 12.0 66.2 30.1 0.6 13.8	283 42 12.2 82.5 34.4 0.6 11.3	208 17 6.8 82.9 24.4 0.3 6.7	62 5 9.2 114.0 32.3 0.4 8.1

```
          N1   N2 |
Within   MEAN 1   |
each     MEAN 2   |     1     |    2     |    3     |   4    |   5
box in   STDEV 1  | APRTMENT |  HOUSE  | APRTMENT |  NEW   | RESALE
table:   COL% MN1 | DOWNTOWN | DOWNTOWN|  SUBURB  | HOUSE  | HOUSE
         % ±SIDEV1|          |         |          | SUBURB | SUBURB
ACTIVITY CODE
```

	1 APRTMENT DOWNTOWN	2 HOUSE DOWNTOWN	3 APRTMENT SUBURB	4 NEW HOUSE SUBURB	5 RESALE HOUSE SUBURB
N1 N2	108 3	94 2	283 4	208 4	62 0
MEAN 2	1.5	0.6	0.6	1.1	0.0
48 PRIVATE ACTVTIES MEAN 1	55.0	30.0	41.3	56.0	0.0
STDEV 1	11.9	4.3	5.1	10.3	0.0
COL% MN1	0.1	0.0	0.0	0.1	0.0
% ±SIDEV1	2.8	2.1	1.4	1.9	0.0
N1 N2	108 20	94 6	283 12	208 14	62 8
MEAN 2	9.0	2.2	2.0	3.0	6.0
49 TRVL PERSNL CARE MEAN 1	48.6	35.0	46.3	45.0	46.8
STDEV 1	25.7	10.5	15.5	15.8	21.6
COL% MN1	0.4	0.1	0.1	0.1	0.3
% ±SIDEV1	14.8	3.2	2.5	3.8	6.5
N1 N2	108 3	94 1	283 4	208 0	62 0
MEAN 2	4.0	1.3	2.9	0.0	0.0
50 FULL-TIME CLASS MEAN 1	145.0	120.0	206.3	0.0	0.0
STDEV 1	25.7	12.3	28.3	0.0	0.0
COL% MN1	0.2	0.1	0.1	0.0	0.0
% ±SIDEV1	2.8	1.1	1.1	0.0	0.0
N1 N2	108 1	94 2	283 3	208 2	62 0
MEAN 2	1.1	4.1	1.3	0.7	0.0
51 SPECIAL COURSES MEAN 1	120.0	195.0	125.0	75.0	0.0
STDEV 1	11.5	33.1	12.8	8.5	0.0
COL% MN1	0.1	0.2	0.1	0.0	0.0
% ±SIDEV1	0.9	2.1	1.1	1.0	0.0
N1 N2	108 0	94 0	283 2	208 0	62 0
MEAN 2	0.0	0.0	1.1	0.0	0.0
52 OCCASIONAL CLASS MEAN 1	0.0	0.0	157.5	0.0	0.0
STDEV 1	0.0	0.0	13.2	0.0	0.0
COL% MN1	0.0	0.0	0.1	0.0	0.0
% ±SIDEV1	0.0	0.0	0.7	0.0	0.0
N1 N2	108 0	94 0	283 0	208 0	62 0
MEAN 2	0.0	0.0	0.0	0.0	0.0
53 UNION+POLTL CLSS MEAN 1	0.0	0.0	0.0	0.0	0.0
STDEV 1	0.0	0.0	0.0	0.0	0.0
COL% MN1	0.0	0.0	0.0	0.0	0.0
% ±SIDEV1	0.0	0.0	0.0	0.0	0.0
N1 N2	108 5	94 4	283 3	208 3	62 0
MEAN 2	7.1	7.5	1.7	0.9	0.0
54 CLASS HOMEWORK MEAN 1	153.0	176.3	165.0	60.0	0.0
STDEV 1	38.5	42.2	19.8	7.3	0.0
COL% MN1	0.3	0.4	0.1	0.0	0.0
% ±SIDEV1	3.7	4.3	1.1	1.4	0.0
N1 N2	108 1	94 1	283 0	208 0	62 1
MEAN 2	1.1	1.6	0.0	0.0	1.2
55 PROFESSL READING MEAN 1	120.0	150.0	0.0	0.0	75.0
STDEV 1	11.5	15.4	0.0	0.0	9.4
COL% MN1	0.1	0.1	0.0	0.0	0.1
% ±SIDEV1	0.9	1.1	0.0	0.0	1.6

Within each box in table:	N1 N2 MEAN 1 MEAN 2 STDEV 1 COL% MN1 % ±STDEV1	1 APRTMENT DOWNTOWN	2 HOUSE DOWNTOWN	3 APRTMENT SUBURB	4 NEW HOUSE SUBURB	5 RESALE HOUSE SUBURB
ACTIVITY CODE						
		108 1	94 1	283 0	208 0	62 1
		2.9	1.6	0.0	0.0	1.2
56		315.0	150.0	0.0	0.0	75.0
OTHER READING		30.2	15.4	0.0	0.0	9.4
		0.1	0.1	0.0	0.0	0.1
		0.9	1.1	0.0	0.0	1.6
		108 0	94 0	283 0	208 0	62 0
		0.0	0.0	0.0	0.0	0.0
57		0.0	0.0	0.0	0.0	0.0
NO EDUCATN RESPN		0.0	0.0	0.0	0.0	0.0
		0.0	0.0	0.0	0.0	0.0
		0.0	0.0	0.0	0.0	0.0
		108 0	94 0	283 0	208 0	62 0
		0.0	0.0	0.0	0.0	0.0
58		0.0	0.0	0.0	0.0	0.0
NO EDUCATN ACTVY		0.0	0.0	0.0	0.0	0.0
		0.0	0.0	0.0	0.0	0.0
		0.0	0.0	0.0	0.0	0.0
		108 6	94 6	283 8	208 1	62 1
		4.6	4.6	1.4	0.1	0.2
59		82.5	72.5	50.6	30.0	15.0
EDUCATION TRAVEL		28.3	20.2	8.8	2.1	1.9
		0.2	0.2	0.1	0.0	0.0
		3.7	6.4	2.8	0.5	0.0
		108 0	94 0	283 0	208 0	62 0
		0.0	0.0	0.0	0.0	0.0
60		0.0	0.0	0.0	0.0	0.0
UNION+PARTY PREP		0.0	0.0	0.0	0.0	0.0
		0.0	0.0	0.0	0.0	0.0
		0.0	0.0	0.0	0.0	0.0
		108 0	94 0	283 0	208 0	62 0
		0.0	0.0	0.0	0.0	0.0
61		0.0	0.0	0.0	0.0	0.0
ELECTED VOL ACTV		0.0	0.0	0.0	0.0	0.0
		0.0	0.0	0.0	0.0	0.0
		0.0	0.0	0.0	0.0	0.0
		108 1	94 1	283 2	208 1	62 0
		1.0	1.3	1.0	1.0	0.0
62		105.0	120.0	135.0	210.0	0.0
MEETINGS		10.1	12.3	11.3	14.5	0.0
		0.0	0.1	0.0	0.0	0.0
		0.9	1.1	0.7	0.5	0.0
		108 0	94 0	283 1	208 0	62 0
		0.0	0.0	0.9	0.0	0.0
63		0.0	0.0	255.0	0.0	0.0
VOL CIVIC ACTVTY		0.0	0.0	15.1	0.0	0.0
		0.0	0.0	0.0	0.0	0.0
		0.0	0.0	0.4	0.0	0.0

Within each box in table:	N1 N2 MEAN 1 MEAN 2 STDEV 1 COL% MN1 %±STDEV1	1 APRTMENT DOWNTOWN	2 HOUSE DOWNTOWN	3 APRTMENT SUBURB	4 NEW HOUSE SUBURB	5 RESALE HOUSE SUBURB
ACTIVITY CODE						
		108 0	94 2	283 0	208 2	62 1
		0.0	2.1	0.0	1.2	1.2
64		0.0	97.5	0.0	127.5	75.0
RELIGOUS GROUPS		0.0	18.5	0.0	14.8	9.4
		0.0	0.1	0.0	0.1	0.1
		0.0	2.1	0.0	1.0	1.6
		108 0	94 1	283 4	208 3	62 0
		0.0	0.8	0.9	0.6	0.0
65		0.0	75.0	63.8	45.0	0.0
RELIGOUS PRACTCE		0.0	7.7	8.2	5.6	0.0
		0.0	0.0	0.0	0.0	0.0
		0.0	1.1	1.4	1.4	0.0
		108 0	94 0	283 0	208 0	62 0
		0.0	0.0	0.0	0.0	0.0
66		0.0	0.0	0.0	0.0	0.0
FACTORY COUNCILS		0.0	0.0	0.0	0.0	0.0
		0.0	0.0	0.0	0.0	0.0
		0.0	0.0	0.0	0.0	0.0
		108 0	94 0	283 0	208 0	62 0
		0.0	0.0	0.0	0.0	0.0
67		0.0	0.0	0.0	0.0	0.0
OTHER ASSOCIATNS		0.0	0.0	0.0	0.0	0.0
		0.0	0.0	0.0	0.0	0.0
		0.0	0.0	0.0	0.0	0.0
		108 0	94 1	283 0	208 0	62 0
		0.0	0.2	0.0	0.0	0.0
68		0.0	15.0	0.0	0.0	0.0
OTHER GROUP ACTV		0.0	1.5	0.0	0.0	0.0
		0.0	0.0	0.0	0.0	0.0
		0.0	1.1	0.0	0.0	0.0
		108 1	94 3	283 7	208 4	62 1
		0.8	1.7	0.8	0.6	0.5
69		90.0	54.7	32.1	30.0	30.0
GROUP ACTV TRAVL		8.6	9.9	5.7	4.1	3.8
		0.0	0.1	0.0	0.0	0.0
		0.9	3.2	2.5	1.9	1.6
		108 1	94 1	283 2	208 1	62 0
		0.6	2.2	1.5	0.1	0.0
70		60.0	210.0	210.0	15.0	0.0
SPORTS EVENTS		5.7	21.5	18.3	1.0	0.0
		0.0	0.1	0.1	0.0	0.0
		0.9	1.1	0.7	0.5	0.0
		108 2	94 0	283 3	208 0	62 1
		3.3	0.0	1.5	0.0	1.9
71		180.0	0.0	145.0	0.0	120.0
PARADES+NGTCLUBS		26.3	0.0	15.2	0.0	15.1
		0.2	0.0	0.1	0.0	0.1
		1.9	0.0	1.1	0.0	1.6

Within each box in table:	N1 N2 MEAN 1 MEAN 2 STDEV 1 COL% MN1 % ±STDEV1	1 APRTMENT DOWNTOWN	2 HOUSE DOWNTOWN	3 APRTMENT SUBURB	4 NEW HOUSE SUBURB	5 RESALE HOUSE SUBURB
ACTIVITY CODE						
		108 2	94 0	283 3	208 3	62 1
		2.4	0.0	1.7	2.4	4.6
72		127.5	0.0	160.0	165.0	285.0
MOVIES		17.2	0.0	16.6	20.2	35.9
		0.1	0.0	0.1	0.1	0.2
		1.9	0.0	1.1	1.4	1.6
		108 1	94 0	283 0	208 4	62 0
		2.4	0.0	0.0	2.8	0.0
73		255.0	0.0	0.0	146.3	0.0
THEATRE+OPERA		24.4	0.0	0.0	20.4	0.0
		0.1	0.0	0.0	0.1	0.0
		0.9	0.0	0.0	1.9	0.0
		108 3	94 3	283 1	208 4	62 1
		1.4	3.2	0.0	2.2	1.0
74		50.0	100.0	14.0	112.5	60.0
MUSEUM+LIBRARY		11.6	20.2	0.8	20.7	7.6
		0.1	0.2	0.0	0.1	0.0
		0.9	3.2	0.0	1.9	1.6
		108 28	94 27	283 75	208 62	62 23
		22.5	24.1	23.3	23.0	35.7
75		86.6	83.7	87.9	77.3	96.3
VISITS+RECEIVING		48.5	52.6	52.3	50.5	78.1
		1.1	1.2	1.1	1.1	1.7
		13.0	11.7	12.7	11.1	16.1
		108 5	94 7	283 25	208 27	62 2
		2.8	8.6	6.5	8.3	1.9
76		60.0	115.7	73.7	64.3	60.0
PARTY WITH MEALS		13.4	43.2	27.2	27.1	11.9
		0.1	0.4	0.3	0.4	0.1
		3.7	4.3	6.4	8.2	1.6
		108 7	94 2	283 3	208 4	62 2
		6.4	1.1	0.8	0.7	2.4
77		98.4	52.5	75.0	37.5	74.0
CAFE+BAR+TEAROOM		26.7	7.7	8.9	6.7	16.9
		0.3	0.1	0.0	0.0	0.1
		6.5	2.1	0.7	1.0	1.6
		108 0	94 0	283 0	208 2	62 0
		0.0	0.0	0.0	2.1	0.0
78		0.0	0.0	0.0	217.5	0.0
ATTEND RECEPTNS		0.0	0.0	0.0	22.2	0.0
		0.0	0.0	0.0	0.1	0.0
		0.0	0.0	0.0	1.0	0.0
		108 25	94 19	283 44	208 40	62 16
		15.1	10.0	9.6	7.8	14.7
79		65.3	49.7	61.7	40.5	57.0
SOCIAL TRAVEL		35.3	27.9	27.5	22.5	35.0
		0.7	0.5	0.5	0.4	0.7
		14.8	8.5	9.5	5.3	14.5

Within each box in table:	N1 N2 MEAN 1 MEAN 2 STDEV 1 COL% MN1 % ±STDEV1	1 APRTMENT DOWNTOWN	2 HOUSE DOWNTOWN	3 APRTMENT SUBURB	4 NEW HOUSE SUBURB	5 RESALE HOUSE SUBURB
ACTIVITY CODE						
		108 3	94 9	283 9	208 7	62 2
		1.4	7.3	2.3	3.1	4.4
80		49.7	76.6	71.7	92.1	135.0
PHYSICL EXERCISE		8.7	26.8	19.5	20.9	27.4
		0.1	0.4	0.1	0.2	0.2
		2.8	8.5	2.1	2.9	3.2
		108 7	94 6	283 15	208 7	62 4
		5.0	4.3	4.5	3.5	8.5
81		77.1	67.5	85.0	102.9	131.3
DRIVES+HUNT+FISH		21.9	18.3	21.2	21.2	46.7
		0.2	0.2	0.2	0.2	0.4
		5.6	6.4	5.3	3.4	6.5
		108 17	94 4	283 22	208 10	62 4
		8.8	2.2	6.0	2.7	2.2
82		55.6	52.5	77.7	55.5	33.5
WALKS+BROWSING		27.8	10.7	26.3	14.3	9.6
		0.4	0.1	0.3	0.1	0.1
		13.0	4.3	6.7	4.3	3.2
		108 0	94 0	283 2	208 1	62 1
		0.0	0.0	0.1	0.3	0.5
83		0.0	0.0	15.0	60.0	30.0
TECHNICAL HOBBY		0.0	0.0	1.3	4.2	3.8
		0.0	0.0	0.0	0.0	0.0
		0.0	0.0	0.7	0.5	1.6
		108 6	94 12	283 30	208 26	62 7
		11.3	12.0	11.3	11.7	23.0
84		202.5	93.8	107.0	93.5	203.3
SEW+KNIT ETC		51.0	38.2	38.7	35.3	83.4
		0.6	0.6	0.6	0.6	1.1
		5.6	7.4	8.5	9.1	11.3
		108 0	94 0	283 3	208 4	62 0
		0.0	0.0	0.8	2.4	0.0
85		0.0	0.0	80.0	123.8	0.0
ARTISTIC ACTIVTY		0.0	0.0	8.4	17.8	0.0
		0.0	0.0	0.0	0.1	0.0
		0.0	0.0	1.1	1.9	0.0
		108 1	94 3	283 2	208 1	62 0
		0.3	1.4	0.3	0.2	0.0
86		30.0	45.0	37.5	45.0	0.0
MUSICAL ACTIVITY		2.9	8.2	3.7	3.1	0.0
		0.0	0.1	0.0	0.0	0.0
		0.9	3.2	0.7	0.5	0.0
		108 2	94 2	283 6	208 6	62 4
		1.1	2.9	2.0	3.2	4.1
87		60.0	135.0	95.0	112.5	63.5
SOCIETY GAMES		9.1	22.3	14.7	20.6	21.6
		0.1	0.1	0.1	0.2	0.2
		1.9	2.1	2.1	2.9	4.8

Within each box in table:

N1 N2	
MEAN 1	
MEAN 2	
STDEV 1	
COL% MN1	
%±STDEV1	

ACTIVITY CODE	1 APRTMENT DOWNTOWN	2 HOUSE DOWNTOWN	3 APRTMENT SUBURB	4 NEW HOUSE SUBURB	5 RESALE HOUSE SUBURB
88 OTHER LEISURE	108 1	94 0	283 1	208 7	62 0
	0.4	0.0	0.7	2.6	0.0
	45.0	0.0	195.0	77.1	0.0
	4.3	0.0	11.6	20.6	0.0
	0.0	0.0	0.0	0.1	0.0
	0.9	0.0	0.4	3.4	0.0
89 ACTV LEISR TRAVL	108 8	94 12	283 18	208 12	62 1
	4.7	8.4	3.0	2.2	0.2
	63.8	66.2	46.6	38.7	15.0
	24.7	29.2	16.4	10.7	1.9
	0.2	0.4	0.1	0.1	0.0
	3.7	10.6	3.5	3.4	0.0
90 RADIO LISTENING	108 0	94 3	283 2	208 3	62 1
	0.0	1.4	0.6	0.3	2.2
	0.0	45.0	82.5	20.0	135.0
	0.0	8.2	6.9	2.5	17.0
	0.0	0.1	0.0	0.0	0.1
	0.0	3.2	0.7	1.4	1.6
91 WATCHING TV	108 46	94 34	283 154	208 105	62 29
	41.8	30.0	59.9	50.4	39.0
	98.2	82.9	110.0	99.9	83.3
	63.5	54.1	76.4	63.2	54.2
	2.1	1.5	2.9	2.5	1.8
	17.6	10.6	23.0	22.6	11.3
92 RECORDS+TAPES	108 1	94 0	283 7	208 0	62 1
	0.1	0.0	2.0	0.0	0.7
	15.0	0.0	81.3	0.0	45.0
	1.4	0.0	15.8	0.0	5.7
	0.0	0.0	0.1	0.0	0.0
	0.9	0.0	2.5	0.0	1.6
93 READING BOOKS	108 8	94 14	283 18	208 10	62 7
	7.2	16.9	4.8	3.5	9.2
	97.5	113.6	75.8	72.0	81.4
	34.7	55.0	21.8	17.6	29.3
	0.4	0.9	0.2	0.2	0.4
	4.6	12.8	4.9	3.4	8.1
94 READING MAGAZNES	108 5	94 22	283 41	208 30	62 10
	2.9	16.1	14.0	9.2	12.3
	63.0	68.9	97.0	63.5	76.5
	19.3	38.9	47.5	26.4	32.7
	0.1	0.8	0.7	0.4	0.6
	1.9	11.7	7.8	9.1	12.9
95 READ NEWSPAPERS	108 17	94 20	283 49	208 50	62 16
	8.8	8.3	6.9	10.2	12.8
	55.6	39.0	39.8	42.6	49.7
	29.6	18.1	18.4	21.9	25.0
	0.4	0.4	0.3	0.5	0.6
	6.5	10.6	7.4	10.1	16.1

Within each box in table:	N1 N2 MEAN 1 MEAN 2 STDEV 1 COL% MN1 %±STDEV1	1 APARTMENT DOWNTOWN	2 HOUSE DOWNTOWN	3 APARTMENT SUBURB	4 NEW HOUSE SUBURB	5 RESALE HOUSE SUBURB
ACTIVITY CODE						
96 CONVERSATIONS		108 26 9.7 40.3 20.7 0.5 1.9	94 41 35.4 81.2 54.9 1.8 22.3	283 82 19.8 68.2 43.0 1.0 10.2	208 77 26.7 72.2 49.7 1.3 16.3	62 27 28.7 65.9 42.2 1.3 16.1
97 WRITE+READ MAIL		108 2 1.1 60.0 9.1 0.1 1.9	94 8 7.5 88.1 31.7 0.4 8.5	283 10 1.6 45.0 10.0 0.1 2.1	208 9 1.9 43.2 9.8 0.1 3.4	62 5 3.4 42.0 12.8 0.2 6.5
98 RELAXING		108 48 23.5 52.8 45.2 1.2 9.3	94 39 24.1 58.0 49.5 1.2 9.6	283 119 30.2 71.8 60.1 1.5 11.0	208 54 22.1 85.3 62.5 1.1 7.2	62 27 24.7 56.7 43.1 1.2 9.7
99 PASSV LEISR TRAV		108 2 0.8 45.0 6.4 0.0 1.9	94 1 0.2 15.0 1.5 0.0 1.1	283 2 0.2 22.5 2.0 0.0 0.7	208 0 0.0 0.0 0.0 0.0 0.0	62 0 0.0 0.0 0.0 0.0 0.0

N1, total number of people who answered time-budget questions; N2, number of people who supplied answers for this activity; Mean 1, total time spent for this activity, divided by N1; Mean 2, total time spent for this activity, divided by N2; STDEV 1, standard deviation using mean 1 and N1; COL% MN1, this activity's mean 1 % of column sum of mean 1; % + STDEV1, percentage of answers above 1 row STDEV (using row mean 1, N1).

The typical way of representing information on categories of people from time budgets is to compute an arithmetic mean of time usage, either hours or minutes devoted to that task by any particular group. Obviously, the arithmetic mean for one group, such as the apartment downtown group, can be compared with any other group, such as the house downtown group. However, the first question that arises is whether the mean should be computed based on all the people in the category or on just those persons in the category who actually did the activity during the day in question. The argument in favor of the former is that it gives a picture which characterizes the average emphasis within that whole group. The disadvantage of the former, and hence the advantage of the latter, is that it distorts the actual amount of time which the participants devote to the activity, whereas the latter type of arithmetic mean would be a realistic representation of how much time people devote to the activity, *if* they in fact do it. The reader can see in Table 1 that only 79 out of 108 residents of the high-rise apartment worked in a remunerative position on the day in question; in comparison, only 25 of the 94 female heads of downtown single-family households worked for pay.

If the arithmetic mean based on the total number of persons in the category of housing were to be used, so as to indicate differences in emphasis between categories of movers, one can then certainly see from mean 1, the top center figure in each box, that an average of 265.7 minutes was devoted by downtown apartment women to work in the day in question, in contrast to only 87.3 minutes by those living in downtown houses. A striking picture of differential work emphasis emerges from this set of data, at the very outset. Such a comparision does not appear as stark if we examine the arithmetic mean calculated on the basis of only those who actually did the activity. Mean 2, located directly under mean 1, shows that if a female head of household does work there is very little difference among categories of mover on how long a workday she puts in.

A mean figure, however, does not indicate whether the figures that went into the mean represented a lot of people who were doing just about the same thing or whether, instead, they represented people who devote very different amounts of time to something like work, where the measure of central tendency, such as the mean, is only an indication of the "middle" of a range of behaviors. Hence measures of dispersion indicate how wide the differences are among people in a specific category (i.e., how far away from the mean given percentages of the population tend to be). The standard deviation, computed here with respect to mean 1, indicates how many minutes above or below the mean one would have to look in order to include about two thirds of the persons in the category. In the case of wives moving to downtown apartments, the standard deviation, found under mean 2, is 182.9 minutes, which indicates that about two thirds of the ladies in that category work between 82.8 minutes and 448.6 minutes a day. This is a very wide range, indicating that in fact there is considerable variation among the

persons in this category, something that the mean does not indicate. One can easily understand this case, since 29 persons in that category do not work at all and hence contribute zero minutes to the calculation of the arithmetic mean.

The next-to-last figure from the bottom of every cell is simply a percentage of the number of minutes devoted to the activity that are reported during the day concerned (which, as discussed earlier, does not always equal 24 hours). The average amount of time is sometimes put in percentage form so as to represent a standard measure, which is easier to use as input into some formulas than numbers representing minutes or hours. This percentage figure, however, shows nothing more or less than does mean 1.

Finally, indications of central tendency and dispersion do not indicate whether a disproportionate number of persons in one category are very highly engaged in that activity regardless of the presence of a number of nonparticipants. This information would at least tell us whether people in one or another category had burning interests or obligations with respect to given activities. Although there is no standard measure for such an emphasis, we constructed one, which we called the *index of activity emphasis*. It is computed by calculating the standard deviation for all the persons with respect to a given activity, regardless of their residential category, and then isolating all individuals who devote more time to this activity than mean 2, plus one standard deviation. We then ask what percentage within each of the specific categories of movers consists of the "heavy" time users so identified. This figure, multiplied by 100, is the index of activity emphasis, found at the bottom of every cell in the table. Through inspection, one can see that slightly over 50 percent of those in the apartment downtown category are heavy users of work time, as compared to only 17 percent of those in the house downtown category. The index of activity emphasis normally correlates quite highly with mean 1; but at times it is a useful supplementary measure, as it does point to a different aspect of time usage.

Although we have concentrated on just two cells in this rather large table, the reader can picture how one would go about comparing different types of movers with respect to their pre-move behavioral differences. Some of our many expectations were upheld by these figures, and others were not. But in any case, figures such as these make tests possible. The reader may test some of his own pet theories on Table 3.

Although Table 3 indicates group differences in activity from place to place, the same can be done from time to time. Since we interviewed the group of people at each of three points in time, we can observe the behavioral changes of these people. Table 4 presents time-budget results as they vary both from place to place and from time to time. This tells us whether people moving to particular destination environments change their behavioral emphases in ways that we might expect. In the case of Table 4, figures representing mean 1 and the total number of persons in the category are the ones presented, as our interest was on intergroup comparison, not on the time devoted only by actual users.

We have been led, for example, to expect from other questions asked these people before their move that those moving to downtown apartments would increase the amount of time devoted to physical exercise and decrease commuting time to work. We expected that those moving to downtown houses would by and large maintain a low commuting time to work and increase the amount of time devoted to gardening and use of the city's cultural facilities. We expected that those moving to suburban apartments would increase only the amount of time devoted to physical exercise, while in contrast those moving to single-family homes in the suburbs would increase the amount of time that

would be spent on gardening, housekeeping, and entertaining.

Construction of a table like Table 2 enables the reader to determine whether specific activities such as these indeed do follow either hypothetical expectations or people's own expectations. In the present case, for example, all our expectations were fulfilled to one degree or another (as were our expectations for the husbands; their data are not displayed here).

However, analysis of time usage that includes *more* than two points in time provides the researcher an opportunity to discover *patterns* of change. The differences in the *patterns* in which people's expectations were shown to be fulfilled is worthy of some comment. In some cases the expectation was fulfilled immediately after the move and stayed relatively stable or even declined thereafter. In these instances we were dealing with uses of time that compensated for an explicit deficit in the lives of the people, thus bringing about these changes, or the change was a direct result of the exigencies of moving.

In the former case, apartment dwellers who chose their residences with the hope that they might participate more fully in physical exercise had in fact demonstrated less practice of this pursuit in their previous residence than had the people moving to any of the other categories of environment.

Similarly, wives who moved to downtown apartments had been the most disadvantaged vis-à-vis travel time to work compared to wives in the other categories. Hence the immediate change in these categories of activity for these persons was a direct and immediate consequence of moving; it is no wonder in this instance that the *wife* is the one in the downtown apartment family who enjoys the greatest decline in commuting time.

Regarding the latter case of changes due to the exigencies of moving, wives moving to new suburban homes were very likely forced to put in

Table 4

Average time (minutes) spent pursuing activities by housing type and location: wife weekday (based on number who answered time budget in trend).

ACTIVITY CODE	PHASE 1 APRTMENT DOWNTOWN	PHASE 1 HOUSE DOWNTOWN	PHASE 1 APRTMENT SUBURB	PHASE 1 HOUSE SUBURB	PHASE 2 APRTMENT DOWNTOWN	PHASE 2 HOUSE DOWNTOWN	PHASE 2 APRTMENT SUBURB	PHASE 2 HOUSE SUBURB	PHASE 3 APRTMENT DOWNTOWN	PHASE 3 HOUSE DOWNTOWN	PHASE 3 APRTMENT SUBURB	PHASE 3 HOUSE SUBURB
0 NORMAL PROF WORK	256.60 / 78	84.56 / 80	137.51 / 221	70.22 / 207	244.94 / 79	94.72 / 79	144.86 / 219	76.52 / 207	252.95 / 66	85.50 / 80	172.84 / 197	82.81 / 215
1 PROF WORK - HOME	2.88 / 78	0.94 / 80	2.71 / 221	6.09 / 207	3.23 / 79	3.99 / 79	1.78 / 219	1.59 / 207	8.86 / 66	14.81 / 80	8.22 / 197	3.28 / 215
2 OVERTIME WORK	3.27 / 78	0.00 / 80	0.20 / 221	0.36 / 207	1.33 / 79	0.00 / 79	0.00 / 219	0.00 / 207	1.14 / 66	0.00 / 80	0.00 / 197	1.19 / 215
3 WORK DISPLCEMNTS	3.85 / 78	0.00 / 80	1.09 / 221	0.87 / 207	13.67 / 79	8.16 / 79	2.12 / 219	2.10 / 207	0.00 / 66	0.00 / 80	0.00 / 197	1.12 / 215
4 WORK INTERRUPTNS	0.00 / 78	0.00 / 80	0.00 / 221	0.00 / 207	0.00 / 79	0.00 / 79	0.00 / 219	0.00 / 207	0.00 / 66	0.00 / 80	0.00 / 197	0.00 / 215
5 AUXILIARY WORK	0.00 / 78	2.25 / 80	1.76 / 221	2.17 / 207	4.37 / 79	1.90 / 79	2.26 / 219	6.45 / 207	0.00 / 66	1.13 / 80	0.00 / 197	1.26 / 215
6 WORKPLACE MEALS	23.85 / 78	5.81 / 80	9.71 / 221	6.16 / 207	21.84 / 79	7.97 / 79	15.96 / 219	8.77 / 207	26.59 / 66	4.50 / 80	13.02 / 197	6.00 / 215
7 BEFORE-AFTER WRK	8.65 / 78	0.94 / 80	6.38 / 221	2.61 / 207	7.22 / 79	3.04 / 79	4.17 / 219	2.10 / 207	3.18 / 66	0.38 / 80	2.89 / 197	1.60 / 215
8 REGULAR WRK BRKS	25.19 / 78	6.19 / 80	17.51 / 221	5.22 / 207	12.15 / 79	4.18 / 79	12.47 / 219	3.84 / 207	8.18 / 66	4.88 / 80	18.05 / 197	4.67 / 215
9 WORKPLACE TRAVEL	55.17 / 78	16.13 / 80	25.44 / 221	13.54 / 207	41.96 / 79	17.09 / 79	30.54 / 219	17.53 / 207	59.09 / 66	14.81 / 80	34.17 / 197	17.58 / 215
10 FOOD PREPARATION	33.05 / 78	69.51 / 80	69.69 / 221	77.51 / 207	41.01 / 79	64.32 / 79	60.48 / 219	82.80 / 207	45.42 / 66	66.15 / 80	65.76 / 197	78.04 / 215
11 WASHING DISHES	19.04 / 78	27.19 / 80	29.86 / 221	37.31 / 207	24.11 / 79	30.18 / 79	27.53 / 219	23.77 / 207	22.26 / 66	24.75 / 80	34.94 / 197	34.40 / 215
12 INDOOR CLEANING	31.91 / 78	63.75 / 80	68.07 / 221	77.45 / 207	45.95 / 79	73.66 / 79	76.99 / 219	100.29 / 207	26.33 / 66	54.55 / 80	56.95 / 197	61.12 / 215
13 OUTDOOR CLEANING	0.00 / 78	1.13 / 80	0.95 / 221	0.36 / 207	0.00 / 79	2.47 / 79	0.89 / 219	1.09 / 207	0.00 / 66	1.50 / 80	0.23 / 197	2.65 / 215
14 LAUNDRY+IRONING	14.04 / 78	26.25 / 80	40.44 / 221	36.67 / 207	20.13 / 79	56.76 / 79	28.35 / 219	36.96 / 207	13.39 / 66	24.75 / 80	20.71 / 197	36.00 / 215
15 CLOTHES REPAIR	0.00 / 78	0.75 / 80	1.70 / 221	4.49 / 207	0.57 / 79	0.95 / 79	1.51 / 219	2.83 / 207	0.91 / 66	3.38 / 80	0.99 / 197	3.63 / 215
16 HOME REPAIRS	20.38 / 78	40.88 / 80	22.33 / 221	28.62 / 207	0.76 / 79	18.97 / 79	5.48 / 219	16.73 / 207	2.27 / 66	5.63 / 80	2.59 / 197	5.23 / 215

	PHASE 1				PHASE 2				PHASE 3			
ACTIVITY CODE	APRTMENT DOWNTOWN	HOUSE DOWNTOWN	APRTMENT SUBURB	HOUSE SUBURB	APRTMENT DOWNTOWN	HOUSE DOWNTOWN	APRTMENT SUBURB	HOUSE SUBURB	APRTMENT DOWNTOWN	HOUSE DOWNTOWN	APRTMENT SUBURB	HOUSE SUBURB
17 GARDEN-ANIMALS	0.00 78	8.25 80	2.71 221	5.36 207	0.00 79	8.35 79	1.50 219	5.94 207	0.00 66	6.56 80	2.28 197	5.09 215
18 HEAT+WATER CARE	0.00 78	0.00 80	0.00 221	0.00 207	0.00 79	0.00 79	0.00 219	0.00 207	0.00 66	0.00 80	0.00 197	0.00 215
19 OTHER HSHLD CARE	0.38 78	1.31 80	0.75 221	0.94 207	0.38 79	2.09 79	0.62 219	1.52 207	0.00 66	0.38 80	0.00 197	1.40 215
20 BABY CARE	7.88 78	37.86 80	31.42 221	34.64 207	17.47 79	23.91 79	32.94 219	31.09 207	31.35 66	20.44 80	31.44 197	15.84 215
21 OLDER CHILD CARE	2.12 78	36.16 80	29.80 221	42.89 207	2.85 79	27.15 79	25.88 219	42.24 207	3.86 66	42.54 80	35.99 197	42.34 215
22 SCHOOL WORK SUPR	0.77 78	1.69 80	0.54 221	1.88 207	0.19 79	1.52 79	0.34 219	2.39 207	0.00 66	9.38 80	1.22 197	3.77 215
23 CHILD READG+TALK	0.77 78	2.44 80	2.51 221	3.62 207	0.19 79	3.04 79	3.22 219	7.83 207	0.68 66	7.31 80	1.90 197	3.97 215
24 INDOOR GAMES	0.96 78	4.50 80	5.97 221	6.01 207	1.14 79	3.23 79	6.37 219	6.81 207	1.59 66	6.17 80	8.37 197	6.42 215
25 OUTDR GAMES+WALK	0.00 78	8.63 80	6.11 221	11.74 207	2.28 79	5.13 79	10.13 219	6.09 207	4.32 66	5.81 80	5.71 197	2.86 215
26 MEDICAL CARE	0.38 78	4.50 80	0.00 221	1.59 207	0.57 79	2.85 79	0.96 219	1.09 207	0.17 66	0.17 80	1.21 197	2.72 215
27 OTHER CHILD CARE	0.00 78	0.56 80	1.15 221	2.82 207	2.09 79	3.04 79	1.30 219	3.04 207	0.91 66	0.00 80	0.23 197	0.48 215
28	0.00 78	0.00 80	0.00 221	0.07 207	0.00 79	0.00 79	0.00 219	0.00 207	0.00 66	1.50 80	0.08 197	0.00 215
29 ACCOMPANY CHILD	0.19 78	3.94 80	2.23 221	6.88 207	2.28 79	12.71 79	2.81 219	7.68 207	3.64 66	11.72 80	6.92 197	11.35 215
30 EVERYDAY PURCHSE	16.15 78	18.54 80	14.59 221	21.87 207	20.70 79	33.04 79	30.47 219	34.05 207	29.53 66	38.22 80	22.46 197	42.47 215
31 DURABLE PURCHASE	3.85 78	3.19 80	4.82 221	11.81 207	0.76 79	8.54 79	3.70 219	1.74 207	4.09 66	0.38 80	2.13 197	2.72 215
32 OUT PERSONL CARE	0.00 78	0.38 80	0.75 221	3.91 207	0.00 79	3.23 79	1.10 219	2.90 207	2.05 66	5.81 80	1.29 197	2.37 215
33 OUT MEDICAL CARE	2.12 78	0.56 80	2.58 221	0.80 207	0.95 79	1.71 79	1.92 219	1.01 207	1.82 66	3.56 80	2.21 197	2.16 215

ACTIVITY CODE	PHASE 1				PHASE 2				PHASE 3			
	APRTMENT DOWNTOWN	HOUSE DOWNTOWN	APRTMENT SUBURB	HOUSE SUBURB	APRTMENT DOWNTOWN	HOUSE DOWNTOWN	APRTMENT SUBURB	HOUSE SUBURB	APRTMENT DOWNTOWN	HOUSE DOWNTOWN	APRTMENT SUBURB	HOUSE SUBURB
34 ADMIN SERVICES	2.69 / 78	0.75 / 80	1.56 / 221	0.86 / 207	4.75 / 79	3.23 / 79	1.03 / 219	1.96 / 207	0.91 / 66	0.94 / 80	2.21 / 197	2.30 / 215
35 REPAIR+SERVICES	1.54 / 78	0.38 / 80	1.22 / 221	2.32 / 207	0.38 / 79	2.09 / 79	1.03 / 219	1.15 / 207	3.86 / 66	3.94 / 80	0.30 / 197	2.44 / 215
36 PURCHASE WAITING	0.19 / 78	0.75 / 80	0.41 / 221	1.67 / 207	2.47 / 79	0.00 / 79	0.62 / 219	0.00 / 207	0.45 / 66	0.00 / 80	0.76 / 197	0.28 / 215
37 OTHERS+CONTRACTS	2.88 / 78	5.81 / 80	0.41 / 221	4.13 / 207	0.00 / 79	0.00 / 79	0.00 / 219	0.00 / 207	0.00 / 66	0.00 / 80	0.00 / 197	0.00 / 215
38 SELL+SHOW HOUSE	0.00 / 78	0.00 / 80	0.88 / 221	2.75 / 207	0.00 / 79	0.00 / 79	0.00 / 219	0.00 / 207	0.00 / 66	0.00 / 80	0.15 / 197	0.14 / 215
39 TRAVEL FOR GOODS	25.95 / 78	15.54 / 80	22.31 / 221	26.05 / 207	11.20 / 79	18.23 / 79	9.77 / 219	12.88 / 207	11.36 / 66	14.60 / 80	7.77 / 197	13.71 / 215
40 PERSONAL HYGIENE	52.29 / 78	35.60 / 80	47.91 / 221	36.81 / 207	43.47 / 79	113.72 / 79	121.71 / 219	61.01 / 207	42.24 / 66	38.44 / 80	34.87 / 197	39.20 / 215
41 HOME MEDICARE	0.00 / 78	0.00 / 80	0.00 / 221	0.80 / 207	0.00 / 79	0.00 / 79	0.21 / 219	1.88 / 207	0.00 / 66	0.19 / 80	0.00 / 197	0.00 / 215
42 CARE TO ADULTS	0.77 / 78	1.50 / 80	4.07 / 221	1.67 / 207	0.76 / 79	1.71 / 79	1.85 / 219	1.59 / 207	0.00 / 66	0.00 / 80	0.23 / 197	0.14 / 215
43 HOME MEALS+SNCKS	63.44 / 78	97.55 / 80	79.52 / 221	86.69 / 207	64.16 / 79	115.25 / 79	75.26 / 219	92.07 / 207	60.85 / 66	93.32 / 80	85.71 / 197	99.16 / 215
44 OUTSIDE MEALS	18.83 / 78	14.44 / 80	7.06 / 221	6.52 / 207	17.66 / 79	3.61 / 79	6.16 / 219	1.59 / 207	2.50 / 66	2.63 / 80	1.82 / 197	4.26 / 215
45 NIGHT SLEEP	1120.74 / 78	1030.09 / 80	1096.35 / 221	1153.90 / 207	1293.42 / 79	1276.71 / 79	1209.44 / 219	1142.45 / 207	1054.77 / 66	1052.63 / 80	1107.17 / 197	1044.20 / 215
46 DAY SLEEP HOUR+	4.42 / 78	1.13 / 80	5.02 / 221	3.55 / 207	9.87 / 79	12.72 / 79	5.82 / 219	4.28 / 207	1.36 / 66	5.63 / 80	5.79 / 197	12.28 / 215
47 NAP OR REST	4.81 / 78	10.50 / 80	13.10 / 221	8.26 / 207	4.18 / 79	3.42 / 79	2.95 / 219	3.19 / 207	1.36 / 66	11.06 / 80	6.55 / 197	5.44 / 215
48 PRIVATE ACTVTIES	0.38 / 78	0.38 / 80	0.75 / 221	0.43 / 207	0.57 / 79	0.95 / 79	15.75 / 219	0.14 / 207	0.91 / 66	2.25 / 80	0.76 / 197	0.98 / 215
49 TRVL PERSNL CARE	9.19 / 78	2.44 / 80	2.17 / 221	3.77 / 207	4.37 / 79	1.90 / 79	1.50 / 219	2.32 / 207	0.00 / 66	0.00 / 80	0.00 / 197	0.21 / 215
50 FULL-TIME CLASS	5.58 / 78	1.50 / 80	3.73 / 221	0.00 / 207	5.51 / 79	0.00 / 79	2.95 / 219	0.00 / 207	14.09 / 66	14.63 / 80	0.53 / 197	0.00 / 215

	PHASE 1				PHASE 2				PHASE 3			
ACTIVITY CODE	APRTMENT DOWNTOWN	HOUSE DOWNTOWN	APRTMENT SUBURB	HOUSE SUBURB	APRTMENT DOWNTOWN	HOUSE DOWNTOWN	APRTMENT SUBURB	HOUSE SUBURB	APRTMENT DOWNTOWN	HOUSE DOWNTOWN	APRTMENT SUBURB	HOUSE SUBURB
51 SPECIAL COURSES	1.54 / 78	0.94 / 80	0.54 / 221	0.58 / 207	4.37 / 79	7.97 / 79	0.62 / 219	1.52 / 207	6.82 / 66	10.88 / 80	3.05 / 197	1.95 / 215
52 OCCASIONAL CLASS	0.00 / 78	0.00 / 80	1.43 / 221	0.00 / 207	0.76 / 79	0.00 / 79	0.00 / 219	0.00 / 207	0.00 / 66	3.56 / 80	0.91 / 197	0.00 / 215
53 UNION+POLTL CLSS	0.00 / 78	0.00 / 80	0.00 / 221	0.00 / 207	0.00 / 79	0.00 / 79	0.00 / 219	0.00 / 207	0.00 / 66	0.00 / 80	0.00 / 197	0.00 / 215
54 CLASS HOMEWORK	9.81 / 78	8.81 / 80	0.61 / 221	0.58 / 207	8.54 / 79	0.38 / 79	0.55 / 219	0.58 / 207	5.68 / 66	6.75 / 80	0.91 / 197	3.07 / 215
55 PROFESSL READING	1.54 / 78	1.88 / 80	0.00 / 221	0.36 / 207	0.00 / 79	0.00 / 79	0.96 / 219	0.00 / 207	0.00 / 66	0.00 / 80	0.00 / 197	0.00 / 215
56 OTHER READING	4.04 / 78	1.88 / 80	0.00 / 221	0.36 / 207	0.00 / 79	0.38 / 79	0.00 / 219	0.87 / 207	0.00 / 66	0.00 / 80	0.00 / 197	0.00 / 215
57 NO EDUCATN RESPN	0.00 / 78	0.00 / 80	0.00 / 221	0.00 / 207	0.00 / 79	0.00 / 79	0.00 / 219	0.00 / 207	0.00 / 66	0.00 / 80	0.00 / 197	0.00 / 215
58 NO EDUCATN ACTVY	0.00 / 78	0.00 / 80	0.00 / 221	0.00 / 207	0.00 / 79	0.00 / 79	0.00 / 219	0.00 / 207	0.00 / 66	0.00 / 80	0.00 / 197	0.00 / 215
59 EDUCATION TRAVEL	6.35 / 78	5.44 / 80	1.70 / 221	0.22 / 207	3.99 / 79	3.42 / 79	2.47 / 219	1.23 / 207	6.36 / 66	6.92 / 80	1.22 / 197	0.28 / 215
60 UNION+PARTY PREP	0.00 / 78	0.00 / 80	0.00 / 221	0.00 / 207	0.00 / 79	0.00 / 79	0.00 / 219	0.00 / 207	0.00 / 66	0.00 / 80	0.00 / 197	1.33 / 215
61 ELECTED VOL ACTV	0.00 / 78	0.00 / 80	0.00 / 221	0.00 / 207	0.00 / 79	0.00 / 79	0.00 / 219	0.00 / 207	0.00 / 66	0.00 / 80	0.00 / 197	0.00 / 215
62 MEETINGS	0.00 / 78	1.50 / 80	0.61 / 221	1.01 / 207	3.42 / 79	1.33 / 79	1.64 / 219	0.94 / 207	0.00 / 66	0.00 / 80	1.90 / 197	0.00 / 215
63 VOL CIVIC ACTVTY	0.00 / 78	0.00 / 80	1.15 / 221	0.00 / 207	0.00 / 79	0.00 / 79	0.00 / 219	0.00 / 207	0.00 / 66	1.31 / 80	1.52 / 197	1.46 / 215
64 RELIGOUS GROUPS	0.00 / 78	2.44 / 80	0.00 / 221	0.36 / 207	0.00 / 79	0.00 / 79	0.00 / 219	0.00 / 207	0.00 / 66	0.00 / 80	0.00 / 197	0.70 / 215
65 RELIGOUS PRACTCE	0.00 / 78	0.94 / 80	1.02 / 221	0.36 / 207	0.00 / 79	0.00 / 79	0.00 / 219	1.74 / 207	0.00 / 66	0.00 / 80	0.83 / 197	1.32 / 215
66 FACTORY COUNCILS	0.00 / 78	0.00 / 80	0.00 / 221	0.00 / 207	0.00 / 79	0.00 / 79	0.00 / 219	0.00 / 207	0.00 / 66	0.00 / 80	0.00 / 197	0.00 / 215
67 OTHER ASSOCIATNS	0.00 / 78	0.00 / 80	0.00 / 221	0.00 / 207	0.00 / 79	3.23 / 79	0.34 / 219	1.52 / 207	0.00 / 66	1.13 / 80	1.37 / 197	3.56 / 215

ACTIVITY CODE	PHASE 1 APRTMENT DOWNTOWN	PHASE 1 HOUSE DOWNTOWN	PHASE 1 APRTMENT SUBURB	PHASE 1 HOUSE SUBURB	PHASE 2 APRTMENT DOWNTOWN	PHASE 2 HOUSE DOWNTOWN	PHASE 2 APRTMENT SUBURB	PHASE 2 HOUSE SUBURB	PHASE 3 APRTMENT DOWNTOWN	PHASE 3 HOUSE DOWNTOWN	PHASE 3 APRTMENT SUBURB	PHASE 3 HOUSE SUBURB
68 OTHER GROUP ACTV	0.00 / 78	0.19 / 80	0.00 / 221	0.00 / 207	0.00 / 79	0.00 / 79	0.00 / 219	0.29 / 207	0.00 / 66	0.00 / 80	0.30 / 197	0.14 / 215
69 GROUP ACTV TRAVL	0.00 / 78	2.05 / 80	0.81 / 221	0.43 / 207	0.95 / 79	1.14 / 79	0.89 / 219	0.80 / 207	0.00 / 66	0.55 / 80	1.82 / 197	0.97 / 215
70 SPORTS EVENTS	0.77 / 78	0.00 / 80	0.68 / 221	0.00 / 207	0.00 / 79	0.57 / 79	0.00 / 219	1.52 / 207	0.00 / 66	0.00 / 80	0.00 / 197	0.63 / 215
71 PARADES+NGTCLUBS	1.35 / 78	0.00 / 80	1.97 / 221	0.00 / 207	0.00 / 79	0.00 / 79	0.00 / 219	0.00 / 207	0.00 / 66	0.00 / 80	0.53 / 197	0.28 / 215
72 MOVIES	1.54 / 78	0.00 / 80	0.54 / 221	1.96 / 207	2.28 / 79	1.70 / 79	1.37 / 219	0.80 / 207	2.03 / 66	2.25 / 80	0.00 / 197	3.07 / 215
73 THEATRE+OPERA	3.27 / 78	0.00 / 80	0.00 / 221	2.83 / 207	0.00 / 79	0.00 / 79	0.00 / 219	0.00 / 207	0.00 / 66	0.00 / 80	0.00 / 197	0.00 / 215
74 MUSEUM+LIBRARY	0.38 / 78	3.75 / 80	0.06 / 221	2.46 / 207	0.57 / 79	4.54 / 79	0.27 / 219	1.30 / 207	1.59 / 66	2.42 / 80	0.61 / 197	1.05 / 215
75 VISITS+RECEIVING	27.65 / 78	26.95 / 80	26.37 / 221	27.92 / 207	9.27 / 79	21.76 / 79	23.44 / 219	26.55 / 207	28.92 / 66	46.24 / 80	30.50 / 197	38.28 / 215
76 PARTY WITH MEALS	3.08 / 78	9.75 / 80	6.85 / 221	6.14 / 207	1.87 / 79	16.27 / 79	15.04 / 219	9.68 / 207	0.00 / 66	2.63 / 80	0.23 / 197	0.70 / 215
77 CAFE+BAR+TEAROOM	6.91 / 78	1.31 / 80	0.95 / 221	1.44 / 207	7.95 / 79	0.19 / 79	2.60 / 219	3.33 / 207	12.95 / 66	10.30 / 80	4.34 / 197	8.07 / 215
78 ATTEND RECEPTNS	0.00 / 78	0.00 / 80	0.00 / 221	2.10 / 207	0.00 / 79	0.00 / 79	0.00 / 219	0.00 / 207	4.55 / 66	0.00 / 80	0.00 / 197	0.00 / 215
79 SOCIAL TRAVEL	13.44 / 78	11.05 / 80	10.17 / 221	10.14 / 207	4.11 / 79	9.85 / 79	6.90 / 219	4.11 / 207	5.21 / 66	10.06 / 80	6.45 / 197	8.99 / 215
80 PHYSICL EXERCISE	1.91 / 78	6.36 / 80	2.17 / 221	4.42 / 207	5.13 / 79	5.70 / 79	5.20 / 219	4.78 / 207	6.12 / 66	10.30 / 80	6.24 / 197	5.79 / 215
81 DRIVES+HUNT+FISH	3.27 / 78	5.06 / 80	3.80 / 221	3.99 / 207	0.57 / 79	2.08 / 79	7.19 / 219	1.81 / 207	0.68 / 66	0.75 / 80	2.97 / 197	4.88 / 215
82 WALKS+BROWSING	8.85 / 78	2.63 / 80	6.58 / 221	2.82 / 207	5.32 / 79	7.58 / 79	4.58 / 219	5.43 / 207	6.36 / 66	4.30 / 80	6.24 / 197	1.88 / 215
83 TECHNICAL HOBBY	0.00 / 78	0.00 / 80	0.14 / 221	0.43 / 207	0.38 / 79	0.00 / 79	0.00 / 219	0.00 / 207	0.00 / 66	0.00 / 80	0.84 / 197	0.00 / 215
84 SEW+KNIT ETC	12.12 / 78	11.63 / 80	11.54 / 221	13.55 / 207	10.63 / 79	19.75 / 79	11.30 / 219	19.86 / 207	10.68 / 66	13.69 / 80	18.58 / 197	15.90 / 215

	PHASE 1				PHASE 2				PHASE 3			
ACTIVITY CODE	APRTMENT DOWNTOWN	HOUSE DOWNTOWN	APRTMENT SUBURB	HOUSE SUBURB	APRTMENT DOWNTOWN	HOUSE DOWNTOWN	APRTMENT SUBURB	HOUSE SUBURB	APRTMENT DOWNTOWN	HOUSE DOWNTOWN	APRTMENT SUBURB	HOUSE SUBURB
85 ARTISTIC ACTIVTY	0.00 / 78	0.00 / 80	0.34 / 221	2.39 / 207	0.00 / 79	0.00 / 79	0.00 / 219	0.36 / 207	4.55 / 66	0.75 / 80	0.91 / 197	1.81 / 215
86 MUSICAL ACTIVITY	0.38 / 78	1.69 / 80	0.07 / 221	0.00 / 207	0.00 / 79	0.19 / 79	0.27 / 219	0.94 / 207	0.45 / 66	0.94 / 80	0.00 / 197	0.98 / 215
87 SOCIETY GAMES	1.54 / 78	0.00 / 80	2.58 / 221	4.20 / 207	8.14 / 79	0.76 / 79	2.40 / 219	2.39 / 207	2.05 / 66	3.00 / 80	1.83 / 197	4.88 / 215
88 OTHER LEISURE	0.58 / 78	0.00 / 80	0.88 / 221	1.52 / 207	0.00 / 79	0.00 / 79	0.00 / 219	0.00 / 207	0.00 / 66	0.00 / 80	0.00 / 197	0.00 / 215
89 ACTV LEISR TRAVL	5.96 / 78	7.49 / 80	3.19 / 221	2.17 / 207	0.19 / 79	3.03 / 79	1.16 / 219	3.17 / 207	1.14 / 66	3.19 / 80	2.58 / 197	2.15 / 215
90 RADIO LISTENING	0.00 / 78	1.69 / 80	0.41 / 221	0.87 / 207	0.19 / 79	0.19 / 79	0.68 / 219	0.51 / 207	0.23 / 66	2.06 / 80	1.22 / 197	0.14 / 215
91 WATCHING TV	41.54 / 78	29.42 / 80	59.38 / 221	44.93 / 207	73.10 / 79	33.41 / 79	87.40 / 219	54.20 / 207	55.23 / 66	34.67 / 80	83.90 / 197	64.18 / 215
92 RECORDS+TAPES	0.19 / 78	0.00 / 80	2.44 / 221	0.22 / 207	0.00 / 79	0.00 / 79	0.82 / 219	0.87 / 207	0.00 / 66	0.19 / 80	2.13 / 197	0.70 / 215
93 READING BOOKS	10.00 / 78	16.13 / 80	5.77 / 221	4.49 / 207	11.39 / 79	1.90 / 79	1.92 / 219	5.29 / 207	2.05 / 66	2.25 / 80	2.13 / 197	3.91 / 215
94 READING MAGAZNES	2.88 / 78	18.19 / 80	15.34 / 221	11.52 / 207	16.52 / 79	22.78 / 79	12.40 / 219	29.93 / 207	24.09 / 66	28.50 / 80	13.10 / 197	18.69 / 215
95 READ NEWSPAPERS	9.62 / 78	6.94 / 80	6.99 / 221	12.10 / 207	11.96 / 79	8.54 / 79	6.02 / 219	13.99 / 207	9.32 / 66	18.38 / 80	9.21 / 197	19.26 / 215
96 CONVERSATIONS	8.45 / 78	39.36 / 80	20.96 / 221	28.58 / 207	23.52 / 79	35.82 / 79	26.00 / 219	25.70 / 207	16.59 / 66	30.00 / 80	16.43 / 197	30.13 / 215
97 WRITE+READ MAIL	0.38 / 78	8.81 / 80	1.63 / 221	1.95 / 207	8.73 / 79	5.49 / 79	1.30 / 219	7.25 / 207	3.64 / 66	7.69 / 80	4.72 / 197	4.19 / 215
98 RELAXING	24.41 / 78	23.97 / 80	27.94 / 221	24.85 / 207	10.63 / 79	29.01 / 79	21.23 / 219	22.67 / 207	19.09 / 66	16.30 / 80	16.52 / 197	9.00 / 215
99 PASSV LEISR TRAV	1.15 / 78	0.19 / 80	0.14 / 221	0.00 / 207	0.00 / 79	0.00 / 79	0.00 / 219	0.07 / 207	0.00 / 66	0.00 / 80	0.00 / 197	0.00 / 215

more time on housework after moving into a new home. Once this had been done for a reasonable period of time after the move, certainly within the first year and two months, then it is understandable how time devoted to housework could begin to decline again.

A second pattern of change includes great increases in expected time usage only after the families have been in their new homes for some time. This usually reflects some high degree of actual activity emphasis in their previous residence, as mediated by the initial impact of making a move. For example, families moving to suburban houses were found to participate more in gardening previous to their move than did those moving to other types of homes; husbands moving to downtown houses were more devoted to cultural pastimes than were the other groups of men. Although these moves were to help create even more fruitful circumstances for the pursuit of these activities, and this trend did in fact occur, there was no immediate increase of any significance in these pursuits. That the expectations were fulfilled in the longer view, but not in the shorter, is almost certainly because these activities could be postponed during the rigors of early settlement until after immediate problems, such as housekeeping, were solved.

It is highly important that the expectations of those moving to downtown apartments are satisfied immediately, and that those moving to homes, particularly suburban homes, are satisfied more slowly, since the length of residence in high-rise apartments is almost always considered a more temporary arrangement in Toronto than is movement to a single-family house. Even at the time they moved, most of the persons in this study who moved to high-rise apartments expected to be moving again within the next 5 years; the proportion among those moving into homes was just the reverse. This "instant fruition" of a temporary apartment residence, as compared to the longer-run advantage taken of the more permanent detached housing, is indicated by findings which show that those who moved to suburban houses took the longest to feel at ease in their new surroundings after the move.

It is definitely open to question, however, whether representation of longitudinal change in time usage is best achieved by resorting to *aggregate* uses of time data, with slight differences in the number of persons contributing to the totals of any one point in time. Hence one check of the preceding conclusions is to use only those individuals who responded at all three points in time and to analyze whether individuals changed in their personal use of time devoted to the activity in question in the direction observed in the aggregate figures. In short, we need to know whether the averages are merely a fiction based on substantial changes in time by a few people, or whether they reflect a number of individual changes in the direction observed spread more widely throughout the sample.

The kind of table illustrated by Table 5, on those who moved to high-rise apartments downtown, shows the distribution of individual changes. In every case for this group, a greater percentage of persons increased or decreased their devotion of time to an activity in the direction expected than did the opposite.

One can also perform the manipulations just described on phenomena other than the activity data in the time budget. For example, Table 6 follows the same format as Table 5 for the downtown apartment group, but indicates instead the changes in the amount of time people spend with particular persons rather than in particular types of activity. It shows at the least, for example, a decrease in the amount of time spent alone and an increase in time spent with children, indicative of a demographic trend characterizing this group.

We also used the time budget as the basis for graphic presentations, as we wanted to "see"

Table 5
Change in time spent pursuing activities—phase 1 to phase 3[a]

WIFE-WEEKDAY   APT CESSATION   N = 65

ACTIVITY	CESSATION N	%	-(50-99) N	%	-(10-49) N	%	-(0-9) N	%	NO CHANGE N	%	+(0-9) N	%	+(10-49) N	%	+(50-99) N	%	+(100-199) N	%	+(200+) N	%	COMMENCEMENT N	%
0	11	16.92	1	1.54	9	13.85	4	6.15	12	18.46	4	6.15	8	12.31	4	6.15	3	4.62	0	0.0	9	13.85
1	1	1.54	0	0.0	0	0.0	0	0.0	57	87.69	0	0.0	0	0.0	0	0.0	0	0.0	0	0.0	7	10.77
2	2	3.08	0	0.0	0	0.0	0	0.0	62	95.38	0	0.0	0	0.0	0	0.0	0	0.0	0	0.0	1	1.54
3	3	4.62	0	0.0	0	0.0	0	0.0	62	95.38	0	0.0	0	0.0	0	0.0	0	0.0	0	0.0	0	0.0
4	0	0.0	0	0.0	0	0.0	0	0.0	65	100.00	0	0.0	0	0.0	0	0.0	0	0.0	0	0.0	0	0.0
5	13	20.00	5	7.69	0	0.0	0	0.0	27	41.54	0	0.0	0	0.0	1	1.54	2	3.08	1	1.54	14	21.54
6	12	18.46	3	4.62	2	3.08	0	0.0	49	75.38	0	0.0	0	0.0	0	0.0	3	4.62	0	0.0	3	4.62
7	15	23.08	3	4.62	0	0.0	0	0.0	38	58.46	0	0.0	0	0.0	0	0.0	3	4.62	0	0.0	6	9.23
8	11	16.92	8	12.31	13	13.85	0	0.0	17	26.15	0	0.0	5	7.69	2	3.08	8	12.31	1	1.54	8	12.31
10	9	13.85	4	6.15	9	9.23	0	0.0	15	23.08	0	0.0	3	4.62	4	6.15	6	9.23	0	0.0	13	20.00
11	17	26.15	3	4.62	3	4.62	0	0.0	15	23.08	0	0.0	1	1.54	0	0.0	1	1.54	1	1.54	15	25.23
12	14	21.54	6	9.23	1	1.54	0	0.0	22	33.85	0	0.0	1	1.54	4	6.15	1	1.54	2	3.08	19	29.23
13	0	0.0	0	0.0	0	0.0	0	0.0	65	100.00	0	0.0	0	0.0	0	0.0	0	0.0	0	0.0	0	0.0
14	10	15.38	1	1.54	0	0.0	0	0.0	42	64.62	0	0.0	1	1.54	0	0.0	0	0.0	0	0.0	11	16.92
15	12	18.46	0	0.0	0	0.0	0	0.0	51	78.46	0	0.0	0	0.0	0	0.0	0	0.0	1	1.54	1	1.54
16	0	0.0	0	0.0	0	0.0	0	0.0	65	100.00	0	0.0	0	0.0	0	0.0	0	0.0	0	0.0	2	3.08
17	2	3.08	0	0.0	0	0.0	0	0.0	65	100.00	0	0.0	0	0.0	0	0.0	0	0.0	0	0.0	0	0.0
18	2	3.08	0	0.0	0	0.0	0	0.0	52	80.00	0	0.0	0	0.0	0	0.0	0	0.0	0	0.0	0	0.0
20	3	3.08	0	0.0	0	0.0	0	0.0	60	92.31	0	0.0	2	3.08	1	1.54	0	0.0	0	0.0	12	12.31
21	1	3.08	0	0.0	0	0.0	0	0.0	64	98.46	0	0.0	0	0.0	0	0.0	0	0.0	1	1.54	2	3.08
22	2	0.0	0	0.0	1	1.54	0	0.0	61	93.85	0	0.0	0	0.0	0	0.0	0	0.0	0	0.0	0	0.0
24	0	0.0	0	0.0	0	0.0	0	0.0	63	96.92	0	0.0	0	0.0	0	0.0	0	0.0	2	3.08	2	3.08
25	0	0.0	0	0.0	0	0.0	0	0.0	64	98.46	0	0.0	0	0.0	0	0.0	0	0.0	1	1.54	1	1.54
27	0	1.54	0	0.0	0	0.0	0	0.0	65	100.00	0	0.0	0	0.0	0	0.0	0	0.0	0	0.0	0	0.0
29	1	1.54	0	0.0	0	0.0	0	0.0	28	43.08	0	0.0	0	0.0	0	0.0	2	3.08	1	1.54	4	6.15
30	15	23.08	1	1.54	0	0.0	0	0.0	55	84.62	0	0.0	0	0.0	0	0.0	0	0.0	18	27.65
31	6	9.23	0	0.0	0	0.0	0	0.0	64	98.46	0	0.0	0	0.0	0	0.0	1	1.54
32	3	4.62	0	0.0	0	0.0	0	0.0	60	92.31	0	0.0	0	0.0	0	0.0	3	3.08
34	2	3.08	0	0.0	0	0.0	0	0.0	60	92.31	0	0.0	0	0.0	0	0.0	3	4.62
35	0	3.08	0	0.0	0	0.0	0	0.0	60	92.31	0	0.0	0	0.0	0	0.0	3	1.54
37	0	0.0	0	0.0	0	0.0	0	0.0	63	96.92	0	0.0	0	0.0	0	0.0	0	0.0
38	0	0.0	0	0.0	0	0.0	0	0.0	65	100.00	0	0.0	0	0.0	2	3.08	12	18.46
39	16	24.62	4	6.15	1	1.54	0	0.0	29	44.62	0	0.0	3	4.62	1	1.54	6	9.23
40	4	6.15	16	24.62	16	24.62	0	0.0	7	10.77	0	0.0	11	16.92	8	12.31	5	7.69
41	0	0.0	0	0.0	0	0.0	0	0.0	65	100.00	0	0.0	0	0.0	0	0.0
42	2	3.08	7	26.15	6	9.23	0	0.0	7	10.77	0	0.0	3	4.62	6	9.23	6	9.23	2	3.08
44	18	27.65	1	0.0	12	18.46	9	13.85	43	66.15	11	16.92	14	21.54	4	6.15	1	1.54	4	6.15
45	1	1.54	0	0.0	0	0.0	0	0.0	62	95.38	0	0.0	0	0.0	0	0.0	1	1.54	3	4.62
46	3	4.62	1	1.54	0	0.0	0	0.0	58	89.23	0	0.0	0	0.0	0	0.0	1	1.54
47	5	7.69	1	1.54	0	0.0	0	0.0	58	89.23	0	0.0	0	0.0	0	0.0	0	0.0
48	1	1.54	0	0.0	0	0.0	0	0.0	56	86.92	0	0.0	0	0.0	0	0.0	1	1.54
49	9	13.85	0	0.0	0	0.0	0	0.0	56	86.15	0	0.0	0	0.0	0	0.0	0	0.0

Table 5 (continued)

CHANGE IN TIME SPENT PERSUING ACTIVITIES --- PHASE 1 TO PHASE 2
YA5C CURRENT HOUSING TYPE AND LCCATICN
WIFE-WEEKDAY   APT DOWNTOWN   N= 65

ACTIVITY	CESSATION N	%	-(50-99) N	%	-(10-49) N	%	-(0-9) N	%	NO CHANGE N	%	+(0-9) N	%	+(10-49) N	%	+(50-99) N	%	+(100-199) N	%	+(200+) N	%	COMMENCEMENT N	%
50	0	0.0	0	0.0	0	0.0	0	0.0	62	95.38	0	0.0	0	0.0	0	0.0	2	3.08	0	0.0	1	1.54
51	1	1.54	0	0.0	0	0.0	0	0.0	61	93.85	0	0.0	0	0.0	0	0.0	0	0.0	0	0.0	3	4.62
52	0	0.0	0	0.0	0	0.0	0	0.0	65	100.00	0	0.0	0	0.0	0	0.0	0	0.0	0	0.0	0	0.0
53	0	0.0	0	0.0	0	0.0	0	0.0	65	100.00	0	0.0	0	0.0	0	0.0	0	0.0	0	0.0	0	0.0
54	3	4.62	0	0.0	1	1.54	0	0.0	58	89.23	0	0.0	0	0.0	0	0.0	0	0.0	0	0.0	3	4.62
55	1	1.54	0	0.0	0	0.0	0	0.0	64	98.46	0	0.0	0	0.0	0	0.0	0	0.0	0	0.0	0	0.0
56	1	1.54	0	0.0	0	0.0	0	0.0	64	98.46	0	0.0	0	0.0	0	0.0	0	0.0	0	0.0	0	0.0
57	0	0.0	0	0.0	0	0.0	0	0.0	65	100.00	0	0.0	0	0.0	0	0.0	0	0.0	0	0.0	0	0.0
58	0	0.0	0	0.0	0	0.0	0	0.0	65	100.00	0	0.0	0	0.0	0	0.0	0	0.0	0	0.0	0	0.0
59	3	4.62	2	3.08	0	0.0	0	0.0	55	84.62	0	0.0	0	0.0	0	0.0	0	0.0	0	0.0	5	7.69
60	0	0.0	0	0.0	0	0.0	0	0.0	65	100.00	0	0.0	0	0.0	0	0.0	0	0.0	0	0.0	0	0.0
61	0	0.0	0	0.0	0	0.0	0	0.0	65	100.00	0	0.0	0	0.0	0	0.0	0	0.0	0	0.0	0	0.0
62	0	0.0	0	0.0	0	0.0	0	0.0	65	100.00	0	0.0	0	0.0	0	0.0	0	0.0	0	0.0	0	0.0
63	0	0.0	0	0.0	0	0.0	0	0.0	65	100.00	0	0.0	0	0.0	0	0.0	0	0.0	0	0.0	0	0.0
64	0	0.0	0	0.0	0	0.0	0	0.0	65	100.00	0	0.0	0	0.0	0	0.0	0	0.0	0	0.0	0	0.0
65	0	0.0	0	0.0	0	0.0	0	0.0	64	98.46	0	0.0	0	0.0	0	0.0	0	0.0	0	0.0	1	1.54
66	0	0.0	0	0.0	0	0.0	0	0.0	63	96.92	0	0.0	0	0.0	0	0.0	0	0.0	0	0.0	0	0.0
67	1	1.54	0	0.0	0	0.0	0	0.0	64	98.46	0	0.0	0	0.0	0	0.0	0	0.0	0	0.0	0	0.0
68	1	1.54	0	0.0	0	0.0	0	0.0	64	98.46	0	0.0	0	0.0	0	0.0	0	0.0	0	0.0	0	0.0
70	1	1.54	0	0.0	0	0.0	0	0.0	62	95.38	0	0.0	0	0.0	0	0.0	1	1.54	0	0.0	1	1.54
71	1	1.54	0	0.0	0	0.0	0	0.0	64	98.46	0	0.0	0	0.0	0	0.0	0	0.0	0	0.0	0	0.0
72	1	1.54	0	0.0	0	0.0	0	0.0	62	95.38	0	0.0	1	1.54	1	1.54	0	0.0	0	0.0	1	1.54
75	2	3.08	0	0.0	0	0.0	0	0.0	62	95.38	0	0.0	0	0.0	0	0.0	0	0.0	0	0.0	1	1.54
76	12	18.46	1	1.54	0	0.0	0	0.0	34	52.31	1	1.54	1	1.54	1	1.54	1	1.54	0	0.0	15	23.08
77	3	4.62	1	1.54	0	0.0	0	0.0	62	95.38	0	0.0	0	0.0	0	0.0	0	0.0	0	0.0	0	0.0
78	0	0.0	0	0.0	1	1.54	0	0.0	48	73.85	0	0.0	0	0.0	0	0.0	0	0.0	0	0.0	12	18.46
79	10	15.38	0	0.0	0	0.0	0	0.0	46	70.77	0	0.0	0	0.0	0	0.0	1	1.54	0	0.0	8	12.31
80	3	4.62	0	0.0	0	0.0	0	0.0	44	67.69	0	0.0	0	0.0	0	0.0	0	0.0	0	0.0	4	6.15
81	3	4.62	0	0.0	1	1.54	0	0.0	58	89.23	0	0.0	0	0.0	0	0.0	0	0.0	0	0.0	2	3.08
82	8	12.31	0	0.0	0	0.0	0	0.0	48	73.85	0	0.0	0	0.0	0	0.0	0	0.0	0	0.0	8	12.85
84	2	3.08	0	0.0	1	1.54	1	1.54	56	86.15	1	1.54	1	1.54	0	0.0	0	0.0	0	0.0	5	7.69
85	1	1.54	0	0.0	0	0.0	0	0.0	64	98.46	0	0.0	0	0.0	0	0.0	0	0.0	0	0.0	1	1.54
87	2	3.08	0	0.0	0	0.0	0	0.0	60	92.31	0	0.0	0	0.0	0	0.0	0	0.0	0	0.0	1	1.54
88	1	1.54	0	0.0	2	3.08	0	0.0	60	92.31	0	0.0	0	0.0	0	0.0	0	0.0	0	0.0	3	4.62
89	5	7.69	0	0.0	0	0.0	0	0.0	59	90.77	0	0.0	0	0.0	0	0.0	0	0.0	0	0.0	1	1.54
90	0	0.0	0	0.0	0	0.0	0	0.0	65	100.00	0	0.0	0	0.0	0	0.0	0	0.0	0	0.0	0	0.0
91	12	12.31	6	9.23	5	7.69	1	1.54	16	27.69	0	0.0	0	0.0	0	0.0	1	1.54	6	9.23	19	29.23
92	1	1.54	0	0.0	0	0.0	0	0.0	64	98.46	0	0.0	0	0.0	0	0.0	0	0.0	0	0.0	0	0.0
93	9	13.85	0	0.0	0	0.0	0	0.0	54	83.08	0	0.0	0	0.0	0	0.0	0	0.0	0	0.0	2	3.08
95	2	3.08	2	3.08	2	3.08	0	0.0	44	67.69	0	0.0	0	0.0	0	0.0	1	1.54	1	1.54	18	27.69
96	12	18.46	0	0.0	0	0.0	0	0.0	47	72.31	0	0.0	1	1.54	1	1.54	0	0.0	3	4.62	13	6.15
97	1	1.54	0	0.0	0	0.0	0	0.0	58	89.23	0	0.0	0	0.0	0	0.0	0	0.0	0	0.0	6	20.00
98	18	27.69	3	4.62	0	0.0	0	0.0	25	38.46	0	0.0	1	1.54	1	1.54	1	1.54	5	7.69	12	18.46
99	2	3.08	0	0.0	0	0.0	0	0.0	63	96.92	0	0.0	0	0.0	0	0.0	0	0.0	0	0.0	0	0.0

a The data are for a weekday, from wives who live in downtown apartments. N equals the number of people who answered the time budget.

Table 6

Change in time spent with specific types of person, in specific location, and in combination thereof—phase 1 to phase 2[a]

WIFE—WEEKDAY — APT DOWNTOWN N = 65

PERSONS PRESENT	CESSATION N	%	-(50-99) N	%	-(10-49) N	%	-(0-9) N	%	NO CHANGE N	%	+(0-9) N	%	+(10-49) N	%	+(50-99) N	%	+(100-199) N	%	+(200+) N	%	COMMENCEMENT N	%
1	1	1.54	21	32.31	6	9.23	3	4.62	0	0.0	2	3.08	5	7.69	3	4.62	6	9.23	12	18.46	6	9.23
2	2	3.08	2	3.08	0	0.0	0	0.0	24	36.92	0	0.0	0	0.0	2	3.08	0	0.0	1	1.54	34	52.31
3	2	3.08	4	6.15	14	21.54	1	1.54	1	1.54	4	6.15	6	9.23	8	12.31	7	10.77	17	26.15	1	1.54
4	2	3.08	1	1.54	0	0.0	0	0.0	49	75.38	0	0.0	0	0.0	2	3.08	1	1.54	1	1.54	8	12.31
5	6	9.23	1	1.54	2	3.08	0	0.0	43	66.15	4	6.15	4	6.15	0	0.0	1	1.54	1	1.54	7	10.77
6	4	6.15	0	0.0	0	0.0	0	0.0	61	93.85	0	0.0	0	0.0	0	0.0	0	0.0	0	0.0	0	0.0
7	10	15.38	2	3.08	0	0.0	0	0.0	46	70.77	0	0.0	0	0.0	0	0.0	0	0.0	1	1.54	6	9.23
8	8	12.31	1	1.54	2	3.08	0	0.0	30	46.15	0	0.0	1	1.54	1	1.54	2	3.08	1	1.54	15	25.23
9	8	12.31	1	1.54	5	7.69	1	1.54	11	16.92	2	3.08	4	6.15	5	7.69	6	9.23	10	15.38	12	18.46

LOCATION

LOCATION	CESSATION N	%	-(50-99) N	%	-(10-49) N	%	-(0-9) N	%	NO CHANGE N	%	+(0-9) N	%	+(10-49) N	%	+(50-99) N	%	+(100-199) N	%	+(200+) N	%	COMMENCEMENT N	%
1	0	0.0	0	0.0	14	21.54	6	9.23	1	1.54	11	16.92	15	23.08	11	16.92	5	7.69	2	3.08	0	0.0
2	5	7.69	0	0.0	0	0.0	0	0.0	54	83.08	0	0.0	0	0.0	0	0.0	0	0.0	0	0.0	4	5.23
3	6	9.23	1	1.54	0	0.0	0	0.0	53	81.54	0	0.0	0	0.0	2	3.08	0	0.0	0	0.0	5	7.69
4	13	20.00	1	1.54	7	10.77	3	4.62	12	18.46	9	13.85	9	13.85	2	3.08	0	0.0	0	0.0	9	13.85
5	18	27.69	8	12.31	2	3.08	0	0.0	48	73.85	0	0.0	5	7.69	4	6.15	2	3.08	3	4.62	10	15.38
6	4	6.15	0	0.0	0	0.0	0	0.0	55	84.62	0	0.0	0	0.0	0	0.0	0	0.0	0	0.0	6	5.23
7	6	9.23	0	0.0	0	0.0	0	0.0	7	10.77	0	0.0	0	0.0	7	10.77	3	4.62	8	12.31	7	10.77
8			4	6.15					6	9.23												
9			0	0.0					59	90.77											0	0.0

COMBINATION OF PERSONS PRESENT AND LOCATION

COMBINATION	CESSATION N	%	-(50-99) N	%	-(10-49) N	%	-(0-9) N	%	NO CHANGE N	%	+(0-9) N	%	+(10-49) N	%	+(50-99) N	%	+(100-199) N	%	+(200+) N	%	COMMENCEMENT N	%
1	0	0.0	0	0.0	9	13.85	4	6.15	1	1.54	4	6.15	9	13.85	10	15.38	10	15.38	18	27.69	0	0.0
2	13	20.00	1	1.54	0	0.0	0	0.0	43	66.15	0	0.0	0	0.0	0	0.0	0	0.0	0	0.0	8	12.31
3	1	1.54	30	46.15	8	12.31	0	0.0	1	1.54	1	1.54	4	6.15	3	4.62	2	3.08	12	18.46	3	4.62
4	8	12.31	2	3.08	0	0.0	0	0.0	38	58.46	1	1.54	0	0.0	0	0.0	2	3.08	0	0.0	17	26.15
5	10	15.38	0	0.0	1	1.54	1	1.54	39	60.00	0	0.0	0	0.0	0	0.0	1	1.54	0	0.0	17	26.00
6	10	15.38	3	4.62	4	6.15	0	0.0	7	10.77	3	4.62	4	6.15	6	9.23	4	6.15	9	13.85	15	22.08

a The data are for a weekday, from wives who live in downtown apartments. N equals the number of people who answered the time budget.

Persons present: 1, all alone; 2, alone in crowd; 3, with spouse only; 4, with spouse and children; 5, with children only; 6, with other household adult; 7, with nonhousehold relatives; 8, with friends and neighbors; 9, with work associates.

Location: 1, at home; 2, around the home; 3, in neighborhood; 4, place of work; 5, another's home; 6, business or public places; 7, streets and parks; 8, in transit; 9, other.

Persons + location (combinations of above in order, as follows): 1, person codes 1-6 + location code 1; 2, person codes 1-6 + location codes 2 and 3; 3, person codes 1-6 + location codes 4-9; 4, person codes 7-9 + location code 1; 5, person codes 7-9 + location codes 2 and 3; 6, person codes 7-9 + location codes 4-9.

what people's daily rounds of activities consisted of and to assess whether one or another group of movers had a different *range* of daily activity. With the help of a CalComp plotter, we were able to indicate the relationship among people's homes and those places where they went during the course of the day. Graphic presentations may represent specific types of activities or, on the other hand, the general pattern of movement characterizing people's daily lives.

The differences in spatial orientation reflected in the time-budget data between husband and wife in suburban homes is indicated in Maps 1 and 2.[3] Far more trips are recorded for husbands, even though fewer respond to the interview. They also travel farther and are more likely to visit the city center. The difference in orientation on a daily basis to downtown commercial facilities between those wives living in suburban homes as compared to downtown homes, the same percentage of whom hold jobs, is shown in Maps 3 and 4.

Besides the specific content portrayed in the maps, they indicate directionality, which can explain the orientation of differential subgroups under investigation. This is still another possible by-product of time-budget analysis, and may be particularly useful in assessing any differences that may actually be present among subgroups when overt length and use of time may look similar.

One might speculate concerning some of the advantages the time budget had for this particular task, as well as particular weaknesses that other methods might hope to surpass. Besides its demonstrated manipulability in the production of various kinds of quantitative analyses, as well as their graphic presentation, the time budget may have measured two phenomena that direct questions might have had more difficulty in tapping accurately. They are time devoted to housework and time spent alone. Each of these is a highly normative situation, which the ordinary person does not normally estimate correctly when faced with a direct question. Yet, in the context of a day's events, it is evident that respondents can provide information in bits and pieces, which when assembled in analysis is highly useful in operationalizing the pattern of life. Thus everyday phenomena about which we rarely think in anything resembling a synoptic form are major strengths in time-budget methodology, which direct questions are far less likely to assess.

However, when the phenomena observed occur only rarely, the time budget will produce only indirect evidence on them. Although aggregate data may nonetheless provide indexes of change, which may be substantiated by more direct measures, these indicators are highly imprecise if the odds are low that an activity will be performed during the period for which time budgets are administered. For example, in the current study, very little time was spent on the weekday in question on cultural activities. If a man goes to the opera, for example, five times a year in Toronto, this is very frequent; he may in fact choose a residence on the basis of good access to the opera and other such attractions, even though the study of one or several days of his time is highly unlikely to include a record of such a visit.

Thus time-budget studies that require investigation into infrequently performed activities should be based on a longer period of time than just 1 or 2 days. Since this is impractical in terms of administration, if any degree of detail, let alone a complete inventory, is desired concerning rarely performed activities, more *direct* questions could be used.

Even on a frequent and regular task such as shopping, one performed regularly but not normally daily in Canadian cities, there is a great difference in detail between what one may find from the time budget and what can be assessed through separate, direct questions. Although the

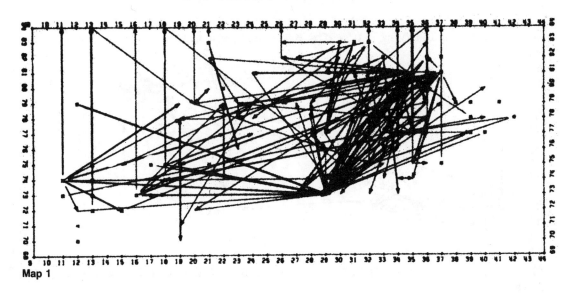

Map 1

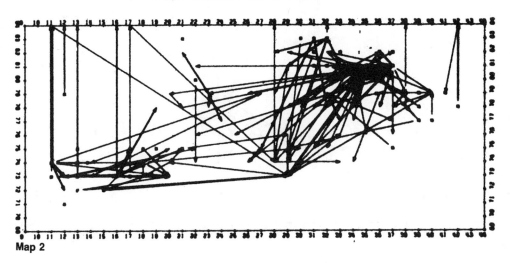

Map 2

HOUSE   SUBURBS
TIME BUDGET: WIFE WEEKDAY: COMMERCIAL TRIPS

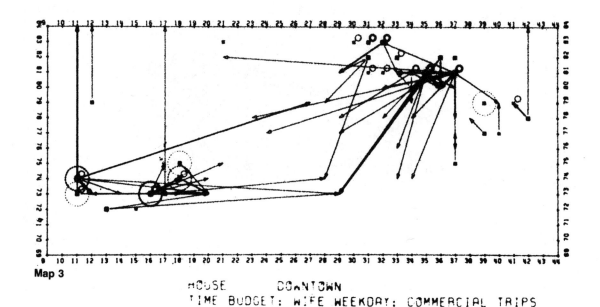

Map 3

HOUSE   DOWNTOWN
TIME BUDGET: WIFE WEEKDAY: COMMERCIAL TRIPS

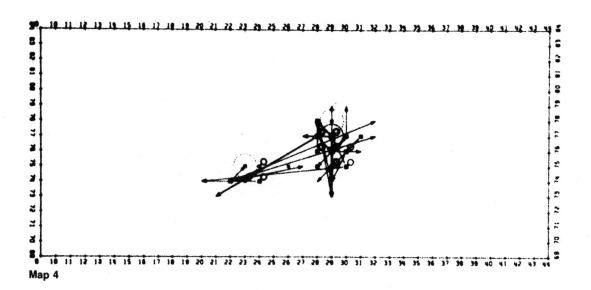

Map 4

time budget may be fully satisfactory in providing data that would "index" one subgroup of a population in contrast to another, this may not be enough for some purposes. For example, if one were to compare Maps 3, 4, 5, and 6, the difference in detail is clear, even though the former two maps, produced from time-budget data, refer to all commerce visited during a weekday, while the latter two, taken from direct questions, refer only to where women shop for their groceries. Each type of map may differentiate the two residential subgroups of wives, but the latter provide much greater indication on where exactly people usually go. This latter information

may be very much more important in studies addressing questions different from those covered in the present paper.

The applicability of the time budget to environmental concerns certainly does not stand or fall on a single study, let alone a few examples from it. The overall aim of this paper was (1) to identify the time-budget methodology, (2) to indicate its relevance to design questions, (3) to indicate some of the procedures followed in its use, (4) to provide a warning as to some of its major pitfalls, (5) to indicate briefly its history of use, and (6) to provide concrete evidence of one such usage.

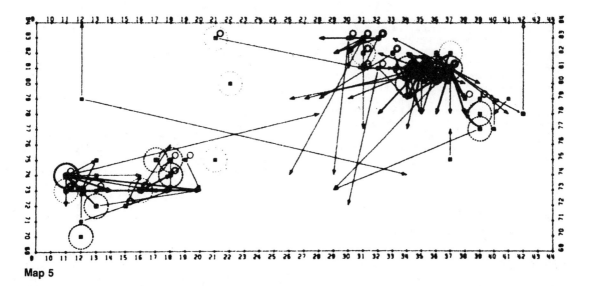

HOUSE   SUBURBS
WHERE GO FOR GROCERIES

Map 5

HOUSE   DOWNTOWN
WHERE GO FOR GROCERIES

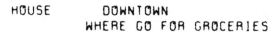

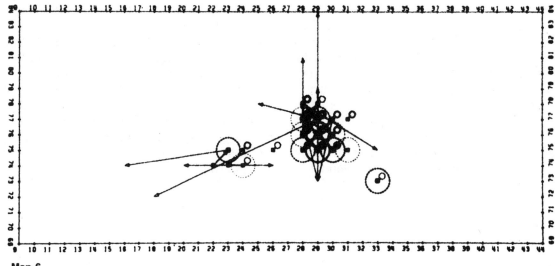

Map 6

NOTES

1. For a more detailed account, see Ottensmann (1972).
2. Michelson, as principal investigator, is grateful to the many persons who have been associated with the project, "The Physical Environment as Attraction and Determinant: Social Effects in Housing," whose primary sponsor is Central Mortgage and Housing Corporation (Canada). Support has also been received from The Canada Council. Among those who made a direct contribution to the data in this chapter are June Steele, Don Rogers, Colin Stafford, Les Cseh, and Cathy Barth. Interviewing was conducted by York University Survey Research Centre, as was part of the coding of interview materials, with the remainder done by RECON Ltd.
3. The key to Maps 1–6 is as follows: origin of lines, locations of respondent' home; lines and arrows, straight-line distance between respondent home and location visits, if greater than 1 mile; small circle, commercial facilities visited that are located in same block as home; large dashed circle, commerical facilities visited that are located within same 1-mile grid as respondent home, although greater than one block away.

REFERENCES

4. Aas, D. 1973. "Explorations with Alternative Methodologies For Data on Time Use." The 2nd colloquium of the Research Group on time-budgets and social activities. Berlin (GDR).
5. Anderson, E., and C. Fitzsimmons. 1960. "Use of Time and Money by Employed Homemakers." *Journal of Home Economics,* vol. 52.
6. Anderson, James. 1970. "Time Budgets and Human Geography: Notes and References." Discussion Paper 36. London: Graduate School of Geography, London School of Economics.
7. Anderson, James. "Space-Time Budgets: Potentialities and Limitations." Discussion Paper 33. London: Graduate School of Geography, London School of Economics, n.d.
8. Anderson, James, and John Goddard. "Some Current Approaches to Human Geography in Sweden." Discussion Paper 33. London: Graduate School of Geography, London School of Economics, n.d.
9. Apali, N. "Some Problems of Sacrifice of Time for the Customer at Shopping in Retail Trade — Results of Corresponding Investigations in GDR's Stores." Fachschule für Binnenhandel, Dresden, n.d.
10. Artiomov, V. A., B. P. Kutyriov, V. D. Patrushev. 1970. "Free Time: Problems and Perspectives. *Society and Leisure,* vol. 3.
11. Bachy, C. 1972. "Le Budget-temps des medecins." Paper presented to the Research Group in Time-Budgets and Social Activities, European Coordination Centre for Research and Documentation in Social Sciences, Brussels.

12. Becker, G. 1965. "A Theory of the Allocation of Time." *Economic Journal,* vol. 75.
13. Bell, Wendell. 1958. "Social Choice, Life Styles, and Suburban Residence," in W. M. Dobriner (ed.), *The Suburban Community.* New York: Putnam.
14. Bell, Wendell. 1968. "The City, the Suburb, and a Theory of Social Choice," in Scott Greer, D. L. McElrath, D. W. Minar, and Peter Orleans (eds.), *The New Urbanization.* New York: St. Martin's.
15. Berger, B. M. 1963. "The Sociology of Leisure: Some Suggestions," in E. O. Smigel (ed.), *Work and Leisure: A Contemporary Social Problem.* New Haven, Conn.: College & University Press.
16. Beshers, James. 1962. *Urban Social Structure.* New York: Free Press.
17. Brail, R. K. 1969. "Activity System Investigations: Strategy for Model Design." University of North Carolina unpublished Ph.D. dissertation.
18. Broadbent, T. A. "An Activity Analysis Framework for Urban Planning." London: Centre for Environmental Studies, working paper, n.d.
19. Brown, G., and M. Rutter. 1966. "The Measurement of Family Activities and Relationships." *Human Relations,* vol. 19.
20. Bull, N. 1965. "Work: Effect on Number and Duration of Activities per Day." Vancouver, B.C.: University of British Columbia unpublished M.A. thesis.
21. Busch, C. 1970. "Domaines d'applications majeures de la methode des budgets-temps dans l'optique d'une sociologie du temps libre ou d'une sociologie de la vie quotidienne." *Society and Leisure,* vol. 3.
22. Chapin, F. S. 1965. *Urban Land Use Planning.* Urbana, Ill.: University of Illinois Press.
23. Chapin, F. S. 1966a. "Time Budget Studies and City Planning." Paper presented at the Time-Budget Round-Table at the Sixth World Congress of Sociology, Evian.
24. Chapin, F. S. 1966b. "The Use of Time Budgets in the Study of Urban Living Patterns." *Research Previews,* vol. 13.
25. Chapin, F. S. 1968a. "Activity Systems and Urban Structure: A Working Schema." *Journal of the American Institute of Planners,* vol. 34.
26. Chapin, F. S. 1968b. "Activity Systems as a Source of Inputs for Land Use Models," in G. C. Hemmens (ed.), *Urban Development Models.* Washington, D.C.: Highway Research Board.
27. Chapin, F. S. 1970. "Activity Analysis of the Human Use of Urban Space." *Town and Country Planning,* July/August.
28. Chapin, F. S. 1970b. "Some Exploratory Directions in Time-Budget Research." Paper presented at the Seventh World Congress of Sociology, Varna.
29. Chapin, F. S. 1971. "Free Time Activities and the Quality of Urban Life." *Journal of the American Institute of Planners,* vol. 37.
30. Chapin, F. S., and H. C. Hightower. 1965. "Household Activity Patterns and Land Use." *Journal of the American Institute of Planners,* vol. 31.
31. Chapin, F. S., and H. C. Hightower. 1966. *Household Activity Systems: A Pilot Investigation.* Chapel Hill, N.C.: Centre for Urban and Regional Studies, Institute for Research in Social Science, University of North Carolina.
32. Chapin, F. S., and T. H. Logan. 1968. "Patterns of Time and Space Use," in H. S. Perloff (ed.), *The Quality of the Urban Environment.* Baltimore: The Johns Hopkins Press, for Resources for the Future, Inc.
33. Chapin, F. S., and R. K. Brail. 1969. "Human Activity Systems in the Metropolitan United States." *Environment and Behavior,* vol. 1
34. Converse, P. E. 1966. "Gross Similarities and Differences in Time Allocations: A Progress Report." Paper presented for the Round Table on Time Budgets of the Sixth World Congress of Sociology, Evian.
35. Converse, P. E. 1968. "Time Budgets," in David Sills (ed.), *International Encyclopedia of Social Sciences,* vol. 16. New York: Macmillan.
36. Cullen, I. G. 1973. "Space, Time and the Disruption of Behaviour in Cities." *Society and Leisure,* vol. 1.
37. Cullen, I., V. Godson, and S. Major. 1971. "The Structure of Activity Patterns." Papers to be presented at the London meetings of the Regional Science Association.
38. Cullen, I., and V. Godson. 1972. *Network of Urban Activities: The Structure of Activity Patterns.* Research Paper 1. London: Joint Unit for Planning Research.
39. Cullen, I., and V. Nichols. "Networks Project: Report on the Tabulations of the Pilot Time-Budget Survey of the Bartlett School of Architecture." Seminar Paper 14, Second Series. London: Joint Unit for Planning Research, n.d.
40. Dahlgren, Rune, Jan Hellberg, and Goran Lindberg. 1971. Boendeaktiviteter och Omgivning. Lund: Institutionen för Byggnadsfunktionslära, Tekniska Högskolan; Lund.
41. De Grazia, S. 1964. *Of Time, Work, and Leisure.* New York: Doubleday.
42. Doob, L. W. 1971. *Patterning of Time.* New Haven, Conn.: Yale University Press.
43. Duncan, O. D., and Beverly Duncan. 1957. "Residential Distribution and Occupational Stratification," in P. K. Hatt and A. L. Reiss (eds.), *Cities and Society.* New York: Free Press.
44. Elliott, D. H., A. S. Harvey, and D. Procos. 1973. An Overview of the Halifax Time-Budget Study Prepared for the Second Annual Colloquium of the Working Group on Time-Budgets and Social Activities. Berlin, D.D.R.
45. Fava, S. F. 1956. "Suburbanism as a Way of Life." *American Sociological Review,* vol. 21, no. 1.
46. Feldheim, P., and G. Manz. 1973. "Time-Budgets and Social Activities." *Society and Leisure,* vol. 1.
47. Feldman, A. S., and Charles Tilly. 1960. "The Interaction of Social and Physical Space." *American Sociological Review,* vol. 25.

48. Fisk, G. 1964. "The Personable Disposable Time: The Psychology of Occupational Differences in the Use of Leisure." *The Frontiers of Management Psychology*. New York: Harper & Row.

49. Foley, D. L. 1964. "An Approach to Metropolitan Spatial Structure," in M. M. Webber (ed.), *Explorations into Urban Structure*. Philadelphia: University of Pennsylvania Press.

50. Foote, N. 1961. "Methods for Studying Meaning in Use of Time," in R. W. Kleemeier (ed.), *Aging and Leisure*. New York: Oxford University Press.

51. Foote, N., and R. Meyersohn. 1959. "Allocations of Time Among Family Activities." Paper presented at the Fourth World Congress of Sociology, Stresa.

52. Gans, H. J. 1967. *The Levittowners*. New York: Random House.

53. Goodey, Brian. 1972. "Displays for Mating." *Design and Environment*, vol. 3 (summer).

54. Goody, J. 1968. "Time: Social Organization," in D. Sills (ed.), *International Encyclopedia of the Social Sciences*, vol. 16. New York: Macmillan.

55. Govaerts, F. 1969. *Leisirs des femmes et temps libre*. Brussels: Université Libre de Bruxelles.

56. Govaerts, F. 1973. "Connaissance sociologique du loisir et concept de fonction. Etude critique." *Society and Leisure*, vol. 1.

57. Gronau, R. 1973. "The Intrafamily Allocation of Time: The Value of the Housewives Time." *American Economic Review*, vol. 63, no. 4 (Sept.).

58. Gross, E. 1963. "A Functional Approach to Leisure Analysis," in E. O. Smigel (ed.), *Work and Leisure: A Contemporary Social Problem*. New Haven, Conn.: College & University Press.

59. Grushin, B. 1967. *Free Time. Current Problems*. Moscow: Mysl Publishing House.

60. Hägerstrand, Torsten. 1970. "What About People in Regional Science?". Papers and Proceedings of the Regional Science Association, vol. 24 (Jan.).

61. Hammer, P. G., and F. S. Chapin. 1972. *Human Time Allocation: A Case Study of Washington, D.C.* Chapel Hill, N.C.: Centre for Urban and Regional Studies, Institute for Research in Social Science, University of North Carolina.

62. Havighurst, R. J. 1961. "The Nature and Values of Meaningful Free-Time Activity," in R. W. Kleemeier (ed.), *Aging and Leisure*. New York: Oxford University Press.

63. Hemmens, G. C. 1966. *The Structure of Urban Activity Linkages*. Chapel Hill, N.C.: Centre for Urban and Regional Studies, Institute for Research in Social Science, University of North Carolina.

64. Hemmens, G. C. 1970. "Analysis and Simulation of Urban Activity Patterns." *Socio-Economic Planning Sciences*, vol. 4.

65. Henry, Jules. 1965. "White People's Time, Colored People's Time." *Trans-Action*, vol. 11.

66. Hightower, H. C. 1965. "Recreational Activity Analysis: Toward a Spatial and Aspatial Methodology for Urban Planning." Chapel Hill, N.C.: University of North Carolina. Unpublished Ph.D. dissertation.

67. Hitchcock, J. R. 1968. "Urbanness and Daily Activity Patterns." Chapel Hill, N.C.: University of North Carolina. Unpublished Ph.D. dissertation.

68. Holman, M. A. 1961. "A National Time-Budget for the Year 2000." *Sociology and Social Research*, vol. 46.

69. Horton, J. 1967. "Time and Cool People." *Trans-Action*, vol. 4.

70. Hungarian Central Statistical Office. 1965. *The Twenty-four Hours of the Day (Analysis of 12,000 Time Budgets)*, English version. Budapest: Hungarian Central Statistical Office.

71. Javeau, Claude. 1970. *Les vingt-quatre heures du Belge*. Brussels: Université Libre de Bruxelles.

72. Javeau, Claude. 1973. "Le role des reductions dans l'analyse des budget-temps." *Society and Leisure*, vol. 1.

73. Johannis, T. B., Jr., and C. N. Bull. 1971. "Non-work Time and Leisure: Three Areas of Future Growth and Development." *Society and Leisure*, vol. 2.

74. Kolaja, Jiri. 1969. *Social System and Time and Space: An Introduction to the Theory of Recurrent Behavior*. Pittsburgh: Duquesne University Press.

75. Kranz, P. 1970. "What Do People Do All Day?". *Behavioral Science*, vol. 15.

76. Larrabee, E., and R. Meyersohn (eds.), 1958. *Mass Leisure*. New York: Free Press.

77. Leibowitz, A. S. 1972. *Women's Allocation of Time to Market and Non-market Activities: Differences by Education*. Unpublished Ph.D. dissertation. Ann Arbor, Mich.: University Microfilms.

78. Lemel, V. 1972. "How Urbanites Budget Their Time," *Economie et Statistique*.

79. Linder, Staffan. 1970. *The Harried Leisure Class*. New York: Columbia University Press.

80. Lippold, G. 1971. "The Influence of Economy on the Increase of Leisure." *Society and Leisure*, vol. 2.

81. Lippold, G. 1973a. Personality Formation and Time Budget in the G.D.R. Between 1965 and 1972. Berlin-Karlshorst, D.D.R.: Bruno Leuschner Hochschule fur Okonomie.

82. Lippold, G. 1973b. "The Utilization of Time Budget Data for Planning." *Society and Leisure*, vol. 1.

83. Lundberg, George et al. 1934. *Leisure: A Suburban Study*. New York: Columbia University Press.

84. Macmurray, T. 1971. "Aspects of Time and the Study of Activity Patterns." *Town Planning Review*, vol. 42.

85. Manz, G. 1973. "People's Requirement and Use of Time." *Society and Leisure*, vol. 1.

86. Maric, D. 1972. "Picture, Country by Country and Branch by Branch, of Actual Duration of Time Worked." Paper presented to the International Conference on New Patterns for Working Time, OECD, Paris, France.

87. McCormick, T. C. 1939. "Quantitative Analysis and Comparison of Living Cultures." *American Sociological*

Review, vol. 4.

88. Meier, R. L. 1959. "Human Time Allocation." *Journal of the American Institute of Planners,* vol. 35.

89. Meyersohn, R. 1966. "Some Observations on Time Budget Research: Comments on the Multinational Comparative Time Budget Research." Paper presented at the Time Budget Round Table, Sixth World Congress of Sociology, Evian.

90. Michelson, W. 1973a. "Discretionary and Nondiscretionary Aspects of Activity and Social Contact in Residential Selection," in L. S. Bourne et al. (eds.), *The Form of Cities in Central Canada: Selected Papers.* Toronto: University of Toronto Press.

91. Michelson, W. 1973b. "Some Inductive Comments on Sociology of Leisure." *Society and Leisure,* vol. V.

92. Michelson, W. 1973c. "The Advent of Multidimensionality in Conceptions of the Quality of Urban Life." Presented to a conference on "The City in History: Idea and Reality," Centre for the Coordination of Ancient and Modern Studies, University of Michigan.

93. Michelson, W. 1973d. "Environmental Change." Research Paper 60. Toronto: Department of Sociology and Centre for Urban and Community Studies, University of Toronto.

94. Michelson, W. 1973e. "The Place of Time in the Longitudinal Evaluation of Spatial Structures by Women." Presented to the Research Group on Time-Budgets and Social Activity, European Coordination Centre for Research and Documentation in Social Sciences, Berlin, D.D.R. Research Paper 61. Toronto: Centre for Urban and Community Studies, University of Toronto.

95. Michelson, W., D. Belgue, and J. Stewart. 1973. "Intentions and Expectations in Differential Residential Selection." *Journal of Marriage and the Family.*

96. Mihovilovic, M. 1969. "Leisure of the Citizens of Zagreb." Publisher: Assembly of Zagreb, Zagreb.

97. Mihovilovic, M. 1972. "Analysis of Some Factors Which Have Influence on Time-Budgets of Employed and Unemployed Women." Paper presented to the International Sociological Association Research Group on Time Budgets and Social Activities, Bruxelles.

98. Mihovilovic, M. 1973a. "Leisure Time of the Adult City Population of Yugoslavia." Standing Conference of Towns of Yugoslavia, Belgrade.

99. Mihovilovic, M. 1973b. "The Influence of Women's Employment on the Family Characteristics and Functioning." Institute for Social Research, University of Zagreb.

100. Moore, W. E. 1963. *Man, Time, and Society.* New York: Wiley.

101. Nakanishi, Naomichi. 1966. *A Report on the How Do People Spend Their Time Survey.* Tokyo: NHK Public Opinion Research Institute.

102. Nakanishi, Naomichi. 1968. *A Study of International Comparison of Time Budget.* Tokyo: NHK Public Opinion Research Institute.

103. Ottensmann, J. 1972. "Systems of Urban Activities: An Interpretative Review of the Literature." Paper prepared for the Centre for Urban and Regional Studies, University of North Carolina at Chapel Hill.

104. Palmer, J. D. 1970. "The Many Clocks of Man." *Natural History,* vol. 79.

105. Park, R. E., Ernest Burgess, and R. D. McKenzie (eds.). 1925. *The City.* Chicago: University of Chicago Press.

106. Patrushev, V. D. (ed.). 1965. *Problems of the Aggregate Time Balance and Results from an Investigation.* Novosibirsk, USSR: Nauka Publishing House.

107. Patrushev, V. D. 1968. "The Time Budget of the Town Population of Socialist and Capitalist Countries." *Philosophic Sciences,* no. 5.

108. Patrushev, V. D. 1970. "Aggregate Time Balance of a Nation (Economic Region) and Its Role in Socioeconomic Planning." Paper submitted to the Seventh World Congress of Sociology, Varna.

109. Patrushev, V. D. 1971. "Aggregate Time Balance of a Nation as a Means of Forecasting the Proportions of Human Activity." *Society and Leisure,* vol. 2.

110. Rehn, G. 1972. "Prospective View on Patterns of Working Time." International Conference on New Patterns for Working Time, OECD, Paris.

111. Riis, J. A. 1890. *How the Other Half Lives.* New York: Scribner.

112. Robinson, J. P. 1967a. "Social Change as Measured by Time-Budgets." *Journal of Leisure Research,* vol. 1.

113. Robinson, J. P. 1967b. "Television and Leisure Time: Yesterday, Today and (Maybe) Tomorrow." Revision of paper given at the American Association of Public Opinion, Survey Research Centre, Institute for Social Research, University of Michigan.

114. Robinson, J. P. 1967c. "Time Expenditure on Sports Across Ten Countries." Paper prepared for the International Workshop on Sociology of Sport, College of Physical Education, University of Illinois.

115. Rossi, P. H. 1955. *Why Families Move.* New York: The Free Press.

116. Skorzynski, Z. 1973. "La Methode des budgets-temps et la planification sociale." *Society and Leisure,* vol. 1.

117. Smigel, E. O. (ed.). 1963. *Work and Leisure: A Contemporary Social Problem.* New Haven, Conn.: College & University Press.

118. Sorokin, P. A., and C. Q. Berger. 1939. *Time Budgets of Human Behavior.* Cambridge, Mass.: Harvard University Press.

119. Staikov, Z. 1970. "Time Budgets as a Methodological Basis for Planning and Forecasting of Social Phenomena." Paper presented at the Seventh World Congress of Sociology, Varna.

120. Staikov, Z. 1973. "Modelling and Programming of Time Budget—Methodological Issues." *Society and Leisure,* vol. 1.

121. Stone, P. J. 1970. "Technical Issues and Solutions Suggested by the International Time Budget Project." Paper presented at the Seventh World Congress of Sociology, Varna.

122. Strzeminska, H. 1973. "Use of Time-Budgets Data for

Diagnosis and Prognosis." *Society and Leisure,* vol. 1.

123. Swedener, Harald, Ingemar Becker, and Uggi Krahg-Schou. 1967. Forslag till Miljö-forsknings program. Stockholm: Stockholms Stads Generalplanberedning.

124. Swedener, H., and D. Yague. 1970. "Proposals for a Nomenclature for Human Activities with Particular Reference to Cultural Activities." *Society and Leisure,* vol. 2.

125. Szalai, A. 1964. "Differential Work and Leisure Time-Budgets as a Basis for Inter-cultural Comparisons." *New Hungarian Quarterly,* vol. 5.

126. Szalai, A. 1965. *International Comparative Time-Budget Study.* Novosibirsk, USSR: Nauka Publishing House.

127. Szalai, A. 1966a. "Differential Evaluation of Time Budgets for Comparative Purposes," in R. Merritt and S. Rokkan (eds.), *Comparing Nations: The Use of Quantitative Data in Cross-National Research.* New Haven, Conn.: Yale University Press.

128. Szalai, A. 1966b. "The Multinational Comparative Time Budget Research Project: A Venture in International Research Cooperation." *American Behavioral Scientist,* vol. 10.

129. Szalai, A. 1966c. "Trends in Comparative Time Budget Research." *The American Behavioral Scientist,* vol. 9, no. 9.

130. Szalai, A. 1968. "Trends in Contemporary Time Budget Research." *The Social Sciences: Problems and Orientation.* The Hague: Mouton UNESCO.

131. Szalai, A. 1972. *The Use of Time.* The Hague: Mouton.

132. Tilly, Charles. 1961. "Occupational Rank and Grade of Residence in a Metropolis." *American Journal of Sociology,* vol. 67.

133. Tomeh, A. K. 1969. "Empirical Considerations on the Problem of Social Integration." *Sociological Inquiry,* vol. 39.

134. Varga, Karoly. 1973. "Achievement, Affiliation and Exposure to Media According to the Sexes." Budapest: Institute of Sociology, Hungarian Academy of Sciences.

135. Von Rosenbladt, B. "Descriptive Validity, Theoretical Relevance, and Some Technical Problems of the Time Budget Data." Institute for Social Research, University of Munster, Dortmunt. Unpublished paper, n.d.

136. Von Rosenbladt, B. "The Meaning of Time Budget Figures: Some Critical Comments on the Basic Tables of the International Time Budget Project." Institute for Social Research, University of Munster, Dortmunt. Unpublished paper, n.d.

137. Walker, K. E. 1969. "Time Spent in Household Work by Homemakers." *Family Economics Review.*

138. Walker, K. E. 1970. "Time-Use Patterns for Household Work Related to Homemakers' Employment." Ithaca, N.Y.: New York State College of Human Ecology, Cornell University.

139. Warner, W. L., et al. 1957. *Social Class in America.* Gloucester, Mass.: Peter Smith.

140. Warner, W. L., and P. S. Lunt. 1941. *The Social Life of a Modern Community.* New Haven, Conn.: Yale University Press.

141. Wheeler, J. O. 1968. "Residential Location by Occupational Status." *Urban Studies,* vol. 5, pp. 26–32.

142. Wunk-Lipinski, Edmund. 1973. *Pattern of Leisure and Development of Women's Personality.* Ministry of Labour, Wages and Social Affairs, Poland.

Photographic Recording of Environmental Behavior

Gerald Davis and Virginia Ayers

Gerald Davis, founder and president of TEAG—The Environmental Analysis Group, Ltd., Vancouver, B.C., Canada, combines in his experience the practice of architecture, business management, survey and behavioral research, and teaching. He spent 10 years in staff and executive positions in a manufacturing company. He taught at Stanford University and practiced architecture for 5 years. He is a member of the Environmental Psychology Program at the University of British Columbia. His present firm bridges between the needs of owners and users and the work of the design professionals.

Virginia Ayers received a B.Arch. from the University of California of Berkeley and an M.Arch., Advanced Studies, from the Massachusetts Institute of Technology after having studied in the social sciences. She has worked for the Center for Environmental Structure, for the Housing Development Administration of New York City, for Gamal El-Zoghby, and is currently architectural programmer with TEAG.

We have written this chapter on photographic methods because there is relatively little literature on the use of photography in research on the interaction between human behavior and the physical environment. Data gathering by photographic methods has been touched on in papers and booklets for legal purposes, but the typical reference is seldom more than a paragraph in length.[1]

This chapter is not an historical review of the development of photographic methods, nor is it a survey of the full range of photographic research that has been undertaken by a variety of students and professionals, who are using everything from simple cameras in remote locations to sophisticated closed-circuit television equipment. It is an attempt to suggest specific techniques developed in the recent past. Some of the equipment mentioned is so new that it will be coming into the general market about the time this book is published.

Our objective is to communicate current thinking and experience, in the hope that researchers and students will work from this material in developing further the state of the art in photographic research.

PHOTOGRAPHY AS A RESEARCH TOOL

Photography Is Only a Part of Research

Photography is only one of the many tools available to the researcher studying behavior in the human milieu. Photography provides economical and comprehensive access to some visually observable aspects of behavior. Behavior can be recorded and analyzed with photography without loss due to observer error, limitations of observer skill, or speed in recording. Crucial moments can be re-created over and over again, and subjected to many types of analysis that are wholly unavailable to the human observer, who can only capture the fleeting moment with notes, sketches, and memory.

Visually observable behavior, however, is only a small part of the complex interactions between people and their milieus. The list of factors that can affect observable behavior seems almost endless: the cultural, social, and physical environments; the expectations, mood, and motivations of the individual; the previous and following experiences of the individual; roles, organizations, and images are examples. What the camera can see and record is only the tip of the iceberg; most of the interaction between the individual and his milieu is invisible.

The camera, however, can give us powerful insights that have previously been unavailable. The camera can expose cues to many nonvisible aspects of the man–milieu interaction. When used in connection with other data, as part of a larger research framework, the camera can be a powerful research tool. Photographic data are often surprisingly rich in information, some of which may not be understood till long after they were obtained. Photographic data provide repeated access to certain aspects of an event, and can be mined time after time for different kinds of treasure. As long as the researcher keeps in perspective the importance of the larger context in selecting, photographing, and analyzing his data, photography can become a major, even a basic, source of research data.

Need for a Conceptual Framework

Any effective research requires a conceptual framework and a rigorous structure of testing and analysis. The individual observer, spending many hours in a particular milieu, working in the context of a defined research plan, skilled in perceiving and recording, must make many hard judgments, moment by moment, as to what is important, what is relevant, and what is simply background for his study. Over time, however, the skilled observer, the anthropologist, the sociologist, the environmental psychologist, or members of other relevant disciplines, all come to understand the meanings of behavior in a particular milieu in the light of their prior studies, and of the paradigms within which their current study is operating. They observe within the limitations of their research project. They perceive within the limitations of their understanding. Thus their records are hemmed in by the double limitations of their perceptions and their project. To a considerable degree the camera can free them from these limitations because of the comprehensiveness of its images, which include data that may not have been perceived as significant, or not understood, at the time of photography.

Even the camera, however, is limited by the photographer. He selects what to photograph and how to photograph it. Although he is much less confined than with written records, he is still constrained by the conceptual framework for his study. Without a conceptual framework, implicit or explicit, the researcher only photographs bits and pieces that may or may not be relevant to any future analysis or understanding. But if the researcher has a general understanding of the milieu, often developed from direct observation of people in settings, then the photographic data may provide new conceptual opportunities. Because of the comprehensiveness of typical photographic data and the ability to "re-create" events over and over again during analysis, the researcher with photographic methods has unusual opportunities to enrich his concept, or even to modify it, *after* his initial photographic data gathering. He may, however, as discussed on pages 245–270, need to reiterate his data gathering to confirm the later developments of his conceptual framework.

In short, think first, observe second, and only then start to photograph.

General Advantages of Photographic Methods

For recording the visual aspects of behavior, photography can provide much greater accuracy and much more information about complex or brief events than visual observation with written notes. In particular, photography can record complex sequences of events, in fine detail, where even several skilled observers working as a team would miss significant data. And photography can often permit the gathering of data less obtrusively and less expensively than other means.

In analysis of data, photography permits the juxtaposition of similar events that occurred at different times or in different locations, so that similarities, and even replicability, can be more easily perceived and tested. The photographic data can be analyzed in the isolation of the projection room, free from the distractions and interruptions of the real-life context. A particular event can be made to recur many times, unchanged,

so that the analyst can concentrate on a different aspect each time without losing the rest of the data; in effect, he can dismember the event without destroying it. When using time-lapse photography, the analyst can study the same event at several speeds, taking advantage of the way that different aspects of behavior tend to dominate perception at different projection speeds. Photographic images can be superimposed with grids or templates for statistical or formal analysis, which would be impossible to do during the real event in the field.

Photography can permit improved observational effectiveness. By allowing the researcher to study an event in depth of detail, photography allows the observer to understand and deal with more simultaneous aspects of the event. What had been perceived as "distractions" often become significant research content. His understanding of the event then becomes more comprehensive and more accurate. This can be cumulative. As the researcher increases his analytical skills in working with the film and gains new insights into the behavior under study, he also increases his effectiveness in observing and filming the relevant events.

Photography communicates not only to the initial researcher, but also to those who use the results of his research. When the researcher has identified the prototypical images of the man–milieu relationship he is studying, he can with his film re-create selected events in simulated "real time." Since many of those who design our environments are visually oriented, the visual real-time image permits a much more effective communication than reams of words and intellectual abstractions.

Photography Is Rarely Effective Without Other Research Methods

What can be observed with the naked eye, or with the camera, is usually only a small part of the total data needed for any research problem. In a few instances we have found that a person who already fully understands the context can define a problem so that the only *new* data needed can be gathered photographically. As an example, a picture can be used to determine the degree of crowding in a public place. From photographs of people standing waiting outside a courtroom, the minimum normal interpersonal distance can be determined. The interpretation and use of the data, however, depend on an understanding of the context, including the cultural and social milieu.

Examples of Using Photography in Research

For some types of photography, the researcher can make specific judgments in advance of the camera work, specifying what to photograph and how. The research team doing such photography will require relatively less training and understanding of the research objectives than for some of the later examples we shall give.

Inventory of a physical environment The camera can record spaces, buildings, or interiors economically, accurately, quickly, and comprehensively. Space inventories require very systematic structured photographic procedures, with careful logging of exposures and coordination with plans and diagrams of the spaces inventoried. Unless special methods are used, the data usually do not include dimensions for scaling. They are, however, an excellent reference record, particularly as a base or data control. Normally, at least two wide-angle photographs are taken of each space from diagonally opposite directions. For interior spaces, one is usually taken from the entrance and the other from the opposite side (Figure 1).

Photographing people or things for later counting A single person with a camera can photograph a large number of people or vehicles

moving past a particular place or present at a particular location, when accurate tabulation directly at the moment would be impractical or difficult. At a later time, the time-lapse film or 35mm slides can be studied frame by frame, often with astonishing accuracy (Figure 2). Photographs of moving crowds can be overlaid with grids, and accurate counts and densities calculated. The film often permits further analysis, such as counting movements of particular individuals in the crowd, or estimates of crowd composition by sex, approximate age, and so on. Crowds may also be studied in specialized locations, such as elevators, where secondary data like the number of handbags carried is important, and may be determined from the film.

Study of selected details of an activity or function When an activity or function such as the use of a telephone at a desk is generally understood in its context, photographic data can be a powerful tool for detailed analysis (Figure 3). Time and motion studies that yield information about how tasks are performed and the sequences of motions are an example of this use of photography in research. We have used photography to help us study selected details of queuing behavior at a bank, at an airport check-in counter, and at the counter (interface zone) in the office of a university registrar.

For these three types of photography, the camera work can usually be planned in advance, and often the camera can be left to operate untended for many minutes or for whole portions of a day. There are a number of other types of photography, however, for which the choices of subjects to photograph or the choices of behavior that are relevant to the research objectives are made primarily at the time of photography. These types of photography, five of which are listed next, require that the photographer fully understand the research project, its objectives, content, and proposed kinds of analysis. We have

Figure 1

Inventory of a physical environment. These two prints are copied from 35mm color slides taken from opposite ends of a courtroom. They show almost all the furniture and equipment normally in place in the courtroom. They also show many aspects of the physical structure and fittings of the space itself, including exposed structural members (concrete columns and beams), wall finishes (including their color, on the original 35mm slides), the radiators under the windows, the lighting fixtures, and so on. This information on the physical structure and fittings was used by the architects and engineers in planning the remodeling of the space.

A total of five slides were taken to inventory this courtroom, of which these two were the main slides and suitable for black-and-white reproduction. One other slide showed the "window wall," with its curtains, but presented technical problems for copying in black-and-white, owing to the high brightness contrast between the actual window areas and their surrounds, and the intervening walls. (For photographs of walls with unshaded windows we normally use the same exposure setting as for the rest of the space near the windows, and let the image through the window "wash out.") Of the other two slides, one

showed the public seating area largely hidden at the rear of the left slide, and the other showed details of the judge's bench.

The arrangement of the courtroom is clearly shown in the whole series. Judge's bench, table for the attorneys, box for the witness, box for the prisoners, chairs for press and official visitors, and chairs and table for court officials are all clearly identifiable. This visual information was part of a series used in discussions with members of the judiciary, the bar, and others during the planning of new facilities, and related "rules of practice." From this visual information it was clear that such a courtroom arrangement, although acceptable for a county court, would not be suitable for a small claims court because, among other things, there is need for more seating for members of the public awaiting the start of their case.

Because the photographs used in this type of research are generally color slides or colored Super-8 movie film, we had to make intermediate black-and-white negatives for the prints shown herein. This resulted in a loss of sharpness, compared to the colored images actually used for research. (All photos in this chapter are by the authors, except where specified.)

found that the research team itself needs to do the photography for these kinds of research.

Study of a sequential experience We take 35mm slides as we walk through, or ride through, an environment, recording and revealing our visual and spatial experiences. Photography such as this allows the researcher to record and study the space sequence and the behavior of people

in the space in an orderly and logical way, and also to communicate his perceptions to others. Events, behaviors, and objects that may have escaped his attention while he walked and photographed are recorded for future analysis. By his overall selection of camera angles, vistas, glances to right or to left, a skillful photographic researcher can preserve the spatial sequences, with emphasis and detail; as he perceived them, but with a richness that no amount of sketching or remembering can equal.

We have used sequential presentations for a freeway, for the main street of a large city, for a walk through the urban core of a provincial capital, to compare the urban scales of cities in Europe and in North America, to evaluate a complex of university buildings, to study a shopping center, to evaluate an office-landscape installation, and for many other purposes. Readers can find some examples in Cullen (1961, p. 18, an illustration of serial vision; and p. 20, the sequence in New Delhi) and in Appleyard et al. (1964, p. 14, approach to the United Nations Building on the East River Drive in New York City).

Study of the visual components of the image of a place The researcher can use photography to record, analyze, and communicate the essential visual elements that contribute to the image or aura of a particular place or envi-

Figure 2
Photographing people or things for later counting. Time-lapse photographs, two exposures (or "frames") per second, were taken of the entrances to the courthouse and of the public sidewalk in front, so that accurate counts could be developed of people entering, leaving, and passing the building. Every 15 minutes a set of 35mm slides was taken from the same view-points to provide supporting detail of the context. These black-and-white prints are made from the 35mm slides.

The picture at the left duplicates a frame from the Super-8 time-lapse film, and shows an individual standing at the top of the steps, apparently ready to walk down, while another person enters the field of view from below, approaching the steps. The use of the time-lapse camera is important, as illustrated by the full sequence of which this is an excerpt. The full sequence shows that the individual at the top of the steps came out of the door behind him, paused for a few seconds to look around the area, and returned inside. The objective of this photographic study

was to determine the courthouse population continuously throughout the day, as well as the flows of people through the various entrances; therefore, it was important to know that this person never really left the courthouse precinct. This sequence, and others like it, were also useful to the architect in raising the design question: What view-points should be provided so that people can see others approaching a courthouse building? Another appropriate question is: What type of door, screen, or other separation is appropriate between the "inside" and the "outside" of the courthouse precinct?

The slide of the sidewalk, shown at the right, includes a walking "band" passing the courthouse, and indicates the kinds of pedestrian traffic and sound sources to be expected at this location. It also shows, as does the Super-8 film, the numbers of people passing a given point at a given time.

The 35mm slides were taken with a 105mm lens.

ronment (Figure 4). Sometimes the objective is to synthesize what are the basic components of the image under study; what gives the place its visual mood and character. This photographic data may be particularly useful when correlated with the answers to interviews about how users of the place perceive it. If these responses can be correlated further with the intentions and/or perceptions of planners, designers, and owners, wholly new understandings may be achieved.

Alternatively, photographs of places with known images can often be used to study and anticipate perceptions and objectives for a proposed project. For existing environments, changes in color or finish, additions to structure, or changes in landscape can be evaluated by using such tools as the Environmental Adjective Check List, if before-and-after photographs are available.

Analysis of functional systems, including activities and physical components Slides and film can show how people use space and facilities in various activities. Time-lapse, time-sampling and various detailed motion-picture films can show the interrelations between activities and their physical environments. Combining both wide angle and telephoto in 35mm slides may give telling evidence of effective planning, or of "misfits" (Figure 5). These pictures may often be taken at the same time as a space inventory. This is an ad hoc use of photography instead of using photography systematically to inventory.

Half a day with photographic equipment in a baggage sorting area revealed the reality of how the system really worked, as distinct from what was intended and what management understood. Film of a street intersection where many accidents have been recorded revealed the elements of driver practice and physical construction that contribute to the accident pattern.

Figure 3
Study of selected details of an activity or function. We were studying behavior during the midday period in a shopping mall that had been created by closing a business street to vehicular traffic. The "street furniture" includes kiosks, restaurants, stairs to the upper levels of some buildings, seating, displays, and this grouping of symbolic rocks. (Each rock had been selected from one of the provinces of Canada.)

The 35mm slide on the left, taken with a 24mm wide-angle lens, shows the rock garden in its context of the wider mall, with sidewalk and passers-by.

The 35mm slide on the right, taken from a slightly more distant vantage point with a 105mm lens, shows details of how the rock garden is actually used during the lunch period.

Figure 4
Study of the visual components of the "image" of a place. We photographed this shopping mall to record and synthesize into a usable record the basic visual components of its "image." The fact of such noontime happenings as a band concert contributed to that image. People stood around, listening and watching. Others passed by, aware of the "happening" but uninvolved. There was enough room for passers-by outside the circle of on-lookers.

Some people could sit and enjoy the performance, alone or with friends.
In the left 35mm slide, taken with the 24mm wide-angle lens, we recorded the general context. In the right 35mm slide, taken with the 105mm long-focus lens, we recorded specific details that gave focus and emphasis to the component of "image" that we wished to illustrate.

Understanding individual behavior, group dynamics, and roles Film can be particularly effective in tracking and recording individual or group behavior in a particular place, or over a particular time cycle (Figure 6). A time-sampling camera in the room of a hospital patient, at the nurses' station, or in the hospital corridor could explain much that a self-recorded diary, or even an observer, would miss. A time-sampling camera in the room of a college student can reveal much about the design of the room and its furnishings that hours of interview and observation would overlook. Photographic recording of the movements of particular individuals in a small-claims courthouse revealed complexities of normal routines that not even the staff had perceived in years on the job. Tracking visitors through a museum with photographic equipment emphasized the strengths and weaknesses of exhibit design that unaided observers had missed.

Understanding behavior in specific environments Photographic recording can be particularly useful in analyzing behavior that exists only for a few instants, but recurs frequently in a variety of contexts. When people approach and step on an escalator or moving sidewalk and when they leave it, the transitional behavior lasts only for seconds. It is, however, behavior that urban dwellers repeat many times in different locations; and it is behavior that is little understood, even by those who have frequently experienced or observed it. By selecting contexts so that certain variables are controlled, the research can compare accurately many different aspects of behavior with only small amounts of film. From this study, predictions of behavior can be made. An example of this research is described later.

These five categories of research using photography all require that the photographer fully understand the research content and objectives.

Figure 5
Analysis of functional systems, including activities and physical components. These two 35mm slides, both taken with the 24mm wide-angle lens, give evidence of "misfits," failures in the physical planning and arrangements of furnishings and equipment. In the left slide (taken by Billy C. Ellis), a storeroom is used as an office and as storage space for the worker's bicycle. The owner of the bicycle reported that he had no safe place elsewhere in the building to park his bicycle with confidence that it would not be "stripped." This picture was taken during a photo survey of the building.

The slide on the right was taken during a photographic inventory of the offices of a firm of stockbrokers in the course of planning their move to new offices. The secretary was explaining that one of her functions was to process invoices and correspondence which were mailed in window envelopes. Several days each month, when she handled large mailouts, she used far more envelopes than could be stored in the open drawer on which her hand rests. She therefore kept a pile of cartons, full of envelopes, on the floor near her work station. There was no alternative suitable storage within the large workspace of her office. In planning the new layout, this slide was used with the notes taken at the same time, to ascertain that appropriate storage would, in the future, be available to her.

We have found one category of research that, in addition, requires exceptional photographic skills, since the situation may make other photographic methods difficult to apply. Furthermore, this last category may require special sensitivity on the part of the researcher to the behavior and perceptions of those around him.

Participant observation using photographic recording We have used photography as a basic adjunct to our participant observation work. This is easiest when we can participate naturally as tourists or visitors, so that taking pictures is a normal and accepted part of our role. Behavior in many public places, in resorts and hotels (Figure 7), and in some semi-private locations can be effectively recorded in this way. Often note taking is more difficult than photography, and we must retire periodically to a private place to dictate or write our notes and photolog. There are a few situations, such as during a courtroom trial, when photography is generally illegal. There are many borderline cases, however, where photography is legal, if permitted by the owner or management. An example of the latter situation occurred in participant observation for a project in a group of branch banks. Because photography was generally forbidden in the banks, taking pictures would attract so much attention to the photographer, even with official permission, that he could no longer observe the banking activities as a normal participant customer. It was therefore necessary to have one person, identified to management,

Figure 6
Understanding individual behavior and group dynamics and roles. These prints are taken from a Super-8 time-lapse film of the secretarial and receptionist area in an office (taken by Donald L. Derezinski). The battery-powered clock on the wall does not show well in these black-and-white prints made from the Super-8 frames, but in color it indicates that the two pictures were taken only 10 minutes apart. Clearly, there is a problem in keeping a staff member in the area to receive visitors. Also, we noted that whenever someone brought work to one of the women, or discussed something with them, it was distracting to the other. Since these pictures were taken, the work area has been rearranged, and work procedures adjusted, to correct the problems. (With our newer cameras, which print the exact time in hours, minutes, and seconds on each frame of film, we would not have to rely on the wall clock shown here.)

Figure 7
Participant observation using photographic recording. The left picture shows the overall setting at mealtime during a celebration by some of the guests at a resort. The right picture shows the particular seating unit in detail, and how it was used by informally attired guests at the resort. Each picture is part of a separate, but related series dealing with the physical facilities and their utilization. Over 200 pages of single-spaced typewritten transcript from dictation accompanied the photographic data in this study.

take photographs, while another unidentified researcher proceeded with his participant activities. We note that this type of research raises particular ethical issues, which are discussed on pages 257–259.

Photography for Research Is Different from Other Types of Photography

The preceding nine categories of research using photography can hardly be considered all-inclusive. Many readers will have other categories to suggest, and the list will grow in the coming years with new equipment and further experience. We have prepared the chart in Figure 8 to show some of the types of photography that we do *not* consider as photography for research. This chart suggests that the degree of dissemination can vary widely within each of the four general objectives listed. We hope it also emphasizes the very limited aspects of photography that we review in this chapter.

UNDERSTANDING BEHAVIOR ON ESCALATORS AND MOVING SIDEWALKS AT AIRPORTS

In this section we describe a study undertaken specifically to further develop photographic methods of research. In the past we had examined pedestrian flows, queuing, clustering, and other characteristics of pedestrian behavior in airports for concourse design. Because we had found photography to be of use in research in a number of ways, we decided to develop photographic methods that would greatly increase our ability to understand behavior in specific environments.

Escalators and moving sidewalks in airports were selected for photographic study of behavior using time-lapse movies and 35mm slides.[2] This particular method was expected to reveal new insights about behavioral patterns:

1. What characteristics of the area around the beginning of an escalator seem to affect behavior of people who are approaching the escalators?
2. How do people in groups break apart as they approach? What is their relationship to each other when on the escalator and after leaving the escalator?
3. Do people with small children or carrying suitcases behave differently than those who have their hands free?
4. How does the placement of signs, pathways, and obstructions affect the behavior of people approaching, riding, and leaving escalators?

The purpose of the photographic data gathering described in this section was twofold: to reveal technical and procedural problems; and to collect enough data to formulate an outline of theory from which further study could be planned.

Preliminary Findings Regarding the Behavior Under Observation

Even this exploratory first phase, which was phototechnical in emphasis, reveals a number of different kinds of findings that could be expected to come out of later studies.

Typical behavior of escalator users There are typical patterns of behavior for most people on most escalators. For example, people frequently check behind them to see that companions are following safely, sometimes by glancing down at the step to be negotiated, and at other times by glancing around while moving ahead (Figure 9). But as this behavior seems to occur more frequently when getting *on* escalators than getting off, and more frequently getting *off* moving walks than getting on, the checking behavior may be related to the difficulty of the step just negotiated by the first of the companions. There are at least two design implications in this: leave a free zone

DEGREE OF DISSEMINATION

OBJECTIVE OF THE PHOTOGRAPHIC MEDIUM

	PRIVATE	LIMITED DISTRIBUTION	SEMI-PUBLIC	PUBLIC COMMUNICATION
RESEARCH Replicable, pragmatic; Realistic; Photo is a vehicle towards the document; Investigatory	Concept development; Internal data acquisition	Analysis for specific concepts and testing of hypotheses; Enlargement of paradigms; Tool in social research	Application of theory and concepts in practical use	Simulation or communication of reality, as in testing or teaching
DOCUMENTARY Captures "the essential moment"; Realistic; Photo is the total document; Objective emphasis	Private historical data; Espionage; Surveillance	Supplement to social research	Training aid	Political information; Social literature; Newsreel; Photo journalism
REPRESENTATIONAL Controlled reality; Illusory; Illustrative, clarifying; Subjective emphasis		Industrial research and technology; Medical research	Illustration in publication; Law enforcement; Personal identifica-identification; Legal evidence	Political literature, propaganda; Advertising, fashion photography; Persuasion; Cinema; Exhibition
PERSONAL Creative; Illusory; Impressionistic, or expressionistic; Personally interpretative	Private perceptions; Private pornography; Private art	Theraputic Expression; Holiday snapshots; Personal art	Portrait photography; Personal portfolios; Personal display	Art theatre; Photographic publication; Museum display

Figure 8
Uses of the photographic medium. This chart identifies some of the differences between photography for research and other kinds of photography.

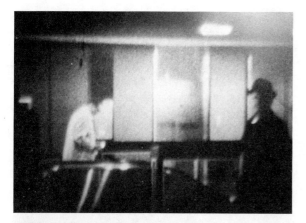

Figure 9
Checking for companions following behind. The man continues watching the escalator step he just got on, while the

in the area where checking for companions is likely to occur; and avoid creating a pedestrian intersection of crossing streams.

Behavior of special populations Although there is a variety of behavior observed on escalators, several kinds appear to be typical of specific populations. We looked for hypotheses associated with fairly permanent physical characteristics, such as people's age and agility, temporary characteristics, such as the type of clothing worn and objects carried, and interactional characteristics, such as the number of people moving as a group and the general nature of their relationships. For example, people who wear glasses tend to tilt their heads farther down than others when stepping on and off. They also tend to hesitate a little longer than others when stepping on. This is one of the conditions that could lower the actual capacity of an escalator below the claims of the manufacturer, who may not take such behavioral characteristics into account.

Environmental influences This category includes not only the physical form of the environment (which in this case was the single aspect covered), but also nonphysical variables of the environment, such as the nature of the surrounding activities, the immediate intentions of users, the various degrees of urgency people have, people's familiarity with the site, and the state of the site in its operational cycle.

One finding about the effect of the physical form on behavior is that a single escalator approached from a free field seems to have two approach zones in which different kinds of be-

companion who follows negotiates the same step. Hypothesis and design implications are discussed in the text. This behavior was filmed at 6 frames per second on Super-8 color film using a Braun Nizo camera. Black-and-white negatives were made from selected frames and printed for publication, unfortunately with great reduction in quality from the originals used in the study.

havior occur. In the outer approach zone, approximately 5 to 10 feet from the first escalator step, most of the gross body movements occur in anticipation of the escalator. In this zone, people in groups start ordering themselves sequentially. Someone may turn around to see if a lagging companion is still within sight. An adult may put

down or pick up a child. It is in the inner approach zone, within approximately 5 feet, that most of the minor adjustments occur in anticipation of the escalator: grabbing a child's hand, switching an object to the other hand, taking a hand out of a pocket, freeing one hand from a two-handed carrier position, or pulling a shoulder bag to the front

Figure 10
This illustration shows outer and inner approach zones. A man puts a child down within an area approximately 5–10 feet from the first escalator step, where other gross movements seem also to take place. The last photo, taken at a different escalator, shows a man taking a child's hand

in an area much closer to the first step. The movie frames were selected from a sequence filmed at 6 frames per second with a Braun Nizo. Simultaneous slides taken at 30-second intervals missed this behavior. The last photo was copied from one of a series of 35mm slides.

to keep it from rubbing against the handrail. Figure 10 shows the behavior of individuals in these two zones.

Implications of mechanization Escalators and moving sidewalks are only two of the many mechanical devices common to our everyday, pedestrian urban environment. A machine demands the same of everyone: the elderly, children, people with canes and crutches, people with poor balance, and people who are afraid, unfamiliar with what to expect, or distracted.

One of the differences between these mechanical devices and other pedestrian experiences is that escalators and moving walks eliminate one kind of choice. For most people, once one is on, one must continue to the end, even if one quickly decides to go back. To the extent that the design increases this loss of choice by removing other alternative means of pedestrian access (stairs, ramps, pathways), the physical form aggravates one of the disadvantages of mechanization.

Implications of general or universal relationships between people and the environment It may be that people develop standard responses to certain kinds of physical settings, and in situations where there is no standard response, they may try modes from other settings. For example, some people who are concerned about the safety of companions will allow the companions to go ahead, which is similar to gesturing someone ahead at a door, and the purpose may not be so much to hold the door open as to hold off pressure from others close behind. Another mode is to lend an arm for the companion to grasp before getting on, and this is very common in stepping off a curb. A more extreme mode is to precede the companion and then turn to lend a firm hand, as in boarding a swaying boat. It is possible, therefore, that physical forms can be created which elicit standard responses inappropriate to the situation, and new designs and new built form might come to be evaluated from the point of view of the standard responses elicited.

Methods

The methods here are those actually used in the study. For a more general discussion of methods and procedures and for the general concepts underlying the procedures developed for this study, see pages 257–270.

Preliminary planning Much of the research strategy could be planned in advance because one member of the team had previously studied behavior on escalators and moving sidewalks, and the other members of the team were already quite familiar with airports and their operations. Because this study was initiated primarily for the sake of developing methodology, we could depend on our previous experience in analyzing the photographs without having to design other research methods as part of the study. Ordinarily, a study like this would involve other methods of research.

As explained later, we used movies to record visually observable behavioral movements. In addition, we took 35mm slides of the same events, to show selected details more clearly than would be possible with Super-8 movies alone. We found this was not necessary in every situation because the informative value of the photographs is affected by such variables as closeness to subject and angle of view. The first iteration using movies at six frames per second, with slides taken simultaneously, was necessary to determine the most effective use of equipment in later iterations (Figure 11).

We used a Braun Nizo S560 camera to take the time-lapse movies. Because the timing mechanism of this camera can be set only approximately and because we wanted to time the duration of events accurately, we photographed in multiples of 30-second time modules; that is, runs of film are 1 minute, or 1½ minutes, or 2 minutes, and so on. Later experience showed that 15-second modules are most appropriate for certain situations and camera angles, because

Figure 11
Super-8 movies with wide-angle lens and telephoto slides taken simultaneously. The first slide, taken on a 30-second time module for the sequence, shows the physical context for the movie shown at the left, and was taken exactly at the time as the first frame shown. The second slide was taken as soon after the first slide as possible, by one person using 35mm cameras mounted with different lenses, both hanging around his neck. This slide shows greater detail than its companion movie frame. Movie frames here are every eighth frame of a movie taken at 6 frames per second. The second slide shows clearly the masking tape applied to the side of the escalator to mark the step-on point in the photograph.

when one is trying to record behavior rather than to take a photographic time sample, film without people present is of little value. A 15-second module allows cutting off the filming sooner after the last person in a given group has passed out of view. New developments in cameras eliminate the necessity of filming multiples of time modules.

Initially, we used a three-person team to gather data: one member to take time-lapse movies; one to take slides with both 35mm cameras; and a third to record on the photolog and read off time modules to the photographers. During the first iteration, we soon found that the team was hampered because each member was not equally familiar with the various tasks. During the second iteration, one person alone was able to handle a movie camera, a 35mm camera, time-modules, and written records effectively.

Before going to the airports, we listed what kinds of specific behavior, situations, and sites should be photographed. This was possible in large part because we were very familiar with the layout of the sites, as well as with the situations and specific behavior expected. These plans did not preclude research decisions being made at the site, but rather meant that the team was better prepared for getting useful data in a short period of time.

Also as part of the preliminary planning, we designed forms to record written data on general environmental conditions, dimensions, population characteristics, the date and location where movies and slides were taken, and with room for a site diagram and general notes. We find that for each new research project a slightly different format is needed. This form, based on photographic forms used earlier, was redesigned after the first iteration. The format used for the second iteration, the photolog, is shown in Figure 12.

The photolog is a book slightly smaller than 8½ by 5½ inches, which fits into a jacket pocket; it opens alternately to two different kinds of pages. Figure 12, left, shows the page that provides space for a diagram of the site and calls for special kinds of notes, with some space for a running log of photography and observation. The alternate pages, Figure 12, right, are a continuation of the running log. A new section, beginning with a diagram and notes, is started at each new site; different viewpoints at a site can be added to the diagram and continued on the running log. Figure 12, left, shows how the log is used to keep track of simultaneous photography by two cameramen, filming in modular time units. Figure 12, right, is an example of records of one researcher filming only when people appear, and includes some observation notes.

Gathering data Before taking any photographs, we first obtained permission from the management, then scouted the site, observing behavior, searching for desirable vantage points, checking light levels, and comparing angles of view in the different lenses. This familiarization with the site, just before actual filming began, enabled us during the photographing to make informal decisions about changes in research design in response to the behavior observed.

Data recorded on the photolog included the site diagram, light-level and color-temperature measurements, escalator dimensions, and the travel time of the escalator.

Photographic data included relevant background information such as: a sign near the escalator indicating the location of a specific site within the airport complex; a television monitor displaying flight information relevant to the people being filmed on the escalators; masking tape placed on the outside of the escalator to indicate the exact stepping-on and stepping-off points; a rectangular trash can situated at the side of an escalator to indicate the exact stepping-on and stepping-off points; a panorama of the site to record the general space; and photographs that show the visual field that subjects would see while being photographed (Figure 13).

The first iteration involved the use of movies and slides simultaneously to record people on

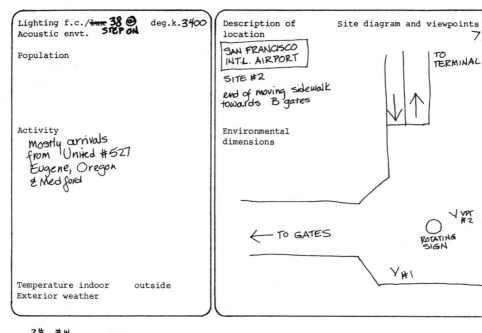

Lighting f.c./~~lux~~ 38 @   deg.k. 3400
STEP ON
Acoustic envt.

Population

Activity
mostly arrivals
from United #527
Eugene, Oregon
& Medford

Temperature indoor   outside
Exterior weather

Description of location

Site diagram and viewpoints

SAN FRANCISCO INT'L. AIRPORT

SITE #2
end of moving sidewalk
towards B gates

Environmental dimensions

7 #3 (MIDDLE OF WALK)
TO TERMINAL
← TO GATES
ROTATING SIGN
V VPT #2
V #1

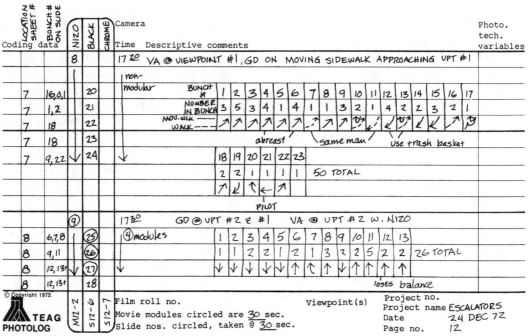

Location sheet #	Bunch # on slide	NIZO	BLACK	CHROME	Camera / Coding data — Time — Descriptive comments																		Photo. tech. variables
		8			17 20 VA @ VIEWPOINT #1, GD ON MOVING SIDEWALK APPROACHING UPT #1																		
					non-modular BUNCH #	1	2	3	4	5	6	7	8	9	10	11	12	13	14	15	16	17	
7	16,0,1		20		NUMBER IN BUNCH	3	5	3	4	1	4	1	1	3	2	1	4	2	2	3	2	1
7	1,2		21		MOV.WLK ⟶ WALK ---	↗	↗	↗	↗	↗	↗	↗	↗	↗	↗	↙	↙	↙	↙	↗	↘	
7	18		22		abreast						same man				use trash basket							
7	18		23																			
7	9,22	↓	24	↓		18	19	20	21	22	23											
						2	2	1	1	1	1	50 TOTAL										
						↗	↙	↑	←	↗												
					PILOT																	
		⑨			17 30 GD @ VPT #2 & #1 VA @ UPT #2 w. NIZO																	
8	6,7,8		㉕		④modules	1	2	3	4	5	6	7	8	9	10	11	12	13				
8	9,11		㉖			1	1	2	2	1	2	1	3	2	2	5	2	2	26 TOTAL			
8	12,13†	↓	㉗	↓		↓	↓	↓	↓	↓	↑	↑	↑	↓	↑	↑	↑	↑			
8	12,13†		28						loses balance												

© Copyright 1972.

⚠ TEAG
PHOTOLOG

M12-2   Ø   S12-7

Film roll no.
Movie modules circled are 30 sec.
Slide nos. circled, taken @ 30 sec.

Viewpoint(s)

Project no.
Project name ESCALATORS
Date   24 DEC 72
Page no.   12

252

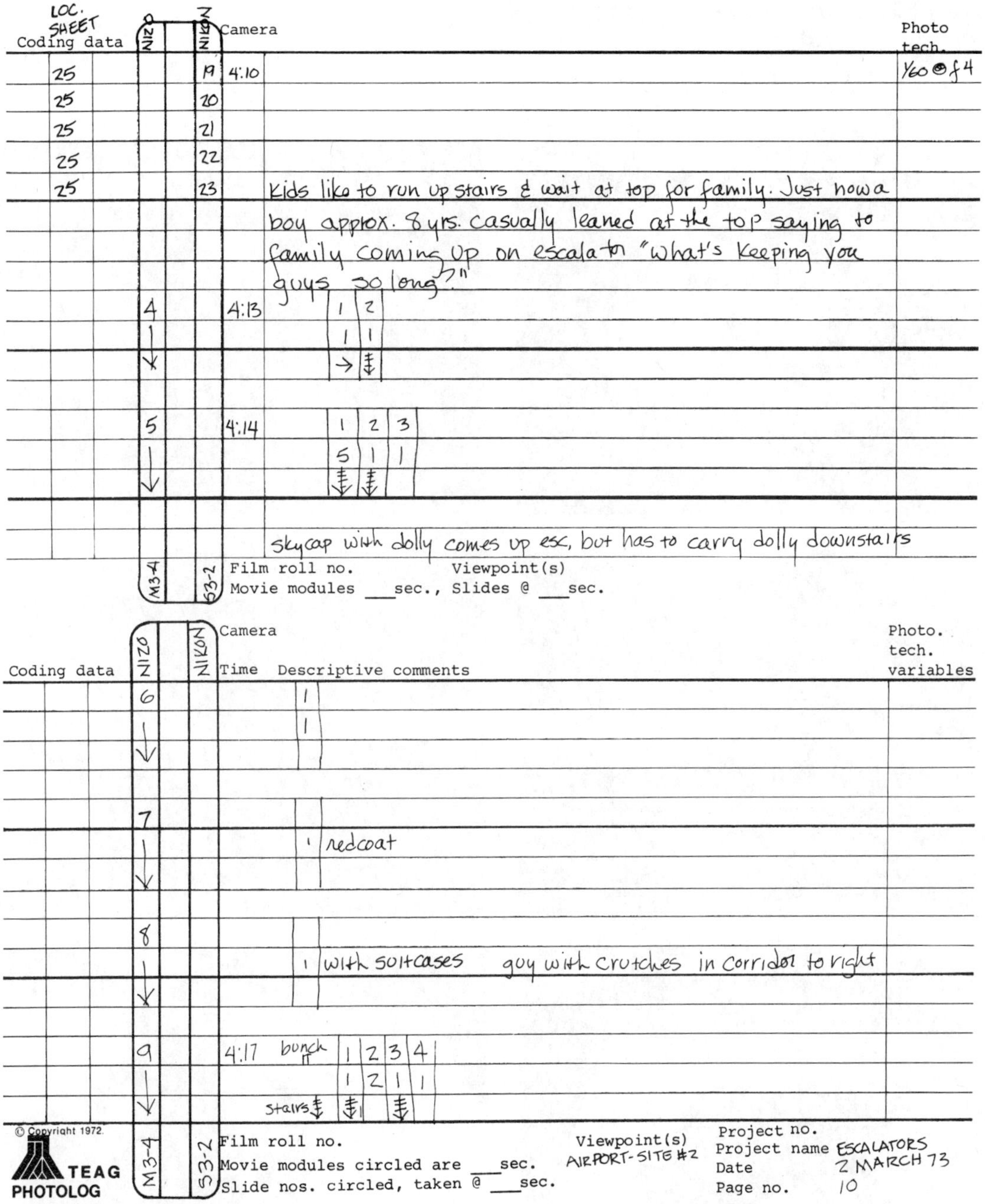

LOC.
SHEET
Coding data
Camera
Photo
tech.

Coding data	NIZO	NIKON	Camera / Time		Photo tech.
25		19	4:10		1/60 @ f 4
25		20			
25		21			
25		22			
25		23			

Kids like to run up stairs & wait at top for family. Just now a boy approx. 8 yrs. casually leaned at the top saying to family coming up on escalator "what's keeping you guys so long?"

| | 4 ↓ ↘ | | 4:13 | 1 2 / 1 1 / → ‡ | |
| | 5 ↓ ↓ | | 4:14 | 1 2 3 / 5 1 1 / ‡ ‡ ‡ | |

skycap with dolly comes up esc, but has to carry dolly downstairs

Film roll no. M3-4   53-2   Viewpoint(s)
Movie modules ___ sec., Slides @ ___ sec.

Coding data	NIZO	NIKON	Camera / Time	Descriptive comments	Photo. tech. variables
	6 ↓			1 / 1	
	7 ↓ ↓			1 / redcoat	
	8 ↓ ↓			1 / with suitcases guy with crutches in corridor to right	
	9 ↓ ↓		4:17 bunch	1 2 3 4 / 1 2 1 1 / stairs ‡ ‡ ‡ ‡	

TEAG
PHOTOLOG

Film roll no. M3-4   53-2
Movie modules circled are ___ sec.
Slide nos. circled, taken @ ___ sec.

Viewpoint(s)
AIRPORT- SITE #2

Project no.
Project name ESCALATORS
Date   2 MARCH 73
Page no.   10

Figure 12
Photologs: These two kinds of pages are used for recording general and specific information about the situations photographed as well as for maintaining a running log of photographs taken. See accompanying text for further discussion.

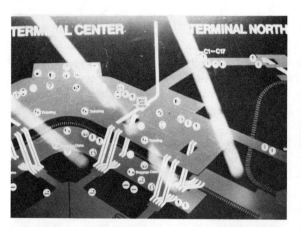

A

B

C

D

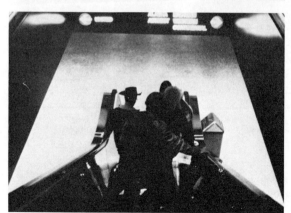

E

F

escalators and moving sidewalks from a variety of angles. As photography is more valuable when context and detail are included on the same film, for the purposes of this study it was found that movies taken from a distance using relatively wide angles of the lens were often more valuable than telephoto shots, because they included more context information per frame without excessive sacrifice of detail. The quality of Super-8 film is grainy, but filmed motion conveys much of the detailed information that we were interested in, and which would be lost in still photographs of such a small size. When filming close to the subjects, the detail information on film was quite clear despite the grainy texture, so slides taken simultaneously from the same viewpoint were found to be redundant (Figure 14).

Some photographic viewpoints were found to be more useful than others in the analysis of many different specific aspects of behavior. For example, some head-on films that clearly showed the hand, foot, and eye movements of people as they approached an escalator, and all on the same piece of film, were rich in behavioral data and thus were valuable for generating hypotheses. Although these very useful viewpoints should be covered by long, continuous runs of film, other viewpoints that yield specific information should also be covered. For example, an overhead shot of people on an escalator gave relatively little information about people's eyes, but gave very clear information about density and the number of escalator steps between arriving passengers who had formed a small queue at the escalator.

The first films were processed and quickly scanned; the recording forms were improved; then one member of the team returned alone to one of the sites to take additional slides, timed movies, and notes covering some additional viewpoints.

Identification coding of films before analysis Organizing slides and movies so that a half-remembered image can be found is not easy. As described later, we identify each slide, film module, and person shown on film by a unique code. Thereafter, for movie film, people could be numbered within bunches, in this case, in the order in which they stepped on or off the escalator.

The coding system separated the data into pieces small enough for the film to be explored heuristically and quickly coded in just the parts of interest; in addition, small errors in counting people were isolated in small pieces of film. Specific frames could then be identified by the bunches or individuals in them if a frame counter was not available, which allowed film to be analyzed on an inexpensive editor. The identification coding was added to the original log made when the film was taken. One of the left-hand columns of the photolog was used for recording which of the bunches of people coded in the films also ap-

---

Figure 13
Photographs of relevant background information. A: A layout diagram displays the layout of the facility and shows the site of the photos precisely at the "you are here" arrow. The glass-covered diagram mounted at a slope is difficult to photograph because of reflected ceiling lights, and is perhaps also difficult to see. B: Alphanumeric display gives relevant flight information for groups of people in the area being studied. C and D: Two slides combining to make a panoramic view of a site, taken with 50mm rather than a wide-angle lens. Interiors are often fairly dim, and it is sometimes difficult to get proper exposures where illumination is uneven. Again, the original color slides revealed more than these reproductions can. E and F: Two slides of a time series showing the moving view-point of potential subjects. The far face of the trash can to the right of the escalator conveniently marks the step-off point very clearly for photos taken on the lower level.

Figure 14
Movies alone are sometimes sufficient. Slides, although sharper than movie frames, are sometimes unnecessary when the angle of view and closeness to subject cap- **tures much of the detail of interest. The motion captured in movies often reveals more behavioral information than much clearer single shots.**

peared in slides taken at the same time. This system was the only feasible way then available to identify specific frames in Super-8 films, because we had not yet obtained the digital-time-readout camera described later.

Heuristic analysis The nature of the analysis depends on the purpose of the research. In this study we were engaged in exploratory research. Therefore, the analysis was planned to elicit insights, generate hypotheses, and generally increase observational skills.

Initial viewings of photographic material are often exciting, but this excitement soon wears off as the analyst realizes both the limitations of the data obtained and the large number of bits of information that have to be coded and correlated. There are several systematic ways of beginning the analysis:

1. By taking a fairly rich piece of film and brain-dumping with it, noting all ideas that occur, and trying to be explicit about bits of behavior that are so common they are difficult to see.
2. By viewing a segment of film at many different

speeds, forward and backward, in order to see more each time.
3. By scanning a lot of material with only one hypothesis or point of view in mind. This is difficult in the face of so much rich material (it is impossible unless one is already very familiar with the material), but it is worthwhile; even the inevitable distracting insights tend to be useful.

In this study, it seemed that the films on which fairly unusual events occurred were more useful for heuristic analysis. Other films that showed many examples of specific kinds of behavior were more valuable for use in preliminary testing of hypotheses by the transfer of information to charts and matrices, graphs showing relative frequencies, and other rough summaries of data. Very often, hypotheses generated from heuristic analysis have called for further iterations of data gathering, both by photographic and by other methods. In this study, quasi-quantitative methods of analysis were used only to the extent that they helped give direction to the development of concepts about behavior. Most of the analysis was intuitive in nature.[3]

METHODS AND RELEVANT CONCERNS

In this section we discuss some of the specific working methods that we have used when applying photographic methods to research problems. We also discuss ethical and professional concerns that we feel must be respected by the researcher.

Being Ethical

Using photographs of people in behavioral research raises significant ethical questions. The earlier they are recognized, the easier it is to modify the research design so that the information needed can be gathered ethically. An essay by Shils (1959, p. 129) sets out some of the general standards of ethics that should be considered in social research. Shils separates the ethical concerns of observation into two parts: first, the wrongfulness of any manipulation of subjects, and, second, the intrusion "without a person's consent, or his knowing co-operation, into the reserved sphere of his individuality." In addition to consideration of the right of privacy of individuals, one must also be aware of intrusions into the privacy of groups, communities, and organizations. For all these, the degree of privacy required may vary from territory to territory or from situation to situation.

When photographing for research, there are a number of possible situations:

1. The subjects are aware of the study and agree to participate or knowingly cooperate.
2. The subjects (or potential subjects) are aware of the photography and prefer not to be included—for "good" reasons, "bad" reasons, no reasons, or just "on principle."
3. The subjects are aware that they are being studied, but the researcher does not know

how they feel about it.
4. The subjects might not know that they are being studied.

Certainly the first situation is preferable, but it can sometimes be difficult to achieve without distorting the behavior being observed. In some situations, one can ask subjects for permission to use the information either after the pictures are taken or else far enough in advance for the behavior to become "natural" when it is photographed. Unfortunately, the latter is not always possible; and proceeding without obtaining explicit permission in advance is not so much a "compromise" of the situation as a decision to involve the subject regardless of his feelings. Even when permission is given, it is ethically revokable at any time without cause. And that permission is not necessarily open-ended; it does not cover situations not explicitly understood when permission was given or implications that may surface later.

When subjects prefer not to be included in the study, sometimes the researcher can press for reasons for refusal. Out of the discussion, permission to photograph may eventually be granted, subject to certain conditions. For example, collecting certain kinds of information may be excluded, or confidentiality may be guaranteed, or all data may be submitted for approval before use or retention. Some subjects volunteer readily when they know others have refused (if more subjects shy away because they know others have, perhaps the study should be reexamined). In situations where the researcher can gradually become known, permission is often granted eventually, although it might have been withheld at first.

If one cannot know how potential subjects feel about being photographed, it is wise to offer them an easy way out. This can be done physically, by offering an alternative path out of the range of the camera, or socially, by providing an acceptable reason or by setting fixed times when photographs will be taken. Then people who do not want to be included can arrange to be absent. The researcher can simply stop photographing when there is any reluctance or hesitation. If subjects notice the photography and understand what is being done before they come into view, they usually have time to decide whether to participate or not. A small number of people usually duck out of the way if given the chance (these people seem to be different from those who step out of the way from concern about "spoiling" the pictures). If filming head-on would catch subjects by surprise, it is sometimes acceptable to stand in the stream of traffic (without obstructing) and film people's backs as they pass. This may not provide all the information one would like in a single sequence (e.g., no eye movements), but filming head-on could be so disruptive of behavior as to be a waste of time and film; in addition, it very likely would be a serious invasion of privacy.

If people do not know that photographs are being taken, the researcher cannot really know how to be responsible for the information collected. There is also the risk of missing some of the behavioral context. Even if people object to being photographed, knowing *why* can tell the researcher significant things about the situation.

It seems that, in general, photographic research methods should avoid exposing publicly the identity or specific actions of particular people unless they have given permission, or are public figures, or are making a "public action." In specific situations, however, the legal and ethical limitations will vary, and careful judgment is required.

The following are a few guidelines we have found useful in trying to be ethical in our research.

1. Wherever possible, ask the management for permission to photograph the site. Even in public places, security is much tighter than it has been, and it is wise to identify oneself and explain one's purpose in advance. Frequently, one discovers useful background information in the process. The manager of the site can give permission only as far as he is concerned; he cannot speak for the subjects, and there may also be other kinds of permission required (e.g., parent's permission to photograph children).

2. Avoid photographing people in a way that manipulates or interferes with what usually takes place. For example, to mark an important visual line on photographs, we moved a trash can a few inches without significantly changing the function of the situation. There are numerous inconvenient situations occurring all the time that one might take advantage of, but *creating* inconvenient situations is ethically questionable. Unfortunately, sometimes just the act of photographing manipulates people, and even prevents them from doing what you expect them to do. For example, frequently in public places people stop outside the camera range to wait until filming stops, out of courtesy, so that they will not "ruin" the pictures. This shows that they do not fully understand why the photography is taking place, and therefore are not giving their fully knowing consent.

3. Although it can seem a waste of time, we find it is valuable to try to respond to people who are curious about what we are doing. Our explanation not only can help get explicit permission from potential subjects, but also frequently can elicit interesting comments on the situation under study. A person who bothers to ask what we are doing is probably someone familiar enough with the situation to know that our activity is unusual. If people are curious enough to ask questions, there is a chance that they are sensitive observers and could have valuable insights to share. In this

sense, respecting the ethical demands of the situation has occasional unexpected rewards. And if the photographic team is challenged with eye contact rather than with words, similar indications of openness and deference to the rights of others can still take place on a nonverbal level.

It is important to try to develop sensitivity to potential subjects' unspoken concerns about serious or nonhobby photography as soon as possible in every study. The need for greater sensitivity is brought to light with the first uses of the cameras, even during the first efforts to define the technical aspects of the photography for a particular study, such as finding out what lenses are best for capturing both hand gestures and interpersonal distance at the same time. And just as each study may require different uses of the photographic equipment, each study may also raise different concerns in potential subjects and require different responses from the researchers.

We have found it useful to begin our first test photographs on "home territory," because a high degree of sensitivity already exists in such situations, and it seems to be much easier to develop sensitivity in a research context. In one's neighborhood, the park one uses, one's school, one's workplace, there is a natural commitment to respect the feelings of others who share in using these places important in one's own life, and one is aware of wanting others to be as considerate as oneself in their use and examination of the same places. One is more likely to take greater pains in answering questions as clearly and as completely as possible (which is a very good basis for conducting a study in places less familiar to the researcher).

Potential subjects can become questioning or can be put at ease by the physical appearance of the photographer. Hopefully, normal appearance is not too different from that of the potential subjects; if it is too different, probably someone else should be gathering the information, because the cultural gap between the research team and the subjects is too great. One need not literally follow the line, "when in Rome do as the Romans do," but doing so does convey an acceptance, if not a respect, that is absolutely necessary.

4. A final caution comes from Collier (1967, p. 44) rather than from our own experience. In one instance Collier used photographs of a group to study community interaction, but rather than showing the photographs only to a trusted key informant, or just to those photographed, he gave in to requests to show them to many others. Unfortunately, this created gossip and misunderstandings. To avoid similar problems in the future, he recommends that "Pictures made in the public domain can be fed back into the public domain. Pictures made in private circumstances should be shown *only to people in these circumstances.* . . ."

The Research Team

We have found that the research under discussion is better conducted by an integrated small team, rather than by a single individual, or by groups of people assigned specific tasks at various stages of the research. A single small group of researchers, bringing complementary experience, skills, and insights to the tasks, seems to be much more effective and more economical both for designing and conducting the research, including the selection of specific data, and for creative analysis. In this respect, we find that research utilizing photography to study interactions between human behavior and the environment is significantly different from research using other methods.

As an example, research that involves questionnaires, field interviews, or diaries is often conducted with a hierarchy of staffs: the researcher director, who designs the research and gives general direction; several research assistants, who undertake specific tasks, such as drafting the questionnaire or interview guide, directing the field crews, or preparing the computer programs for tabulation and analysis; the statistician, who draws the sample; and the field crews of skilled interviewers, who are trained to conduct each interview exactly like all the other interviews for the project to ensure replicability. At a university, a faculty member may assign each of many students the responsibility for conducting a small number of interviews, using the skills he is teaching at that time; although the individual interviews so obtained may vary in quality and validity, the ensemble of all interviews may provide a sufficiently valid data base to permit analysis and the drawing of reasonable conclusions. Some service companies maintain trained staffs in the field who can take questionnaires prepared by a researcher, administer them consistently and effectively, and return the completed material for analysis within a matter of a few weeks, or even in just a few days in case of urgency.

In all these examples, the people who are doing the interviewing or other data gathering are relatively independent, or separate, from those who utilize the data for analysis and the development of conclusions. The separation usually does not adversely affect the quality of the data base.

This separation does not seem acceptable when using photographic methods. So far, we have found it essential for the individuals who plan the research to participate actively in both the fieldwork and the detailed analysis of the photographic material.

If the film is to be rich in relevant information, many judgments must be made on the spot, in the field, at the time of photographing. These judgments include selecting camera locations, angles of view, background and other contextual information to be filmed, depth of field and exposure duration to emphasize one aspect or another of the subject area, and specific events or time periods for photographing. Such judgments can only be made by people who understand in depth the objectives and content of the overall research project, and who also know how the data will be analyzed and correlated. People who work at arm's length from the researchers, such as most students or professional survey fieldworkers, cannot have this depth of understanding.

The researchers, then, must do their own photography; therefore, they must have sufficient skill in photography that the process of taking the photographs does not distract them from the research purposes of their work. When operation of the cameras becomes second nature, the researcher can concentrate on the content of the data he is collecting by photographic methods.

Perhaps in years to come there will be skilled researchers who are also skilled photographers, and who can overcome this problem sufficiently to hire out as fieldworkers for the photographic aspects of a research project. They will require a higher degree of training and of general skills than is the case for today's survey teams. First, however, photographic methods will have to achieve general acceptance, and many people will have to become skilled in the full range of methods discussed in this chapter. We expect in 1974 to undertake a pilot project to determine if some parts of the analysis can be conducted by people who were not present when the film was exposed, although some of the photographic team will provide continuity through the project, from start to finish. (In our experience, the analysis is typically much more time-consuming and repetitive than the taking of the photographic data; therefore, studies will be greatly speeded up if we can use additional people effectively during detailed tabulations and analysis from the films.)

There are many advantages to having only *one*

person take the photographs. Often, the photography must occur at a remote location to which travel is expensive, particularly if several people must be sent. A single person may be much less obtrusive than several people with cameras, and therefore have less effect on the behavior being photographed. A single person will have a consistent approach to the selection of the subject matter, the inclusion of context, and the sequencing of images, so analysis becomes easier because of this consistency.

Unfortunately, we have found that a single person quickly loses touch either with the real event or with the process of recording and photographing. For a single individual to overcome this problem, he or she must be so skilled both in the techniques of photography and in technical observation and recording that these operations become second nature, almost subliminal. Only then can the researcher concentrate on the selection and content of the behavior being studied.

In our experience, the optimum approach is to gather data with a photographic team of two, who possess complementary skills and background. A fully qualified team of three photographic researchers may permit greater control and replicability of data and other observations. The third person must be fully integrated into the team, however, and not function simply as an added-on "support staff member." All members of the team must have the same perception of what is happening among the people being observed, so that time signals, cues, and responses to unexpected new information or new events are consistent for all the photographic and context data. Adding a clerk just to take down written notes and to call out time signals can be counterproductive, because the clerk-assistant will not understand the consequences of events observed. We have found that such a clerk-assistant often misinterprets instructions from the other researchers, who, under the pressures of

recognizing and photographing "the precise moment" of a significant event, cannot pause to explain to a subordinate. The clerk-assistant can only try to watch what the researchers are doing and guess at what they consider important at that particular moment.

If the nature of the behavior to be photographed or the place in which the behavior occurs requires that more than three photographic researchers be working simultaneously, we suggest that, if possible, the study be designed to limit each work session to not more than four photographers. A larger team does permit obtaining photographic data from more camera locations (points of view) or to cover more types of data content. Unfortunately, the more people there are on the photographic team, the greater the difficulty in establishing adequate intercommunication among what each team-member is observing or perceiving, and even between what each considers important and seeks to record (photograph).

Another problem with using a large team is that the amount of film to be analyzed may increase arithmetically, but the amount of time for analysis may increase almost exponentially, owing to the need for more complex cross-correlation of films. Since the bulk of the time involved in photographic methods is consumed in the analysis of the film, every effort must be made to limit exposed film to what is really necessary for the understanding that is sought.

The actual photographic skills required have been, in our experience, quite modest, although some individuals have distinctly more aptitude and interest than others. And although only modest skills are required, they must be second nature to researchers. We use only a few types of equipment so that we do not have to make mental adjustments repeatedly in the course of a single photographic session. We drill ourselves and our associates on practice assignments and on field tests so that problems of correct exposure, lighting, camera angle, and similar technical matters can be resolved before we have to deal with the content data of the study. So far, we believe that it is easier to teach a good research observer to use the photographic equipment than to train a good photographer to select and photograph the data that have research significance. Since most projects have limited budgets for time and money, we have abandoned attempts to add photographic specialists to the research team; instead, we "grow" our own photographers out of the research group.

Some researchers, however, seem to have real difficulty in achieving the necessary photographic competence. Picture taking for them never seems to become second nature, easy and relaxed. They become intimidated by the gadgetry, and are always forgetting one minor technical step or another, so that their films are out of focus, incorrectly exposed, jerky, or otherwise unsuitable for analysis. Some people find the need for the accurate recording and coding of film data and field notes an unacceptable personal discipline.

Others may be excellent photographers, but because they lack a solid grounding in behavioral theory and research concepts, they produce photographs that are of very limited research value. A news photographer, however skillful, has entirely different objectives from a research photographer. A commercial photographer, with a background of advertising and industrial work, may have great difficulty in selecting camera angles and moments of activity that reflect the particular behavioral problem under study. As one successful and creative architectural photographer commented,

I've spent all my professional life making buildings look beautiful, even if I had to leave the people out of most of the pictures. Now I have to stop thinking about creating beautiful images out of the buildings I photograph, and try to capture what the ordinary visitor or user sees, experiences, does. I have been practicing a specialized creative art-form. Photography for research seems almost the opposite.

To use photographic methods in studying behavior, the researcher needs to synthesize two distinct sets of method and approach. He needs the general skills and insights of the experienced behavioral researcher and he needs a limited but specialized set of photographic skills, polished to the point that he does not ever think consciously about the techniques, but only the content, of his work. When the researcher achieves this synthesis, and many researchers do not find it difficult, he can expect to achieve results of unexpected potency, insight, and replicability.

Information About the Context of the Photographs

Photographic methods of data gathering are only part of a comprehensive research effort. Analyzing data collected by photographic means is effective only when sufficient information about the context is available to ensure that interpretation is accurate and complete, not misled by half-understood details. For example, the interpretation of behavior in queues at a counter may be quite different if one is told that the length of the queue is normal, or if one learns that for the period of observation the counter is understaffed temporarily and that people are waiting for abnormally long periods.

We find that we are often studying behavior in one small area of a larger building or place. Often we use long-focus lenses, or come quite close to the behavior under study, to obtain detail information about body and limb movement, eye motion, and the like. At the same time we can gather a "visual" statement of the observable context by using wide-angle lenses to photograph the subjects in the overall environment (Figure 15). We also try to move through the same path that our subjects are following, and photograph the environment from their point of view, as they would perceive it. Thus the most direct and obvious context data are collected with cameras at the time of

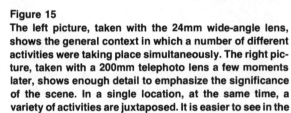

Figure 15
The left picture, taken with the 24mm wide-angle lens, shows the general context in which a number of different activities were taking place simultaneously. The right picture, taken with a 200mm telephoto lens a few moments later, shows enough detail to emphasize the significance of the scene. In a single location, at the same time, a variety of activities are juxtaposed. It is easier to see in the right-hand, detailed picture that a wedding reception is taking place, a badminton game is underway behind the bridal couple and their party, and behind the grassed badminton court is a swimming-pool area with people sunbathing. Through all this activity stroll people who are present but who are not participating in any of these activities.

the basic photographic recording of behavior. The camera also provides an economical means of capturing detail on information displays (building plans showing "you are here," or television-screen displays of aircraft arrival and departure times at an airport). Some data can be included directly in the photographed image, for example, by putting measured markers in the field of view of the camera to indicate distances, by placing a portable, battery-operated wall-clock into the field of view of the camera, by using a camera that prints directly onto the film the time of exposure to the nearest minute or second, or by close-ups of a fellow researcher with various scales or measurement data. These methods can often provide more information more economically and faster than trying to write down all the relevant readings and descriptions.

Certain basic information about each photographic data-gathering session is best recorded on a consistent, routine basis. We have de-veloped a photolog form, which we vary slightly from project to project as our experience grows; it provides a complete summary and index of *all* film exposed, by whatever means and for whatever purpose (see Figure 12). The photolog contains critical measurements of distance, light level, temperature, and the like, brief comments on subject matter for identification, and additional notes most conveniently added close to the identification of the film they explain. We also use the photolog to note specific photographic data (exposure time, f-stop, lens focal length, etc.) to aid us in improving our technique in the future. We find it important to note the general weather, the time of day, and other factors that might affect how people dress or behave, to explain what we will see later in the film.

Floor plans, landscape or street plans, diagrams of function, and pamphlets or other printed matter about the place are often hard to obtain, but very valuable when they exist. They can make analysis much easier by giving hard data to index by. For convenience of access, and consistency of storage, we often photograph key elements of such printed material with a close-up lens, such as the 55mm Micro-Nikkor-P Auto lens. When plans are not available, they should be created by the researcher, even if only in rough, diagrammatic form, to permit the plotting of angles of view for particular photographic sequences at the time the photographs are taken (Figure 16).

Most of the contextual information, however, is likely to come from other forms of behavioral research—interviews, observation, tracking, secondary data such as tabulations of activity, questionnaires, and, importantly, the researcher's own participation in the environment and behavior. Findings should be carefully recorded in a preplanned format corresponding to the specific research objectives and to the site; the format for recording participant observation in a hotel or a resort might be quite different from the records for a drugstore, bank, or law court.

As an example, when studying behavior of departing air passengers in gate lobbies at an airport, we found that a significant proportion of the passengers on certain routes were flying for the first time in their lives, and that between 1 and 2 percent were not only flying for the first time, but were flying to attend a funeral. For the occasional traveler, the unfamiliar experience of air travel may be a deeply emotional experience or it may be associated with holiday or excitement. These people will behave quite differently from the peripatetic businessman who has experienced the ritual of flight loading many times, and endures it with the minimum of personal involvement. Without this kind of understanding, the analyst could draw quite misleading conclusions from film taken in airport gate lobbies.

When practicable, interviews with the individuals being photographed tend to give the richest information as to what they think they are doing,

or at least as to what they are prepared to divulge about what they do. Often, however, the individuals cannot be interviewed, for example, when the interviewing process would change their behavior, or when the interviewing process would cause an unacceptable delay to the respondents. In such instances, the researcher may interview other, similar people behaving similarly; they act as surrogates for those he photographs.

A specialized kind of understanding about an environment or behavior pattern can be obtained from people knowledgeable about the environment, such as a social worker in a community context or an airport manager or an airline official at an airport. They can explain what political or social forces underlie a particular group behavior in a specific cultural milieu, or what management decisions affected particular architectural or operational decisions. The architect for a particular environment can often provide the rationale for many aspects of the environmental design, including the circumstances that led to particular observable problems.

From these *background* sources of context information, the researcher can come to understand *why* events occur that to the uninformed would seem dysfunctional. He may learn that directional signs erected to lead people through one stage of remodeling have not been changed since the remodeling was completed and the routing changed; or that baffle walls in a passageway, which prevent people from understanding where they are going, were erected after project completion by the building management to reduce air flows and heat loss through the passageway, without thought to the effect on the people using the passageway.

The manager of an airport will know of the peaks of activity at specific locations, and of the problems in planning and layout that cause recurrent difficulties, congestion, or other dysfunctions. He will know of breakdowns of equipment, or of the rearrangement of gate assignments,

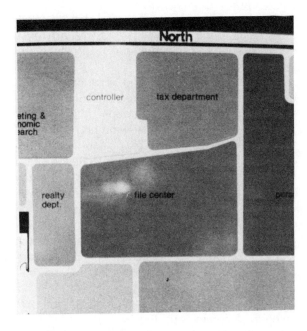

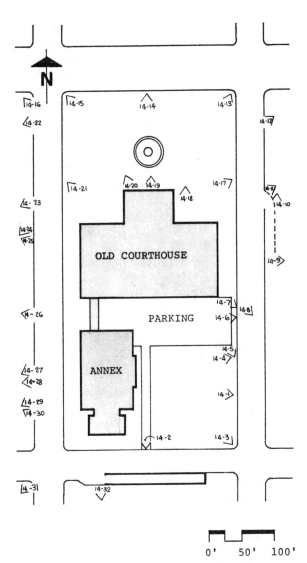

Figure 16
The left picture shows a portion of the layout plan for an installation of office landscape. This plan was mounted on the wall of the elevator lobby for the information of visitors to the floor, showing where each department is located in the layout. Each department is coded in a different color. The right-hand diagram was created by the researcher as part of the photo inventory of the exterior of a historical building that was to be remodeled. The location and direction for each photograph taken is indicated on the plan.

which have been ordered to meet a particular weather situation, aircraft delays, and the like. This information enables the researcher to better understand the content of his photographic data on the behavior of passengers and staff at the airport. In the same way, the staff of an airline knows why a particular flight (airplane arrival or departure) is crowded or partly empty, or why the people on a particular flight are rushed or frustrated or otherwise behaving abnormally.

People entering a building lobby from the outside will behave quite differently if the tempera-

ture outside is 20 degrees warmer. Recording of outside environmental data will help the researcher understand the use of doors, use of clothing, body movement and speed, and other behaviors that affect the use of the environment under study, but which are external to it.

We suggest that the researcher use a measuring tape calibrated both in inches and centimeters for taking critical distances, such as the width of an escalator. We suggest that in addition to recording light level in foot-candles and lux, the researcher should also record the temperature of the light in degrees Kelvin, as suggestive of mood and character. We have also found that by using a single film type throughout our work, both in still photography and motion picture, and by using a single, well-controlled laboratory for all our processing, we can compare somewhat the "color feel" of lighting from the film itself. By holding the photographic variables constant, differences in lighting quality and contrast are emphasized.

It is outside the scope of this chapter to discuss in detail the various other research methods for obtaining contextual information to use in analyzing the photographic data. The essential point is that the photographic data cannot be examined in isolation from their context.

Exposing Behavior by Means of Photography

We find that photography allows us to *perceive* behavior that we otherwise only see; furthermore, photography allows us to identify and understand replicable relationships between environment and behavior that were otherwise invisible or misunderstood.

Simple still photographs, the frozen instant, have long provided profound and often haunting insights into human life and behavior. In the past generation, such artists as Dorothea Lange and Cartier-Bresson have documented the human fact in ways that touch every observer. They have created single images that make an implicit general statement in the mind of each observer.

The researcher using photography, however, seeks to make an *explicit*, replicable statement of fact, to substantiate, embellish, or overthrow a paradigm. He cannot leave it to those reading his report to provide background and specific interpretation of his photographic images. Although

his photographs may be beautiful, his art must never distort the reality; instead, his art must serve reality by exposing it more explicitly, more insightfully.

In our first research using photography, we used only still photographs, usually 35mm slides. We soon learned to take groups of slides of a particular behavioral event—wide angle to show the overall scene, telephoto or close-up to show details of pose or action, and time series to show changes or sequences of events. We found, however, that 35mm time series were expensive, cumbersome to analyze, and, without a motor drive on the camera, difficult to obtain. As an example, a sequence on behavior at an elevator lobby, taken one exposure every 15 seconds, failed to give us some essential information, because the interval between exposures was so long that some people were missed entirely, going in or coming out (Figure 17).

We then started using Super-8 motion pictures in conjunction with 35mm slides, because the movies gave us the actual content of the movement or gesture that a single 35mm slide could only "freeze." With movies we could also go back in time and study the events or behavior that led up to the crucial moment we were studying. This led to much better understanding and analysis.

We were now faced with a new problem—we were inundated with data. To reduce the number of frames of film to analyze, we used a camera that exposed from six frames per second down to one frame per minute. We usually ran it at four or six frames per second. We find that four frames per second gives sufficient information about the content of a movement or gesture, but we settled on six frames per second as our standard because we found one projector that would show our film at this speed. With it, we could project the film at the same speed we had exposed it, and so simulate real time. The projector could also be operated one frame at a time, for detailed analysis, and at 18 or 54 frames per second. It could operate backward and forward in any of these modes. Finally, by scraping away a bit of the emulsion on the sprocket side of the film, we could so code the film that the projector would stop at any significant point we wanted to index for easy access and analysis. Because this projector will not operate at four frames per second, we still use half again more film than we feel we need, but this is the best compromise we have found so far in the equipment commercially available.

We find that running the film at various speeds reveals various kinds of information. Patterns and flows of behavior are often not perceived by the observer at the site, or by the analyst when projecting at the same speed used in exposing the film; but these patterns and flows become immediately obvious when the film is run at 18 or 54 frames per second. In some cases we want to understand the causes of a particular event. We

then watch the film till the event occurs, and then run it backward to understand the actions leading up to it. An example of this is a study of how people claim bags at airports. By starting with the moment a passenger lifts his bag off the claim device, we can run backward in time, on film, to learn when his bag first arrived at the claim device (carousel or racetrack), when he first arrived in the claim area, and what helped or hindered his recognizing and removing his bag.

Taking film at very slow speeds, such as one or two frames per second, is useful for other purposes. With 3,600 frames on a single roll, we can photograph a doorway or other control point and count accurately the people or vehicles moving past, even in large numbers, for an extended period. We can also understand the nature and many of the causes of such congestion as may occur.

Sometimes we need more accurate informa-

Figure 17
The need for short intervals between time-series pictures is particularly important when studying some kinds of behavior. These two pictures were taken 15 seconds apart as part of a series lasting about 10 minutes. There has been almost a complete change in population of the elevator lobby during this period, and the one person present at both photographs is the owner of the suitcases shown at the right of the right-hand (later) picture. She was

"watching them" while her traveling companion went in search of a porter. Not only has there been a change of population, but we do not know where the people in the left picture went or where the people in the right picture came from. Had we taken a time series with Super-8 film at 6 frames per second, our film cost per 10 minutes would have been roughly the same, but we would have had usable information in much greater depth and continuity.

tion about what happens in a particular location than can be provided by diaries. If many people use the location, or if we need detailed content knowledge about behavior, a time-sampling camera may be valuable. We have a camera that allows us to select the duration of each sample period, the number of frames to be exposed during each sample period, and the interval between sample periods. We have used it, for instance, in studying activities in an office, with the camera exposing three or six frames during 1 second, with an interval of 59 seconds before the next group of frames was exposed. A portable wall clock in the field of view of the camera provided time coding.

When the exact duration of an activity or the exact time of an event is important, we use a camera that shows on each frame in digits at the bottom the time in hours, minutes, and seconds of that particular frame. This is particularly useful in studying capacities of spaces, densities of crowds, speeds of movement, and causes of congestion.

The Super-8 film format has the limitation, however, that relatively little detail can be obtained, owing to the small film size of the single frame. We therefore usually take 35mm slides concurrently with the Super-8 film to provide context data and supplementary detail; then the Super-8 has only the burden of informing us about behavior and movement.

We make a point of using the same film in both the 35mm still cameras and the Super-8 movie cameras. In this way, we have similar color balance and detail, and comparative analysis is facilitated. We have tried using black-and-white film in very low light situations, and also using portable black-and-white closed-circuit television equipment. These latter experiences have been generally less satisfactory, because the absence of color greatly reduces the amount of available information needed for analysis. As an example, when a man claims his suitcase at an airport, it is almost impossible to distinguish that bag from many others unless we can see its color.

Avoid Distorting the Behavior Being Photographed

It seems a truism that the researcher should affect the subject of his photography as little as possible, or he may affect the validity of his data and analyses. We have found two approaches most fruitful in avoiding this problem. The choice between them will depend in part on the physical environment and technical considerations, including layout, camera angles needed, and so on. The choice will also be affected by the ethical considerations discussed earlier.

We usually try to be as unobtrusive as possible. We use light-weight hand-held cameras and if possible dress to blend into the scene. We have always worked with the available light, without special floodlights or spotlights. These constraints limit our choices of what and when to photograph, but we have found that with a normal speed of ASA 160 (23 Din) we have got most of the pictures we needed. Occasionally, we need to identify ourselves to those being photographed, or we need to use a tripod at some unusual location. If we must make ourselves obvious, we find that it is sometimes desirable to put up a sign explaining what we are doing, such as "traffic study" or "baggage study," so that people who do notice us will understand and accept our presence and our photography.

As mentioned earlier, we try to avoid any direct contact with the subjects of the photography, at least until after the film has been exposed. We find that interviews often make people think twice about what they would otherwise do naturally, and so behave in different ways than if they had not been interviewed. When, for ethical or other reasons, we have to establish our presence and the fact of our photography before we can work, we find that people need a little time to get used to us before they return to normal behavior. In an office, the people who normally work there may disregard us after a few minutes; the visitor from another part of the building may accept our photography, but still act a little differently, and so distort our data. These are problems that we must face and resolve on each separate study.

Cataloging and Retrieving Photographic Data

The general principle in identification and retrieval is that any 35mm slide, or any print from a negative, or any frame of Super-8 film can be referred to in a way that differentiates it from every other exposure in the data. We start with the roll of film, whatever its type or source, and identify it with

1. The initials of the photographer, which tells us which sequence of photologs to consult.
2. The year and month in which the roll was started.
3. The exposure number or frame number within the roll. (On Super-8 film, where the time indication is included in the image, we use that for frame identification; otherwise, the counting by modules of time is more complex, as noted in the example on escalators discussed before.)

Thus a 35mm slide might be coded GD-74-8-33-27. This means the 27th slide on the 33rd role started in August 1974, by Gerald Davis. This is marked on the mount of the slide in a simplified way, using a date stamp to give year and month, and the day of the month when known. The slide technician only has to write the initials, the roll number, and the exposure number within the roll. This coding matches to the written coding in the photolog, and so provides a cross reference for access in serial fashion.

We have tried having a processing laboratory imprint a serial number along the side of Super-8 film, one impression per foot of film. This has not proved satisfactory, because the printing is often illegible, cannot be read when the frame is projected, obscures some of the detail on the side of the film, and does not reproduce when a copy of the film is made.

We avoid any cutting or mutilation of original film. If we want to make a special film for presentation, we have the film copied and cut up the duplicate. This is important, because often the researcher will need to return to the original film for additional data, additional analysis, or some other purpose. If the film has been mutilated, it is no longer possible to work from a complete statement and sequence of the behavior that was photographed. We use the photolog as our index when we wish to retrieve special sequences for copying or special analysis. Unfortunately, at this time selected pieces of film cannot be copied from a film without duplicating the entire 50-foot roll. Even if this were possible, we would still preserve our originals intact.

Cycles of Photography in the Course of Research

It seems impossible to avoid repeating that photography is only one tool of research and that its value is magnified when it is used in conjunction with other research methods. Photography simply adds another dimension to the data base and another mode to the analysis for a particular research study. When the researcher chooses to use photography among his methods, we find he usually follows a cyclical development in planning and executing his work. First, he has to define what is to be examined; then he must understand the limits that his photographic tools impose on what he can learn; thereafter, he comes to deal with the content of the behavior under study.

As an example, the researcher starts by defining his conceptual framework with the participation of the research team, especially those who will be involved in the photography and analysis. It is then possible to plan the specific sites and settings that might be suitable for photographic data gathering. Thereafter, sites can be scouted, anomalies noted, questions raised, and problems identified before obtaining permission to photograph, if required; then the personnel for the team are assigned and trained. Preliminary interviews with people operating at the site, managers, staff, and the planners and architects are useful at this point. Concurrently, a start can be made on selecting camera angles, selecting and checking the applicability of particular cameras and lenses, and identifying supplementary equipment that will be needed. Interviews and other context-gathering activity proceeds as appropriate. A sampling plan will be developed to ensure that the behavior actually photographed is representative of the more general range of behavior under study.

The first main photographic phase will include the use of photologs, the recording of measurements, weather, and other site information, and the many background actions mentioned earlier. Once the initial mass of film has been processed, the heavy work really starts. We find that many hours of analysis and conceptual development are required for each hour spent photographing. (Indeed, in planning project budgets, it is the analysis time that gives us the greatest difficulties.)

After the initial phase of analysis, a synthesis is developed, which may support the initial conceptual framework or which may require its reconsideration. Perhaps new insights will arise that require reiteration of the preceding steps to achieve a new, more advanced conceptual framework, or to confirm a hypothesis arising out of the earlier work. One aspect of using photographic methods is that they are something like Pandora's box: they tend to expose so much that was not understood before that there is a strong temptation to explore newly identified issues that were not part of the original project or assignment. In our experience, we have never been satisfied with a single full iteration.

EQUIPMENT

Technical improvements in photographic equipment occur so rapidly that by the time this book is published the list of specific equipment we use will have changed. The emphasis in this section will therefore be on the types of equipment and the reasons for our choices, rather than on the specific brand names or models actually used at the time of writing. We assume that the reader will have a new and wider range of options when he purchases equipment for projects a year or two in the future (Figure 18).

Equipment for Still Photography

We have found that 35mm is the most effective and economical standard, yielding high-quality images at acceptable cost. Particularly because color is so important a part of the photographic information, both as content and for identification during analysis, the 35mm color transparency slide has become our standard format. Black-and-white film is used only rarely to duplicate material already photographed in color to obtain acceptable prints for printing in reports.

We use "through-the-lens reflex" cameras, selected so that the image on the ground glass is exactly the whole image appearing on the exposed film. It is also important to be able to select the specific angle of view, from a wide angle that shows the context or larger environment under study to a telephoto or long focus that emphasizes detail. This need usually requires changing lenses, unless, as we do, the photographer has two cameras, each with one

Figure 18
Much of the photographic equipment we carry with us is shown above, as well as the Super-8 film editor and to its left, at the top of the picture, part of the Super-8 MFS-8 projector. At the right of the picture is the small tape recorder and microphone and a corner of the larger Uher tape recorder sometimes used in our work. The Super-8 movie camera lying on its side is the Nizo S-560. The two Nikon FTn cameras and some of the lenses are shown, together with the two light meters. The hand counter and the measuring tape are examples of the additional equipment that we recommend.

of the two lenses most commonly used.

We therefore normally work with two 35mm reflexes, each loaded with film of the same speed (ASA 160 color, 23 Din); both cameras are the same model and operate identically, except that one has a black trim, the other chrome. It is important that the two cameras operate identically; under the pressure of capturing a particular movement or behavior on both cameras, there is always the risk of confusion and error if the photographer must remember the different ways that two cameras operate. Having identical cameras reduces the probability of mistakes occurring repeatedly 6 inches behind the camera. For the same reason, we also use lenses on the two cameras of about the same "speed" (i.e., lenses which at their widest aperture admit about the same relative amount of light to the film). This gives us similar exposure readings on both cameras. Again, having

one camera with black trim and one with chrome trim also allows us to distinguish easily between them when keeping log records of what is exposed on the film in each particular camera body.

One camera is normally fitted with a 24mm f/2.8 lens. This gives a wide-angle view adequate to record most interiors, and yet not so wide that serious distortion of vertical lines appears at the sides, as is the case with the "fisheye" lenses. It is usually important to keep the back of the camera, and thereby the film, in a vertical plane when photographing buildings or interiors, so that the vertical lines of the photographic subject are aligned with the edges of the view-finder screen; this will reduce perspective distortion and make the pictures look more "real."

The other camera is normally fitted with a 105mm f/2.5 lens. This lens provides a detailed view of a small portion of the field of coverage of the 24mm wide-angle lens, yet is compact enough to fit in the normal carrying case. It is also fast enough (takes pictures in dim light) that it can be hand-held in normal interior lighting (no need for a tripod). Although we do not recommend this for the inexperienced photographer, we have regularly obtained satisfactory results using this lens at an exposure of 1/30 second.

Because the two cameras hanging around the neck may bang into each other as one walks or shifts about, we keep the strap on one as short as possible, and the strap on the other as long as possible, and so save much damage.

We normally have a third lens in a carrying case hanging from one or the other camera strap for use in special situations of very low light level. The third lens we carry is a 55mm f/1.2. When photographing dark storerooms or gloomy corridors, this lens is invaluable. It also is quite adequate for much night photography, even when held by hand at 1/8 second or longer.

We have standardized at this time on Nikon equipment, but find it quite heavy and noisy. Hauling around 20 pounds or more of photographic gear on the neck is very tiring; also, the cameras are quite noisy, causing problems when the photographer wishes to be "unobtrusive." Of course, anyone walking around with two big Nikons is likely to attract some attention in most situations.

We find the through-the-lens, center-weighted light metering of the Nikon fully adequate for most uses, and the speed and convenience of the built-in meter is important for much photography where it is essential to capture a fleeting movement or gesture. We do use a separate meter for some work. We have not, however, found the advanced "spot meters" with a 1 degree angle of view sufficiently valuable to warrant the additional weight and complexity they introduce to what should be almost a subliminal activity—the actual picture taking.

We also use a third camera for taking 35mm slides, the very lightweight Rollie 35. This camera is carried in the briefcase or large purse as a matter of course—it is always there. Frequently we find that a situation develops before our eyes or an opportunity to record a behavior or environment opens up at a time when it is not expected, and we do not have our two big cameras with us. The highly portable small camera has allowed us to photograph how people arrange themselves at lunch across a large public plaza, when by chance we were in an office overlooking the open space. It allowed us to capture on film unexpected sets of behavior when people started driving out of a parking lot at the end of a day during a heavy snowfall. It allowed us to record seating patterns in a conference room where photography was permitted, but where the large cameras were too bulky to bring along, and perhaps too intimidating also. And it has frequently allowed us to take pictures in a participant observer role when the larger cameras

would have made us seem professional. Some other newer equipment on the market, such as the new Olympus series, might be even more effective for these purposes.

Equipment for Motion-Picture Photography

As with still photography, we have selected format and equipment that permit high-enough-quality images at acceptable cost, with equipment and processing readily available. All our motion-picture photography is taken in the Super-8 format. We use color reversal film matching that for our 35mm transparency slides (ASA 160 color, 23 Din). Occasionally, in very dark situations, we may have the film specially processed to permit exposure at ASA 400, or use black-and-white film with a rating of ASA 400. We use these alternatives rarely, however, because the loss of information in the processed film is so great.

At present, we have five motion-picture cameras purchased at different times and for different purposes. As noted above, we normally expose at six frames per second. (The camera makes six exposures, uniformly spaced in time, during each second.) However, the several cameras have various individual technical characteristics that permit us to gather different kinds of data with different cameras, according to the research problem at hand.

Our most flexible camera permits the operator to run it at the normal speed of 18 frames per second, at 24 or 54 frames per second, at any speed below about six frames per second down to one each 2 minutes, or in single frames. The latter range of speeds is not calibrated, but set by the camera operator by turning a dial and adjusting until the desired speed is achieved. The camera operates on batteries, and there is some slowing down of the exposure rate as the batteries discharge over several hours of continuous operation. The camera has a zoom lens, permitting shifts in focal length (and thereby changes in the angle of view) from moderately wide angle (7mm) to telephoto (56mm). The lens is fast enough (lets enough light in onto the film at f/1.8) to permit satisfactory results with our normal film in most interior public places. The camera is the Braun Nizo S-560. Although it is the second most expensive of our cameras, it is a stock item, available in many camera shops "off the shelf."

This camera works well for many research uses, but its greatest value is its adaptability to a variety of situations. It was successfully used for the escalator study described above, although the problem of analysis and film identification was complicated because the exposure rate (frames per second) is not precisely calibrated at the slower speeds, and because clock time or other identification was not shown directly on the film. (With some of the film, we might have been able to show clock time by using one of the new battery-operated portable wall clocks.) By applying varying degrees of ingenuity for coding and time identification, we have used this camera in studying the behavior of crowds, both standing and in movement; waiting behavior of office workers; behavior at interface zones between workers and visitors, such as at counters; cordon counts, to determine the number of people and/or vehicles passing a certain point during prescribed time periods; and other similarly diverse situations.

Motion-picture cameras with the designation XL generally have shutters that remain open for an extra-long time at each frame. Instead of what used to be a norm of 1/30-second exposure, the period may be enough longer that the camera can be used in very dim light. The disadvantage of the XL camera type is that, when photographing human behavior with these longer exposures, rapid movement of the person being photographed shows as a blur on the film.

If the light is very dim, however, the researcher may have no alternative but to accept some blurring of movement, particularly arm and leg motion, as the price of getting any behavior data at all on film. We have two Kodak XL cameras, which have been modified to run at a standard speed of six frames per second, giving each exposure a duration of 1/19 second. The cameras are relatively inexpensive to purchase and to modify, but we use them only in special low-light situations.

Research into behavior patterns using diaries is discussed elsewhere in this book. Photography allows an alternative method of obtaining similar data, and we have a Super-8 movie camera that has been specially modified to perform this research function. This time-sampling camera will photograph in time-lapse mode, as many frames as desired over any desired period, and then pause for as long as desired before photographing another period of activity. As an example, we have run it in an office to study the use of a space or the behavior of specific workers in specific tasks. The camera was set to expose three or six frames per second over a duration of 1 or 2 seconds, and to do this once a minute. With approximately 3,600 frames in a single roll of Super-8 film, the camera can be operated automatically for about 10 hours, and thus record an entire working day without being touched. Although each burst of exposures caused a perceptible sound, we find that it is audible only at close range and is quickly accepted as "background sound" by those normally in the area near the camera. The short burst of 1 or 2 seconds of activity is long enough for the researcher to determine what activity is being performed, with a richness of data on location; activity; position and movement of individuals; use of furniture, equipment, tools, and space; personal interaction and interpersonal distance; and other relevant factors far exceeding what the typical respondent will write down on a "diary" form. Furthermore, by recording such data photographically at intervals as short as 1 minute, we have a data base of very high precision and rich enough to permit evaluation, even with a small number of subjects. When the camera is recording group activity, as in an office, reception area, living area, or public space, it can provide a data base almost unobtainable by any other method. The camera is relatively inexpensive, being a modification of a standard mass-produced unit.[4]

Some research problems require precise information on the time that a particular photograph was taken. An example is the baggage-claiming study mentioned earlier. It was necessary to determine the length of time that each bag was on the claim device at the airport before it was claimed, and the length of time each passenger was in the claim area before he recognized and removed his bag from the claim device and left the baggage-claiming area. Various times, such as first event, median event, and last event, for these actions had to be determined accurately for various types of airplane load, point of origin, and so on, so that standards could be set for use in computer models of future airport operations. The researcher is greatly helped if the time information is recorded directly on the film with the photographic image of the event; this is much more accurate and much easier for analysis than the time-consuming methods we have outlined. From the same source mentioned in the footnote to the previous paragraph, we have obtained a digital-time-readout camera which operates at the standard six frames per second, and which prints in a band across the bottom of each frame (picture) up to six red digits indicating the hour, minute, and second in real time. Even if the camera is stopped between events, the clock continues to operate, so that the real-time chronology of the events is maintained. Our camera supplier is now developing a unit that

will combine the features of the time-sampling camera with the digital-time-readout camera. We expect the unit to be commercially available at moderate cost well before publication of this book.

All our Super-8 motion-picture cameras have automatic light-meter controls regulating the exposure, and allow a form of manual override. This is needed in situations where the subject of interest is illuminated differently from the overall average brightness of the picture field, as when the people being photographed are in silhouette against a window or bright background.

Equipment for Viewing 35mm Slides

The initial viewing of 35mm slides usually occurs when the packet of 20 or 36 slides, in cardboard mounts, is received from the processing laboratory. Immediately upon receipt, an identifying number is put on each slide mount to differentiate that slide from all others in the files. We have found the use of a light table almost essential for this work. Our light tables are quite inexpensive; they are ordinary fluorescent light fixtures, size 2 by 4 feet, with a sheet of ¼-inch-thick, flat, translucent plastic substituted for the normal lens of the lighting fixture. Since the brightness of ¼-inch plastic is still too great for comfort, we place large sheets of paper over the light surface, which also gives us other advantages. The paper can be marked up with notes, guidelines, or other information to aid in sorting and analyzing the slides; the paper also protects the plastic from dirt and scratches and is easily and cheaply replaced.

Thoughtful analysis of the slides, particularly in conjunction with the time-lapse film, usually requires enlargement of the image by projection. (Prints are expensive, require excessive processing time, are cumbersome to file, and lose much of the detail of the original transparency.) The selection of a projector is difficult, since economical equipment rarely meets the special requirements of the researcher.

We have set as a primary requirement that the projector must not damage the slide even when a single slide is projected for long periods of time during analysis, perhaps for 1 or 2 hours without interruption. One measure of potential degradation of the slide image is the buildup of heat *in* the slide; above a specified temperature for each film and processing method, the image-bearing emulsion becomes soft and liable to damage, the plastic base that supports the emulsion may expand or buckle beyond recovery, and fading or other color change may occur. Many camera shops keep on hand a special thermometer slide consisting of two sheets of glass with a thermocouple mounted between them. When this slide is inserted in a projector, the silhouette of the thermocouple, with a read-out in degrees Fahrenheit, is projected on the screen, indicating the temperature of the thermometer slide at that moment. Many popular projectors come within 10 or even 5 degrees F. of the maximum allowable temperature for the slide that is recommended by such film manufacturers as Eastman Kodak.

A second requirement of importance to the analyst is that he should be able to access and project any particular slide in a group with reasonable convenience; also, while projecting a sequence of slides, he should be able to go back easily to look at an earlier slide in the sequence. The ability to project a single slide, inserted manually, is a useful convenience.

High-quality projection lenses and variable brightness of the projection bulb are also important. The projection lens must resolve all the detail that the color film can record. A choice of focal lengths is of value, but for most analytical work we recommend a projection lens in the range of 90 to 100mm (not longer than 4 inches). This will give a big enough image on the screen for the analyst to be able to read the detail while staying close to the projector. A longer focal length, up to as much as 7 inches, is sometimes useful when projecting from the rear of a room to a large group. It is then that the researcher will need maximum bulb brightness.

We often take two photographs of a single scene, one of the left half and one of the right half, so as to record a full wide angle of view as perceived by the human eye using peripheral vision. Therefore, we need to project the two images side by side, simultaneously, with matching projection equipment. The effect is of a super-wide-angle projection, which almost envelops the viewer when he is placed between the projectors, and at a distance from the screen about two thirds the width of the combined image. Thus two matching projectors are required. At the time we purchased our slide-projection equipment, the Leitz Color 250 projector seemed the best compromise for our needs.

Equipment for Viewing Super-8 Motion-Picture Film

Much of our work, often including the first review of newly processed film, is done on a portable hand editor. The editor is particularly useful for technical work, such as the manual coding of film when we are counting people in "bunches." The viewer allows us to run through the film rapidly, stopping or adjusting speed at will, to look at one or more sequences over and over again. The viewer permits one person to work quietly and effectively without disturbing others nearby. It also provides one convenient projected image of good brightness for use in making a black-and-white negative (with a 35mm camera) of a single frame in the movie film.

High optical resolution, high brightness of the projected image, and maximum screen size are the primary criteria in selecting a viewer. The threading and film track must also minimize wear and tear on the irreplaceable original film. At present we use Braun SB 1 Super-8 editors.

When projecting Super-8 film for analysis, the researcher has so many technical requirements that most amateur Super-8 movie projectors prove quite inadequate. He needs to project the time lapse in real time, that is, about four to six frames per second. He needs to be able to run the film at several faster speeds to find the various patterns of movement in his data. (The ability to simulate the real time of events at different, but controlled speeds, is a powerful tool. It allows a whole range of insights not possible with a manually operated table editor.) He needs to be able to stop the film at any frame and hold a single frame on the screen for an extended period of analysis, sometimes up to half an hour or more. He needs to be able to code the film so that it will stop at predetermined points for use in later analysis or in presentation. He needs to be able to do all the preceding not only in forward motion, but also in reverse motion. And the film must stay in focus in any of these modes. (Unfortunately, this cannot be taken for granted.) Finally, he needs as many as possible of the controls available on a remote-control unit, so that he can examine the projected image close up, while the projector responds to instructions to change the image in view.

The only projector we have found that meets these needs and is readily available and affordable is the Kodak Ektagraphic MFS-8. It has standard operating speeds of 6, 18, and 54 frames-per-second, plus single, frame-at-a-time viewing. It also provides all the other functions listed previously. Unfortunately, it is somewhat noisy, and at the end of a day of analysis we really notice the fatigue this causes. It is also expensive to operate, because the projection bulb unit costs about $1 for each hour of manufacturer's estimated bulb life. Because its standard slow speed is six frames per second, it also causes us to use more film than we feel is

necessary to record and understand most behavior. (As noted earlier, we have found that four frames per second gives sufficient information, but we often shoot at six frames per second so that we can simulate real time when projecting for analysis.) We expect that a modified projector, matching speeds exactly to the cameras described earlier, will soon be available from the same source as the cameras.

Other Equipment and Services

Slide storage and retrieval is basic to any analytical work. We store slides in plastic sheets, 8½ by 11 inches, which have pockets accepting twenty 35mm slides per sheet. The sheets have three holes punched for standard ring binders. These sheets protect the slides from dust and fingerprints; but we suspect that they may eventually cause some damage to the emulsion, which can stick to the plastic under pressure, heat, or humidity. We hope to find a better solution that is still as lightweight, economical, and easy to rearrange or sequence in analysis. (Heavy metal cabinets, some fireproofed and with built-in light sources for viewing, have been on the market for years. We have not used them because of their high cost, weight, and bulk, and because of the low portability of the groups of slides in their racks. These cabinets seem better suited for those who are more concerned about individual, highly valuable, archive slides.) We insert the slides in pairs, left and right, in two columns down each plastic sheet, and record on each slide the location of the slide in its "home" storage sheet and the identification of the overall sheet. In this way, any slide that has been removed from a sequence can easily be refiled in its original location.

A splicer for assembling segments of Super-8 movie film is frequently used. (We never cut up original film, only copies.) Splicing permits the grouping of relevant events into a single sequence for easier analysis or presentation. We use any good-quality standard unit, such as the Kodak Universal Splicer.

Light meters are important for recording context data. We measure illumination levels in footcandles (lumens per square foot) and in the international system unit, hecotolux (hundreds of lumens per square meter), using the General Electric type 213 meter. It is relatively inexpensive and lightweight, and sufficiently accurate for our needs up to this time. We measure light "temperature," or color, with the Gossen Sixtacolor meter, which reads in degrees Kelvin.

Film processing is a continuous problem for us. It is essential that the 35mm slides be returned to us with each slide numbered as to its sequence within the roll for coordination with our photolog. It is also essential that the processing provide a consistent color balance, even when slides taken at the same time but with different cameras are processed on different days, or in different places. And of course, the film must be returned free of scratches, tears, or blemishes, and mounted square in the cardboard frame. We have had great difficulty finding commercial processors in different parts of North America that comply with all these requirements. Our present standard procedure is that all film is delivered by hand to Kodak. (We try to avoid using the mails or long-distance shipments because of the lack of control over temperature during shipment.) We find that the Kodak laboratories provide the most consistent single source of processing across the continent (although we have had excellent results with a few individual processors in scattered locations).

Apparently, Super-8 movie film, being mainly for the amateur market, does not receive the same care in processing that is given to the 35mm slide. Again, we have found Kodak our most consistent source of processing. Quality control in the color balance and resolution of de-

tail in duplicates is generally much poorer than for 35mm slides. A first-generation copy is often quite different from the original, and the color balance may vary during the length of a single roll. A second-generation copy is usually at the low end of acceptability for any purpose.

The researcher should not forget the many accessory items needed in his fieldwork. We normally carry a measuring tape reading in inches and in centimeters; lined note pads in a folder or on a clipboard; a stopwatch; portable, battery-operated wall clocks; masking tape and drafting tape for putting up marks and signs that will show on the film, such as indicators of distance or scale, or the mark opposite the first moving step on an escalator; hand-operated counters; pencils; ball-point and felt-tip pens, and colored pencils or pens, all for a variety of uses, including marking on the tape mentioned earlier; spare file folders; bulldog clamps; plastic bags to hold rolls of film and other items; film containers (each for one 35mm cassette) with tape on them on which one can write the serial identification number of the film roll; a shoulder bag for items such as these; clothing with many pockets; and, of course, a supply of the photolog forms developed for the particular research project.

Herewith we add a word of caution to the reader: effective utilization of all the above-noted accessories in conjunction with the two Nikons, the digital-readout time-lapse camera, and large purse containing the smaller camera requires that the researcher have the strength and endurance of an Olympic athlete.

DIRECTIONS FOR THE FUTURE

Because research using *photographic* methods to study behavior in the human milieu is so new, we must assume that techniques and applications will grow in number and breadth in the coming years. Our own experience and understanding have greatly increased in the recent past. It may be of value to consider some potential directions for future development.

Future Applications

We expect that photographic methods will rapidly become commonplace in fields now dominated by the interview, observer recording, and diaries. In particular, we expect developments in the whole family of methods associated with observation, including tracking, counting, planned note taking, and similar unobtrusive approaches to data collection, hopefully within ethical limitations. We expect that the camera will make accessible many subject areas of research that, heretofore, have received little attention because of cost or analytical problems. And we expect that interest in photographic methods will grow rapidly for a few years, as researchers come to learn the strengths and limitations of these methods.

Training and field experience will be necessary before researchers can expand substantially the actual use of new photographic methods. We anticipate specific institutional and internship programs for graduate students in the immediate future.

Because photographic methods make economically feasible some research projects that are of government interest, we expect a growth in grants to fund both the studies and some equipment acquisition. Applications could include housing, urban studies, health fields, transportation, office and administrative activities, business management, public, and private security, service and marketing analysis, and a host of others.

Future Equipment

We expect that major equipment manufacturers, such as Kodak, will probably not enter this field directly in the next year or two, but that small companies will offer a wider range of modifications to standard mass-produced equipment.

There is an urgent need for standardization, as between analysis–projection film speeds and the operating speeds of the cameras. Since sophisticated equipment modification tends to be less expensive when accomplished electronically than by mechanical means, those cameras which lend themselves to electronic changes will probably become standard.

We suggest that certain time-lapse speeds will probably become standard, such as six or four frames per second, one frame per second, and one frame per minute. For time sampling, we may expect intervals of ½, 1, and 2 minutes, and some rather longer period to become norms. The standards will probably arise out of the experience of the researchers in analytical procedures, however, rather than for technical reasons, because within these ranges it is the number of different standards, rather than the nature of any particular standard, that appears to determine the cost of the modifications.

Now that the microcircuitry is readily available "off the shelf," we expect that most new research cameras will include the digital-time-readout image printed directly on the film as part of the photographic image. Although for Super-8 film about six digits seems maximum with present films and technology, we hope to see at least four additional digits to identify month and day, available on 35mm still cameras.

One present gap in the range of available accessories is equipment to make economical prints from short strips or from single frames of Super-8 film. This could be a boon for the analysis and reporting of research.

NOTES

1. There are some interesting, longer accounts of photographic research, for example, Whyte's brief account (1972) of research in progress on the uses of plazas and public open spaces in New York City, but he does not

describe how the study was designed or is being conducted. An account of an older study, by Collier (1967), offers many insights into ways in which photography can be used as an integral part of anthropological kinds of research. However, the technical information is out of date and the book describes methods of little relevance to individuals designing or prescribing built environments.

2. Data were gathered over 11 days of the holiday season, December 1972–January 1973, at two airports, the Seattle Tacoma International Airport and the San Francisco International Airport. Francoise Szigeti participated with the authors in this study.

3. For an example of quasi-quantitative analysis from photographs, see Chapter 7 of Collier (1967).

4. For information on price, delivery, and technical details, contact Mr. Robert W. Watler, President, Western Precision Products, Ltd., 1855 West 4th Ave., Vancouver, B.C., Canada, V6J 1M4. The time-sample camera is model K 101 C/3 and the digital-time-readout camera is model K 102 A/1.

REFERENCES

5. Appleyard, Donald, Kevin Lynch, and J. R. Myer. 1964. *The View from the Road*. Cambridge, Mass.: MIT Press.

6. Collier, John, Jr. 1967. *Visual Anthropology: Photography as a Research Method*. New York: Holt, Rinehart and Winston.

7. Cullen, Gordon. 1961. *Townscape*. New York: Van Nostrand Reinhold.

8. Shils, E. A. 1959. "Social Inquiry and the Autonomy of the Individual," pp. 114 –115 in Daniel Lerner (ed.), *The Human Meaning of the Social Sciences*. New York: World Publishing Company.

9. Whyte, W. H., Jr. 1972. "Please Just a Nice Place to Sit." *The New York Times Magazine* (Dec. 3), pp. 20 ff.

Observing Environmental Behavior: The Behavior Setting

Dagfinn Ås

Dagfinn Ås (who sometimes spells his name Aas) is a member of the research staff of the Norwegian Building Research Institute in Oslo. In this position, he has been in the vanguard of Scandinavian researchers in the application of empirical techniques to the study of housing. He has studied sociology at the University of Michigan, been a visiting professor at the University of Missouri, and lectured in both the United States and Canada. Mr. Ås has also been active recently in the use and application of time-budget techniques.

LOOKING OR ASKING

A social scientist has many tools in his box. Like most specialists, he prefers some to others. Furthermore, some are appealing because they can be used for more than one problem, however imperfectly. He may not always use his toolbox to its full potential.

The social scientist favors the technique of questioning. The sociologist, for example, will design a questionnaire for just about any problem, and the social psychologist will invariably start out by interviewing persons.

This kind of social scientist might be a very good interrogator, but he will be a very bad detective. To be a good detective one must surely be able to get information out of suspects and other persons, but one must also be able to follow concrete leads in the environment. One must be a good and accurate observer.

Observation, and observational methods, can be seen as basically and theoretically very distinct from the methods of questioning. Through observational methods, we tap a somewhat different universe. The two approaches relate to each other, however, as we shall see; but here let me continue to stress differences, as such emphasis will facilitate the analysis of each.

The observation–questioning dichotomy can be seen as related to the "outside–inside" question. The objects of study are behaving persons, and we have the choice of describing them from the outside through an observer or from the inside by asking the behaving persons to give us *their* descriptions and experiences. As all persons are able to assume the observer's role vis-à-vis oneself, we can in theory obtain observational information by asking the subjects under study to act as our observers. This is actually more than a hypothetical approach; we often do this in our studies. The kind of information obtained this way, however, should be called *quasi-observational information*.

We can readily observe verbal behavior, but it is primarily against *nonverbal behavior* that observational methods are directed. Verbal behavior or speech is not bound by the specific environment in which it takes place. At the breakfast table, for example, the conversation might center on problems of international politics, although in most families the conversation consists of utterances directed toward the children and their misbehavior. From the observer's point of view, these and other situations will be classified under the same heading: breakfast.

It is, however, students of verbal behavior who have provided us with a set of concepts that perhaps best captures the essence of observation distinct from questioning. Kenneth Pike (1954–1960), in his quest for a unified theory for both verbal and nonverbal behavior, has brought to the foreground the concept of *etic* and *emic*.

An emic standpoint is one that is oriented toward the actors or subjects under study and *their* interpretation of the events that take place. It is the classical anthropological approach, where you rely heavily upon informants that supply the meaning and interpretation of the activities observed. It is, in short, the subjective approach to cultural events.

The etic approach, in contrast, is external or alien. The etic standpoint calls for observations from the outside and from far enough away to see the shape of the events (and thereby similarities across cultures), even if the meaning of the same events to the "natives" differs from yours.

It is interesting to note that it is easier to "identify" with an emic approach: it is the "warm" approach, whereas the etic point of view is cold and detached. This might in some way help to explain why social scientists tend to favor the emic approach; they let the subjects themselves provide essential information, themselves taking the role of those who order and present it.

OBSERVING AND DESIGNING

Although the debate still rages in some quarters over the question of whether the designer is an artist, I take as my point of departure that the designer first and foremost provides solutions to questions of form and function. He is supposed to shape the environment so that certain activities can take place and so that certain human needs are satisfied. It follows from this that the designer must obtain information from or about the people for whom he is designing.

Being part of the same culture will of course make it possible for the designer to make good guesses about desired activities and needs. It is, however, a well-established fact that persons in the design profession are recruited from certain population groups more often than from others. He or she will know first of all the subculture of which he or she is a member, and know it better than any other in the society. The necessity of obtaining information from and about the people he is designing for is quite real.

Such information can be provided at very different levels of generality, and it is my argument that it is not sufficient to have access to a list of common human *needs,* even if this were to prove possible. This is too general and too far removed from the environmental elements under discussion—or design solutions. It is through *activities* that needs are satisfied, and it is at this level that it is meaningful to talk about fit or correspondence between humans and their environment.

In designing new structures, whether a residential area or a central business district, one will always try to improve on past practices. So if information from the inhabitants themselves is needed, direct attention should be focused on how best to obtain it. It is, however, a great misunderstanding to believe that information of this kind is already in the hands of a wide range of persons, and that the job of the researcher is just that of assembling it.

It is important to obtain information on the inhabitants' ideas, but this information is insufficient. In addition, we shall need information obtained in an independent manner on the activities themselves. Throughout this chapter we shall spell out how and why.

This stress on the need for such information does not mean that the designer himself and his role become unimportant. Quite the contrary: in my opinion, the demand on the designer as a creative force will be stronger rather than weaker in a situation where data are present on and from the inhabitants.

ACTIVITY AND EXPERIENCE

To this point, I have intentionally tried to present the contrast between observation and questioning. The observant reader will also have noticed that I seem to favor the etic approach and the role of the observer rather than the one of the questioner. He is right; let me add, however, that this is a timebound and strategic stance. At present, in environmental research, we have a long way to go to come fully to grips with our man-made and men-built environment. The current need is greater for developmental work in the area of observational techniques than with respect to methods to tap attitudes, beliefs, and all that comes under the heading of experience.

One reason for this imbalance in the development of different methods is that the social scientist has previously left the environment largely outside his studies and concentrated on humans and their interpersonal relationships. For these kinds of problems, the various techniques that include questioning are usually well adapted. It is first when you try to bring environmental factors into the sociological analysis that the relative underdevelopment of observational methods is uncovered.

In studies of environmental problems, however, it is of fundamental importance not only to obtain a description of environmental facts, but also to obtain information about the inhabitant's own reactions to these conditions; in short, their experience. On these grounds we cannot perform our studies relying only on etic information, however desirable. We shall leave this as a reminder lest the reader be led to think that we shall disregard altogether the information coming directly from the people under study. Apart from the question of choosing between information *from* and *about* the persons in question, some comments should be made on the reliability of the information usually obtained.

Quite a few studies have by now shown rather bad correspondence between what people say they do and what they are, in fact, doing. This lack of correspondence comes about for different reasons. On the one hand, we must in many cases expect to receive wrong answers to our questions. This phenomenon has been shown very clearly in a study on magazine reading. After carrying out a regular interview survey on reading habits and magazines, the same people were visited again by somebody who was "collecting wastepaper." Marked differences were observed in types of magazines; they collected many more low-prestige magazines than were reported in the interviews to be read.

However, most discrepancies are not due to deliberate misrepresentations of fact, as in the above case. People will, on the whole, report their activities truthfully; but owing to such processes as selective perception, they will not report on the facts themselves, only on their *interpretation* of the facts.

A person's interpretation of reality is of great importance for the person himself, and if the problem at hand is that of predicting his attitudes, we would do best to rely on his own report of his behavior rather than observational records of his behavior. However, the designer or student of environmental design will seldom be confronted with this task.

BEHAVIOR AND ACTIVITY

Before going further we must try to define or more carefully explain what the concept of activity stands for. The word is part of our everyday language and thereby supposedly understood. This is not too helpful, however, since we bring to the word a series of different associations. Furthermore, we need to define the *entities* of our concern and their environment, as our primary concern regards the relations between the two.

We can easily identify and describe the elements and parts of our daily environment: the houses, the gardens, the trees, the street, the car. Such descriptions can be performed on different levels, as most elements are to be seen as parts of parts of parts: the car, the wheels, the spokes, and so on. Some of these levels stand out and constitute units of seemingly greater importance: the car, for example.

Most people will agree with these simple classifications, but in spite of this simplicity it has proved very difficult indeed to spell out the principles behind such discriminations between units and their environment. Roger Barker has been able to do this relatively well by referring to the different levels of phenomena in science. The environment of an entity, according to Barker, "is made up of those parts of the *outside* regions with which the entity is coupled by laws on a different level from those which govern the entity itself" (Barker, 1960, p. 8). The trailer that moves with the car is part of the moving unit and does not constitute the environment. So however, does a person's hearing aid and the person's clothing. Please note that this attempt at definition operates within a "frozen" world; the concept of time is not involved.

If we introduce the concept of *time* and apply it to our field of inquiry, we are confronted with a different set of entities. The various behaviors of the person, rather than his features, will be the phenomena that are perceived. It is the activities that take place and the events that unfold which catch one's attention. We are confronted with persons, activities, and environment—not only the first and the third, as before. To move forward, then, let us deal with the newcomer: *activity*.

Instead of saying that an activity or behavior has environmental coordinates in space and time (which is somewhat better than not recognizing the environment at all), my main point is that all behavior implies *an interaction* between persons and environment. Furthermore, the reality in which we live, and which we as researchers study, is one of activities. Seen in this perspective, characteristics of persons or objects in their environment are relevant in so far as they impinge on the events that take place, a point stressed as well in Michelson's introduction and in the chapter by Michelson and Reed.

Now then, if activities are to be seen as the unit of analysis instead of, for example, individuals, the problem of definition becomes more acute. There is not a corresponding clarity in our language (our thinking) with respect to behavioral units or what constitutes one activity as distinct from another in the same behavior stream.

We must necessarily clarify this problem before we go on to discuss various techniques of observing it. I shall rely here quite heavily on Marvin Harris (1964), who is one who has dealt with the problem, and also on Roger Barker.

Being alive and awake, we are in constant interaction with our environment and are each and every one of us "emitting" a stream of behavior. We are engaged in many dissimilar behaviors to the extent we can cut and divide this stream of behavior in smaller time segments. If I should describe what I did just after getting out of bed this morning, a first way of dividing the behavior stream would go like this: turning off the alarm clock, going to the bathroom, washing my hands and face, putting on a robe, bringing in the morning paper, putting on the coffee pot, sitting down to read the morning news, and so on. Furthermore, each of these behaviors could be subdivided into small bits and segments. For example, "putting on the coffee pot"; enter the kitchen, open the cupboard, take out the pot, turn on the water, fill the pot with water, turn off the water faucet, put the pot on the stove, turn on the stove, open the cupboard, take out the can, open the can, open the drawer, take out the spoon, spoon coffee from the can into the pot. The next behavior is actually part of this sequence, as I watch the coffee pot while reading the morning newspaper. If we wanted to go on to even more detailed levels of description, we could do that, too. At some point, however, we

reach a level where the human sense organs give in. There is a final level beyond which we cannot go; there is a smallest unit of observable behavior.

Marvin Harris, in his search for the smallest unit of behavior, notes that "...every motion of a bodypart is necessarily associated with some spatio-temporally contiguous and continuous alteration of things in the body's immediate environment" (Harris, 1964, p. 28). This provides our definition of the smallest unit of behavior, for which Harris proposes the name "actone." He suggests a three-point definition:

1. The units must consist of a bit of body-motion *and* an environmental effect produced by that motion.

2. Neither the environmental effect nor the body-motion will be so small as to fall below an observer's naked visual or auditory thresholds.

3. All observers will agree that the particular unit has occurred when and only when it has occurred (Harris, 1964, p. 36).

This attempt at defining might help in clarifying the issue at hand and in backing up the proposition that behavior implies an interaction of humans and their environment. It does not help much beyond that, however, because it can be demonstrated easily that a record of observations at the level of actones is not very useful. As Harris puts it: "Common sense and actual ethnographic practice suggest that certain kinds of people emit certain kinds of actones in the presence of certain kinds of objects at certain times and places" (Harris, 1964, p. 53).

In order that an observational record make sense, it is necessary to obtain information on the type of actor involved, the place he is in, at what time the behavior takes place, and what kinds of objects are handled. No degree of detail is more correct than any other for the observational record. The student of design and design research will most often need to use observational records more general than those of my morning activities. Observational studies of activities imply much more than dealing with and detailing streams of behavior: we have to include substantive portions of the physical matrix of the environment.

HUMAN OBSERVERS AS INSTRUMENTS OF RESEARCH

It is well to be aware of the fact that human beings are involved in all research ventures, although seldom recognized as an instrument of research. In our context, however, we should specify the limitations that we work under when employed as observers and recorders.

When this problem is dealt with in the literature, it is usually under the heading "bias." In my opinion the danger of distortion is overemphasized, and the observer is generally not recognized as the "carefully coordinated system of censors" which he can truthfully be designated as being. All research instruments must be calibrated; so also with the human observer. We usually call this training. His awareness of certain features in the environment must be heightened while he might be asked to disregard other features.

Speaking of instrumentation and calibrating, we should state more precisely what we are talking about. I will do this by again quoting Marvin Harris:

Indeed, the instrument I propose as the basic research tool in behavioral studies cannot, in a strict physicalist sense, be regarded as a piece of observational apparatus at all. This instrument is the observer's eye. As a secondary piece of equipment, to be used in more restricted circumstances, I should like to put forward the observer's ear. And as tertiary apparata, to be used under yet more restricted occasions, I should like to propose the use of the observer's digital sense of touch and his olfactory receptors. Cameras, stop-watches, tape-measures, balance-scales, tape-records, and pedometers may also prove useful for more refined analysis of the behavior stream. But these ought to be employed after observers' eyes and ears have been applied to

the relevant portion of the field of inquiry (Harris, 1964, p. 32).

It goes without saying that there must be a close correspondence between the real-life phenomena that are the objects of the observers and their observational records. We will, however, never ask that they be identical; we are usually confronted with such complicated phenomena that a reduction in the amount of information present is of paramount importance.

Regardless of the particular techniques that the researcher makes use of, he can take one of two positions in his role of "observer and data generator." He can take the very passive role of translator. He will have at his disposal a set of coding categories which he applies to the real word and consequently records the result of this application. The other major role is an active one where he will stimulate his environment and record the reaction to that. These two roles have been called by others *transducer* and *operator* and their products are referred to as T-data and O-data, respectively, (Barker, 1965; Ashby, 1956).

The observer will typically be given the role of the transducer, while those doing any kinds of questioning most often fall into the role of the operator. The two roles each have their representatives and defenders. The one working with experimental methods, say in a laboratory, will to an extreme degree adhere to the role of the operator. Someone out to describe the life and existence of people in existing communities will try as best he can to follow the role of the transducer. The latter is clearly the most difficult role to play, as it ideally implies noninterference. The observer of everyday life and activities will typically be confronted with such great amounts of data that he will have to operate with heavy "filters." He must disregard many aspects of the situation to be studied in order to manage the recording itself. By his sheer presence, however, he often runs the risk of direct interference, without intending it.

So far we have talked about the human observer as if he was another piece of physical equipment. It is possible to design the observer's role this narrowly, but it is hardly a proper use of such "instruments," as they are capable of much more. To make use of the observer's other capabilities, those of reasoning and interpreting, does not necessarily violate the role of the transducer. The point is that while the observer is still operating as a translator and coder of information, he is, at the same time, being involved in the analysis of the data. The data he delivers will not be just "raw material" but partly refined material to be processed further by other researchers.

It is an old dictum in social science that behavior is purposeful and goal directed. It follows that recording of behavior and activities should, to be complete, be followed by a statement of purpose. At this point, however, we encounter a sharp disagreement among students of activities and behavior. Roger Barker argues that it is both necessary and possible to record behavior as the actors experience it, by interpretation of the activities. Marvin Harris, representing the opposite view, is sharp on this point. He argues that "the extension of the emic view point to nonverbal behavior is doomed to generate nothing but intuitive, culture-bound and subjective descriptions (Harris 1964, p. 148).

What is at stake here is that if the observer is a native of the culture he is out to study, he cannot avoid identification and understanding. A recording of this is possible. This kind of information will have a varying degree of reliability, and it is important to make clear that this is an interpretation on the part of the observer. It might, and often will, correspond to the people's own interpretation of the situation. This, however, does not mean that the information must be classified as emic.

There is no scientific reason why we should exclude interpretive material by observers, but we must never equate this kind of information with the more straight observational data.

MAJOR STRATEGIES FOR OBSERVATION

As we have stated, observing and describing behavior implies an identification of segments of the behavior stream. We have earlier given examples of detailed reporting of this; let us now go to the other extreme and give some examples of the most general reporting that we can do.

The dichotomy between the sleeping and awake conditions encompasses the most general categories for a daily cycle. Studies have shown, however, that human beings sleep pretty much the same number of minutes (close to 8 hours) everywhere in the world. The dichotomy of being at home versus being in other localities will depend heavily on the person being male or female, employed or not, having children or not, and so on.

Another good example of very broad categories of behavior is the "four kinds of time" proposed by Claude Javeau (1970). The four are: (1) necessary time—sleep, meals, and personal hygiene; (2) contracted time—work and education; (3) forced time—travel, shopping, family work, housework, upkeep of possessions, and so on; and (4) free time—all kinds of recreational activities. Again, studies show a great similarity across nations. The first two kinds of time appear very stable; the relation between the latter two seems to be a very useful indicator of life styles.

Analysis at this aggregate level, however, will require observations at a more detailed level, so let us now turn to examples of the most used and most useful observational units of behavior. Both Roger Barker and Marvin Harris have provided lists of possible levels of description, with names for each. Both propose use of the term *episode* for one level. In Harris's scheme, this is defined as "an actone for which four stage-coordinates have been supplied, corresponding roughly to answers to questions of who, what, when and where" (Harris, 1964, p. 70).

When dealing with behavior streams of individuals, this is very basic unit, and observation on this level is perfectly possible to perform. With these episodes as building blocks, we can isolate chains of episodes and single episodes that constitute important nodes in the stream of behavior. These nodes will correspond to cutting points whenever broader categories of behavior are sought. Note, however, that the unit of analysis here is the individual, and this is not necessarily the correct unit for all studies. We shall return to this shortly.

The four "stage coordinates" or descriptive dimensions—type of actor (who), behavioral objects (what), time (when), and place (where)—provide us with a way of keeping separate different research approaches. By concentrating more on one than the others—to hold one constant and let the others vary —we can see how these approaches are related.

On a very general level the observant reader will see that this also gives rise to the distinction between disciplines: the student of history will concentrate on the dimension of time, the geographer will do the same with the spatial dimension, the ethnographer will concentrate on behavioral objects, and the social psychologist will let the behaving individual be at the center of attention.

In the present context, it does not make much sense to hold the time dimension constant; we made quite a point of the fact that this element is part of any observational record. However, if we concentrate on a given location or space and perform continuous recordings of (varying) actors and their behavior, we obtain information that is very relevant for environmental studies.

We shall deal with this kind of approach at length below.

A very different kind of approach is the one where the actor is "held constant" and space will vary to the extent that the particular individual moves around. The kind of data obtained this way corresponds to what is elsewhere called the time budget.

There is a logical third approach where one holds constant a movable object or physical entity and follows it on its course as it is handled by different people in different places.

It is, however, the first two approaches that form the two major techniques for describing daily and recurrent behavior. The choice between the two is a fundamental one, as it will to a large degree determine the analysis to follow. The person can constitute the unit of analysis only under the second of these strategies.

In an actual case, in following the one or the other of these strategies, one will still have lots of "elbow room" or different techniques to choose from in order to carry out a particular study. There are differences in the particular role of the observer and the specific techniques he uses that form the basis for differential names attached to observational techniques.

Participant observation is one such name that might need special mention, as it is a well-known term but perhaps often misunderstood. The term refers to a situation where the observer attaches himself to a situation that he is going to study in a real sense. He lets himself be employed by the factory he is going to study, he manages to be taken into the street-corner gang he is out to study. In short, he adopts a role similar to the ones played by the persons under study. He will thereby have access to all relevant "places" and will also have an opportunity to experience directly the environment and conditions of life in these situations.

The old ideal of noninterference suggests that observers should not tell their new companions about their real aims. This is a "hot" issue, as there is, of course, an element of deceit involved here. This is an issue under constant debate and cannot be resolved finally one way or the other.

The behavior of the people under study will not necessarily change because of the presence of an observer. The information conveyed to the observer will, however, typically be different. The difference will not necessarily be with respect to content; the observer will, however, either receive more or less information than other persons in the group, depending on the degree of mutual trust.

In our culture, with its particular political system, the private sphere of each individual or family will in some cases be a critical matter. Not all research ventures are to the benefit of the people studied, and it is just proper that they take measures to keep the observer out of sectors of their life.

Unobtrusiveness will be a general goal for development work in the area of observational methods. The disguised observer performing his participant observations might be quite unobtrusive. If however, use of the results from his study could be used to the disadvantage of the people studied, the present author will not defend these research activities. The role of the participant observer could be taken both in studies of individual behavior and in studies of behavior in certain locations.

Let me come back to this basic dichotomy and present a second form of observation, called *systematic observation.* Under systematic observation, the observer does not participate but rather records what he sees in as complete detail as possible *while the activity is in progress.* It is intensive and follows a prearranged system of recording—hence "systematic observation." However, this approach requires a form of sampling of the universe to be potentially observed because of its intensity. The student of behavior is only interested in space that is inhabited. Other kinds of space are of no interest unless it constitutes part of the "view" from inhabited space and thereby is linked to some behavior. Furthermore, sleep is considered an activity, but for many practical reasons we shall often disregard this. The behavior to be studied, therefore, will take place during periods when humans are up and moving about.

The behavior of a particular community will "start" as the first person awakes. The particular community will consist of a certain set of fixed "arenas" of behavior. They come into the picture to the extent that they are populated. They are not part of our behavioral universe if they are not populated, and the communal day will "end" when the last person goes to bed. For this set of behaviors and situations, we are in need of a concept. I propose this be called the *milieu,* as distinct from the concept of the environment, which refers to the surroundings or the supporting receptacle of the activities and behaviors that constitute a particular milieu.

We shall never be able to study total milieus in the way that all activity can be observed. This, however, will never be necessary, as we can sample from this universe as other research ventures do in other universes. This sampling is complex owing to the fact that the dimensions along which we can sample will be interdependent. To recapitulate, our sampling dimensions are (1) places, (2) times, and (3) persons. It is evident, however, that subgroups of the population will favor the use of particular arenas; some arenas will be in continuous use while others will be active at certain times only. Finally, if all ages of the population are included, the activity patterns will differ over the time of the day. If we then go beyond the daily cycle, there are additional difficulties associated with the weekly or the seasonal cycle.

Very little development work has been done with respect to this kind of sampling. No fixed rules exist with respect to sample "size" and no technique for computing "sampling error" is accessible. Let us present some examples to illustrate these problems.

If, for example, we wanted to study and possibly compare a set of schools with the aim of studying the impact of some structural aspects of the buildings on behavior systems, observational methods would be called for. We would necessarily have to design some system of sampling the actors, the places, and the times. We would have to observe and study both teachers' restrooms, as well as corridors, and we would have to visit sessions in the morning as well as in the afternoon.

Apart from sampling of the time dimensions, we could choose to literally follow some of the pupils and teachers in their daily routine at the school. The opposite technique would be to sample the places or arenas of activity. Observation would then cover all activity in these places within certain time periods. As soon as you work with particular environments complex enough to include more than one activity arena, we at least theoretically have some choice of approaches. I say theoretically because you will not always have access to individuals, whereas it is relatively easy, at least in the Western cultures, to have access to various locations or spaces.

Unless certain actors are to be at the center of attention, the sampling of space will have to be coupled with the sampling of time. This can be exemplified with two typical examples of observing activities out-of-doors in residential areas or smaller communities.

Preliminary scouting will typically precede any systematic study based on observations. Finding various arenas of an area is a relatively easy affair. Concrete clues will be present and will indicate activity arenas even if no activity is going on. One basic technique, then, will be to design a path for the observer to follow at specified times of the day. He will arrive at a certain number of arenas at specified times and have at his disposal a certain number of minutes in which to scan the arena, to observe the actors, and to categorize them and their behavior. The arena must be mapped in advance and a border line must be defined, inside which the observations are to be performed. Entering the observations directly onto special maps of the same arena is often found to be helpful. This is very practical, for example, in connection with observing children at play. Special symbols or a shorthand will be relatively easy to develop and use in such studies.

The other main technique for observing out-of-door activities is to center the attention on the concrete pathways and lines of communication, and to make use of a moving rather than stationary observer. The preliminary scouting can be designed so as to first map the concrete environmental barriers, the corresponding doors and portals, and the specially built roads and paths. Not much scouting is needed in order to provide special maps for the pathways of an area. In order to be able to gather a set of observations at a given point in time, this technique typically requires many observers. They will each be allocated a pathway with a defined area on both sides of it. Each will travel this path within a relatively short time period and observe and record actors and activities. The observations will be made and recorded as persons are "hit" by an imaginary line perpendicular to the observer's movements along the pathway. Again, a sampling of the time of day will be necessary to provide a full record. This technique can be seen as a simulation of the individuals' behaviors and is therefore a variant of the technique of holding constant the person or actors involved.

Each of the dimensions space, time, and population can be used singly as a first sampling variable, defining a territory, a time period, or a subpopulation to be studied. In this early period of development, we badly need studies that can also provide frameworks: studies that embrace total populations, whole communities, and which span the yearly cycle of human behavior. We turn to this now, and we will use the rest of this chapter to discuss the concept of the behavior setting and how to go about describing it. Although the behavior-setting approach is but one form of systematic observation, and hence even a smaller subsegment of all forms of observation, it has undergone considerable pioneer work of relevance to design and planning research.

THE ENVIRONMENT, THE MILIEU, AND THE BEHAVIOR SETTING

Environment and environmental studies are terms that are seen more and more in various publications. They are, however, somewhat unspecific terms that require more clarification. In our modern society we see that more and more of our daily environments are built environments. Not only that, we are constantly better able to control and shape the environment. Technological changes over time have made it possible to change the environment on a much larger scale than before, and changes in the social organization of certain sectors of society have resulted in very large building projects. Large geographic areas, for example, are planned, shaped, and built in a unified manner. Planning at this level requires information on day-to-day behavior that has not been systematically assembled before.

In some of these newly built environments, we encounter social problems at present at a scale not known previously. The human being is well known for his adaptability to various environments, but it has lately been clear to more and more people that how we shape and build our environment might have great consequences for the inhabitants. The question put to the researcher therefore is: Does it matter how we shape and build our environments?

To answer this question we have to ask additional questions: How can we study the consequences of given environmental structures? In what way can different consequences be demonstrated?

The traditional social scientist would probably try to assess the degree of satisfaction (happiness) of the inhabitants of the different environmental structures. This would be illuminating, but unless we perform more detailed and careful studies of the people's activities, daily life, and existence, we would be at a loss to formulate action programs, whether for planning new areas or improving old ones. It is at this point that the behavior-setting approach is so central. A survey of the behavior settings in a given area is a very direct description of what we have called life and existence, or milieu.

We asked above about the "consequences" of certain environmental factors. At this point we should make clear that the built environment, or for that matter the total physical environment, is to be seen as a set of *input factors*. There are other such inputs; and broadly speaking the population and its characteristics is a second set of inputs. A third broad class of inputs will be the social organization that prevails. An assessment of consequences will necessarily have to deal with *output factors*.

It is in order to capture this aspect that we have introduced the word "milieu." The word is not totally unknown, but it might be possible to build into it a more precise meaning, which at the same time sets it off from the concept of environment. The concept environment is needed in its own right as a synonym for, but a better concept than, surroundings. The concept of milieu, however, will also need clarification and specification. At the most general level, we can say that *the milieu consists of a set of behavior settings*.

THE DEFINITION OF BEHAVIOR SETTINGS

The Eskimos have very many concepts for snow, and this is an often-used example of the correspondence between language and the conditions of life of a people. For important aspects of life, we have a necessary number of differentiated concepts. In our present-day changing society, however, we are confronted with serious environmental problems, and we seem to lack concepts for expressing this, or even thinking about it.

It is very easy to be lead astray by one's own language in believing that there is a reality corresponding to concepts we have invented. At the same time, we do not, in fact, perceive phenomena for which no concept exists, even if this were to be a very concrete aspect of our own environment.

The concept of behavior setting is just this; it refers to something very real and concrete in our environment. We all know this phenomenon, but we have not had a proper frame of reference for understanding it. The new concept has had a crystallizing effect for theory and research on persons and their daily environment. It is for many a completely new thought to consider the drugstore, the Sunday mass, a game of football, and the weekly scout meeting as phenomena of the same class. It is, however, very easy to communicate the idea of the behavior setting, as with the well-known egg of Columbus; once demonstrated, it is readily understood and accepted.

Barker and his associates arrived at a new understanding of the importance of the environmental forces through work in the area of child psychology. As he himself expresses it:

When we made long records of children's behavior in the real-life settings in accordance with a traditional person-centered approach, we found that some attributes of behavior varied less across children within settings than across settings within the days of children. We found, in short, that we could predict some aspects of children's behavior more adequately from knowledge of the behavior characteristics of the drugstores, arithmetic classes, and basketball games they inhabited than from knowledge of the behavior tendencies of particular children (Barker, 1968, p. 4).

This insight shatters the traditional border of the science of psychology, and Barker has found it necessary to call the field in which he works *ecological* psychology, to explicitly make the point that environmental factors are fundamental. Behavior settings are accordingly *ecological units.*

It is not possible to present a short definition of the concept behavior setting, as Barker's own definition covers five pages in his book *Ecological Psychology* (1968). The definition is made up of seven separate parts. We will quote the first in full:

A behavior setting consists of one or more *standing patterns of behavior.* Many units of behavior have been identified: reflex, actone, action, molar unit, and group activity are examples. A standing pattern of behavior is another behavior unit. It is a bounded pattern in the behavior of men, en masse. Examples in the Midwest are a basketball game, a worship service, a piano lesson. A standing pattern of behavior is not a common behavior element among disparate behavior elements, such as the twang in Midwestern speech or the custom in small American towns of greeting strangers when they are encountered on the street. A standing pattern of behavior is a discrete behavior entity with univocal temporal–spatial coordinates; a basketball game, a worship service, or a piano lesson has, in each case, a precise and delimited position in time and space. Furthermore, a standing pattern of behavior is not a characteristic of the particular individuals involved; it is an extra-individual behavior phenomenon; it has unique characteristics that persist when the participants change (Barker, 1968, p. 18).

The second point of Barker's definition includes the following: "The behavior patterns of a behavior setting are attached to particular constellations of nonbehavioral phenomena." And Barker goes on to specify the fundamental point that behavior must be seen as an interaction of persons and environmental elements.

The environmental elements can be seen to be surrounding or enclosing the behavior and also similar in structure so as to fit the behavior that takes place. This coupling of persons with their environment is so fundamental that Barker has found it fitting to invent a special new concept in order to refer to it; he calls it "synomorphy."

We have indicated above that new ways of thinking require new concepts, and this is why Barker has found it necessary to introduce a whole set of new and partly strange-sounding words. A given behavior setting, for example the drugstore, is a very complex entity. A detailed description requires that it is split up in parts. As a system of behavior settings, however, it does *not* split in persons and things; it splits into synomorphs.

DESCRIBING THE BEHAVIOR SETTING

The concept of synomorphs, the elements that refer to behavior-in-environment, cuts across all kinds of situations of human activity. When we talk of behavior settings, however, we first of all refer to *public* situations outside the private home or family. Theoretically, there is no reason why we cannot apply the ecological point of view to family activities, but it makes also a lot of sense to distinguish between a private and a public sphere. In this way the number of behavior settings in a given area or community could vary from practically zero upward.

The sheer number of behavior settings is the first measure a survey will yield. This measure is important in its own right, as it is in some cases a direct measure of the richness of the milieu. An example: some people have criticized sharply some of the new residential districts in urban areas of Scandinavia. They might have well-equipped and modern dwellings, but the quality of life in these areas is said to be low. A survey of behavior settings would most probably

substantiate these claims as the number of settings would be very low. Very little goes on.

Extent and amount can, however, be measured in more than one way. First, a given setting can occur frequently or very seldom. The Fourth of July celebration will necessarily take place only once a year, but others can of course be freely scheduled often or seldom. The same setting, when functioning, can be a very short affair, or it can go on throughout most of the day, like the drugstore or other shops. Finally, the setting can have many participants or very few. These dimensions (number, occurrence, duration, and population) can be seen as separate measures; but they can also be combined to form composite measures. Barker has himself proposed to combine number, occurrence, and duration into a general ecological resource index.

There is, of course, no fixed number of descriptive dimensions for the behavior settings. This is dependent upon what the researcher is out to test. He will have to select the descriptive dimensions that fit his aims and hypotheses.

In his explorations in Midwest and Yordale, Barker has not had any such explicit set of hypotheses in mind. Rather he has worked like the natural scientist out to systematize a set of new species. He says himself that: "The number of behavior settings . . . is analogous to the number of acres of land in Midwest Country. The number of genotypes (types of behavior settings) . . . is analogous to the number of types of soil in the country" (Barker, 1968, p. 109). He adopts a naive stance and tries to code and register the concrete reality with as little distortion and prestructuring as possible.

He then suggests that apart from counting the number, occurrence, duration, and population, it is important (and possible) to register *the functional positions of inhabitants*. By this is meant that the setting provides for a set of roles to play; some are leaders and direct the events to a very great extent, like the minister at Sunday mass in church. For most settings it is possible to isolate some persons in the roles of leaders, and there will be other roles with different degrees of power, all the way to the other extreme, the on-looker. The setting itself, then, can be judged to be one where few or many take an active part in the activities. A community with many settings that offer active participation would, from a particular value point, be judged better than one where only roles are available for the partici-pants. Barker goes on (1968, pp. 27–28) to de-scribe a set of 11 *action patterns,* whose pres-ence or not, he argues, can readily be observed and recorded. This corresponds to categories of behavior that we all make use of in reporting on activities: aesthetic, business, educational, gov-ernmental, nutritional, personal appearance, physical health, professional, recreational, reli-gious, social action pattern. Closely associated with these patterns are a set of *behavior mechanisms* that further illuminate the concrete activities: affective, gross motor, manipulation, verbal, and thinking.

Finally, Barker suggests that the settings can be judged with respect to the degree of *pressure* put on people to participate, the degree of *autonomy* the setting has when it comes to in-fluence from outside the community, and the degree to which it caters to the needs of differ-ent population subgroups. The latter dimension is called *welfare*.

For students of human activities, Barker's suggestions of descriptive dimensions are very useful, but they must be seen as just one set of possible dimensions. This field of inquiry is new and largely unexplored.

The behavior within the behavior settings is highly predictable. It can be seen as program-med, and consequently there will be persons (leaders mostly) that are carriers of these pro-grams. We can expect, however, that a particu-lar activity which in one community is sponsored by a church organization, somewhere else would be within the domain of labor unions. What in one community is sponsored by private business concerns will elsewhere be offered by a public body. For comparative purposes the identification of sponsors will be important. The point above relates to the problem of change and innovation. Even if Barker is largely correct in saying that the distribution of types of be-havior settings is analogous to soil types in the land, changes have and will take place. New set-tings will appear and others will die. It will be necessary to study how particular sets of be-havior settings correspond to and are supported by the economic and political institutions in the particular culture of which the communities are located. In this way, few of the behavior settings will be high on Barker's scale of autonomy.

MAKING A SURVEY OF BEHAVIOR SETTINGS

By now it should be clear that the behavior-setting concept is very general and can be ap-plied in very different research situations (Fig-ures 1–3). In his original work, Roger Barker ap-plied his concept in studies of total towns. These towns are relatively small (800 persons), and he has studied first in the United States and Eng-land (Barker, 1973). It makes a lot of sense to have the study area correspond to a concrete, bordered community, but it is perfectly possible to make a similar study in territories delineated differently. It would even be possible to apply the behavior-setting concept in the study of particu-lar, selected population groups, whose needs are under consideration. An interesting use of the behavior-setting concept has been made in connection with studies of institutions like schools. We shall comment upon this below.

Finally, we shall give an example of how the concept can be used in studying certain sectors of public life.

Behavior settings:

18.1   Elementary Upper School Basketball Game
18.2   Elementary Upper School Basketball Game out of town
18.3   Elementary Upper School Basketball Practice
18.4   Elementary Upper School Basketball Tournament
18.5   High School Boys Basketball Game
18.6   High School Boys Basketball Game out of town including Tournament at Patton
18.7   High School Boys Basketball Practice
18.8   High School Freshman Boys Basketball Tournament out of town
18.9   High School Freshman and Sophomore Girls Basketball Game
18.10 High School Freshman and Sophomore Girls Basketball Game out of town
18.11 High School Girls Basketball Practice
18.12 High School Girls and Freshman Boys Basketball Game
18.13 High School Girls and Freshman Boys Basketball Game out of town
18.14 Midwest Town Team Basketball Game

Figure 1
Some behavior settings in a high school. (Excerpted, with permission of the publisher, from *Ecological Psychology: Concepts and Methods for Studying the Environment of Human Behavior* by Roger G. Barker [Stanford: Stanford University Press, 1968], p. 98.

First, let us comment upon behavior-setting surveys of concrete geographic areas, whether total communities or particular areas in larger communities. For a given survey we can isolate three distinct steps: (1) scouting and mapping, (2) recording and describing, and (3) analysis and reporting.

There is no set procedure for the scouting phase, but it is possible to give some general advice. In this phase, work with registers and all kinds of documented information, direct observation, and interviewing are approaches that should be used, in combination as appropriate.

Maps of the area are logical points on departure, but if there is access to aerial photos, this is, of course, a vastly better starting point. From the latter, provided the proper scale is available, it is easy to see and map lines of communication. It is further usually possible to distinguish between residential areas and business districts.

Probably indoor activity arenas will show up as special structures.

On the basis of work with maps and photos, actual observation in the field is the critical step. The observer should follow all communication-lines and paths in order to record all concrete clues to behavior settings. It is remarkable how much information can be picked up this way. Signs and posted notices are of particular help, and bulletin boards of all kinds are there to be mined. The public settings advertise themselves, and the pedestrian observer will typically come from the field with a filled notebook.

Another source of information to be used will be documents, publications, and newspapers. If there is a local newspaper, the researcher should reserve ample time to read it. Both the advertising section and columns of local news are a great help. The Yellow Pages of the telephone directory and other publications that include listings of institutions are of course other sources.

The scouting will not have lasted long before the structure of the given community is revealed, with the key persons indicated. Interviewing these and other informants will complete the register of possible behavior settings being built up by the project. Informants are easily located by "snowballing"; the interviewed person is asked to suggest other persons for interviewing, and this is kept up until few new names come up. Leaders of central institutions such as churches, schools, local chambers of commerce, and all forms of governmental offices should be contacted.

Barker's complete survey covered the yearly cycle. A behavior setting was recorded if and only if it had at least one occurrence a year. If we want to formulate general conclusions about life and existence in a given area or community, we must cover the yearly cycle. Seasonal changes of activity are so great that any shorter time period than a year would presently create

Name: *High School Boys Basketball Game*

Genotype # 1-3: 0 · 1 · 8	Genotype Commonality # 8: 9	Locus 16: 1	
B S # 4-6: 0 · 0 · 5	Authority System 13-14: 0 · 1	No. of Occurr. 17-19: 0 · 0 · 8	
Genotype Date 7: 3	Class of Authority Systems 15: 4	Survey # 20: 5	

Occupancy Time of Town Subgroups				Max. Penetration of Subgroups		ACTION PATTERN RATINGS	
Group	No. P	Hours	OT Code	Group			
Inf	3	24	21-22: 0 · 4	Inf	21: 1	Aes: 53: 0	
Presch	12	54	23-24: 0 · 5	Presch	22: 2	Bus 54: 1	
Y S	10	87	25-26: 0 · 6	Y S	23: 2	Prof 55: 1	
O S	18	258	27-28: 0 · 9	O S	24: 4	Educ 56: 1	
Town Child	43	423	29-30: 1 · 1			Govt 57: 1	
Adol	63	1720	31-32: 1 · 7	Adol	25: 4	Nutr 58: 1	
Adult	72	1676	33-34: 1 · 7	Adult	26: 5		
Aged	7	81	35-36: 0 · 6	Aged	27: 2	PersAp 60: 2	
Town Total	185	3900	37-38: 2 · 3	Grand Max	28: 5		
Males	97	2264	39-40: 1 · 9	Males	29: 5	PhysH 62: 2	
Female	88	1636	41-42: 1 · 7	Females	30: 4	Rec 63: 8	
I	35	600	43-44: 1 · 2	I	31: 4	Rel 64: 0	
II	105	2236	45-46: 1 · 9	II	32: 5	Soc 65: 6	
III	42	1014	47-48: 1 · 4	III	33: 4	MECHANISM RATINGS AffB 66: 9	
N-G	3	50	49-50: 0 · 5	N-G	34: 4	GroMot 67: 7	

POPULATION (number)		PERFORMERS (number)			
				Manip 68: 7	
Town Child 51-53: 0 · 4 · 3		Town Child 35-36: 0 · 1		Talk 69: 9	
Out Child 54-56: 1 · 8 · 7		Out Child 37-38: 0 · 0		Think 70: 4	
Total Child 57-59: 2 · 3 · 0		Tot Child 39-40: 0 · 1		GEN RICH 71-72: 23	
Town Total 60-62: 1 · 8 · 5		Town Total 41-42: 5 · 3		PRESSURE RATING Children 73: 4	
Out Total 63-65: 9 · 3 · 7		Out Total 43-45: 2 · 4 · 9		Adolesc 74: 2	
Grand Total 66-69: 1 · 1 · 2 · 2		Grand Tot 46-48: 3 · 0 · 2		WELFARE RATING Children 75: 0	
Grand O.T. (code) 71-73: 0 · 3 · 1	70: blank	Perf/Pop 49-50: 2 · 7		Adolesc 76: 3	
Total Duration 74-77: 0 · 0 · 2 · 4		Aver. No. 51-52: 8 · 4		AUTONOMY RATING wtd 79: 7	
Average Attendance 78-80: 3 · 6 · 3					

Figure 2
Data sheet of behavior setting 18.5, high school boys basketball game. (Excerpted, with permission of the publisher, from *Ecological Psychology: Concepts and Methods for Studying the Environment of Human Behavior* by Roger G. Barker [Stanford: Stanford University Press, 1968], p. 99.)

TABLE 5.3. *Behavior Setting Genotypes of Midwest, 1963–64. Number* (N),
Occurrence (O), *Duration* (D), *Ecological Resource Index* (ERI),
Occupancy Time of Town Residents (Town OT), *and Occupancy
Time of All Inhabitants* (Total OT) *of Behavior Settings
in Each Genotype**

No.	Genotype	N	Resource Measures			Output Measures	
			O	D	ERI	Town OT	Total OT
1.	Abstract and Title Company Offices	1	305	2,500	0.52	4,054	4,606
2.	Agricultural Advisors Offices	1	250	2,040	0.43	5,206	6,559
4.	Agronomy Classes	2	4	13	0.08	72	341
5.	Animal Feed Mills	1	310	3,344	0.62	8,998	16,881
6.	Animal Feed Stores	1	307	2,736	0.55	5,857	8,127
7.	Animal Husbandry Classes	4	6	20	0.16	23	394
8.	Athletic Equipment Rooms	2	265	180	0.26	284	412
9.	Attorneys Offices	4	1,155	7,250	1.72	20,584	23,347
10.	Auction Sales	2	3	14	0.08	485	1,645
11.	Auditing and Investigating Co. Offices	1	250	2,000	0.47	2,320	2,380
12.	Automobile Washing Services	2	3	18	0.08	113	143
13.	Award Ceremonies	3	3	5	0.12	176	283
14.	Bakery Services, to Order	1	50	200	0.09	242	242
15.	Banks	1	305	1,750	0.43	26,499	36,860
16.	Barbershops	2	450	3,600	0.78	2,760	7,601
17.	Baseball Games	16	71	167	0.67	6,781	13,691
18.	Basketball Games	14	124	272	0.64	14,164	36,058
19.	Beauty Shops	1	305	3,329	0.62	13,099	15,549
20.	Billiard Parlors and Taverns	1	308	4,300	0.73	21,330	39,212
22.	Bowling Games, Ten Pins	25	725	3,204	1.77	23,862	41,214
24.	Building, Construction, Repair Services	6	1,135	9,160	2.00	14,155	19,564

* The complete, alphabetized, and numbered genotype list covers two survey years, 1954–55 and 1963–64. Genotypes that were present in the former year and absent in the latter year are omitted from the 1963–64 list; hence the genotype numbers are not consecutive. The occupancy times reported are from the coded values (see Appendix 1).

Figure 3
Behavior setting genotypes. (Excerpted, with permission of the publisher, from *Ecological Psychology: Concepts and Methods for Studying the Environment of Human Behavior* by Roger G. Barker [Stanford: Stanford University Press, 1968], p. 110.)

unsurmountable difficulties. I used the phrase "presently," as it is to be expected that if these kinds of surveys were performed on a large scale in different cultures, there is reason to believe that certain invariances could be established so that more limited surveys could be made possible.

A scouting phase of the sort sketched here will have led to a list of potential behavior settings. For each there will be available one or more of the following items of information: Name of leader(s), responsible organizations/institutions, and address. The work ahead now consists of a detailed registration and description of each setting.

At this point in a survey we should carefully assess the available resources in order to use them most effectively. The detailed registration and description is a time-consuming job. If the number of field workers is small, carrying out a survey will take a very long time. This in itself is not bad, as there is a whole series of advantages in performing these recordings throughout the year, as it and its behavior settings unfold.

We have mentioned the possibility of describing the activities going on within an institution like a school in terms of behavior settings. The corresponding scouting period would necessarily be quite different from that described, as full coverage would be easy to obtain.

It is perfectly possible to map the various behavior settings that take place in a school over the day, and also for longer periods of time. In this situation, direct observation might be the best method to use, provided that one can satisfactorily solve the problem of sampling. A study of more than one school would show the same kinds of settings. The difference between schools would be that the larger schools would have more settings of the same kind functioning simultaneously (classes) and also that some of the settings would have a greater number of participants. In the small school we shall find that a relatively greater number of persons will participate in more different settings than in the large school. The school might be so small that particular settings such as the school brass band or other usual school setting are not to be found or that they function badly, for lack of participants.

The problem of "manning," or rather "undermanning" and "overmanning" of settings, has been illuminated particularly well in studies of schools (Barker and Gump, 1964). But the question is a general one: most settings will operate at their best with an optimum number of participants.

The overmanned behavior settings seem to be the most problematic ones, at least from the participants' point of view. Besides the direct problem of crowding, the overmanned setting in the school will lead to a situation in which many pupils do not find the necessary number of meaningful roles to play. The challenge is not there, and the level of expectations will be low; as he is not really needed at the school, so he might as well drop out.

In the beginning of this chapter we made a distinction between real observations and quasi-observational records. The latter refers to description given by persons who themselves have been present at a given event. The reason we call it "observational" is that the information asked for is the kind that an observer could see and record; no attitudes, beliefs, evaluations, or other experiential information are included. Any extensive behavior-setting survey will have to rely on this kind of information; there are clearcut limitations as to how much information of this kind can be obtained through straight observations. One should take care, however, to include straight observation of enough different settings to satisfy oneself that the registration instrument (data sheet, questionnaire, etc.) is functional.

In his publication Barker does not give much information on the research process itself. We know, however, that the field work in each of his towns took place over a relatively long period of time.

To turn from Barker's work to our own, we can illustrate a somewhat different approach taken from a study of social–cultural activities in the town of Stavanger, Norway, 1972–1973 (Rosenlund and Ås, 1972–1974). This study is one of a series of studies of different European towns initiated by the Council of Europe. All studies center on the role of the local municipality as a provider (source and/or obstructive force) of sociocultural activities. The results of the study will first of all be fed back to the various decision-making bodies in the town to help them improve existing policies concerning the development of local cultural life and, very specifically, needed facilities.

Besides other information, a careful description of the present supply of sociocultural activities was needed: the kind of activities provided, their organization and content, participation rates, duration, sponsors, economic aspects, and so on. Various methods were necessary to cover all this, but most of it could be covered by carrying out an inventory of on-going sociocultural activities after the model of the behavior-setting survey. Parallel with this study, a separate interview study of people's leisure-time behavior is carried out, so to cover both the *supply* and the *demand* side of the total culture consumption.

The town of Stavanger has about 70,000 inhabitants, and the study aimed at covering the whole town. The term "social-cultural activities" indicates a frame of reference that goes beyond what traditionally is called cultural activities. At the outset the following sectors to be covered were selected: theatre, music, exhibitions, film, social–humanitarian events, politics, education, religion, and sports. The scouting period indicated that the events we were interested in were supported, arranged, and directed by organiza-

tions rather than particular individuals. The first phase of the study then consisted of establishing a complete register of such organizations in the town. A list of about 800 organizations was compiled in this way.

It was at the outset estimated that at least 20,000 single sociocultural events would take place in the town throughout the year. Even this number of events, which turned out to be *less than one fourth of the actual number,* is a large number to handle in a single study. A total survey could not be carried out, therefore, without participation from very many people. The very same organizations that we had listed were invited to participate in the study, and a network of rapporteurs was established. These people were asked to fill in simple data sheets on the single arrangements or events they sponsored. This registration was designed to be a day-to-day affair. We were able to recruit between four and five hundred such rapporteurs.

For various reasons, this very large network could not be maintained for an indefinite period. After three months of operation it was evident that the field work operated under severe strains. The day-to-day registration was consequently called to a halt. We had then obtained information on about half the organizations and their activities. The information, was very detailed, however.

The alternative method, which the project turned to in the next phase, is to contact representatives of the organizations directly and obtain information through interviews. By using this method, less detailed information results. It is not possible to obtain accurate information on, for example, participation rates of different population groups, details on their programs and concrete activities, and so on. The interviews were carried out over the telephone and the operation took one full month to finish.

We lack information from some organizations,

but this two-stage operation resulted in a set of data that is relatively complete. All in all the 841 organizations showed to be responsible for about 4,000 types of arrangements throughout one year, and the total number of events turned out to be about 83,000.

In Barker's writings will be found detailed instructions on how to identify and define the single setting and how to distinguish between related settings. He also presents criteria by which one can group the settings into categories or types. In large-scale studies such as the one described above, a certain degree of violence to these principles is unavoidable. If interviewing dominates, and the information is more quasi-observational than straight, the data will accordingly be influenced very much by the concepts used by the respondents. A given organization will have its own names for its various arranged events. Some of these were one-time events, but many followed a regular schedule over the year. Our units, then, are more general than the single setting but not as general as the *genotype,* which Barker recommends as the unit to be counted.

I have argued earlier that a behavior-setting survey would be an alternative method to studies of time use. There ought to be, then, a high degree of similarity between the time devoted to a given class of activities when described by these two different methods. Such a similarity seems to be present in our data. In the Stavanger study we have information on both durations and number of participants for the different events. A straight multiplication of averages for this for the 83,000 arranged events results in an average of 22 minutes daily spent on sociocultural activities per person in the town. We used the total number of inhabitants (70,000) as the final divisor. Although no representative study of time use has been performed in Stavanger (or in Norway for that mat-

ter), a recent multinational study of time use indicates that many countries show corresponding averages of 20–30 minutes per day for similar activities (Szalai et al., 1972).

BEHAVIOR-SETTING SURVEYS IN THE DESIGN PROCESS

We listed above a series of situations in which a behavior-setting survey could be used; towns, areas, institutions, and so on. It is now only proper to review a similar list of the motives for making such surveys and their possible uses for the designer and the student of environmental design.

The original works of Roger Barker were carried out for traditional scientific reasons. Development of theory is here the all-important motive. In my opinion there is nothing as practical as good theory, and the first contribution lies in the new insight which this theory provides.

A second contribution lies in the fact that a new research tool is provided. The techniques of the behavior-setting survey are sufficiently developed to be considered research tools. In the quoted study of small and big schools, the concepts and methods made a meaningful comparison of institutions possible by providing a unit of analysis within these institutions. In the study of sociocultural activities it was possible to survey with the same instrument phenomena usually considered to be different.

The student and practitioner of design will profit from both these contributions. The insight provided by the theory makes it possible to better grasp the meaning of activity. The theory stresses the fact that the environment is *part* of the activities and that activity is a vital part of the environment. Furthermore, stress is put on the dimension of *time:* behavior and activity are segments of time and can be seen as sequences and strings of related actions.

The environmental designer will typically not carry out full-fledged inventories of behavior settings in an area. Such inventories can be carried out in a very detailed manner as well as simplified by just counting the settings as being present or not. General surveys that do not probe deeply can very well be considered part of the data-gathering phase in a design process, such as for the provision of cultural facilities. The "student of environmental design" that I here define as much as a researcher as a designer will, I hope, go further and participate in the continuing development of the behavior-setting survey as well as other observational methods. His toolbox is not complete without tools of this kind.

The environment is a very concrete phenomenon that we must learn to handle as realistically and sensitively in our research and design as we try to in our daily life.

REFERENCES

1. Ashby, W. R. 1956. *An Introduction to Cybernetics*. New York: Wiley.

2. Barker, R. G. 1960. "Ecology and Motivation," in M. R. Jones (ed.), *Nebraska Symposium on Motivation*. Lincoln, Nebr.: University of Nebraska Press.

3. Barker, R. G. 1965. "Explorations in Ecological Psychology." *American Psychologist*, no. 1, pp. 1–13.

4. Barker, R. G. 1968. *Ecological Psychology*. Stanford, Calif.: Stanford University Press.

5. Barker, R. G. 1973. *Qualities of Community Life*. San Francisco: Jossey-Bass.

6. Barker, R. G., and P. V. Gump. 1964. *Big School, Small School: High School Size and Student Behavior*. Stanford, Calif.: Stanford University Press.

7. Harris, Marvin. 1964. *The Nature of Cultural Things,* New York: Random House.

8. Javeau, Claude. 1970. *Les vingt-quatre heures du Belge, Bruxelles*. Brussels: L'Institut de Sociologie, Université Libre de Bruxelles.

9. Pike, Kenneth. 1954–60. *Language in Relation to a Unified Theory of the Structure of Human Behavior,* vols. 1–3. Glendale, Calif.: Summer Institute of Linguistics.

10. Rosenlund, Lennart, and Dagfinn Ås. 1972–1974. Unpublished study. Stavanger: Rogaland Distriktshøjskole.

11. Szalai, Alexander, et al. 1972. *The Use of Time*. The Hague: Mouton.

Index